Irwin Bernstein

Evolutionary Psychology

D0166149

Evolutionary Psychology

The Ultimate Origins
of Human Behavior

Jack A. Palmer

University of Louisiana at Monroe

Linda K. Palmer

Edition Naam USA

Allyn and Bacon

Boston • London • Toronto • Sydney • Tokyo • Singapore

Executive Editor: *Carolyn Merrill*
Editorial Assistant: *Jonathan Bender*
Senior Marketing Manager: *Caroline Croley*
Editorial Production Service: *Bernadine Richey Publishing Services*
Manufacturing Buyer: *Joanne Sweeney*
Cover Administrator: *Kristina Mose-Libon*
Electronic Composition: *Omegatype Typography, Inc.*

Copyright © 2002 by Allyn & Bacon
A Pearson Education Company
75 Arlington Street
Boston, MA 02116

Internet: www.ablongman.com

All rights reserved. No part of the material protected by this copyright notice may be reproduced or utilized in any form or by any means, electronic or mechanical, including photocopying, recording, or by any information storage and retrieval system, without written permission from the copyright holder.

Between the time Website information is gathered and published, some sites may have closed. Also, the transcription of URLs can result in typographical errors. The publisher would appreciate notification where these occur so that they may be corrected in subsequent editions.

Library of Congress Cataloging-in-Publication Data

Palmer, Jack A.
    Evolutionary psychology : the ultimate origins of human behavior / Jack A. Palmer, Linda K. Palmer
        p.   cm.
    Includes bibliographical references (p.) and index.
    ISBN 0-205-27868-X (softcover)
    1. Genetic psychology.   I. Palmer, Linda K.   II. Title.

BF701 .P27 2001
155.7—dc21

                                                                                2001046075

Printed in the United States of America

10   9   8   7   6   5   4   3   2   1   06   05   04   03   02   01

To the memory of our son Adam Jalal Palmer,
who through his profound dedication to the spiritual life
knew the true scope and potential of science.
And in memory of Faye Palmer Cone and Marian Fairchild Gill,
who lovingly demonstrated throughout their lives
a natural understanding of the importance of nurturing children
and of bringing to fruition nature's latent potentials.
And to our daughter Nani Faye Palmer,
who is working with love and humility toward
creating a brighter future for humanity.

Contents

Preface   xiii

Acknowledgments   xv

1 *Origins: The Roots of Evolutionary Psychology*   **1**

    Darwin's Theory   **2**
        Solving the Great Puzzle   2
        Basic Tenet's of Darwin's Theory   5

    The Modern Synthesis   **6**
        Mendel's Laws   6
        Mutations   7
        DNA   9

    Behavior as a Function of Evolution   **11**
        William James   11
        The Abuse of Darwinism   11
        Environmental Determinism   12
        Ethology   14
        Altruism and Sociobiology   15
        Evolutionary Psychology   16
        The Methods of Evolutionary Psychology   18

    Summary   **23**

    Discussion Questions   **24**

    Key Terms   **25**

    Additional Reading   **25**

2 *From Big Bang to Big Brain*   **26**

    Life in the Universe   **26**

    The Beginning   **28**

Vertebrate Life   **31**

Hominid Evolution   **34**
   Africa: Cradle of Human Evolution   34
   Bipedalism   38
   The First Humans   42

Summary   **47**

Discussion Questions   **47**

Key Terms   **47**

Additional Reading   **48**

3   *Encephalization and the Emergence of Mind*   **49**

The Prime Movers in Hominid Encephalization   **50**
   Machiavellian Intelligence   51
   Ice Ages   53
   Ballistic Hunting   56
   Language   57
   Intraspecific Competition   59

The Modular Brain   **60**
   Localization of Function   62
   Laterality   65

The Modular Mind   **67**
   Fear Learning   67
   Social Reasoning   69
      Problem 1   *69*
      Problem 2   *70*
      Problem 3   *70*
      Problem 4   *71*
   Gender Differences   72

Summary   **77**

Discussion Questions   **77**

Key Terms   **78**

Additional Reading   **78**

4   *Language: Crown Jewel of Communication*   **79**

The Nature of Language   **80**
   Animal Communication   81
   Animal Language Studies   82
   Feral Children   85

Language Acquisition   **88**
Developmental Stages   88
Critical Periods   90

Language Evolution   **91**
Universals   92
Ancient Origins   97
Conceptual Domains   102

Summary   **104**

Discussion Questions   **105**

Key Terms   **105**

Additional Reading   **105**

5   *Mating and Reproduction*   **106**

Sexual Selection   **107**
The Evolutionary Basis of Sex Differences in Human Behavior   109
Mate Selection Criteria   111
The Preferences of Men   *111*
The Preferences of Women   *112*

The Aesthetics of Attraction   **115**
Symmetry   115
Waist-Hip Ratio   116
The Masculine Ideal   119
The Feminine Ideal   120

Human Pheromones   **120**
Menstrual Synchronicity   121
Major Histocompatibility Complex Preferences   122
Male Pheromones   123
Female Pheromones   124

Jealousy and Mate-Guarding   **124**

Sperm Wars   **126**

Sexual Orientation   **129**

Pair-Bonding Strategies   **132**
Limerence: Short-Term Pair Bonding   132
Long-Term Pair Bonding   135

Summary   **136**

Discussion Questions   **138**

Key Terms   **138**

Additional Reading   **138**

6   *Ontogeny*   **140**

Prenatal Development   **141**
Why Ontogeny Seems to Recapitulate Phylogeny   141
Regulator Genes   142
The Adaptive Function of Morning Sickness   142
Mother–Fetus Competition   145

Postnatal Development   **146**
A Priori Mind   146
Parent–Infant Conflicts of Interest   150
Incest Avoidance   152
Evolved Contingency Mechanisms   153
   Childhood Experience and Adult Reproductive Strategy   *154*
   Childhood Experience and Adult Personality   *155*
   Birth Order and Adult Personality   *156*
Optimizing Cognitive Potential   158
The Adaptive Function of Menopause   160

Summary   **160**

Discussion Questions   **162**

Key Terms   **162**

Additional Reading   **162**

7   *Social Order and Disorder*   **164**

*Dominance Hierarchies: The Coordination of Affiliation
and Aggression*   **165**
The Biochemistry of Status and the Function of Mood States   173
   Serotonin   *173*
   Testosterone   *177*
   Stress Hormones   *178*

The Evolution of Compassion   **180**
Kin Selection and Altruism   180
Reciprocal Altruism   183
Universal Morality and Ethics   185

Summary   **187**

Discussion Questions   **188**

Key Terms   **188**

Additional Reading   **189**

8 *Personality and Psychopathology*   **191**

Early Personality Theorists   **192**

Contemporary Approaches to Personality Theory   **193**
The Case-Study Research Paradigm: The Clinical Approach
to Personality   193
Trait Theory   194
Factor Analysis: A Major Tool of Correlational Research   194

The Three-Factor Model of Personality   **196**

The Five-Factor Model of Personality   **197**

Evolutionary Theory and Personality   **198**
The Adaptive Significance of Personality Traits   198
Phylogeny and Ontogeny of Personality   200

Personality and Abnormal Behavior   **204**
Axis I Psychiatric Diagnoses   205
    Schizophrenia   *205*
    Depression   *207*
    Anxiety   *208*
Axis II Personality Disorders   209
    Antisocial and Histrionic Personality Disorders   *210*
    Borderline Personality Disorder   *211*
    The Other Axis II Personality Disorders   *212*

Summary   **214**

Discussion Questions   **215**

Key Terms   **215**

Additional Reading   **216**

9 *The Creative Impulse: The Origins of Technology
and Art*   **217**

Tool-Use   **218**
In Nonhuman Animals   218
The Hominid Archaeological Record   223
Tool-Use as a Selective Force in Human Evolution   225
Assessment of Hominid Cognitive Ability   227

Aesthetic Manipulation   **227**
Pleistocene Art   228
The Adaptive Significance of Art   230

Consciousness and the Symbolic Universe   236

Summary   241

Discussion Questions   242

Key Terms   242

Additional Reading   242

10   *Ancient Mammal in a Brave New World*   244

Mismatch Theory   245

Stress: Then and Now   249

Mental Health   252

Indoctrination, Nationalism, and War   253

Better Living through Chemistry: Psychopharmacology   258
The Origins of Substance Abuse   258
Psychopharmacology   260

The New Eugenics: Genetic Engineering   265

Summary   268

Discussion Questions   269

Key Terms   270

Additional Reading   270

Appendix A: Wason Selection Tasks for Cheater Detection (Cosmides & Tooby, 1992)   271

Cheater Version   271

Altruistic Version   272

Appendix B: Neurotransmitters: A Primer   273

Glossary   277

Bibliography   289

Index   305

Preface

In the distant future I see open fields for far more important researches.
Psychology will be based on a new foundation, that of the necessary
acquirement of each mental power and capacity by gradation.
—Charles Darwin

Evolutionary psychology is the study of the adaptive significance of behavior and attempts to explain how certain behaviors developed over time in order to secure survival and increase the probability of survival of one's progeny. Darwin's words, penned over a century ago, make the point that each level of cognitive and behavioral complexity is acquired slowly, gradually, through generation upon generation, over eons of time. William James, author of the first psychology textbook, founded his subdiscipline of functionalism on Darwin's basic assertion that behavior, just like morphology, is shaped by selective pressure, and that traits such as consciousness and the ability to plan and to problem solve were highly adaptive traits that developed in the human species as a result of natural selection. What evolutionary psychology offers that is very different from other perspectives is the idea that many of the behaviors that we view as negative or harmful (e.g., jealousy, anger, greed) as well as those we view as positive and helpful (e.g., love, compassion, loyalty) are not the result of external forces such as punishment and reward, although external forces may bring these behaviors to fruition: These behaviors are the result of our intrinsic, biological human nature. Moreover, even the subtlest and most esoteric of human behaviors such as aesthetic sense, self-reflexive consciousness, and a striving for meaning are explainable as the result of the laws of natural selection.

As we enter the twenty-first century, the scientific investigation of human behavior has been ongoing for well over a hundred years. However, much confusion continues to exist regarding how best to explain human behavior. Part of the problem stems from the mistaken idea that evolutionary accounts of behavior are mutually exclusive to more traditional explanations of behavior based on proximate (immediate) mechanisms. Both explanations have veracity, but to fully understand behavior each explanation must be integrated into the greater whole. This book weaves evolutionary explanations into a framework that incorporates ontogeny and physiological mechanisms, as well as immediate causation, in order to arrive at the clearest and most complete explanation possible for the myriad behaviors exhibited by our species.

This book reviews how evolutionary psychology explains and predicts human behavior in a variety of contexts such as gender-dependent preferences and strategies in mate selection, negotiation of social interactions, development and maintenance of social hierarchies, adaptiveness of mood states, and triggering of different behavioral strategies by differential childhood experiences. The primary topics addressed are human origins, evolution of the human brain and mind, language, mating and reproduction, ontogeny, social behavior, origins of tool use and art, and the challenges of adjusting our evolved minds and behavior to the modern environment.

Modern evolutionary theory has the capacity to link the social sciences to each other and to the natural sciences. At the present time, there is no overarching theory or prevailing paradigm that links the social sciences together or that even enables the prevailing theories of the various disciplines of social sciences to be completely congruent with each other. One of the reasons that evolutionary psychology has become such a "hot topic" in recent years is its potential to provide explanations and predictions for a wide variety of disciplines including anthropology, economics, psychology, sociology, and other social sciences. Evolutionary theory may well be the framework within which the social sciences can develop congruent, complimentary paradigms of behavior in the same way that the various disciplines of the natural sciences have laws that are complimentary, congruent, and nonconflictual.

Given that evolutionary psychology has tremendous explanatory power and that it has the potential to become the premier theory of the social sciences, graduate students and undergraduates in psychology and other social science disciplines are increasingly required to study and understand basic, evolutionary tenets as they apply to individual human behavior as well as to human institutions. This book is appropriate as a primary text for courses in evolutionary psychology, as well as a supplementary text for courses such as social psychology, comparative psychology, physiological psychology, and developmental psychology. Both graduate and undergraduate students will find it to be valuable reading, and it will allow them to obtain quickly a background in the paradigm of evolutionary psychology.

Acknowledgments

Many people gave generously of their time and energy to help us in this project. To everyone who provided support, we are deeply indebted to you. We especially want to thank all the graduate and undergraduate students at University of Louisiana at Monroe and Willamette University who assisted in preparation of materials, particularly the students of the evolutionary psychology seminars and classes and the graduate assistants who worked on this project. We are very grateful to our reviewers, whose comments have greatly improved the text. We wish to thank Sean Wakely for his warm support and enthusiasm when the project was just getting off the ground, and to all the staff at Allyn and Bacon who have given their assistance. Our deep gratitude goes to Russell Gardner, Devendra Singh, and Delbert Thiessen for their advice, encouragement, and helpful commentary. Many thanks to Daniel Povinelli for his thought-provoking work and discussions. Special thanks to Roger Thomas and Irwin Bernstein for their mentoring in comparative cognition and primate behavior at the University of Georgia and the Yerkes Primate Research Station. We are very thankful to David Williamson and Arlen Zander for their help and support, particularly in securing a sabbatical that benefited this work. We are especially grateful to William McCown for his expert contributions on personality theory, as well as for his friendship and support. We feel a very special and deep gratitude to Elsa Poetker, Joseph Poetker, and Mukund Shah for their priceless friendship and ongoing support throughout difficult times. An extra-special thank-you to everyone at Lighthouse Farm Oregon for their love and for providing a unique refuge and retreat. Our eternal gratitude goes to Adam Jalal Palmer and Nani Faye Palmer for all their help, support, and love. Reviewers for Palmer and Palmer, *Evolutionary Psychology:* Elaine Baker, Marshall University, Gordon M. Burghardt, University of Tennessee, J. Timothy Cannon, University of Scranton, Casey Dorman, United States International University, Russell Gardner, University of Texas Medical Branch, Christopher D. Horvath, Illinois State University, Cathleen B. Hunt, University of Arizona, Robert A. Johnston, College of William and Mary, J. J. Jordan, Francis Marion University, Ralph J. McKenna, Hendrix College, Marilee Monnot, Oklahoma City University, John K. Pearce, Brighton-Allston Mental Health Center, Dean G. Pruitt, State University of New York, Buffalo, Devendra Singh, University of Texas, Dorothy Tennov, University of Bridgeport, and Delbert Thiessen, University of Texas.

1

Origins: The Roots of Evolutionary Psychology

EURIPIDES:
I taught them all these knowing ways
By chopping logic in my plays,
And making all my speakers try
*To reason out the **How** and **Why**.*
So now the people trace the springs,
The sources and the roots of things,
And manage all their households too
Far better than they used to do,
Scanning and searching "What's amiss?"
And, "Why was that?" And, "How is this?"
                    —Aristophanes, *The Frogs* (405 B.C.).

Chapter Questions

1. Do all living things come from a single common ancestor?
2. Why do living things come in such an enormous variety of forms?
3. How did two English naturalists, working independently of each other, discover the process of natural selection and grasp its sweeping implications?
4. Does natural selection shape the behavior of organisms including people?

Darwin's Theory

Solving the Great Puzzle

In 1831 a young naturalist named Charles Darwin set sail aboard the *H.M.S. Beagle* (Darwin, 1887). During the following five years the Beagle carried Darwin to remote parts of the world allowing him to witness firsthand a variety of astonishing natural phenomena. Although other educated and intelligent people had beheld similar sights, Charles Darwin was the first to grasp the profound implications of what he saw. Among the wonders he witnessed were the bizarre creatures inhabiting a group of volcanic landmasses off the coast of Equador called the Galapagos Islands. The creatures he observed included gigantic tortoises hundreds of time larger in mass than the tortoises living on the nearby South American Continent (*galapagos* is the Spanish word for turtle). Another strange fact noted by Darwin was that each island had its own unique species of giant tortoise (see Figure 1.1).

The islands were also home to marine iguanas, large, odd-looking reptiles that made a living by feeding on seaweed and algae beneath the icy waters of the Pacific Ocean. Inland, amid the islands arid volcanic wastelands, land iguanas made a living by cropping cactus. Both species of Galapagos iguanas were similar to the common iguanas inhabiting the South American mainland, yet each species had its own distinct morphology, physiology, and behavior. The same was true of numerous other species inhabiting the islands. Darwin identified dozens of new bird species, once again similar to mainland species but with their own unique

FIGURE 1.1   Charles Darwin

variations. One species of finch had a behavioral answer to the question of how to make a living like a woodpecker. Instead of developing a long pointed beak and jackhammer pecking capability, this particular finch had retained its basic finch body but with a different behavioral repertoire from that of other finches. In order to catch the insect larvae hidden deep in the tissues of plants, these creatures would carefully select a long cactus spine or thorn and use this as a tool to probe plant crevices until a tasty grub could be located and impaled.

The unusual life forms of the Galapagos, although fascinating, were only one small part of a much bigger puzzle (Darwin, 1968). In Argentina, Darwin had found the fossilized bones of an elephant sized creature called Megatherium. These giants no longer existed in South America or anywhere else, but very similar, albeit teddy-bear-sized, animals called tree sloths could still be found in the forests of that continent. This same pattern of apparent relatedness existed between numerous other extinct fossil forms and present day living animals. In some cases there was a great degree of similarity. In fact, some of the fossils were virtually identical to extant (living) animals. In other cases the differences were so great that only an expert in skeletal morphology could detect features common to both fossil and modern species.

During the course of its five-year voyage, the *Beagle* carried Darwin to Australia where all the indigenous mammals are marsupials. Unlike eutherian mammals, which nourish their unborn offspring by way of a special gestational organ called a placenta (Darwin, 1871), marsupials give birth to their young when the babies are still in a very undeveloped state. These embryo-like offspring climb up their mother's belly seeking the warmth and security of their mother's pouch. Only a lucky few from any given birth cohort are destined to find haven in the pouch where they can latch on to a milk-exuding teat. The majority of the marsupial newborn never make it to the pouch and quickly perish. Outside of Australia, marsupials are a rarity, with the opossum being the most common marsupial to share environments with placental mammals.

In Australia, Darwin found very few native placental mammals, but marsupials occupied many of the same ecological niches that were filled by placental mammals elsewhere in the world (Darwin, 1968). For example kangaroos occupied a niche filled by deer or antelopes in the Americas, Eurasia, or Africa. The Tasmanian Devil occupied the medium-sized predator niche. The rich variety of marsupial life in Australia and its highly restricted presence on the rest of the earth gave Darwin another piece to the big puzzle.

But even stranger phenomena awaited Darwin down under. Two of the native species (the duckbill platypus and the echidna) were monotremes (egg-laying mammals). Whereas marsupials were rare outside of Australia and its neighboring landmasses, monotremes were nonexistent. The reproductive physiology of the marsupials, though rare, could be found in the rest of the world. Only in Australia could one find furry, warm-blooded quadrupeds that reproduced by laying eggs. Bipedal, warm-blooded egg-layers were in abundance throughout the world, but birds are not that similar to monotremes (the duckbill of the platypus is only superficially similar to the bill of certain waterfowl). Monotreme reproductive physiology most closely resembles that of a class of cold-blooded quadrupeds, the reptiles. The monotremes represented an altogether different sort of taxonomic bridge. They represented a link not just between species within a genus or between families or orders. They showed characteristics common to two distinct classes of vertebrates, the mammals and the reptiles (Darwin, 1871). This was a very important puzzle piece for Darwin.

Charles Darwin's grandfather, Erasmus Darwin, had argued that all living things were connected by common descent from a single ancestral organism (Darwin, 1887). One test for this idea would be the existence of transitional forms at every taxonomic level. The animals of the Galapagos, which clearly resembled mainland species while being simultaneously strangely different, supported the idea of new species radiating from a common ancestor. The resemblance between fossil giant sloths and living tree sloths supported the idea that many of the transitional forms had become extinct leaving only the indelible mark of their existence in the fossil record. The monotremes represented forms that were transitional between reptiles and mammals, and the marsupials represented a transitional link between monotremes and placental mammals. Furthermore, the way in which very similar ecological niches were filled by very different sorts of organisms on the South American mainland, the Galapagos islands, and the Australian continent supported the idea first put forward by Erasmus that organisms will change over time in order to adapt to their environments. What Erasmus had failed to do was to come up with a mechanism that could explain how this adaptive change came about. It was the destiny of his grandson Charles to be the first to explain the origins of the myriad life forms on this planet, including our own.

After returning to his native England, Charles Darwin found the requisite puzzle pieces necessary to fathom the grand whole that they represented (Darwin, 1887). The progressive morphing of organisms into very different organisms was not a phenomenon unique to the natural world. Many of Darwin's countrymen had demonstrated remarkable success in altering the form and function of a variety of domesticated plants and animals. Their technique, called selective breeding, consisted of simply retaining those individual animals or plants that possessed certain desirable characteristics and using them for breeding stock. By repeating this process over numerous generations, wild cattle were transformed into walking milk factories with giant distended udders, and wolves evolved into poodles and cocker spaniels. The mechanism behind these sorts of transformations was a selective process engendered by goal-directed human intelligence. Darwin saw the organismic transformations of nature as the product of a very different sort of selective process.

What this selective process was occurred to Darwin in 1838 after he read *An Essay on the Principle of Population,* a 1798 publication by Thomas Malthus, a British political economist. Malthus, who was also a clergyman, was deeply distressed by the sight of thousands of slum dwellers living in grinding poverty (Darwin, 1859). He observed that the ability of humans and other creatures to reproduce far exceeds their ability to accrue resources. Malthus argued that populations would tend to increase exponentially but food resources would remain constant or at best increase arithmetically. He further argued that the inevitable disaster that would result from this process could only be circumvented by moral restraint (sexual abstinence), or failing that, war, famine or disease. The predilection of almost all living things for excessive fecundity as described by Malthus was the key puzzle piece that allowed all the other errant pieces in Darwin's puzzle to fall in place producing a coherent and comprehensive whole. This grand whole was Darwin's Theory of Natural Selection or, as it was to be known sometime later, Darwin's Theory of Evolution.

Darwin procrastinated in presenting his theory to the scientific community for such a long period of time that evolution theory almost came to be associated with the name of another English naturalist (Milner, 1990). In 1858 Darwin received correspondence from Alfred Russel Wallace, who was living in the Moluccan Islands. The letter basically outlined the theory of natural selection in much the same way Darwin had described it in his much longer, but unfinished, manuscript. Like Darwin, Wallace had been influenced by the work of Malthus and the geologist, Charles Lyell, who argued that gradual change over vast periods of time could produce dramatic changes. Unlike Darwin, who came to the idea of evolution in part from studies of selective breeding in domestic animals, Wallace got the idea from his observations of the natural distribution of living populations including human tribal groups and their competition for resources.

When Darwin read Wallace's manuscript he was dismayed that he was about to be scooped by another. He appealed to his friends, Sir Charles Lyell and the botanist Sir Joseph Hooker. These prestigious scientists used their influence to make an arrangement that would insure that Darwin's name would be associated with the Theory of Natural Selection. Excerpts from the manuscripts of both Wallace and Darwin were issued in a joint publication in July 1858, and Wallace's contribution was titled "On the Tendency of Varieties to Depart Indefinitely from the Original Type." Darwin then rushed to complete *The Origin of Species* which was published in 1859. Under the modern conventions of science, Wallace should be credited with discovering the theory of natural selection since his completed manuscript was the first to explicitly lay out the theory. However, without Darwin's painstakingly meticulous attempt to preempt every conceivable criticism against his theory and his extraordinary ability to build alliances and coalitions within the scientific community, the theory of natural selection may have been rejected or ignored for decades. It was through Darwin's efforts that in a very short period of time he was able to reshape and revolutionize Western thought.

Basic Tenets of Darwin's Theory

1. Organisms produce an excess of offspring, many more than are required to replace the parents.
2. The individuals within a population of organisms show a range of variability across numerous physiological and behavioral traits.

3. Because of the inherent variability between individuals within a population, some individuals will be better able to survive and reproduce while others will be less suited to survive and reproduce.
4. Because of the differential survival and reproduction of individuals with certain characteristics these adaptive characteristics will come to be more and more prevalent with each succeeding generation.
5. Eventually, as a result of natural selection, enough change may accrue in a population to make it reproductively isolated from other populations, hence the origin of new species.

The simple but elegant theory of natural selection was essentially correct as Charles Darwin and Alfred Russel Wallace conceived it 150 years ago (Milner, 1990). Unfortunately, in the nineteenth century there was no science of genetics, and gene theory is crucial to the theory of natural selection. In Darwin's time most biologists believed in "blending inheritance," the idea that parental traits mixed in their offspring the same way different colored paints would smoothly blend together. If this were true, it would mean that any new adaptive trait could not increase in a population because successive blending from generation to generation would wash it away. The erroneous belief in blending inheritance made it difficult for Darwin to defend natural selection as the major driving force in evolution. Fortunately for Darwin's theory, one of his contemporaries, Father Gregor Mendel, demonstrated that hereditary traits were transmitted as units that did not blend (particulate inheritance). Unfortunately for Darwin the man, Mendel's discoveries were ignored by science until they were rediscovered some years after Darwin's death.

The Modern Synthesis

In 1865 Gregor Mendel, an Austrian monk, published a paper summarizing his many years of hybridization experiments with peas (Strickberger, 1990). The paper implied that parental characteristics do not blend in their progeny but are transmitted as discrete units. Mendel's work was ignored by his contemporaries, and it was not until 16 years after his death in 1899 that three scientists doing hybridization experiments rediscovered Mendel's classic paper. These researchers were able to use Mendel's 1865 publication to interpret their own findings. In genetic nomenclature, the principles of inheritance are known as Mendel's Laws. Gregor Mendel never explicitly formulated these laws, instead they were read into his writings by subsequent researchers after they discovered the classic 3:1 ratio for themselves.

Mendel's Laws

1. *The Law of Segregation or Particulate Inheritance:* The members of a pair of homologous (AA) chromosomes segregate during meiosis and are distributed to different gametes. A hybrid or heterozygote (Aa) transmits to each mature sex cell (gamete) only one factor (A or a) of the pair received from the parents, not both factors and not a blend of the two.

2. *The Law of Independent Assortment:* Each member of a pair of homologous chromosomes segregates during meiosis independently of the members of other pairs, so that alleles carried on different chromosomes are distributed randomly to the gametes. (see Figure 1.2)

Mutations

Following the rediscovery of particulate inheritance it was found that inheritable changes in genes, termed mutations, could occur spontaneously and randomly without regard to the environment (Strickberger, 1990). Because mutations were seen to be the only source of genetic novelty, many geneticists believed that evolution was driven onward by the random accumulation of favorable mutational changes, an idea labeled mutationism. The geneticist Hugo De Vries had the erroneous belief that macromutations could produce a new species in one generation with no transitional forms. The idea of natural selection as the primary driving force in evolution fell out of vogue during the early years of the twentieth century.

Even while mutationism was rising in popularity, the scientific groundwork that would ultimately vindicate Darwinism was being laid by Sewall Wright, J.B.S. Haldane, and several other geneticists, all working independently (Strickberger, 1990). They showed that any given gene is adaptive only under certain environmental conditions. If conditions change over time, the gene may become maladaptive. The vast store of genes potentially available for inheritance by the next generation constitutes the gene pool. Sexual reproduction ensures that the genes are randomly reshuffled in each generation, a process termed recombination. When a population is in a state of equilibrium, the gene frequency (the frequency of occurrence of each gene in proportion to the total number of genes in the gene pool) remains the same, even though the genes are recombined in different ways in each individual. When the gene frequencies in the pool shift in a sustained, directional manner, evolution is occurring. Mutations provide the gene pool with a continuous supply of new genes (since mutations were unknown to Darwin, the original source of new variability was a mystery to him). It is through the process of natural selection that the gene frequencies change so that advantageous genes occur in greater proportions.

Despite the mathematical support that was developed for this view of evolution, most evolutionists adhered to the theory of evolution by random mutations until the late 1930s (Milner, 1990). In 1937, Theodosius Dobzhansky published *Genetics and the Origin of Species*, extending the mathematical arguments with a wide range of empirical evidence. By experimentally manipulating laboratory environments, he was able to observe adaptive genetic changes in large populations of fruit flies (evolution). Dobzhansky established that modern genetic theory is compatible with Darwinian selection. Natural selection is the chief cause of persistent changes in gene frequencies and therefore of evolutionary changes in a population's characteristics. In the remaining decades of the twentieth century the research findings from all fields of biological and paleontological science have added ever-increasing support to the revitalized Darwinian theory of evolution.

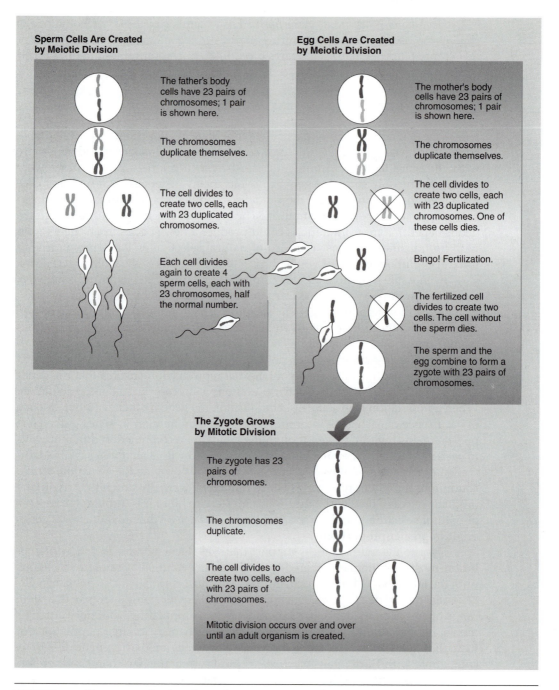

FIGURE 1.2 Gamete production through meiosis, zygote formation, and cell division. (Drawing adapted from J. Pinel's *Biopsychology*, p. 37, © 2000 by Allyn & Bacon. Used by permission of Allyn & Bacon.)

DNA

In 1953, James Watson and Francis Crick were able to deduce the structure of deoxyribonucleic acid (DNA), the molecule of heredity (Crick, 1981). DNA is in the form of a twisted ladder (a spiral helix) the rungs of which consist of nucleotide base pairs. Adenine is paired with thymine, and cytosine is paired with guanine (see Figure 1.3). The power of DNA comes from its capacity to code for protein production and its capacity to replicate itself. A sequence of three adjacent nucleotides codes for a particular amino acid, a protein building block. The proteins that are assembled from the total sequence of amino acids direct the biochemical pathways of development and metabolism in an organism (see Figure 1.4).

The second important characteristic of DNA is its ability to replicate itself. Before a cell divides, the DNA ladder uncoils itself and splits apart at the nucleotide seam. Each separate strand carries a series of unpaired nucleotides that begin

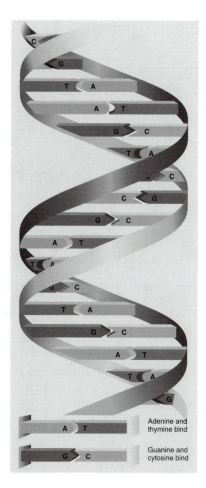

FIGURE 1.3   DNA, the replicator molecule: As a DNA molecule breaks into separate strands, each isolated nucleotide base attracts a complimentary base, thus the adenine attracts a new thiamine, the thiamine a new adenine, etc. The end result is two new DNA molecules that are perfect replicas of the original. (Drawing adapted from J. Pinel's *Biopsychology,* p. 40, © 2000 by Allyn & Bacon. Used by permission of Allyn & Bacon.)

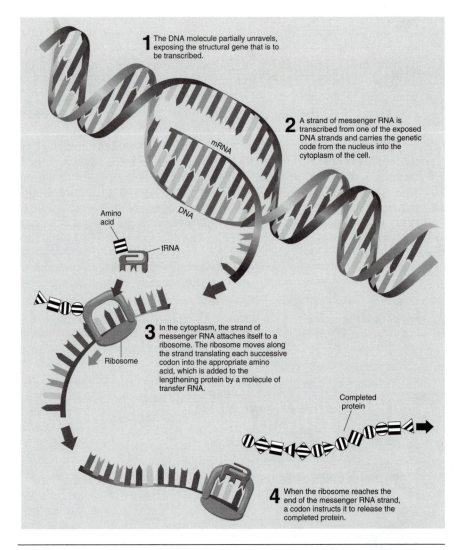

The DNA molecule partially unravels, exposing the structural gene that is to be transcribed.

A strand of messenger RNA is transcribed from one of the exposed DNA strands and carries the genetic code from the nucleus into the cytoplasm of the cell.

mRNA

DNA

Amino acid

tRNA

In the cytoplasm, the strand of messenger RNA attaches itself to a ribosome. The ribosome moves along the strand translating each successive codon into the appropriate amino acid, which is added to the lengthening protein by a molecule of transfer RNA.

Ribosome

Completed protein

When the ribosome reaches the end of the messenger RNA strand, a codon instructs it to release the completed protein.

FIGURE 1.4   The translation of genetic information into the machinery of life, i.e., the transcription of proteins. (Drawing adapted from J. Pinel's *Biopsychology*, p. 41, © 2000 by Allyn & Bacon. Used by permission of Allyn & Bacon.)

to attract their complementary nucleotides. Each adenine attracts a thymine and each cytosine attracts a guanine and so on until the two half strands become two complete strands of DNA. It is DNA's capacity as a replicator molecule that makes reproduction possible in every living thing from simple microbe to complex multi-cellular organism.

Mutations are now known to be changes in the nucleotide base pair sequences that affect the expression of protein manufacture (Strickberger, 1990). A gene is defined as a specific sequence of nucleotides along a chromosome coding for a particular polypeptide or protein. Natural selection operates to favor or suppress a particular gene according to how strongly its protein product contributes to the reproductive success of the organism. These findings have made possible the study of evolution at the molecular level, tracing the history of changes in particular genes, in gene organization, and constructing molecular phylogenies based on DNA similarities between taxonomic groups. Today, evolutionary studies extend into all branches of biology. As Dobzhansky pointed out, nothing in biology makes sense except in the light of evolution.

Behavior as a Function of Evolution

William James

The year 1890 saw the publication of the first psychology textbook, *Principles of Psychology*, by the American philosopher and psychologist William James. The work advanced the principle of functionalism, which argued that complex mental functions including higher order consciousness exist for the same reason that complex morphological and physiological characteristics exist. They exist because they had adaptive significance in the ancestors of the organisms that presently display them. Higher order consciousness enabled a human to have a mental construct of self and to visualize his or her "self" in various situations including a projected future scenario. For example, a human ancestor that could make projections about food shortages that would occur with the change of seasons might lay in stocks of nonperishable foods during a time of abundance. Individuals who displayed behavior of this type would have an enormous advantage over individuals who failed to anticipate changes in their personal situation.

William James (1890) argued that humans show more behavioral plasticity than other animals because we have more instincts than they do, not fewer. We tend to be ignorant of the existence of these instincts because they work so well in processing information and structuring our minds that it is difficult to perceive their action or conceive of their reality (Cosmides & Tooby, 1997). Consequently, we take "normal" behavior for granted not realizing that "normal" behavior needs to be explained just as any other behavior. This "instinct blindness" has always been a major hurdle to overcome in the study of psychology. James clearly recognized the essential role played by natural selection in shaping patterns of complex human behavior. Ironically, almost a century would pass before mainstream behavioral science would again turn to the evolutionary perspective as a means to understanding human psychology. The reasons for this hiatus have to do with the misuse and misunderstanding of Darwinian theory.

The Abuse of Darwinism

During the latter part of the nineteenth century the views of Herbert Spencer, an English philosopher, became popular among many wealthy industrialists in

Europe and America. Spencer used the concept of natural selection as an ethical justification for *laissez-faire* capitalism (Milner, 1990). It was Spencer who coined the phrase "survival of the fittest" although it is often mistakenly attributed to Darwin. Spencer's philosophy of Social Darwinism was used to justify the exploitation of the poor by the dominant affluent classes. Numerous millionaires during this period readily embraced what they believed was scientific vindication of their capitalist excesses. Paradoxically, proponents of Marxism also called themselves Social Darwinists, emphasizing the parallel between competition in nature and the struggle of the working classes. The German evolutionist Ernst Haeckel believed that humans must conform to nature's processes, no matter how ruthless. Years after Haeckel's death, Adolph Hitler and his fellow Nazis took this twisted view to its horrific extreme with the enactment of official government policies aimed at the extermination of "unfit" races. Hitler declared, "Nature is cruel, therefore I am cruel."

Hitler's statement epitomizes the naturalistic fallacy, the argument that because something exists in nature it is a correct model for human behavior (Wright, 1994). In Darwinian terms, "Nature" is both blind and indifferent to the fate of her children. For self-aware creatures like ourselves to use the existence of something in nature as a justification for our conscious decisions is nothing but a deluded rationalization, a grievous error. Examples can be found in nature of almost any conceivable social system or pattern of individual behavior, but this does not mean that these are good or desirable patterns for human behavior. Who, for example, would hold up the dung beetle as an example of an ideal natural diet for humans? Because of the misuse of evolutionary theory by the so-called Social Darwinists and some fascist extremists, the idea of genetic determinism came to be strongly associated with biological explanations of behavior.

Genetic determinism argues that "genes are destiny" (Wright, 1994). According to this view, whatever qualities a man or woman possessed, whether exceptional or defective, good or bad, were hardwired in their genome. Many believed that applying biological principles to humans was a way of advocating the doctrine of genetic determinism and therefore supporting the maintenance of the status quo. In the case of the industrialist Social Darwinists, the Eugenicists, and many others who distorted evolutionary theory to suit their own agendas, the latter charge was certainly true. Unfortunately for science, these abuses set the stage for an equally extreme swing in the direction of environmental determinism.

Environmental Determinism

Extreme environmentalism argues that all complex behavior is the result of learned associations and reinforcement contingencies. In psychology, this view was manifested in the behaviorist perspective, founded by the Russian physiologist, Ivan Pavlov. In America, behaviorism was popularized by John Watson and later made pragmatic by B. F. Skinner. The major success story derived from Pavlovian conditioning theory was the technique of systematic desensitization, which was a way of extinguishing the maladaptive associations, displayed in phobias. Skinner's operant conditioning approach, based on reinforcement of desired behaviors, has proven itself to be a powerful method for shaping certain behaviors in innumerable species. In humans it has been especially useful in training mentally retarded individuals to function with minimal supervision. Despite the practical merits of the behaviorist techniques, the behaviorists never produced the revolutions in individual behavior and consequently human society envisioned by Skinner. This failure was not from a lack of trying. Numerous individuals were attracted to behaviorism's mechanistic, and some would say overly simplistic, approach to behavior, and many ardently believed Skinner's claim that we could build a utopian society if we could insure that only "proper" behaviors were reinforced. A realization of the practical limits of the behaviorist approach to shaping behavior slowly emerged during the 1950s and 1960s, while the dreams of Skinnerian utopias slowly died. The greatest failure of behaviorism was not its utility, which was actually its strong suit, but its abysmal failure to explain human behavior. Behaviorism opted for an ideological stance that guaranteed its eventual failure from the very beginning when it divorced itself from biology, declaring that biological principles were essentially irrelevant to understanding behavior. This was tantamount to a fish declaring water was irrelevant to its existence.

In a similar anti-biology vein, anthropology adapted the perspective that human behavior is infinitely malleable and that individuals are shaped in their totality by the culture in which they grow up (Allman, 1994). Franz Boas and Margaret Mead were proponents of this cultural relativist perspective. This perspective, which was originated by Boas, was in part a reaction to the elitist views that prevailed in academic circles around the turn of the century (Holloway, 1997). At this time, most European and American scholars believed that cultures could be ranked in a developmental hierarchy from low to high with the highest tier of course being occupied by "civilized" westerners. By advocating an egalitarian perspective on culture, Franz Boas improved both the ethical integrity and the science of anthropology. Through transcending attitudes of racism and cultural supremacy anthropology made enormous gains in objectivity. Unfortunately, in their efforts to distance themselves from the cultural chauvinism of the nineteenth century, the cultural relativists went overboard in their empowerment of culture as the primary shaper of human behavior.

The cultural relativist anthropologists concentrated on delineating the differences between human cultural groups while ignoring the similarities (Allman, 1994). They viewed culture as though it was some disembodied entity that shaped people rather than being shaped by them. From their perspective, biology (e.g., evolution, genetics, neurophysiology) was irrelevant to any discussion of human behavior. Incredibly, some of the advocates of extreme environmentalism not only viewed humans as *tabulae rasae* (blank slates to be inscribed by the environment) but all other organisms as well. Fortunately for science, while most American social scientists were under the thrall of behaviorism and cultural relativism, some European researchers were making great strides in a discipline called ethology.

Ethology

In 1973, the three founders of ethology, the study of animal behavior, Konrad Lorenz of Austria, Nikolaas Tinbergen of the Netherlands, and Karl von Frisch of West Germany shared the Nobel Prize in physiology and medicine (Kimble, 1994). Karl von Frisch in his study of honey bee "language" demonstrated that a highly flexible and adaptive system of complex symbolic communication could be genetically encoded in the individual members of a social group. Lorenz studied a phenomenon called filial imprinting. Imprinting is a special form of learned attachment that occurs in social animals during a time of heightened sensitivity called a critical period. For example, during the first 36 hours after goslings hatch they will imprint on the first large moving object they encounter. Normally this would be their mother, but if a human scientist manipulates the situation such that the goslings encounter him or his dog during the critical period the goslings faithfully flock to and follow either a featherless biped or a furry quadruped until they are fully grown. Birds also sexually imprint during a critical period that occurs when they become sexually mature. Birds reared from a young age by humans often come to identify humans as appropriate mating partners, ignoring opposite sex members of their own species. Before Lorenz elucidated the complex mechanisms involved, filial attachment and sexual attraction in animals would have been attributed to "instinct" or learning based on reinforcement contingencies.

The third Nobel laureate Niko Tinbergen said that any behavior could be explained from the perspective of several different levels of analysis (Tinbergen, 1951). These different levels of explanation were not mutually exclusive and all of them together were needed to fully understand a given behavior. The first three explanations that follow can be thought of as answers to how questions. The fourth, the evolutionary explanation, answers the question "why does the behavior exist?"

1. **Proximate Causation:** Proximate causation focuses on the immediate factors (e.g., physiological or neurobiological) that produce a behavior. A detailed analysis of which neural pathways become active just prior to and during a behavior and how the organism's internal biochemistry including various hormone levels influences the activity of those neural pathways would provide a proximate explanation of that behavior. A simplistic version of a proximate explanation for a behavior would be the stimulus-response interpretation favored by behaviorist psychologists.
2. **Ontogeny:** An ontogenetic or developmental explanation of behavior looks at the interaction of environmental influences with genetic information from conception onward. Ordinary learning would fall under the rubric of ontogeny as well as critical period learning. Moreover, early exposure to environmental insults (e.g., radiation or chemicals) can have a profound and irreversible impact on behavior as well as physiology.
3. **Function:** A functional explanation of behavior seeks to specify the adaptive significance of a pattern of behavior. Behavior that has an adaptive function

should by definition enhance the survival of that organism and/or increase its reproductive fitness. Behavior that has an adaptive function is clearly linked to the evolutionary process. However, the present day function of a behavior may not be the same function the behavior fulfilled during thousands of generations of natural selection. Moreover, many individuals express behavior patterns that are clearly maladaptive in the present day although the underlying predispositions for these behaviors may have resulted in adaptive behavior patterns in ancestral environments.

4. **Evolutionary history:** An evolutionary explanation of behavior is based on the idea that behaviors that have an adaptive function will be concentrated in the behavioral repertoire of an organism as a result of eons of natural selection. Organisms that are closely related phylogenetically are likely to share many behavioral tendencies.

Altruism and Sociobiology

In almost all animal societies examples can be found of seemingly selfless service rendered by one individual toward another. Honeybee workers for example literally work themselves to death procuring resources for the hive and when they sting intruders in defense of the hive it is a kamikaze act that is invariably fatal. In numerous species of social animals, sentinels will sound a warning at sight of a predator thereby aiding their group mates but putting themselves at higher risk. Apparently unselfish behavior of this kind that does not benefit an individual and may even be harmful to the individual but that enhances the welfare of others is called altruism. Darwin attempted to reconcile altruism with natural selection by arguing that the performer of an altruistic act, though damaging its own reproductive success to some degree, nevertheless contributes to the survival of others of the species. How such sacrifice could be selected for was unclear to Darwin; eventually, the genes predisposing altruism should become rare and then go extinct, since their possessors are reproducing less often than animals lacking them.

The first major advance in understanding altruism came during the early sixties when British biologist W. D. Hamilton developed the concept of kin selection or inclusive fitness (Hamilton, 1963). His theory shows with mathematical precision that individuals within a species can best enhance their own reproductive success by aiding their close relatives so long as the gain conferred on the recipient is much greater than the cost to the donor. For selection of altruistic genes to occur, K must be greater than the reciprocal of r where r equals the coefficient of relationship of the recipient to the altruist ($K > 1/r$). Since full siblings have $r = \frac{1}{2}$ (due to the law of independent assortment) genes causing altruistic behavior towards brothers and sisters to be selected only if the behavior and the circumstances are generally such that the gain is more than twice the loss. Ideally, an animal would suffer no loss in reproductive fitness if it sacrificed its life to save the lives of two of its siblings. Many heretofore inexplicable behaviors in social animals can be explained in this way.

However, altruism often occurs in the absence of close genetic relatedness; that is, it can involve individuals that are not direct kin. R. L. Trivers, an American biologist, proposed that reciprocal altruism can account for such cases (Trivers, 1971). According to this concept, individuals in need receive aid on the "understanding" that they will reciprocate such aid. One chimpanzee will groom another, removing parasites from areas the receiver could not reach, because later the roles will be exchanged. For reciprocal altruism to work, however, the members of the group need to be able to identify and exclude any cheaters who simply accept the boons but never return the favor. Conditions conducive to facilitating such systems are most likely to occur in small groups, such as those of primates, including primitive human societies. The English biologist John Maynard Smith (1982), using computer simulations, demonstrated how reciprocal altruism can evolve in a species that is completely selfish at the outset because of the greater reproductive success conferred by such altruistic behavior.

These various theories and supporting data were brought together by the American biologist E. O. Wilson in *Sociobiology: The New Synthesis* (1975), a book that has become the holy writ of sociobiology as a distinct field of study. In its chapter on the evolution of human behavior, the book also helped to make sociobiology the target of critics who leveled charges of genetic determinism against its proponents. Wilson's speculations that our ethical and moral systems, even our aesthetic sense all have an evolutionary basis did not sit well with the *tabula rasa* camp. However, his suppositions that humans are designed by natural selection to be easily indoctrinated, to have innate sex differences in behavior, and to have a predisposition for warfare and genocide had an infuriating effect on Wilson's critics. E. O. Wilson, an innocuous Harvard biology professor, was not only attacked in print for his views but suffered physical assaults as well. The term sociobiology came to be associated with a number of negative connotations such as racism and sexism and few nontenured academics risked being branded as advocates of sociobiological theories. The coining of a new term for the investigation of human behavior from an evolutionary perspective may have been in part motivated by a desire of its practitioners to distance themselves from the connotative baggage that had been acquired by sociobiology. The new term was *evolutionary psychology.*

Evolutionary Psychology

According to Leda Cosmides and John Tooby, codirectors of the Center for Evolutionary Psychology at the University of California at Santa Barbara, evolutionary psychology differs from sociobiology because it integrates evolutionary biology with cognitive science (Small, 1995). Evolutionary psychology views the mind as a set of information-processing machines that were designed by natural selection to solve adaptive problems faced by our hunter-gatherer ancestors.

David Buss, an evolutionary psychologist at the University of Texas, sums it up in the following statement: "Sociobiology bypassed the mind and focused on behavior, whereas evolutionary psychology views the mind—that is, our evolved

BOX 1.1 • *Through a Glass Darwinian*   *The Abuse of Evolutionary Psychology*

Since its inception, the field of evolutionary psychology, like its previous incarnations, has had to weather a firestorm of criticism. Criticism, of course, plays a vital role in the development of good science. Unfortunately, much of the criticism leveled at evolutionary psychology ignores the body of empirical data and logical inference upon which it is based. In fact, evolutionary psychology is often treated as though it were a sort of heretical philosophy instead of a scientific discipline seeking to understand human behavior. One particularly vociferous critic, who somehow parlayed his expertise in the paleontology of snails into an omniscient understanding of primate evolution and psychology to level scathing criticism at the entire field of evolutionary psychology. This is not to say, that people who are not trained experts in a particular scientific discipline can not make insightful critiques and other valuable contributions. Unfortunately, the critiques of this particular snail researcher were not motivated by concerns for scientific veracity. The articles that were written by this individual, attacking evolutionary psychology, were propaganda pieces, emotionally manipulative but rationally incoherent.

What is the heresy inherent in evolutionary psychology that evokes such extreme reaction? After all, the basic tenet of evolutionary psychology is that humans, like every other animal species have evolved behavioral predispositions. These predispositions are the product of a long process of adaptive evolution. They exist because, in general, the behavior they engendered enhanced the survival and/or reproduction of those who possessed such predispositions. If the critics were simply the same anti-evolutionist crowd that has been making specious arguments against Darwinian theory since Darwin's time there would be no mystery about it. Most anti-evolutionists are adherents of fundamentalist religious beliefs that leave no room for evolutionary theory. For

these people, a failure to oppose Darwinism, would simply be dishonest. In contrast, the most outspoken critics of evolutionary psychology, are avowed atheists who are supposedly staunch supporters of evolutionary theory in general. Why is the evolutionary analysis of the human mind such a threat to these people?

One anti-evolutionary psychology argument, that is often presented, is that the expansion of the human brain over evolutionary time spontaneously created the capacity for language, cognition and every other aspect of complex behavior. The human mind and the environmentally/culturally-programmed giant, blank-slate brain that generated it, mysteriously came into being as a result of a series of unique, unrepeatable accidents that fell outside the mundane process of biological evolution. These critics somehow ignore the vast body of evidence that refutes this view of the human mind. Linguistic and psychological research, over the past few decades, has made it abundantly clear that language and complex cognition do not just spontaneously appear. What is required are very complex, very specialized neural structures that are created by an ontogenetic interaction of specialized genes and environmental stimuli. Those specialized genes are the product of adaptive evolution. Mental functions would not exist, had they not been shaped by natural selection. It's just that simple.

Why, then, is something so obvious being resisted with all the zeal and close mindedness of a holy war? Perhaps this resemblance to religious behavior is more than coincidence. Since before the time of Plato, Western philosophical traditions have typically viewed the mind as synonymous with spirit or soul. The French philosopher Rene Descartes took this perspective to an extreme when he pronounced the human mind/intellect to be a sacred spiritual entity that controlled the machine body at "the seat of

(continued)

BOX 1.1 • (Continued)

the soul," the pineal gland. In marked contrast to the West, Eastern philosophical traditions typically view the mind as a secular entity that acts as an impediment to spiritual progress. Perhaps in the West, the secular academics who have abandoned overt religious beliefs continue to cling to culturally indoctrinated beliefs concerning the sacrosanct nature of the mind. For them, the mind is a carefully guarded ivory tower, full of inviolate mysteries that should never, under any circumstances, be subjected to the impartial, prying lens of science.

psychological mechanisms—as the central locus of adaptation" (Small, 1995; p. 8). Buss further explains the distinction between the two disciplines, describing the sociobiological view of humans as fitness maximizers, while evolutionary psychologists view humans as having species-typical psychological mechanisms that have evolved to facilitate fitness in a probabilistic manner but do not always produce that effect. For example, few unmarried men are seeking to conceive children when they engage in sexual intercourse and when males masturbate after viewing pornography there is not even a remote chance of reproduction, but in both cases the behavior can be explained as the result of an evolved psychological mechanism that generally increased fitness in ancestral situations (Table 1.1).

Cosmides and Tooby (1997), make the following observation:

> Our species lived as hunter-gatherers 1000 times longer than as anything else. The world which seems so familiar to you and me, a world with roads, schools, grocery stores, factories, farms, and nation-states, has lasted for only an eyeblink of time when compared to our entire evolutionary history. The computer age is only a little older than the typical college student, and the industrial revolution is a mere 200 years old. Agriculture first appeared on earth only 10,000 years ago, and it wasn't until about 5,000 years ago that as many as half of the human population engaged in farming rather than hunting and gathering. Natural selection is a slow process, and there just haven't been enough generations for it to design circuits that are well-adapted to our post-industrial life.
>
> In other words, our modern skulls house a stone age mind . . . In saying that our modern skulls house a stone age mind, we do not mean to imply that our minds are unsophisticated. Quite the contrary: they are very sophisticated computers, whose circuits are elegantly designed to solve the kinds of problems our ancestors routinely faced. (p. 11)

The Methods of Evolutionary Psychology

Like many fledgling sciences, evolutionary psychology during its early years was top heavy with speculative theory relative to empirical data. Critics argued that evolutionary models of human behavior were not falsifiable. In other words, evolutionary explanations were considered too flexible and broad to be amenable to

TABLE 1.1 *Evolved Psychological Mechanisms: 10 Illustrations*

Psychological Mechanism	Function	Author(s)
1. Fear of snakes	Avoid poison	Marks (1987)
2. Superior female spatial–location memory	Increase success at foraging/gathering	Silverman and Eals (1992)
3. Male sexual jealousy	Increase paternity certainty	Buss, Larsen, Westen, and Semmelroth (1992) Daly, Wilson, and Weghorst (1982)
4. Preference for foods rich in fats and sugar	Increase caloric intake	Rozin (1976)
5. Female mate preference for economic resources	Provisioning for children	Buss (1989a, 1989b)
6. Male mate preferences for youth, attractiveness, and waist-to-hip ratio	Select mates of high fertility	Buss (1989a, 1989b) Singh (1993)
7. Landscape preferences for savanna-like environments	Motivate individuals to select habitats that provide resources and offer protection	Kaplan (1992) Orians and Heerwagen (1992)
8. Natural language	Communication and manipulation	Pinker and Bloom (1990)
9. Cheater-detection procedure	Prevent being exploited in social contracts	Cosmides (1989)
10. Male desire for sexual variety	Motivate access to more sexual partners	Symons (1979)

(Reprinted from "Evolutionary psychology: A new paradigm for psychological science" by D. M. Buss, from *Psychological Inquiry, 6*(1), p. 6, copyright 1995 by Lawrence Erlbaum Assoc., Inc. Used by permission of Lawrence Erlbaum Assoc., Inc.)

the rigorous testing that is a hallmark of true science. Over the years, however, the base of empirical data supporting the theories of evolutionary psychology has grown steadily. In turn, the adaptationist theories of evolutionary psychology have been increasingly refined resulting in precise, highly testable hypotheses. Ketelaar and Ellis (2000) argue that evolutionary psychology meets the criteria for a progressive scientific research program. Progressive science is evaluated on the basis of the explanatory and predictive power of its theories, its ability to provide coherent explanations of existing phenomena including seemingly anomalous phenomena and to generate novel and accurate predictions that ultimately increase our understanding of the world. The outstanding success of evolutionary psychology in explaining a broad and deep swath of human behavior makes this burgeoning field a prime candidate for unifying the currently disparate social sciences.

All good science begins with observations of the phenomena of interest. In the behavioral sciences, the observations are, of course, generally of the organism's behavior. Ethologists develop a detailed inventory of the types of behavior displayed by the species being studied. This inventory is called an ethogram and it is used to generate specific hypotheses. However, the anatomy and physiology of the organism are also critical to understanding its behavior. For example, someone observing the large, projecting, moist-tipped nose of a ring-tailed lemur (a primitive primate species) might suspect that olfaction played an important role in the social communication of this animal. This conjecture would be confirmed by observing the avid scent-marking engaged in by ring-tailed lemurs. The presence of specialized anatomical and physiological features supporting certain patterns of behavior suggests an evolved adaptive function for the behaviors. This in itself, however, is not conclusive evidence of an evolved adaptation. It is possible that the organism has simply co-opted an existing physiological potential to engage in a novel behavior that was irrelevant to its ancestor's survival.

The hypothesis that the behavior in question promoted the survival of the genes that potentiate it (i.e., the behavior has adaptive significance) requires more rigorous testing. For example a researcher might hypothesize that the ring-tailed lemur scent marks in order to establish territories. To test this hypothesis the researcher could manipulate the ability of the individual animals to scent mark and to detect scent marks. It could then be ascertained what effect these manipulations had on the survival or reproductive capacity of the effected individuals. Obviously the capacity of researchers interested in human behavior to manipulate their subjects in order to test specific hypotheses is much more limited. However, these kinds of limitations are intrinsic to all the sciences dealing with human beings, including biomedical research.

Despite the limitations imposed by ethical constraints in the study of human behavior, there are actually many advantages that are not available with other species. With nonhuman species the researcher is restricted to studying the behavior the animal actually emits, the animal's spoor, and occasionally simple artifacts such as nests. The exceptional capacities of our species for language, culture, and complex technology expand the database for the human ethogram exponentially.

Language enables the researcher to probe individual preferences and tendencies while avoiding the necessity of observing behavior that would usually occur only in private. Language also allows the researcher access to the past. Individuals can be queried about earlier events in their lives. Historical accounts provide general information concerning human tendencies over time periods exceeding individual life spans. Public records documenting births, deaths, marriages, divorces, and criminal acts provide some insight into certain aspects of behavior for several centuries. Archaeological records provide snapshots of behavior from even older periods.

Language and complex cognitive abilities create the capacity for culture. In other words, information can be transmitted and accumulated across generations. Culture embodies the totality of socially transmitted behavior patterns, arts, beliefs, institutions, and all other products of human work and thought. All of these provide clues to understanding human nature and developing testable models concerning evolved psychological mechanisms. Cultural phenomena that are particularly germane to the interests of evolutionary psychologists involve storytelling. All human cultures have a history of oral traditions where legends, myths, philosophical and religious beliefs are transmitted from generation to generation. Recurring motifs common to widely separated cultures provide important clues about universal aspects of the human mind. The invention of writing had the effect of freeze-framing many of these stories or at least making them less subject to change over the course of time. The behavior described in Homer's *Illiad* makes perfect sense to evolutionary psychologists. The epic poem recounts how during the siege of Troy (Illium) the Greek hero Achilles squabbles with his commander in chief, Agamemnon, over possession of some of the spoils of war, the beautiful female captives, Chryseis and Briseis. Many of the psychological patterns depicted in the *Illiad,* such as group territorial conflict and disputes within a male dominance hierarchy over access to fertile females, characterize not only human behavior but the behavior of many nonhuman primate species as well.

In the modern Western world, books, magazines, movies, commercial web sites and television shows are subject to a process similar to natural selection but occurring at a much more rapid pace. The content that sells will be perpetuated while what does not sell will disappear. One by-product of this mercantile selection process is a rich data-source for scientists seeking to understand our evolved psychology. The old cliché that "sex and violence sells" is true because survival and reproduction constitute the essence of evolutionary success. Our ancestors, who by definition were evolutionary successes, had a strong and abiding interest in those aspects of their environment that were most likely to impact the survival of their genes, whether these genes resided in their own bodies or the bodies of their close kin. These evolved interests, preferences and predispositions are very much alive and well in the people of the twenty-first century. In fact, they are so commonplace that they have often been largely overlooked, ignored and misinterpreted by social scientists.

The challenge facing the researcher who has successfully skirted the hurdle of "instinct blindness" that William James warned about in the nineteenth century and who suspects that a commonly recurring pattern of human behavior is an evolved psychological mechanism is one of substantiating their hypothesis. True adaptations must be sorted out from incidental or random evolutionary by-products.

Tooby and Cosmides (2000) list the formal properties of an adaptation as follows: An adaptation is a set of phenotypic characteristics that recurs cross-generationally in a given species. It consistently develops during the life history of the organism as result of specific genes interacting with consistently recurring environmental features. The genes producing the adaptation became established in the species over evolutionary time because the characteristics conferred by these genes enhanced the reproductive capacity of the individuals possessing these genes.

Adaptations evolved as mechanisms to solve problems that were likely to occur in the *environment of evolutionary adaptedness* (EEA) a term coined by Bowlby (1967). The EEA is not a specific time period or location but rather a statistical composite of enduring environmental features that comprised the selective pressures resulting in a particular adaptation. An adaptation may not be currently enhancing reproductive success in a given individual. For a trait to be selected for, it only has to increase the probability of reproductive success. Not every individual in every generation will necessarily experience benefits. Moreover, the environmental features that interact with the requisite genes during ontogeny to manifest the adaptation may not be present during the development of a given individual. For example, children born with severely impaired hearing who have their hearing restored as adults never acquire normal language abilities (Curtiss, 1989).

Another reason an adaptation may fail to produce an adaptive outcome is that new features of the environment may circumvent the original adaptive function of the mechanism. For example, certain drugs can directly stimulate the brain's reinforcement centers. These brain regions are normally activated by survival enhancing activities such as eating when hungry or drinking when thirsty. The direct stimulation of the reinforcement centers opens the way to the very maladaptive behavior patterns associated with drug abuse and addiction (Carlson, 1998).

Because numerous features of the modern environment are of highly recent origin, hypotheses concerning evolved psychological mechanisms in humans must be evaluated from the perspective of the environment in which these mechanisms evolved. Data gathered from studies of contemporary hunter-gatherers have provided invaluable information about lifestyles and concomitant physical and social environments that were typical for our species during the vast majority of its existence. Archaeological evidence provides information about human populations that lived in the past. In fact, the paleoarchaeological record provides critical data on the life style, diet and social organization of the ancestral species that proceeded our own. Thus we can know something about selective pressures that have existed over millions of years of time.

One of the most useful sources of information for understanding adaptive behavior, both in general and within our own species, comes from the study of other animals (Maier, 1998). By studying our closest phylogenetic relatives, the chimpanzees, we can gain insights into which behaviors and capabilities may have been present in our common ancestor living about seven million years ago and which ones were more recently derived during the human evolutionary lineage. Studies of a variety primate species give us important clues about the selective pressures associated with sociality as well as knowledge of which human behavioral tendencies are of ancient primate origin. Even species that are far removed from us phylogentically can shed light on human behavior. For example, no living primate species other than humans forms pair-bonds (mated partners) within a large muti-male, multi-female social group to produce and rear offspring. Many songbird species, on the other hand, do exhibit this type of social organization and studies of their behavior may provide important insights regarding the evolution of human behavior.

Our understanding of proximate physiological mechanisms comes largely from research on other species. Most of our knowledge of the organization and functioning of the nervous system is a result of invasive research on nonhuman animals. Recent developments in noninvasive neuroimaging techniques, such as PET scans and functional MRIs, allow direct study of brain and behavior in humans. It is only by integrating this data with the data gleaned from invasive procedures can we hope to gain a comprehensive understanding of the proximate functioning and evolutionary origins of the human nervous system (Preuss, 2000). Another area where animal research has proven invaluable in contributing to our understanding of human behavioral/physiological adaptations is stress research. Laboratory and field studies have clearly delineated the adaptive functions of the endocrine and nervous systems responses to perceived threats (stressors) as well as the deleterious consequences of chronic stress (Selye, 1956; Sapolsky, 1997).

In summary, the evolutionary psychologist uses a rich plethora of information to identify which aspects of human behavior represent innate psychological mechanisms cobbled together by natural selection. The next step is to substantiate the hypothesized adaptation by generating and verifying specific predictions that are implied by evolved functionality (enhanced reproductive fitness). By the same token, predictions that follow from alternative hypotheses need to be tested and eliminated if possible. Cosmides and Tooby (2000) have used this approach to great advantage in explaining patterns in social contract reasoning that appeared unfathomable except in the context of evolutionary psychology.

In accordance with the methods of modern science, when the testing process is completed, untenable hypotheses are discarded while tenable hypotheses remain for further study. The ultimate test of the validity of a scientific hypothesis is its consistency within the totality of scientific disciplines. The interdisciplinary nature of evolutionary psychology inherently lends itself to producing sound science.

In the next chapter we will look at the origin and development of life on earth beginning with the formation of the universe. We will then focus on the evolution of the hominids from the common ancestor of modern African apes and humans. In order to understand what we are and why we do what we do, we must understand our origins.

Summary

Charles Darwin observed that closely related organisms typically varied across geographic locations separated by physical barriers and across geological periods separated by long time intervals. Darwin reasoned that a process of Natural Selection, analogous to the selective breeding of domestic animals, created differential survival and reproduction of certain individuals within a population. Eventually, over many generations, populations were transformed by natural selection into new species. A second Englishman, Alfred Russel Wallace, independently developed the concept of Natural Selection and the general theory was presented to the scientific community with excerpts from both Darwin and Wallace in 1858.

An unshakable foundation for Darwinian evolution theory was provided by the development of modern genetics. Understanding that traits were transmitted as discrete, nonblending units (genes) led to an understanding of evolution as a sustained, directional shift in population gone frequencies. Spontaneous changes in genes (mutations) provide new raw material for evolutionary change. Delineating the chemical structure of DNA, the molecule of heredity has made it possible to study evolution at the molecular level.

From the inception of evolutionary theory, it was understood that behavioral traits were shaped by Natural Selection just like morphological and physiological traits. Charles Darwin understood this, as did the American philosopher and psychologist William James. William James founded the Functionalist approach in psychology, which is based on the idea that complex mental functions are evolved traits.

This adaptationist approach to human psychology fell out of favor for nearly a century as a consequence of a number of tragic historical events. Darwinian theory was used as a prop to support a number of versions of the Naturalistic fallacy. Social Darwinists argued that the exploitation of the poor by the rich was just the natural order of things and Nazi death camps were created to eliminate "inferior" races. Partially as a result of these abominations, behavioral theories based on environmental determinism were embraced by psychologists (behaviorists) and anthropologists (cultural relativists).

Discoveries in the science of ethology (animal behavior) and sociobiology, such as the concept of inclusive fitness provided the basis for the modern reemergence of an adaptationist approach to human psychology, evolutionary psychology. Evolutionary psychology focuses on the evolved psychological mechanisms that comprise the mind as the central locus of behavioral adaptation. Evolutionary psychologists use information from a variety of sources to identify which aspects of human behavior represent evolved psychological mechanisms. The validity of the hypothesized adaptations is tested by generating and verifying specific predictions that are implied by evolved functionality as well as testing predictions that follow from alternative hypotheses. The interdisciplinary nature of evolutionary psychology gives it an inherently sound scientific basis.

Discussion Questions

1. Why is modern genetic theory (particulate inheritance) so critical to Darwinian Evolutionary theory?

2. Describe a number of twentieth century empirical and theoretical discoveries that would have greatly strengthened William James' Functionalist approach to psychology if they had been known in the nineteenth century.

3. Use Tinberger's four explanations of behavior to explain your own personal dessert preference. Why do humans as a whole show a preference for sweet as well as fatty foods such as ice cream?

Key Terms

altruism
behaviorism
cultural relativist perspective
deoxyribonucleic acid (DNA)
ethology
environment of evolutionary
    adaptedness (EEA)
extreme environmentalism
evolutionary psychology
genetic determinism
genus

families
functionalism
imprinting
inclusive fitness
morphology
mutations
naturalistic fallacy
ontogeny
operant conditioning
orders
particulate inheritance

proximate causation
reciprocal altruism
selective breeding
social Darwinism
sociobiology
species
tabula rasa
taxonomy
Theory of Evolution
Theory of Natural Selection

Additional Reading

The Adapted Mind: Evolutionary Psychology and the Generation of Culture by Jerome H. Barkow, Leda Cosmides, and John Tooby (Editors) (1995).

Human Nature: A Critical Reader by Laura L. Betzig (Editor) (1996).

Mean Genes: From Sex to Money to Food: Taming Our Primal Instincts by Terry Burnham and Jay Phelan (2000).

Evolutionary Psychology: The New Science of the Mind by David M. Buss (1999).

Handbook of Evolutionary Psychology: Ideas, Issues, and Applications edited by Charles Crawford and Dennis Krebs (1997).

Adaptation and Human Behavior: An Anthropological Perspective by Lee Cronk, Napoleon Chagnon, and William Irons (Editors) (2000).

Without Miracles: Universal Selection Theory and the Second Darwinian Revolution by Gary Cziko (1995).

The Autobiography of Charles Darwin 1809–1882 by Charles Darwin.

The Descent of Man by Charles Darwin.

The Origin of Species by Charles Darwin.

The Voyage of the Beagle: Charles Darwin's Journal of Researches by Charles Darwin, et al.

The Selfish Gene by Richard Dawkins (1976).

Darwin's Dangerous Idea by Daniel Dennett (1996).

Human Ethology by Irenaus Eibl-Eibesfeldt (1989).

Introducing Evolutionary Psychology by Dylan Evans (2000).

The Fateful Hoaxing of Margaret Mead: An Historical Analysis of Her Samoan Researches by Derek Freeman (1998).

Emergence: From Chaos to Order by John H. Holland (1999).

New Aspects of Human Ethology by Alain Schmitt, Klaus Atzwanger, and Karl Grammer (Editors) (1997).

Consilience: Unity of Knowledge by Edward Osborne Wilson (1998).

Sociobiology: The New Synthesis, Twenty-fifth Anniversary Edition by Edward Osborne Wilson (2000).

2

From Big Bang to Big Brain

For just as human creations are the products of art, so living objects are manifest in the products of an analogous cause or principle, not external but internal, derived like the hot and the cold from the environing universe. And that the heaven, if it had an origin, was evolved and is maintained by such a cause, there is therefore even more reason to believe, than that mortal animals so originated.

—Aristotle (350 B.C.)

Chapter Questions

1. What is the origin of the universe?
2. Is life unique to Earth?
3. How old is the Earth?
4. When did life first evolve?
5. What were our remote ancestors like?

Life in the Universe

To understand our origins and our place in the grand scheme of things we must first seek some understanding of the nature and origin of the world around us. In an immediate sense this consists of the biosphere of the planet Earth, all the physical properties of this planet, and sun—all of which allow life to exist on Earth. To understand where on the scale from unique to common the Earth lies as a typical planet, it is necessary to compare it with other planets. Until recently this comparison was strictly limited to other planets within our solar system. In the final years of the twentieth century, planets have been discovered orbiting other stars in our galaxy (Flamsteed, 1997). In practical terms, we are still limited to studies of planets in our own solar system since the enormous distances to other star systems precludes the gathering of significant data concerning these other planets. Moreover, any planet large enough to be detected in another star system is probably far too massive to allow the evolution of life. In fact many of the "planets" discovered elsewhere in the galaxy may be brown dwarf stars orbiting a larger primary star. When we compare the earth with the other planets and moons of our solar system, at first glance our home planet appears to be the one oasis for life in an incredibly inhospitable void. Of the inner rocky planets Mercury, Venus, Earth, and Mars, life indisputably exists only on Earth although Mars may harbor simple microbial forms within its crust or fossils of extinct forms. Some Martian meteorites found in Antarctica show microscopic structures that some have claimed to be fossilized Martian microbes (Hecht & Concar, 1996). The Martian terrain shows evidence of water induced erosion from early in its geologic history. The presence of water (a rare phenomenon in the solar system other than on the Earth) greatly enhances the probability that life could have originated on Mars. The only other potential candidate for life in our solar system, Europa, is also the only other celestial body other than Earth to have large quantities of water (Kerr, 1997). Europa, which orbits the gas giant Jupiter, displays a sea of frozen water. The myriad of cracks upon the surface of this ice suggests that liquid water lies beneath the surface.

If the existence of extraterrestrial life in our solar system (either extant or extinct) is corroborated it will have enormous implications for our understanding of the origins of life. If life arose more than once within the same solar system it implies that, in a universe with the physical properties of ours, life tends to readily come into existence. If this assumption is true, the corollary that follows is that among the billions of galaxies each with billions of star systems life must commonly exist throughout the universe. Moreover, given the nature of natural selection to produce organisms of greater behavioral complexity (as discussed in the latter part of this chapter and Chapter Three) it is likely that intelligent species have arisen many times elsewhere in the universe. It is also likely that most of these hypothesized non-earth intelligent species emerged and became extinct before any of our ancestors gazed at the stars and wondered what they were. Given the enormous age of the universe and the relatively recent emergence of *Homo sapiens*, especially the technologically adept *Homo sapiens sapiens*, the odds are good (given the above assumption) for the existence of extraterrestrial intelligences but not so good for their existence during our limited time as a species. When we consider the fact that radio technology was not discovered until the end of the nineteenth century and that it forms the basis for the SETI (Search for Extraterrestrial Intelligence) project, the probability of contacting otherworldly intellects becomes highly remote (Chown, 1997). Considering the history of our own species in regard to contacts between technologically disparate cultures, it is perhaps fortunate that the odds for our encountering a technologically advanced alien species are vanishingly small.

The Beginning

The light that reaches Earth from distant stars and galaxies, regardless of where they are located relative to our solar system, all show a characteristic red shift (Barrow, 1994). This red shift is due to the Doppler effect, a stretching of light waves into longer wavelengths when a light source is moving rapidly away from an observer. The funny thing about this observed red shift is that it is observed in every direction. This means that all distant objects are moving away from our solar system. This is not because the Earth is the center of the universe, rather it is comparable to what happens to the dots on a polka-dot balloon. As that balloon is inflated, the distance of each dot from every other dot increases. The universe is expanding and has been doing so far a long time. Extrapolating backward, cosmologists estimate that all the matter in the universe including all space and time existed as a single minute point some ten to twenty billion years ago. From one unimaginably concentrated point the universe exploded outward in what has become known as the Big Bang.

A crucial test of the validity of the Big Bang theory was the existence of cosmic background radiation. The background radiation is the remnant energy signature from the intense heat generated in the initial moments of the Big Bang. The existence of the background radiation was predicted in 1948 and was confirmed in 1965. The background radiation consists of microwave radiation that can be detected from any direction in space and forms the backdrop for all other radio waves. It has a temperature of 2.7 degrees Kelvin (Taubes, 1997). The ubiquity of this residual energy confirms not only the fact that the universe had an origin (as opposed to having existed forever) but also the fact that its origin was a violent one.

If we give the date of the Big Bang as having occurred 13,500 million years ago, which is suggested by several lines of evidence, the first galaxies came into existence from gigantic clumps of gas about 12,500 million years ago (Calder, 1983). The individual stars that comprised these galaxies were micro-clumps of highly compressed gas. The intense gravitational pressures at the cores of these stars ignited thermonuclear fusion reactions that converted hydrogen into helium with the byproduct radiant energy (Davies, 1994). As the stars aged, they produced heavier elements in their fusion furnaces. In fact all of the elements heavier than hydrogen and helium are the byproducts of stars. Heavier and heavier elements were produced in the fusion furnaces of the stellar cores as the stars aged. All the elements with atomic weights less than iron and including iron were created in this way. Eventually these early stars depleted their fuels to such a degree they could no longer contravene the force of gravity. These collapsed inward upon themselves and then exploded into novas. It was during the nova explosion that the elements with atomic weights higher than that of iron were created. The elementally diverse interstellar gas that remained from these early stars formed the building material that could be incorporated into new solar systems. Clumps of this gas and dust gradually formed as a result of the mutual gravitational attraction of the particles. If the mass of a gas cloud reached a certain critical limit, gravitational pressure started the nuclear fusion process and a new star was born from the remains of previous ones.

In the case of our sun we know that that this birth occurred about 4550 million years ago (Calder, 1983). Our newly formed sun was surrounded by rings of gas and dust that coagulated through collisions and gravitational attraction into the planets. Solar radiation drove the lighter gases outward from the inner portions of the gas ring leaving a mix of heavier elements that would form the inner rocky planets—Mercury, Venus, Earth, and Mars. For tens of millions of years cosmic collisions continued to accrete mass to the bodies of the solar system. About 4500 million years ago the Earth collided with a mass roughly the size of the planet Mars. The material that was ejected into orbit from this violent collision coalesced into Earth's moon. The collisions have continued through to the present although their severity and frequency have consistently waned over time. The record of these impacts is recorded on the cratered face of the Moon. The active geology of Earth and the protective atmosphere that surrounds it have reduced and obscured most of the evidence of cosmic bombardment on Earth's surface. It was the complex chemical mix of materials vented through volcanic activity and raining from space in the form of comets and meteors that allowed interesting things to happen on the newly created Earth.

The tumultuous chemical environment of the early Earth would have been lethal to any existing life forms (Calder, 1983). The atmosphere consisted of methane, ammonia, and water vapor with almost no free oxygen. Corrosive and highly reactive compounds were constantly being spewed onto Earth's surface by volcanism. Natural selection was at work in this pre-life environment (Dawkins, 1989).

Stable molecular compounds persisted while unstable forms were eliminated (Dawkins, 1989). Chains of molecules that could replicate themselves became more common than those that could not. Chains that could replicate themselves quickly and with good fidelity became more common than chains that replicated more slowly and with less accuracy. Of all the elements created in stellar fusion furnaces, carbon in particular demonstrated a great capacity for forming a multitude of intricate molecules. In the 1950s, experiments by Miller and Urey demonstrated that the organic building blocks of life could be readily generated from the type of Earth atmosphere that existed over four billion years ago. The energy sources for these and later experiments were electricity and ultraviolet radiation mirroring the lightning and solar radiation of the pre-biotic Earth. Although laboratory experiments simulating early Earth conditions have produced all the nucleotide bases for DNA and RNA, none of these experiments have succeeded in producing these constituents assembled into highly organized, complex molecules capable of coding for protein production. Despite the failure of biochemists to create simple life forms in the laboratory, most scientists are confident that given the chemically active environment of the natal Earth and thousands of millennia of natural selection the emergence of life from non-life was a straightforward and expected phenomenon.

In fact, by at least 4000 million years ago life existed on Earth. Rocks 3800 million years old suggest the presence of ancient bacteria (Calder, 1983). By 3500 million years ago, photosynthetic bacteria were forming accretions on shallow sea floors called stromatolites. These organisms had evolved the trick of using sunlight to convert carbon dioxide and water into chemical energy releasing oxygen as a waste product. As these photosynthetic organisms proliferated over hundreds of millions of years, the oxygen content of the atmosphere gradually increased. For the anaerobic bacteria that had once been the dominate life on earth, the free oxygen was a deadly poison that had to be dealt with either through cloistering in airless spaces or undergoing radical adaptive change. Today we can still find anaerobic forms living in deep mud and other places untouched by the atmosphere. However, most of the living things on Earth including humans are descended from organisms that adapted to an oxygen-rich atmosphere. The ancestors of eukaryotes (cells with a nuclear membrane) solved the oxygen problem via an evolutionary shortcut (Kimble, 1994). Instead of evolving the necessary physiology themselves they developed a symbiotic relationship with a much smaller bacterium that had already developed biochemistry for oxygen metabolism. The descendents of these oxygen-competent bacteria live on today as the mitochondria inhabiting our cells. The mitochondria have retained their separate heredity through 1800 million years of co-evolution with their host cells. Their function as finely integrated organelles is to use oxygen to manufacture energy for the cells. The presence of mitochondria is absolutely essential to the functioning of eukaryotic cells.

In a similar process of symbiotic co-evolution, photosynthetic bacteria that were incorporated into larger cells became the ancestors of the green plant organelles known as chloroplasts (Kimble, 1994). Possessing both chloroplasts and mitochondria, plants were able to organize themselves into the first multicellular organisms, e.g., seaweed about one millimeter in length, by 1300 million years ago. By 1000 million years ago, seaweed measuring several centimeters in length had evolved.

The first fossil records of multicellular animals date back to 670 million years. These consist of jellyfish and simple worm-like organisms (Calder, 1983). One line of hollow-bodied worms would evolve into vertebrates. Other groups of worms were ancestral to segmented animals (e.g., earthworms and insects) while yet others would give rise to mollusks (e.g., clams and octopuses). Many of these early animals were, from our human perspective, quite bizarre in appearance. The majority of these evolutionary "experiments" were dead-ends whose genetic lineage ended over half a billion years ago. The culling of these early animals may represent the cutting down of central evolutionary branches (phyla) whereas the extinction of species is analogous to pruning twigs from a particular phyletic branch.

With the development of true plants and animals there was an explosion of evolutionary change. For thousands of millions of years the shallow seas of Earth were filled with virtually unchanging microorganisms and then, in what amounts to almost a geologic instant, a broad diversity of plants and animals appeared on the scene. The main reason for this outbreak in evolutionary innovation was the development of a new reproductive strategy called sexual reproduction. Unlike the simple fissioning that characterized asexual reproduction, sexual reproduction required specialized gamete producing cells that split and parceled genetic material into discrete packets. It further required that the organism get together with a cohort to allow its reproductive packets (gametes) to merge with the cohort's reproductive packets. The one clear advantage to this highly involved and convoluted mode of reproduction is that it allows genes to be mixed and swapped on an unprecedented scale (in asexual one-celled organisms, gene exchange sometimes occurs in a process called conjunction, but its effect on gene frequencies is relatively weak). Sexual reproduction allows for accelerated evolutionary change that can keep pace with rapidly changing conditions. Sexual reproduction has a greater capacity for rapid, adaptive, evolutionary change than does asexual reproduction, and this is its great advantage over asexual reproduction.

The shallow seas that teemed with Earth's first experiments in multicellular life were located on or around the ever-moving continental tectonic plates (Svitil, 1997). As these plates moved over the Earth's surface their distance from poles and equator constantly varied. Occasionally tectonic plates collided pushing up huge mountain ranges and causing far-reaching perturbations in the Earth's climate. Mountain building was probably just one variable out of a multitude that was responsible for the periodic ice ages that enshrouded the Earth. It may have been an ice age cooling that allowed for the evolution of multicellular life by thinning out the dense swarms of unicellular organisms. About 535 million years ago, the supercontinent of Gondwanaland shifted through 90 degrees latitude over a 15 million-year period. Over the same period, North America, moving at the rate of several feet per year, journeyed from the South Pole to the equator. It is theorized that this rapid movement was due to the Earth's outer mantle and crust sliding over the liquid core. A spinning sphere like the Earth is most stable when the greatest portion of its mass lies along the equator. The build up of too much mass at the South Pole may have resulted in the rolling over of the entire crust and mantle of the Earth with the inner molten core retaining its original spin and axial tilt. This 15-million-year reorienting of the Earth's surface corresponded to an evolutionary boom known as the Cambrian explosion.

Vertebrate Life

The first vertebrates, jawless bony fishes, appeared 510 million years ago near the end of the Cambrian age (Calder, 1983). By 425 million years ago bony fish had developed jaws. About that time, the heretofore barren terrestrial surface was first colonized by plants. While plants evolved structures that could support their own weight in the open air, certain predatory fish developed muscular fins they could use to "walk" upon the bottom of streams and estuaries. Eventually these fish that were pre-adapted for walking would evolve modified swim bladders that could serve as lungs and other modifications that would make them the first amphibians. Thus vertebrates did not colonize the land until 370 million years ago, tens of millions of years after the arthropods, the first land animals. Vertebrates did not become truly terrestrial until reptiles evolved about 313 million years ago (Calder, 1983). The reptiles laid eggs that were protected from desiccation by special membranes within a leathery or calcified shell.

Homeothermy was probably vital to the survival of the first mammals that appeared about 216 million years ago. A homeotherm or warm-blooded animal retains a constant body temperature whereas a poikilotherm or cold-blooded animal has a body temperature that varies with the temperature of its environment. Dinosaurs and other reptiles, including flying and aquatic types, occupied most of the available ecological niches. The only ecological role the mammals could succeed in was that of a small nocturnal animal. Small bodies lose heat quickly, especially during the relatively cool evening hours. The development of warm-blooded physiology was undoubtedly a boon, if not absolutely critical to the success of the early mammals in their nocturnal niche. The development of homeothermy produced a number of emergent effects such as the evolution of the sex-determining Y chromosome. Another effect was to create the potential for complex and high-powered neural activity. Warm-bloodedness is necessary but not sufficient for the development of large and complex brains in terrestrial animals. Many millions of years would pass before any of the mammalian lineages would show any significant increase in brain size and complexity.

Although the first mammals were egg layers like the modern-day platypus, by 125 million years ago opossum-like marsupials had evolved (Calder, 1983). Like the egg-laying monotreme mammals, they fed their young milk from modified sweat glands. The class Mammalia can be distinguished from all other classes of mammals by this single characteristic. In the marsupials, the young are born in a very undeveloped state. Newly born marsupials, which resemble embryos, must make their way to their mother's pouch and attach themselves to a milk teat in order to survive. Those lucky few that make their way into the pouch remain there until they have developed enough to get about on their own. This relatively wasteful mode of reproduction is necessary in marsupials because of the rudimentary state of the placenta, which allows for a very brief gestation period. The next great event in mammalian evolution was the development of the modern placenta.

The placenta functions as a biological interface between fetus and mother, allowing for nutrient exchange and long-term uterine development. Placental mammals first appeared about 114 million years ago. Mammals remained small, but they started to show adaptive radiation into many different lineages. By 100 million years ago, the ancestors of hoofed mammals had separated from the other lines. The ancestors of primates diverged about 95 million years ago making them among the oldest lines of mammals. The ancestors of carnivores and bats diverged about 90 million years ago, and the ancestors of rodents by 85 million years ago.

The earliest true primate fossils are from a creature called Purgatorius that lived in Montana near the end of the Cretaceous era 69 million years ago (Calder,

1983). Purgatorius undoubtedly eyed the activities of the tyrannosaurs and other reptile giants from the safety of trees. The primates and other mammals may have remained small and insignificant creatures, forever hiding from the giant reptiles they shared the earth with, if not for an incredible catastrophe.

When Darwin wrote *The Origins of Species* he eschewed the role of catastrophic events in shaping the evolution of life (Milner, 1990). This was to emphasize the concept of gradualism that he borrowed from the geologist Charles Lyell. Primarily, Darwin wanted to differentiate his theory of natural selection from the ideas of the proponents of violent and cataclysmic change, such as the biblical flood. In the twentieth century, geologists and biologists had become so fundamentally gradualistic in their thinking that they had a difficult time accepting the evidence of catastrophic events when they found them. Despite overwhelming evidence, the Cretaceous terminal catastrophe was not immediately accepted by the scientific community. With more and more supporting evidence and very little in the way of contradictory evidence, most scientists have come to accept the catastrophe that occurred at the end of the Cretaceous era.

About 65 million years ago, an asteroid measuring two to six miles in diameter crashed into the earth in what is today the Gulf of Mexico of the coast of Yucatan (Calder, 1983). The explosive force of that impact was greater than what would be produced by the simultaneous detonation of all the earth's nuclear armament today. Vast areas of North America were completely incinerated in an instant, but the greatest death toll occurred over the months following the impact. Great amounts of dust and debris were thrown into the upper atmosphere totally obscuring the light from the sun. Without light, photosynthesis stopped and the food chain collapsed. The living things that could survive the long months of cold and darkness included dormant seeds and spores, a few aestivating reptiles like crocodiles and turtles, and small warm-blooded animals (birds and mammals). The dinosaurs and the flying and aquatic reptiles were totally wiped out, and none of their fossils are found above the Cretaceous/Tertiary boundary.

The mass extinctions of 65 million years ago left a world filled with gaping ecological voids (Calder, 1983). Surviving species, particularly mammalian species, quickly evolved to fill these gaps. The Tertiary, the first 64 million years of the Cenozoic era, was a period of remarkable change, both geological and biological. The supercontinent of Pangaea had formed with the collision of Gondwanaland, Euramerica, and Asia around 300 million years ago. Its breakup began 210 million years ago. The North American landmass separated from Europe 60 million years ago and began drifting westward. Australia separated from Antarctica about 50 million years ago to be followed by South America 35 million years ago. About 3 million years ago North and South America drifted into contact with one another.

The biological changes occurring during the Tertiary were equally spectacular (Calder, 1983). Warm-blooded whales had replaced the cold-blooded ichthyosaurs that had dominated the seas during the Mesozoic era. Mammalian herbivores browsed the tops of trees and cropped grass (another new development) in place of long-necked sauropods and menacing ceratopsian dinosaurs. Giant flightless birds occupied the predatory niches vacated by the tyrannosaurs and other reptilian hunters until mammalian carnivores evolved and eventually out-competed them. Members of a very ancient mammalian group known as primates also took advantage of newly available ecological niches.

The term *primate* was coined by Carolus Linnaeus in 1758 in his book *Systema Natura,* which classified all living organisms (Milner, 1990). Primate means *first rank* in Latin, and Linnaeus used this term because it described creatures most closely resembling humans. Linnaeus was, of course, pre-Darwinian in his thinking, and his classification scheme was based on the Aristotelian notion of the *scala natura,* the scale of nature. In the scale of nature, all living things are ranked in a series, with humans at the top, apes and monkeys somewhat below, and so on down the scale to the simpler organisms. Considering the absence of an evolutionary model and the deficits in knowledge in the seventeenth century, Linnaeus did a remarkable job in his classification of the primates. Primates are defined by a host of characteristics. Traits and tendencies found in primates include independent mobility of the digits, opposable digits on hands and feet, the presence of flattened nails rather than claws that are derived from ectodermal tissue, a semi-erect posture that enables hand manipulation, highly developed visual sense including a degree of stereoscopic vision, and a relatively large and complex brain relative to body mass. By 50 million years ago, some of the primates had evolved characteristics typical of modern species, such as a bony ring around their optical orbits and digital nails rather than claws.

Living primates are classified into two sub-orders (Strickberger, 1990). The prosimians, meaning literally before monkeys, and the anthropoids. The prosimians of today include the lemurs, the lorises, and the galago, or bush baby. The prosimians were the first primates to evolve and most of the surviving prosimian species come from the island of Madagascar, which separated from the African mainland millions of years ago. The Anthropoid sub-order includes the monkeys, apes, and humans. Compared to the prosimians, the anthropoids possess a more flattened face, more forward-directed eyes, and a larger, more complex brain. Fossil evidence from Egypt suggests that primitive anthropoids had already evolved by 30 million years ago. Some of these early anthropoids probably island hopped their way to South America, which was much closer to Africa at that time and eventually gave rise to the New World monkeys. On the African continent over the next 10 million years, the anthropoids diverged into two groups, the Old World monkeys and the hominoids, or ape-like forms (Table 2.1).

Hominid Evolution

Africa: Cradle of Human Evolution

15 million years ago, the continent of Africa was covered by tropical forests from east coast to west coast (Leakey, 1994). Living in that forest were a great diversity of primates, including monkeys and apes. In contrast to today's Africa, where only

TABLE 2.1 *Journeys in Deep Time*

In order to gain some perspective on the enormity of geological time imagine the following scenario: A scientist has invented a time-machine that can travel backward in time at the fixed rate of one hundred years for every second experienced by the time-traveler. The table below illustrates how long it will take the scientist time-traveler to reach certain destinations in the past. (BP = before present)

Subjective Time	Real Time	Associated Events
0.98 sec.	1903 AD (98 BP)	First flight of heavier-than-air-craft (airplane)
2.25 sec.	1776 AD (225 BP)	Birth of the United States of America
4.79 sec.	1522 AD (479 BP)	First recorded circumnavigation of the globe
5.46 sec.	1455 AD (546 BP)	Invention of the printing press
7.86 sec.	1215 AD (786 BP)	Magna Carta is signed; Genghis Khan captures Beijing
10.00 sec.	c. 1000 AD (1000 BP)	Vikings colonize North America
15.00 sec.	c. 500 AD (1500 BP)	Birth of Muhammad
16.97 sec.	304 AD (1697 BP)	Huns invade China
20.07 sec.	6 BC (2007 BP)	Birth of Christ
22.05 sec.	204 BC (2205 BP)	The Great Wall of China is completed
23.85 sec.	384 BC (2385 BP)	Birth of Aristotle
25.64 sec.	563 BC (2564 BP)	Birth of Buddha
32.00 sec.	c. 1200 BC (3200 BP)	Olmec pyramids erected in Mexico
46.00 sec.	c. 2600 BC (4600 BP)	The Great Pyramid of Giza is built
50.00 sec.	c. 3000 BC (5000 BP)	Stonehenge is constructed, Sumerians invent writing
55.00 sec.	c. 3500 BC (5500 BP)	The wheel is invented by Sumerians
1 min. 17 sec.	c. 7700 BP	Corn is cultivated in Mexico
1 min. 28 sec.	c. 8800 BP	The earliest known city, Catal Huyuk, rises in Asia Minor
1 min. 30 sec.	c. 10,300 BP	The ice age ends
1 min. 47 sec.	c. 10,700 BP	Goats and sheep are domesticated in the Middle East
2 min.	c. 12,000 BP	The domestic dog is bred from the wolf
3 min.	c. 18,000 BP	Cold peak of latest ice-age; wheat and barley are cultivated in Egypt; gazelles and goats are herded in the Middle East
3 min. 20 sec.	c. 20,000 BP	The bow and arrow is invented in north Africa
4 min. 20 sec.	c. 28,000 BP	The Neanderthals become extinct
5 min.	c. 30,000 BP	The Cosquer cave paintings are created
6 min. 40 sec.	c. 40,000 BP	Modern humans colonize Australia

(continued)

TABLE 2.1   *Continued*

Subjective Time	Real Time	Associated Events
7 min. 50 sec.	c. 40,000 BP	Neanderthals erect a shrine comprised of cave bear skulls in France
10 min.	c. 60,000 BP	Neanderthals bury their dead with flowers from medicinal plants in Iraq
12 min.	c. 72,000 BP	Beginning of the most recent ice age
16 min. 40 sec.	c. 100,000 BP	Anatomically modern humans inhabit South Africa
33 min. 33 sec.	c. 200,000 BP	An archaic *Homo sapiens* crafts a hand ax from a stone so that a fossil sea urchin embedded in it is displayed, showing a concern with aesthetics
50 min.	c. 300,000 BP	Hand axes are made more symmetrically than previously, suggesting improved cognitive abilities
1 hr.	c. 6000,000 BP	The first archaic *Homo sapiens* appears
2 hrs. 46 min.	c. 1 million BP	*Homo erectus* migrates out of Africa
3 hrs. 53 min.	c. 1.4 million BP	*Homo erectus* masters the use of fire
5 hrs.	c. 1.8 million BP	*Homo erectus* appears
6 hrs. 40 min.	c. 2.4 million BP	*Homo habilis* emerges about the same time as early stone tools
10 hrs.	c. 3.6 million BP	Bipedal hominids leave footprints in Laetoli ash
19 hrs. 27 min.	c. 7 million BP	The common ancestor of modern humans and chimpanzees inhabits Africa
1 day, 16 hrs.	c. 15 million BP	The ancestor of orangutans diverges from the ape/human lineage
4 days, 1 hr.	c. 35 million BP	The ancestors of new world primates reach South America from Africa
7 days, 12 hrs.	c. 65 million BP	The earth collides with a large cosmic body resulting in cataclysmic extinctions, including dinosaurs
11 days	c. 95 million BP	The first primates evolve
13 days, 5 hrs.	c. 114 million BP	Placental mammals evolve
20 days, 6 hrs.	c. 175 million BP	Jurassic reptiles flourish, including sauropod dinosaurs that are the largest terrestrial mammals to ever appear on earth
28 days, 9 hrs.	c. 245 million BP	The Permian Age ends with the greatest mass extinction event in Earth's history; 90% of all species become extinct
36 days, 6 hrs.	c. 313 million BP	The first reptiles evolve
49 days, 5 hrs.	c. 425 million BP	The first jawed, bony fishes appear

TABLE 2.1 *Continued*

Subjective Time	Real Time	Associated Events
77 days, 13 hrs.	c. 670 million BP	Jellyfish and flatworms appear
150 days, 11 hrs.	c. 1300 million BP	The earliest plants, in the form of micro-seaweed, evolve
185 days, 5 hrs.	c. 1600 million BP	Blue-green algae (e.g., photosynthetic bacteria) appear
208 days, 8 hrs.	c. 1800 million BP	The symbiotic precursors of modern mitochondria take up residence in the cell bodies of the ancestors of eukaryotic cells
1 year, 86 days, 10 hrs.	c. 3900 million BP	Photosynthetic bacteria evolve
1 year, 98 days	c. 4000 million BP	Life begins on earth
1 year, 161 days, 15 hrs.	c. 4550 million BP	The solar system forms
1 year, 173 days, 5 hrs.	c. 4650 million BP	The supernova that will produce the building blocks of our solar system occurs
3 years, 352 days	c. 12,500 million BP	The first star systems in the universe form
4 years, 102 days, 12 hrs.	c. 13,500 million BP	The "Big Bang," or birth of the universe

a few species of apes survived and most species are monkeys, the Africa at that time was predominately populated by ape species. Just as Darwin predicted (1871), one of these African ape species was the common ancestor of humans and living great apes. Tectonic forces began to tear the continent of Africa apart and, about 12 million years ago, a huge tear running from north to south developed on the African continent. Today we call this tear the Great Rift Valley. The development of the Great Rift Valley had two enormously important biological effects. It created an east-west barrier to animal populations, which promoted evolutionary differentiation on either side of the barrier. Second, it helped cause the development of a rich mosaic of ecological conditions. This ecological mosaic included remnants of forest, stretches of open savanna, and even areas of desert. With the change in the ecology, there was a change in the number of species.

The apes were adapted to a frugivorous diet (fruit-eating), whereas monkeys had evolved to be capable of eating not only ripe fruit, but also green fruit, and fibrous material, such as plant leaves (Leakey, 1994). With the loss of the forest habitat, the monkeys were at an advantage in terms of their diet. The ape species that survive today did so by retreating to forest refuges. These forest refuges served as stable oases in the midst of constantly changing and inhospitable environmental conditions. It is on the border between forest habitat and open savanna that the human line is thought, by some researchers, to have diverged from the ape line. Based on biochemical analysis of DNA, this split probably occurred about

7 million years ago (Sarich, 1983). All of the species that evolved on the human side of the split are referred to as hominids.

Bipedalism

Unlike the apes, who retreated into the dwindling forest as the ecology changed, the hominids evolved adaptations that enabled them to exploit the new conditions. The primary adaptation was the development of bipedalism. When compared to four-legged locomotion, striding on two legs is a relatively slow and inefficient means of getting about. A two-pound rabbit can easily out-run the fastest human. However, comparing bipeds to quadrupeds is not totally valid. We evolved from ape ancestors that were not true quadrupeds. They had adapted to an arboreal lifestyle, which meant that they brachiated when in the trees, and probably knuckle-walked when on the ground, like modern-day chimpanzees and gorillas. When faced with the prospect of traveling across the open savanna from one forest oasis to another, the most efficient means available to these ape-like creatures was bipedal striding. On the other hand, not all the available evidence supports this savanna hypothesis. Recent fossil discoveries indicate that some of the earliest hominid species live in wooded environments. However, bipedalism also offered some other immediate advantages. For one thing, it was a great aid in predator avoidance. Standing upright enabled these early hominids to spot potential predators from a much greater distance. Moreover, standing erect made these creatures appear much more formidable to any predators that may have seen them. The other immediate advantage of bipedalism was that it freed the hands for all sorts of purposes. Food could be carried from one location to another, and simple tools could be wielded.

What may be the earliest known bipedal hominid species was unearthed in a part of the Great Rift Valley in Kenya on October 25, 2000 (Aiello & Collard, 2001). The remains of the creature nicknamed Millennium Man, but officially christened *Orrorin tugenensis*, consisted of bones from at least five different individuals embedded in rock strata dated at more than 6 million years. This species was similar in size to a modern chimpanzee. Its skeletal remains suggest that it was an agile tree climber as well as a terrestrial biped. Its dentition suggests a frugivorous diet typical of apes but the reduced canines and large molars indicate evolutionary trends consistent with human evolution. The next earliest hominid species is represented by a species called *Ardipithecus ramidus*, from Ethiopia, dating from 5.5 to 4.4 million years (Woldegabriel, Haile-Selassie, Renne, Hart, Ambrose, Asfaw, Heiken, & White, 2001; White, Suwa, & Asfaw, 1994). The remains of this creature were found in what is thought to have been a forest environment, but it may have been bipedal. The fact that both Orrorin and Ardipithecus lived in relatively wet, forested environments calls into question the theory that environmental change spurred human evolution by forcing early hominids onto the open savanna, where bipedalism provided a key adaptive advantage. The teeth of *Ardipithecus*, while more human than those of the chimpanzee, are still basically ape-like. *Ardipithecus* probably dined on a menu of soft leaves and fiber-rich fruit.

Australopithecus anamensis (Leakey, Feibel, & McDougall, 1995; Culotta, 1995) is the next oldest hominid species. It dates to about 4.2 million years ago. The leg bones suggest that it was bipedal, but the teeth and jaws are very similar to those of older fossil apes. *Australopithecus anamensis* lived in a dry wooded environment. Its remains were found in Kenya.

Between 3.9 and 3 million years ago, a creature called *Australopithecus afarensis* roamed the African savanna (Johanson & Edey, 1981). The pelvis and leg bones of this hominid were clearly adapted to bipedal walking. The skull of *afarensis* resembles that of a chimpanzee, although the canine teeth were much smaller and the teeth are more human-like in general. The cranial capacity ranges between 375 to 500 cubic centimeters. The bones are very robust, and the finger and toe bones are curved, making them ideal for climbing trees. We can speculate that while *afarensis* moved about the savanna during the day, they sought the refuge of trees to sleep in at night, much like modern day baboons. The height of *afarensis* varied between about 42 inches to about 60 inches. There is evidence that there was strong sexual dimorphism in this species. Males probably weighed almost twice as much as females. More will be said about what this sex-dependent size difference indicates in terms of social organization in the chapter on courtship and reproduction. Since the discovery of *Australopithecus afarensis* many researchers have held the opinion that this species was a direct ancestory of modern humans. However, a recent discovery has seriously weakened this hypothesis.

In 1999, a 3.5 million-year-old skull, showing a unique combination of primitive and derived neurocranial features was found on the western shore of Lake Turkana, Kenya (Leakey et al., 2001). The find represents the oldest, reasonably complete, cranium known for any member of the human family. Its discoverers argued that it was sufficiently distinct from other hominids to belong not only to a new species but to a new genus, as well. They named it *Kenyanthropus platyops,* the flat-faced man of Kenya. *Kenyanthropus platyops* had pronounced cheekbones, small molar teeth and a less protruding jaw than *Australopithecus afarensis* making it much more human looking. However, *Kenyanthropus platyops* also possessed a chimpanzee-sized brain and small ear canals resembling both chimpanzees and *Australopithecus anamensis* of 4.4 million years ago. This mixture of primitive and derived characteristics shows that the evolution of different traits is neither uniform nor consistently progressive. *Kenyanthropus platyops* dentition suggests that it subsisted on soft foods such as fruits and insects, thus exploiting an ecological niche different from that of *Australalopithecus afarensis,* which probably ingested coarser fare such as roots and grasses and lived in drier habitat. It is clear that more than one human-like species coexisted from 3.5 million years ago and the human phylogentic tree appears to be multi-branched and bushy rather than simple and linear.

Hypothesis concerning the behavior of early hominids are generally indirectly inferred from the anatomical characteristics of teeth and other skeletal components. However, occasionally, the fossil record provides a direct glimpse of ancient behavior. Near an ancient volcanic mountain in Laetoli, Tanzania, a layer of fossilized volcanic mud contains tracks of various animals, including saber-tooth tigers, extinct elephants, hyenas, antelopes, and numerous other animals

(Leakey & Harris, 1987). Included in these tracks are three sets of hominid footprints, those of a large individual, a smaller one, and a juvenile. This may perhaps have constituted a family group with the larger individual, the male, walking in front, the smaller, perhaps a female, walking directly in the tracks of the larger individual, and the juvenile walking to their side. The tracks suggest that the young one at one point stopped and turned to look around to the left. The tracks are going north, away from the volcano, which at that time was erupting a spew of ash, which was later moistened by a light rainfall, causing it to harden like cement. The Laetoli footprints date to about 3.6 million years ago, suggesting that the hominids that made the tracks were members of the species *Australopithecus afarensis, Kenyanthropus platyops* or an, as yet, unknown hominid species.

By 3 million years ago, a new species of australopithecine had emerged, called *Australopithecus africanus* (Johanson & Shreeve, 1989). *Africanus* was similar to *afarensis*, but somewhat larger in body size, with a slightly larger brain, ranging between 420 and 500 cubic centimeters. Examination of brain endocasts of *africanus* failed to show a distinct Broca's area, the part of the human brain identified with speech production. The teeth and jaws of *africanus* were larger than those of humans, but their basic shape and structure resembles the human pattern rather than that of apes. The canine teeth have become even smaller in *africanus* than they were in *afarensis*. *Australopithecus africanus* probably made a living as an opportunistic forager and scavenger. How much hunting, if any, these animals did is not clear, but it is clear that they were hunted by other animals. Many of the *africanus* remains bear the marks of predator claws and teeth. They appear to have been preyed upon by leopards, and the younger ones by birds of prey. *Africanus* and *afarensis* are referred to as gracile australopithecines because of their light, slender body build, especially with regard to the teeth and skull. The australopithecines also began to evolve into a robust line with very thick massive jaws and teeth. These robust australopithecines are classified by some paleoanthropologists as species within the genus *Paranthropus* instead of *Australopithecus*.

Australopithecus aethiopicus (*Paranthropus aethiopicus*) lived about 2.6 million years ago (Leakey & Lewin, 1992). This was a robust form of australopithecine. This creature had very massive jaws and teeth and a sagittal crest along the top of its skull, indicating the attachment of extremely large jaw muscles for chewing. Its brain volume was only 410 cubic centimeters. By 2 million years ago, the robust australopithecines had evolved into two species. In South Africa remains of *Australopithecus robustus* (*Paranthropus robustus*) have been found, and in East Africa, remains of *Australopithecus boisei* (*Paranthropus boisei*), originally named Zinjanthropus, have been found. *Robustus* had a massive face, which was flat or dishshaped, no forehead, large brow ridges, and very small front teeth. Its molars were extremely massive, indicating a diet high in coarse or tough food that needed a lot of mastication. The average brain size of this species was about 530 cubic centimeters. There is some suggestion that the *robustus* species may have used simple digging tools. The most massively built of the robust australopithecines was *Australopithecus boisei* (*Paranthropus boisei*). The main difference between it and *robustus* is the increased development of the molars, face, and head. *Robustus* died out about 1 and a half million years ago, and *boisei* persisted until about 1 million years ago, showing that they coexisted with primitive modern humans for over a million years before they became extinct.

The australopithecines split into the gracile and robust lines beginning about 2.75 million years ago (Vrba, 1996). This was also the time when the earth underwent a significant climactic cooling. The robust line adapted to this ecological challenge by becoming highly specialized in terms of procuring food from one very narrow ecological niche. The gracile line, on the other hand, met the challenge by adapting more flexible, more generalized, all purpose behavior patterns. Two and a half million years ago marks the first onset of extensive arctic glaciation, causing the ecology of even the equatorial regions to change drastically (see Figure 2.1).

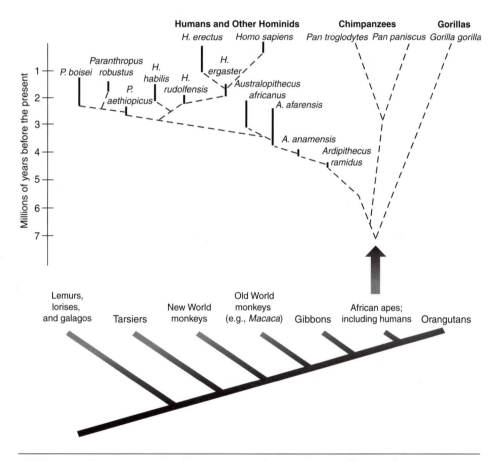

FIGURE 2.1 The phylogenetic tree depicting the emergence of hominids from the African great apes.

(Adapted from "What's human about the human brain" by T. Preuss, from *The New Cognitive Neurosciences*, 2nd edition, Fig. 84.1, © 2000 by The MIT Press. Used by permission of the MIT Press.)

The First Humans

It was at about 2.4 million years ago that we see the emergence of the first member of the genus *Homo*. This species has been dubbed *Homo habilis*, meaning handyman, because of the evidence of stone tools associated with its fossils (Leakey, 1994). *Habilis* was very similar to the australopithecines, except that its face was more prognathous, or forward projecting. The molar teeth were smaller than those of *africanus* but considerably larger than the molars of modern humans. Their average brain size was 650 cubic centimeters, with a range of 500 to 800 cubic centimeters. Moreover, examination of brain endocasts indicates a rudimentary bulge in the Broca's area, the area that is essential for speech production in modern humans. *Habilis* was about 5 feet tall, and probably weighed about 100 pounds. The females were smaller than the males, but *habilis* did not have the pronounced gender-dependent size difference that was seen in the *afarensis* specimens. *Habilis* persisted until about 1.5 million years ago.

Some scientists have argued that *habilis* should be included in the genus *Australopithecus*, not the genus *Homo*. However, examination of the semicircular canals suggests otherwise (Leakey, 1994). The semicircular canals are part of the vestibular system, and contain 3 C-shaped tubes arranged in all the three dimensions in space. In humans, the two vertical canals are significantly enlarged compared to those of apes, indicating adaptation for upright bipedal locomotion. In all species of the genus *Homo*, the inner-ear structure is indistinguishable from that of modern humans. However, in all species of *Australopithecus*, the semicircular canals resemble those of apes. This finding in conjunction with the conical-shaped rib cage of the australopithecines suggests that they were better adapted to walking rather than running.

The status of *Homo habilis* as a taxonomic classification is far from resolved. Many researchers believe that the specimens that are currently lumped together as *Homo habilis* actually represent at least two distinct species of the genus *Homo* (Walker & Shipman, 1996). Those specimens representing the upper end of the range for brain volume are classified by some as *Homo rudolfensis*. In fact, the flat face of *Homo rudolfensis* suggests a close affinity with *Kenyanthropus platyops*, the flat-faced Kenyan that lived 3.5 million years ago in the same region of Africa (Leakey et al., 2001). As more and more fossil evidence comes to light a complete revamping of hominid taxonomies may be in order. The first relatively indisputed species belonging to the genus *Homo* is *Homo erectus*.

Homo erectus appeared about 1.8 million years ago in Africa (Walker & Shipman, 1996). Some *Homo erectus* material found in Java has been dated to be almost as old as some of the oldest African *Homo erectus* specimens. This suggests that shortly after this species evolved, it proceeded to migrate and disperse out of Africa and across Asia as far as the present-day island of Java. Although *Homo erectus* died out in the rest of the world about 300,000 years ago, a few populations may have persisted in Java until about 20,000 years ago. *Erectus* specimens over 1.5 million years old had a brain capacity of about 900 cubic centimeters. More recent specimens between 700,000 to 500,000 years old had about 1100 cubic centimeters of brain tissue. One of the most distinctive characteristics of this species was a very thick brow ridge and a long, low skull. They had protruding jaws, large molar teeth, and no chin. From the neck down, *Homo erectus* closely resembled modern humans. Some of the earliest African specimens indicate that these individuals were well over six feet tall, with very powerful, lanky physiques perfectly adapted to hot equatorial climates and a life-style based on running and walking long distances (Walker & Shipman, 1996). Some researchers place these early African specimens into the species, *Homo ergaster.* Examination of the pelvis and legs indicates that their walking and running may have been much more efficient of that of modern humans. This was mainly because the hips were more narrow and the bones larger and more robust.

The lessened efficiency seen in modern humans in terms of bipedal locomotion was probably necessitated by the need to give birth to larger-brained infants (Walker & Shipman, 1996). Although *erectus* had proportionately smaller brains than modern *Homo sapiens,* this species had already mastered the trick of giving birth to infants with relatively undeveloped brains, and hence, smaller head size. In infant apes, brain growth is relatively slow compared to modern humans, and the brain size basically doubles from infancy to adulthood. In humans and in early members of the genus *Homo,* the infant undergoes a greater than threefold increase in brain mass before it reaches adulthood. The stone tools generally associated with *erectus* are generally more sophisticated than those found in association with *habilis.* The *erectus* tools were typically large cutting instruments with the staple tool being a flat, tear-drop shaped palm-sized stone tool referred to as a hand axe. This stone tool kit shows remarkably little change over the 1.5 million plus years that *Homo erectus* walked our planet. *Homo erectus* was probably the first hominid species to use fire. Hearths dating to 1.42 million years have been discovered in Africa and 750,000-year-old hearths have been found in Europe.

Like all hominid specimens, there is controversy surrounding the exact classification of *Homo erectus.* Some believe there are at least two different species represented by the specimens lumped under *Homo erectus.* These individuals feel that the Asian specimens represent one species, *Homo erectus,* and the specimens from Africa yet a second species, *Homo ergaster.* Even more controversial is the question of the evolutionary relationship between *Homo erectus* and *Homo sapiens sapiens.* Although there are several viable theories surrounding this relationship, what follows is based on what in the author's opinion is supported by the preponderance of evidence at this time.

About one million years ago, *Homo erectus* populations in Africa evolved into a new species, *Homo antecessor* (Bermudez de Castro, Arsuaga, & Carbonell, 1997). Populations of this species migrated north into Europe and remains of *Homo antecessor* have been excavated in caves in Northern Spain. Evidence from artifacts and animal fossils found in association with the *antecessor* remains indicate that these humans were very adept big-game hunters. Tell-tale cut marks on the bones of the Spanish *antecessor* specimens suggests cannibalism.

Geomagnetic dating of the Spanish fossils gives an accurate minimum age of 780 thousand years to these specimens. This makes them among the oldest humans found in Europe. The head of *antecessor* was a curious mixture of both Neanderthal and modern human characteristics. They had the heavy brow ridge, long low brain case, thick chinless lower jaw, and large teeth like Neanderthals, but the face was relatively flat and nonprotruding like that of modern humans. This suggests that the *antecessor* populations that entered Europe eventually evolved into Neanderthal man, *Homo neanderthalensis.*

Homo neanderthalensis was once classified as *Homo sapiens neanderthalencis* based on the belief that they represented a sub-species of modern human. In 1997, analysis of mitochondrial DNA extracted from the first specimen of Neanderthal man ever found indicated that we shared a common ancestor with the Neanderthals about 600 thousand years ago (Lewin, 1997). Based on the DNA evidence and in conjunction with the evidence of the Spanish *Homo antecessor* specimens, the more accurate classification is probably *Homo neanderthalensis* indicating that Neanderthal man was a species separate from our own.

Neanderthal man existed between 230,000 and 28,000 years ago (Trinkhaus & Shipman, 1993). They were found throughout Europe, the Middle East, and Western Asia. The Neanderthals had a brain size slightly greater than that of modern humans, around 1450 cubic centimeters. The structure of the Neanderthal brain is somewhat different from that of modern humans however. The occipital region tends to be enlarged compared to modern humans, and the frontal lobe region appears to be relatively reduced. On the whole, the brain case is relatively longer and lower than that of modern humans, with a marked bulge at the back of the skull. They were very weak chinned and had very protruding jaws. The teeth were very large and robust, but in most fossil specimens they show signs of extreme wear, indicating that the teeth and jaws were used daily to process hides, make tools, or accomplish other tasks. Neanderthals were extremely robust in physique, with bones that were one and one half times as thick as those of modern humans. They clearly show adaptation for cold climate, with very stocky proportions and relatively short extremities. This type of morphology serves to reduce heat loss to a minimum (Walker & Shipman, 1996). The Neanderthals had an efficient stone-tool industry and were very accomplished big-game hunters. Stress and fracture marks on their skeletons indicate that the Neanderthals endured brutally hard lives. The oldest sites of ritual human burial are attributed to the Neanderthals and date back to about 100,000 years ago. This purposeful burying of the dead, often times with accompanying artifacts and perhaps flowers, suggests that these people possessed a higher order level of consciousness. They were self-aware and concerned with the great mystery that surrounds death and life. For the most part, however, it appears that everything the Neanderthals did revolved around a no-nonsense utilitarian approach to life. It was not until the advent of our own species that we see the full flourishing of abstract thought and symbolic communication.

Studies of mitochondrial DNA in modern humans suggests that *Homo sapiens sapiens* arose in Africa about 150,000 years ago (Wilson, 1992; Ingman, Kaessmann, Paabo, & Gyllensten, 2000). Fossil evidence of anatomically modern humans is found in South Africa dating to about 100,000 years ago and in the

BOX 2.1 • *Through a Glass Darwinian*   *The Carnivorous Hominid: Neanderthal Man*

In terms of total calories, the modern American diet, on average, consists of 20 percent to 30 percent meat with the rest of the calories coming from vegetables, fruits, nuts, grains and dairy products. There are also large numbers of Americans with 0 percent meat in their diet. In hunter-gatherer societies meat comprises about 35 percent of the diet with fruits, vegetables, nuts and honey comprising the remaining 65 percent. For *Homo neanderthalensis*, the cold-adapted human species that diverged from our ancestors about 600,000 years ago, meat comprised over 90 percent of the diet (Richards, M. et al., 2000). At least this was the case for some of the last Neanderthals living in Europe.

Chemical analysis of tiny bits of bone from a skull and a jawbone of two Neanderthals, who lived 28,000 years ago, in what is now Croatia, provided chemical signatures of the foods they had eaten. By comparing these chemical signatures with the chemical signatures of the animals that lived at the time, the researchers established just what and how much the Neanderthals ate. They were almost exclusively meat eaters. The analysis indicates that their diet closely matched the diets of the most carnivorous animals from that time period. This level of animal protein consumption makes Neanderthals not only the most carnivorous human species to have ever lived but also the most carnivorous higher primate of all time.

According to Erik Trinkhaus, a member of the research team, "This research puts an end to the argument about whether the Neanderthals were primarily scavengers. Along with their bones we have found large heavy wooden pointed spears, and stone points that must have been crafted skillfully to make thrusting spears for close-in killing. That kind of hunting prowess obviously required the organization of groups of hunters working together in a sophisticated form of social existence. The Neanderthal people were almost certainly very good ambush hunters who possessed the skills and tools to organize hunting parties large enough to fell huge mammoths as well as wolves, cave bears, horses and deer."

Interestingly, some of the key selective pressures proposed to explain the rapid evolution of the human brain appear more applicable to the extinct Neanderthals than to our own species. For example, a dietary shift to a much higher percentage of animal foods, with much more concentrated stores of protein and fat supposedly made expansion of the calorie gobbling brain a possibility. Selection for cognitive abilities for planning and coordinating hunts, the so-called man-the-hunter theory of human brain evolution has probably had one of the longest tenures of any of the various brain evolution theories. Adaptation to climatic change has also been proposed as a mechanism facilitating brain evolution. Certainly, the Neanderthal showed the greatest degree of adaptive specialization for cold of any hominid species. They had stout, compact bodies with short forelimbs. They also had unique nasal and sinus structures for dealing with the cold. We could wrap this up by saying that Neanderthals do, indeed, have the highest average brain capacity of any hominid species, so some or all of the above theories are correct.

But wait, there are a few problems here: (1) Neanderthals are extinct. Apparently, this was the result of coming into contact/competition with our ancestors. (2) When allometric corrections are imposed on the Neanderthal brain it is no longer larger than *Homo sapiens sapiens*. It other words when the greater mass of the Neanderthal body is taken into account, their brain size is proportionately smaller than that of our species. (3) The real interest behind rapid hominid brain evolution was in explaining the evolution of complex mind/complex behavior.

(continued)

BOX 2.1 • (Continued)

The development of sophisticated art-work by our ancestors about 40,000 years ago demonstrated a substantial cognitive gulf separating us from the Neanderthals. Symbolic reasoning, creativity, and sophisticated cultural transmission are hallmarks of our species. Without these abilities and the complex language skills that augment them, we would not be having this discussion. Clearly, the brain evolution theories described above are made problematic by the discovery of Neanderthals carnivorous diet. However, they should not be totally discounted. Like many theories that will be discussed in Chapter 3, they may have something valid to say about human brain evolution, at least in the context of certain time intervals.

Middle East to about 90,000 years ago. Presumably these modern humans evolved from *Homo antecessor* populations that had remained in Africa. The so-called out of Africa theory states that modern humans first arose in Africa and then dispersed throughout the Old World displacing all other populations of humans that were encountered. *Homo sapiens sapiens* entered Western Europe about 35,000 years ago and they co-existed in the same territory with the Neanderthals for a period of about 7000 years (Trinkhaus & Shipman, 1993). After that time, we find no trace of Neanderthal populations. The logical conclusion is that the entry of modern humans into this area was the causal factor in the demise of the Neanderthals, who had lived for tens of thousands of years quite successfully in these regions. There is no archeological evidence of direct conflict between the two species. However, humans have densely occupied this part of the world for thousands of years and it is unlikely that much would remain in the way of artifacts in any open, unprotected location. Most of the modern human artifacts in Europe are found deep within cave sites. It is here that we find some of the most impressive evidence of the use of abstract reasoning and symbolic expression, namely the cave art from the upper Pleistocene.

The cave painting of Western Europe display a variety of Pleistocene animals painted in a very realistic and elegant fashion (Leakey, 1994). The art appears to have been part of a very deep ritualized tradition. Many of the techniques and themes persist for centuries, if not millennia, unchanged. Fine artwork is also expressed in decorated tools, beads, sculptures of human and animals, and musical instruments. At the same time, utilitarian technologies such as hunting tools, scrapers, knives, and clothing, all reached a high level of sophistication. It would seem logical to conclude that the high level of utilitarian and non-utilitarian technology displayed in the upper Pleistocene was a direct result of the emergence of modern morphology and physiology. The modern human brain capacity of about 1350 cubic centimeters was present. The Cro-Magnons, the *Homo sapiens sapiens* living in Western Europe at this time, had very high foreheads, they were tall, their brow ridges were small or absent, they had prominent chins, and lean graceful physiques. However, these basic characteristics first appeared over 100,000 years ago, which raises the question of why did it take over 50,000 years for sophisticated tools and the expression of artwork to emerge. In Chapter 8 we will explore this question in depth.

In the chapter that follows, we will discuss the causal factors in the evolution of bigger and better brains. Then we will explore the nature of the modern human mind.

Summary

The universe began with the Big Bang about 13.5 billion years ago. Our Solar System was formed from the remnants of earlier exploded stars over 4.5 billion years ago. By 4 billion years ago the first life appeared on Earth. Primates appeared about 95 million years ago, 65 million years ago the dinosaurs and numerous other taxonomic groups were exterminated by a cataclysmic asteroid impact opening up a host of ecological niches for the surviving species.

About seven million years ago, the lineage leading to humans and the lineage leading to chimpanzees diverged from a common ancestor. The hominid line (the lineage lending to humans) evolved bipedal locomotion and a split into a gracile line (light boned) and a robust line (heavy boned). The robust line became extinct about one million years ago. The gracile line eventually gave rise to modern humans. The fossil record shows that over a period of about 3 million years, our ancestors evolved from bipedal ape-brained creatures to fully modern humans.

Discussion Questions _____

1. Describe the evolution of the physical universe. Compare and contrast this evolutionary process with the evolution of living things.

2. Currently, there is only one species in the genus *Homo*. This has not always been the case. Give possible reasons for the fact that *sapiens sapiens* is currently the only existing species of human.

3. Science fiction movies typically display intelligent aliens as "humanoid" in appearance. This may be more indicative of the inherent limitations of Hollywood script writers and special effects budgets than any reasoned scientific speculation. How likely is it that self-aware, intelligent beings in other parts of the universe will resemble us physically? What about psychologically?

Key Terms _____

anthropoids	Gondwanaland	*Homo erectus*
Big Bang theory	gracile australopithecines	*Homo habilis*
Cro-Magnon	homeotherm	*Homo neanderthalensis*
doppler effect	hominids	*Homo sapiens sapiens*
eukaryote	*Homo antecessor*	*Kenyanthropus platyops*

Orrorin tugenensis   prosimians   *Systema Natura*
Pangaea   Robust australopithecines
poikilotherm   Scala natura

Additional Reading _____

The History and Geography of Human Genes by L. Luca Cavalli-Sforza, Paolo Menozzi, and Alberto Piazza (1996).

Cosmic Evolution: The Rise of Complexity in Nature by Eric J. Chaisson (2001).

The Descent of Mind: Psychological Perspectives on Hominid Evolution by Michael C. Corballis and Stephen E. G. Lea (Editors) (1999).

The Blind Watchmaker: Why the Evidence of Evolution Reveals a Universe Without Design by Richard Dawkins (1996).

The Extended Phenotype: The Long Reach of the Gene by Richard Dawkins (1990).

Humans Before Humanity: An Evolutionary Perspective by Robert Foley (1997).

Hidden Order: How Adaptation Builds Complexity by John H. Holland and Heather Mimnaugh (Editors) (1996).

Evolutionary Wars: The Battle of Species on Land, at Sea, and in the Air by Charles Kingsley Levy (2000).

Symbiotic Planet: A New View of Evolution by Lynn Margulis (1998).

The Human Revolution: Behavioural and Biological Perspectives on the Origins of Modern Humans by Paul Mellars and Chris Stringer (Editors).

The Riddled Chain: Chance, Coincidence, and Chaos in Human Evolution by Jeffrey Kevin McKee (2000).

Coming Home to the Pleistocene by Florence R. Shepard and Paul H. Shepard (1998).

How Humans Evolved by Robert Boyd and Joan B. Silk (1997).

The Origins of Life: From the Birth of Life to the Origin of Language by John Maynard Smith and Eors Szathmary (1999).

African Exodus: The Origins of Modern Humanity by Christopher Stringer (1997).

Extinct Humans by Ian Tattersall and Jeffrey H. Schwartz (2000).

The Hunting Apes: Meat Eating and the Origins of Human Behavior by Craig B. Stanford (1999).

Neanderthals, Bandits and Farmers: How Agriculture Really Began by Colin Tudge (2000).

The Time Before History: 5 Million Years of Human Impact by Colin Tudge (1997).

3

Encephalization and the Emergence of Mind

It is a law of nature we overlook, that intellectual versatility is the compensation for change, danger, and trouble. An animal perfectly in harmony with its environment is a perfect mechanism. Nature never appeals to intelligence until habit and instinct are useless. There is no intelligence where there is no change and no need of change. Only those animals partake of intelligence that have to meet a huge variety of needs and dangers.

—*The Time Machine* (1895) H. G. Wells

Chapter Questions

1. What unique set of selective forces made humans one of the brainiest species ever to exist on Earth?
2. What is the functional organization of the human brain?
3. What is the basis of the idea that "the mind" consists of a collection of individual components or modules?

The qualities that most set humans apart from all other forms of life are mental qualities. Other species, doubtless, experience pain, fear, sexual desire, and even joy. They are primarily limited to experiencing these states in the present moment. We humans, however, not only have a richer repertoire of subjective sensations but also the ability to represent these feelings abstractly. This allows us, for example, to contemplate a painful experience that occurred months or years in the past or to anticipate the pleasure that will ensue from an event that is expected to occur in the future. This ability to manipulate mental constructs is called cognition.

There appears to be an enormous gap in cognitive ability between humans and other species. We also have three times the brain mass of our closest living primate relatives, the chimpanzees, who are themselves large brained and cognitively complex relative to most other animals. In this chapter we will examine the selective forces that produced the modern human brain. Then we will look at the functional/structural organization of that brain. Lastly, we will take stock of the human mind, as a set of mental modules specialized to adapt us to life in small bands of hunter-gatherers.

The Prime Movers in Hominid Encephalization

One of the common misconceptions concerning the evolutionary process is that it implies progress. People with such a mistaken view of evolution may believe that fish are evolving into amphibians, reptiles are evolving into mammals, and apes will inevitably achieve human status some day. The belief that traits evolve in order to achieve a future goal is referred to as the *teleological error.* When someone argues that birds evolved feathered wings in order to fly or that humans evolved complex brains in order to use tools they are committing the teleological error. The teleological error is a logical fallacy because it implies that future events cause past events.

To understand how birds evolved bodies capable of flight, it is necessary to examine the process as a series of events unconnected to any future outcomes. Feathers were originally modified scales that provided an improved insulating capacity for warm-blooded animals. The low density of these modified scales and certain incidental aerodynamic properties they possessed made them useful in facilitating gliding behavior. Outstretched forelimbs covered with feathers were more advantageous to gliding than those covered with scales. Flight powered by feathered wings developed in birds as a result of natural selection on gliding behavior.

The teleological error is even more likely to be committed when the origins of human capacities are examined. Claiming that our ancestors began walking upright in order that they could use tools is typical example of this error. In fact, the tendency to make the teleological error can be said to be a natural by-product of the evolved mental capacities of the human animal. The human mind has been designed by natural selection to be adept in goal directed behavior. Our minds are so well designed for achieving intended outcomes that we naturally attribute goals and intentions where none exist. Our purposeful manipulation of mental constructs enables us to size up an enormous number of possible solutions to any problem without the time, effort, and risk that would be entailed by actually going through the alternate solutions. This capacity has given humankind an immense advantage over other forms of life. We use it for everything, from rearranging our living room furniture to planning strategy during wartime. The problem, as William James pointed out, is that we are so immersed in this mental process that it colors our perception of reality or in many instances prevents our perception of reality. It is this perceptual blindness that makes it impossible for many people to accept the fact that something as complex as the human brain and as subtle and eloquent as the human mind could be cobbled together by eons of natural selection without plan or purpose. In this chapter we will discuss how this process occurred and describe the end product of this process, namely the modular brain and the modular mind.

Machiavellian Intelligence

Encephalization refers to the amount of brain mass relative to body size. Those species classified as primates are among the most highly encephalized animals on our planet (see Figure 3.1). The relatively large and complex brains of primates can be explained by a number of factors. All living primates are either currently arboreal or descended from arboreal ancestors. Elliot-Smith (1912) proposed the "arboreal theory" to account for the emergence of the primate brain. He argued that the adaptation of terrestrial animals to an arboreal lifestyle necessitated the development of stereoscopic vision and highly manipulative hands. These in turn required a larger and more complex brain. Cartmill (1974) observed that there are many arboreal animals such as tree squirrels that do not have stereoscopic vision or dexterity. Cartmill hypothesized that those primate visual and motor adaptations evolved to facilitate insect predation. He pointed out that forward facing eyes and dexterous forelimbs are also found in cats. The primate brain (as both Elliot-Smith and Cartmill argued) must be relatively large and complex to process stereoscopic vision and coordinate fine manual dexterity. The dexterity, visual capabilities, and brain development of members of the order Primates (e.g., monkeys, apes and humans) generally exceed those of members of the order Carnivora (e.g., cats, canines, and bears). This suggests that neither Cartmill's hypothesis nor the one proposed by Elliot-Smith is entirely adequate for explaining the complexity of the primate brain. Unquestionably both the arboreal lifestyle and the predatory habits of the earliest primates were factors. However, even the combination of these two factors will not suffice to account for the highly developed brains found in monkeys and apes. To understand what the selective forces acting on brain development were, we need to look at the most prominent feature characterizing modern primates. This feature is their extreme sociality.

The importance of sociality can be illustrated as follows: a certain level of complexity is required to judge the location of a tree branch waving in the wind so that it can be successfully grasped, a somewhat higher level of complexity is required to anticipate the movements of a prey animal and successfully capture it, but a much higher level of complexity is required to anticipate the behavior of a member of your own species in response to your behavior. This last is the challenge facing every social animal.

This social intelligence has been called Machiavellian intelligence after the Italian political philosopher, Niccolo Machiavelli (1469–1527), whose how-to writings on governing have turned his name into a synonym for amorality, cunning, and duplicity (Byrne & Whiten, 1988). In his most famous work, *The Prince* (1532),

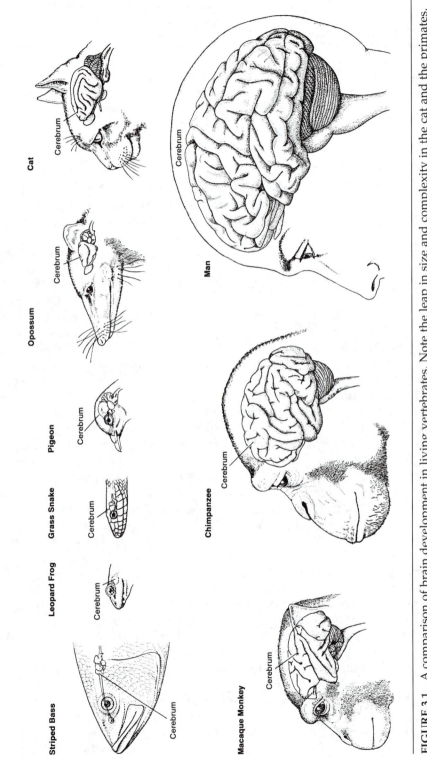

FIGURE 3.1 A comparison of brain development in living vertebrates. Note the leap in size and complexity in the cat and the primates.

he describes the methods by which a prince can gain and hold political power. In Machiavelli's view, a ruler should be concerned only with rules that lead to political success. Traditional ethical rules are perceived as impediments to the acquisition of power. The following quote from *The Prince* typifies Machiavelli's perspective: "Since love and fear can hardly exist together, if we must choose between them, it is far safer to be feared than loved."

When we observe the behavior of non-human primates, particularly Old World monkeys and apes in a social context, it is clear that Machiavellian concerns *do* play a role in their behavior (Byrne & Whiten, 1988). These animals are highly concerned with their position in the social hierarchy and how to better their hierarchical rank. Complex alliances and coalitions are formed to facilitate upward mobility in certain individuals. Unquestionably the most political of all nonhuman animals is the common chimpanzee (DeWall, 1982). Male chimpanzees live in a world of political intrigue that would have impressed Machiavelli himself with its guile, treachery, and ruthless focus on acquiring and maintaining power.

Undoubtedly, the ability to manipulate the behavior of conspecifics played some role in the evolution of brain complexity and intelligence but it is not sufficient in and of itself as an explanation. Chimpanzees are highly encephalized animals yet their brain mass is only about one-third that of our own. Moreover, numerous human studies have failed to find any correlation between Machiavellianism (a strategy of social conduct involving the manipulation of others for social gain against the other's self-interest) and IQ scores or real world material success (Wilson, Near & Miller, 1996).

Social intelligence (both Machiavellian and non-Machiavellian) undoubtedly played a role in the general brain evolution of primates. The common ancestor that we shared with chimpanzees about 7 million years ago was a fairly brainy fellow relative to other animals. However, we must look to other factors in addition to social intelligence to explain the trebling in brain size that occurred in our lineage.

Ice Ages

A number of researchers have postulated that the *Ice Age* played a significant role in human evolution. Ice ages are periods in the Earth's history characterized by large-scale climactic cooling and expansion of glacial ice sheets from the polar regions. Ice ages generally persist for periods of about 100,000 years alternating with warm interglacial periods that last about 10,000 years. Ice ages occur in groupings called glacial epochs that last for millions of years. The Earth has had several glacial epochs during its history. The most recent glacial epoch began about 2.5 million years ago is referred to as the *Ice Age*. The current interglacial period began about 11,500 years ago and most scientists believe it is only an interlude to be followed shortly (in a few centuries or millennia) by a return to cold conditions as we are still living in the *Ice Age* (see Figure 3.2).

Vrba (1996) has argued that the onset of the *Ice Age* corresponds to the emergence of numerous mammalian species, particularly in Africa. Many of the species that appear about 2.5 million years ago show a pronounced increase in body size.

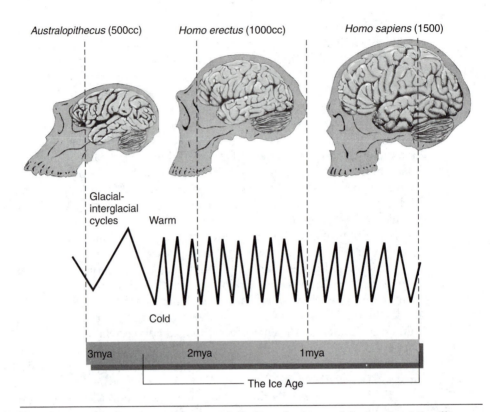

FIGURE 3.2   Hominid encephalization following the onset of the Ice Age 2.5 million years ago.

This is consistent with Bergmann's rule, which holds that warm-blooded animals living in cold climates tend to be larger than their counterparts of the same species living in warm climates. The new species also show changes in body proportions, which is consistent with Allen's rule that states that animals of a given species show reductions in body extremities when living in colder climates. Both Bergmann's and Allen's rules can be viewed as adaptations to climactic change. Vrba believes that it was the massive climactic changes associated with the *Ice Age* producing marked aridity in the African continent and a reduction in forested area that triggered the speciation events not only in bovids and antelopes but also in the hominids. During this time, the hominid line split into the gracile australophithecines and the robust australophithecines.

The changes in body form that occurred were achieved through slight changes in the growth rate and maturation rates during ontogeny. For example, the gracile australophithecine line shows a trend toward neoteny or paedomorphosis. In this condition, juvenile characteristics are retained in the adult animal. Neoteny, thus would be achieved through prolongation of the maturation process, or a suppression of that process. In the robust australophithecines, however, a more rapid onset of maturation would account for the increased thickness of the skull and enlargement of the jaws and teeth. Slight modifications in the activity of various genes during the developmental process are typical of evolutionary changes in complex organisms. This process is referred to as *heterochrony*, which is defined as a phyletic change in the onset and/or timing of development such that the development of a trait or traits in an organism is either accelerated or decelerated relative to the same trait or traits in an ancestor.

Once a certain level of complexity is achieved (i.e., multicellular organization) a more fundamental level of change, such as radically different, gene structures is usually disastrous. Thus the avenue most readily open to evolutionary change is in the control of the expression of existing genes, which is accomplished through slight modifications in the regulator genes. To make an ape more human-like, the genes that control maturation of the skull need to be suppressed, preventing the development of a thick, buttressed skull and huge teeth and maintaining a head that is relatively large in proportion to the body (see Figure 3.3). Not only is the head of adult humans characterized by juvenile features, but the adult

FIGURE 3.3   A comparison of an infant chimpanzee with an adult. The human appearance of the infant ape lends credence to the theory that neoteny or pedamorphosis played a major role in human evolution.

human mind can be considered child-like in its retention of curiosity and plasticity in dealing with the environment. In summation it can be said that the *Ice Age* altered the African ecosystem and triggered the emergence of a plethora of new life forms. However, only one taxonomic lineage led to the highly encephalized organisms called humans. We must continue to look for other factors to account for the evolution of the very complex human brain.

Ballistic Hunting

Calvin (1982) speculates that at least one prime mover in hominid encephalization may have been natural selection for right-handed throwing of stones at prey. Ballistic movements, literally the hurling of a missile at an object, are movements that cannot be modified by feedback. For example, if we were trying to precisely center a thumbtack near the top of a flyer we were posting, we could move it back and forth until we perceived it as being centered. Centering the thumbtack would be a feedback movement. On the other hand, if we tried to place a dart in the exact center of a posted flyer by throwing it from several yards away, this would be a ballistic movement. All of the necessary orchestration and sequencing of muscle contractions must occur appropriately before the dart leaves the hand. Once it is in flight, there is nothing we can do to alter its course. To successfully throw a missile at a target, especially at a moving target, requires complex neural sequencing. Although great apes occasionally throw objects as part of their displays, their accuracy is random. Another difference between ourselves and the great apes is that although individual apes will show a preference for using one hand more than the other, as a species there is no general bias for either right-handedness or left-handedness. In contrast, approximately 89% of all people show a preference for writing with the right hand and also for throwing objects with the right hand.

Sequencing movements that have minimal feedback are not unique to humans. Many species, especially predators that ambush their prey, have to compute all of the requisite muscle contractions that will enable them to hurl their bodies successfully upon their unsuspecting quarry immediately prior to the act. In this type of activity there is no bias toward movements of the right side of the body versus movements of the left side of the body. Hence, no specialization of function rises in one hemisphere over the other. But in a one-arm throwing movement (one-arm movements are more efficient because they provide for greater distance) there is specialization on one side of the body. As to why the preferred side should have become the right side of the body (and hence left hemisphere of the brain) in most people is an area of speculation. Calvin (1982) has made the somewhat tongue-in-cheek suggestion that it may have something to do with cradling infants on the left side where the sound of the maternal heartbeat is loudest. Early hominid females that tended to hold their infants on the left side may have had infants that tended to sleep more soundly, thus making it easier to approach prey and avoid detection from predators. With left-hand cradling, the right arm would more commonly be used in throwing and other complex movements, thus there would be selection for more complex neural development in the left hemisphere of the brain to control these movements. Calvin further argues that the development of this neural sequencing machinery in the left hemisphere provided a foundation that was later co-opted for the development of language behavior. We know that people who suffer stroke damage in the left side often show problems with speech production and language comprehension. They also often show deficits in their ability to sequence things. Sequencing deficits can include things such as sequencing words and understanding the meaning that comes from word order (syntax problems), sequencing facial expressions, and sequencing common behaviors used in day-to-day living. We know from the fossil record that bipedalism developed before major encephalization. Therefore, the subsequent evolution of brain size and complexity in our lineage has to be contributed to prime movers that occurred after this change in locomotion.

Calvin's (1982) ballistic hunting hypothesis does appear to be consistent with many of the facts. However, it places a great emphasis on the idea that hominids became adept to hunting at a very early stage. While it may be possible that these early hominids were following a type of ballistic-hunting lifestyle, the fossil evidence indicates that opportunistic scavenging provided a major source of their food. We can speculate that the left-brain hemisphere, neural-sequencing circuitry initially developed for wielding a club in the right hand. Using a club, even a simple stick or bone implement, would have enabled these small, bipedal hominids to drive lesser scavengers away from carcasses, rush in, cut away small portions with their crude stone tools, and quickly leave the area before larger scavengers approached. Just taking up life on the open savanna would have meant that these creatures would have instantly become highly vulnerable to many of the large predators. While the bipedal gait provided optimal energetic efficiency in terms of covering the greatest distance for the least amount of calories expended, it created a huge deficit in running speed. Being able to wield a club would have transformed a highly vulnerable animal into one that even some of the larger predators would have approached with caution. The neural circuitry that developed for club wielding could have later been selected for the ballistic throwing that is central to Calvin's hypothesis. Once the sequencing pathways were well established in the hominid brain, an evolutionary beachhead existed for another prime mover—language.

Language

Studies of brain laterality in Old World monkeys show they exhibit left-hemisphere dominance for communication and fine motor skills and right-hemisphere dominance for visual processing (Faulk, 1987). This suggests that the bias for the type of specialization Calvin theorizes about was in place long before the hominid stage of human evolution. The ballistic hypothesis of encephalization and language origins remains tenable if we shift the emphasis to the elaboration of preexisting neural tendencies rather than their full-blown inception. Recent studies of brain activity and language show an integral relationship between neural structures involved in communication and motor control such as the caudate nucleus and cerebellum (Willis, 1993).

The role of the cerebellum in language function is particularly intriguing. The cerebellum is the large, highly convoluted structure in the hindbrain. Although it is only about one-tenth the mass of the entire brain, it contains approximately the same number of neurons as the rest of the brain. It has been know for many centuries that the cerebellum is critically involved in controlling posture and coordination of movement. More recently it has been determined that a primary function of the cerebellum is the timing and sequencing of ballistic movements. The cerebellum is one of those areas in the brain that has increased dramatically in size over the past 3 million years, along with other areas such as the neocortex.

The importance of the cerebellum to language function is demonstrated by a genetic anomaly called William's Syndrome. People with William's Syndrome have a cerebral cortex that is only about 80 percent as massive as the cortex of normal people. The cerebellum, however, is normal size and one recently evolved area of the cerebellum, called the neocerebellum, is actually larger than normal. Individuals suffering from this disorder have IQs around 50, which classifies them as mentally retarded. Their language abilities, however, are surprisingly normal. They have good language and vocabulary and are amazingly adept at acquiring new words and new phrases. All of this suggests that the enlarged cerebella in these individuals has something to do with their retention of high-level language skills. It also points to the modularity of both the human brain and the human mind, a topic we shall discuss later in this chapter. The relationship between language, particularly syntax, and ballistic timing seems to be an intimate one. Determining the nature of the selective forces that lead to this relationship may be an area that will remain forever untestable in any ultimate sense.

From one perspective, it's somewhat silly to try to look for one specific factor as being causal in the evolution of hominid encephalization. Natural selection always acts on the whole organism. Each individual had a complex of abilities and tendencies of varying degrees. And the only question central to evolution is whether or not these abilities and tendencies resulted in behavior that allowed these individuals to survive and successfully reproduce. When we look at hominid evolution from this holistic perspective, it immediately raises another question. Over two million years ago our hominid ancestors were highly successful animals. Their ability to survive was on par with or better than that of any other mammalian species living in that part of the world. They certainly had all of the brainpower necessary to survive at that time. What forces pushed toward a tripling of brain mass and a corresponding increase in neural complexity? It seems logical to conclude that those selective forces did not come from the physical environment in terms of predator or climactic change.

One possible explanation is suggested by the correlation that exists between the typical group size of a species and the size of the neocortex in that species (Dunbar, 1996). The neocortex is the cortical tissue that covers the surface of the cerebral hemispheres. It includes the frontal, parietal, occipital and temporal lobes. It is called neocortex, "new" cortex, because it is of relatively recent evolutionary origin. The relationship between group size and neocortical volume is especially prominent in primate species. The neocortex accounts for about 80 percent of the human brain. The highly convoluted surface of the cortex is a result of cramming 2,500 cubic centimeters of brain tissue, averaging about 2 millimeters in depth, into a space compact enough to successfully traverse the birth canal.

Dunbar (1996) has argued that the neocortical expansion is in response to the increased demands of processing social information that occurs with increases in group size. In a social group, each individual must keep track of friends and enemies as well as friends of friends and enemies of friends, etc. These calculations become increasingly complex with each increase in group size. With larger, more complex social groups there is greater demand for Machiavellian intelligence and for a conceptual ability referred to as "theory of mind." Theory of mind refers to the type of conceptual understanding an individual must possess in order to modify behavior in accordance with the assumption that other individuals have the same kind of mind.

Dunbar (1997) posits that language originated as a means to maintain coalitions in increasingly larger groups. In his theory, neocortical expansion was a necessary prerequisite for the inception of language abilities. Once language evolution was under way it led to even greater expansion of the neocortex. Dunbar's theory of language evolution is addressed in greater detail in Chapter 4.

Intraspecific Competition

The greatest selective pressure upon hominid evolution was imposed by the hominids themselves. The main source of this intraspecific selective pressure (intraspecific refers to competition within members of a species) was something that has been termed *runaway sexual selection*. Darwin noted that many extreme characteristics displayed in certain animal species could not be explained as simply the result of natural selection. Darwin believed that traits such as the tail feathers of peacocks and birds of paradise were the result of preferential sexual selection by the females of these species for males that had those qualities in abundance. Darwin first presented these ideas in his book *The Descent of Man and Selection in Relation to Sex* (1871). He believed that sexual selection took two primary forms. The first involved male-male competition for access to females, and the second involved female mate choice for males with certain characteristics (see Chapter 5 for a more complete discussion of sexual selection). Darwin believed that both of these factors played a role in human evolution. Human males are generally larger and stronger than human females because of male-male competition, although this sexual dimorphism was much more pronounced in our remote ancestors. Other secondary sexual characteristics can probably be attributed to female mate choice. One obvious example of a trait that may have been selected for in this way is the male beard. Miller (1998) has theorized that runaway sexual selection explains the runaway encephalization of the human species.

Specifically, Miller argues that hominids developed a preference for novelty and creativity in their courtship displays that resulted in the evolution of mental capacities that were capable of generating these types of complex behaviors. This would explain why the language capabilities and mental capacities of even the simplest hunter-gatherer societies living today far exceed what would be necessary to communicate and function efficiently in this type of lifestyle. Even more credence is lent to Miller's theory when we consider the important role of conversational abilities in modern human courtship.

This is not to say that natural selection did not play a role in the evolution of human mental capacities. Like many of the characteristics that are subject to runaway sexual selection, language and mental capacities became a target of mate choice preferences because it was in the adaptive interest of individuals to mate with members of the opposite sex displaying those abilities. During the glaciation intervals that occurred about every few thousand years during the *Ice Age*, those individuals with greater intelligence and imagination were the ones most likely to solve the adaptive problems imposed by the climactic extremes. Those individuals who continued to prefer these qualities in their mates during the relatively easier interglacial warm-up periods were those whose genes were most likely to survive the harsh culling effects of the cold times that would follow.

The other form of intraspecific competition, namely male-male competition, continued alongside mate preference as a strong selective force. As hominid mental capacities increased, so too did their capacity to compete in terms of physical conflict. Clans and tribes of human ancestors organized themselves to wage war upon their fellows probably long before the *Homo sapiens* stage of evolution had been reached. In those conflicts the groups led by the cleverest, most creative, and quick-witted individuals were probably the ones who prevailed most often. It is probably no coincidence that *Homo sapiens sapiens* is the only living species of hominid that still walks the face of the earth. Those other species of bipedal primates had the misfortune of being too directly competitive with us.

The Modular Brain

The concept of the modular brain (the idea that the brain consists of individual components with specific functions) can be traced back to the early part of the nineteenth century. In 1810 two phrenologists, Gall and Spruzheim, published a book called *The Anatomy and Physiology of the Nervous System*. They were the first to describe the functional role of the cerebral cortex, the corpus callosum, and the decussation of the spinal tracts. The belief system that Gall and Spruzheim founded was called phrenology, and it was based on the idea that by studying the shape and protrusions of the skull one could discern an individual's mental capacity and personality traits. Phrenology has been long since discredited, but the main contribution made by Gall and Spurzheim was the idea that specific areas on the brain have specific functions. This idea has been referred to as localization of function and more recently it has been called the modular brain model.

BOX 3.1 • *Through a Glass Darwinian* *Music and the Modern Brain*

Our ability to experience music is, of course, a function of nervous system physiology. Although the brain's right hemisphere does the majority of work associated with processing music, no single group of neurons is devoted to the task. Different networks of neurons are activated, depending on whether or not the music involves lyrics, whether a person is playing an instrument or simply listening passively (Lemonick, 2000). Neurological research has shown that intensive practice of an instrument leads to a discernible enlargement of parts of the cerebral cortex, the layer of gray matter most closely associated with higher brain function. MRI studies show that the corpus callosum is 10–15% thicker in musicians who began studying music before age seven, compared to nonmusicians and people who began music study later in life (Pantev, Oostenveld, Engellen, Ross, Roberts, & Hoke, 1998). However, the relationship between music ability and other intellectual functions is far from straightforward.

In many people, musical abilities and general cognitive abilities appear to be largely independent processes (Lemonick, 2000). Autistic people are mentally deficient, yet most are proficient musicians and some are even "musical savants" possessed of extraordinary talent. About one per cent of the human population is incapable of processing music at all. This condition is called *amusia* [*a-* = without, *-musia* = music, Latin]. Functional deficits in the more posterior regions of the temporal lobe are implicated in receptive amusia or true tone deafness (Corballis, 1994) Receptive amusics cannot recognize even simple, familiar tunes such as *Frere Jacques*. They can identify specific songs from the lyrics but it makes no difference whether the lyrics are sung or spoken. Expressive amusia, the inability to produce music has been linked to functional deficits in the frontal cortex. Amusics appear to have been born without the neural pathways required for processing music. Neurological tests of

these people fail to show any overt signs of brain damage or short-term-memory impairment and magnetic-resonance-imaging (MRI) scans of their brains look normal.

The fact that amusics appear to possess normal cognitive functioning despite their complete inability to process music is highly intriguing from an evolutionary perspective. It suggests that music ability is a specialized adaptation rather than a biological side effect of other evolved abilities (see Through a Glass Darwinian in Chapter 5). The fact that music ability appears to have been completely deleted from the behavioral repertoire of a few people suggests that it falls under the control of a relatively small number of genes. A capacity for music may have emerged very recently in our evolutionary history (within the last 100,000 years) as a result a few gene mutations and novel combinations. Amusia also provides concrete evidence for the existence of a major behavioral difference that can not be detected physically.

There has been a long-standing debate as to whether or not major changes in human neural organization occurred prior to the Creative Explosion of 40,000 to 50,000 years ago. Fossil evidence exists for morphological modern humans dating to over 120,000 years ago. Genetic studies suggest that our species arose over 150,000 years ago. Yet despite their modern appearance, these humans evidenced no changes in cultural/technological sophistication for tens of thousands of years. A smattering of artwork and tool innovations begin to appear about 50,000 years ago. From that point on, cultural innovation develops at a rapid pace. The level of sophisticated artwork and technology displayed by the Cro-Magnon peoples of Europe during the last Ice Age leaves no question that their minds were as fully modern as their brains. The cultural stagnation that prevailed for the 100,000 years or so prior to the Creative Explosion raises a question concerning the last stages of

(continued)

BOX 3.1 • (Continued)

human-brain evolution. Did microscopic changes occur in neural organization around 50,000 years ago that marked the emergence of the modern human brain? This has certainly been demonstrated to be a viable hypothesis by the existence of hereditary amusia. The fact that a few genes can produce the behavioral capacity for music, without producing detectable changes in the brain, clearly shows that this is a possibility.

Localization of Function

During the latter half of the nineteenth century, physicians Broca and Wernicke discovered brain areas associated with specific language functions. These areas were then named after their discoverers. Broca's area is critical to the production of language, specifically the correct sequencing of words. Wernicke's area is essential to language comprehension. These brain areas were discovered as a result of cerebral vascular accidents, commonly referred to as strokes. In certain individuals it was observed that certain behavioral deficits were associated with damage to specific parts of the brain. Cerebral vascular accidents occur when there is a sudden blockage or hemorrhaging of a blood vessel in the brain. This results in the loss of oxygenated blood flow to a specific region of the brain, and, consequently, the neurons in that region die from lack of oxygen. Correlating particular mental deficits with specific areas of the brain damaged by a stroke continues to be a prime source of evidence for the modular function of the brain.

The manner in which the brain processes visual information provides several good examples of its modular nature. In the condition known as cortical blindness, the occipital lobe region (the striate cortex) has been damaged, and the individual is no longer capable of seeing (see Figure 3.4). Cortical blindness, however, is a much more profound disability than blindness resulting in damage to the eyes. If one loses one's sight as a result of damage to the eyes or optic nerves, one retains one's memory of the sighted world and is still capable of visualizing pictorial representations in the mind's eye. In cortical blindness, not only is a person incapable of sight, he or she loses all memory of vision and cannot even imagine visual stimuli. These individuals no longer have any concept whatsoever of light, color, shape, or visual motion.

The visual process itself can be broken down into a number of sub-modules. Damage to the V4 region of the brain results in the loss of color vision. This condition is called acromatopsia. Individuals who suffer from it can no longer recall what it was like to see color or even conceive of the idea of color. The V5 area of the brain is essential to the processing of movement. Individuals who have suffered stroke damage in this region see the world as a series of still images. For example, while crossing the street they are at high risk because their perception of moving cars is to see them as motionless objects at a great distance and then as another still frame of a motionless object close at hand. They perceive water pouring

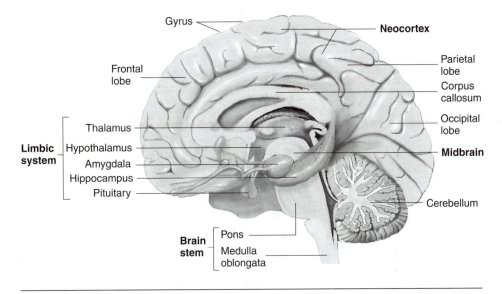

FIGURE 3.4 A side-view of the human brain showing the corpus callosum, the hindbrain (cerebellum and medulla), the limbic system, and the neocortex.

into a cup as a solid arc rather than moving fluid. The ability to integrate the various stimuli into a distinct form comprises yet another visual module in the brain. Individuals with this condition, which is called visual agnosia, can clearly see fine details in whatever they are looking at, but they are unable to comprehend what the whole object represents. One of these individuals was made famous by the neurologist Oliver Sacks (1995) in his book *The Man Who Mistook His Wife for a Hat*. As the book title suggests, this individual was unable to distinguish his wife's head from a hat on a hat rack. The same fellow could not identify simple objects like a glove, yet he could describe in detail the features of the object in a very complex and intellectual fashion. Once again, this underscores the distinction between the logical reasoning parts of the brain and the perceptual facets.

This distinction between logical reasoning and perception is clearly indicated in the examples of individuals suffering from damage to the somatosensory region of the brain. Individuals who have sustained damage to the somatosensory cortex often exhibit a syndrome called contralateral neglect. They no longer receive physical sensations from a particular part of their body. For example, if they have right hemisphere damage their left arm may feel numb, which is not extraordinary. However, these individuals will tend to totally ignore that part of their body that is no longer represented by the somatosensory cortex. For example, they may put their arm through the right sleeve of their shirt and leave the left sleeve dangling. Sacks (1995) gives an account of an individual with such damage who has to be placed back into his bed throughout the night after he winds up on the floor. When questioned, the individual claims that he is trying to get rid of a strange leg that is in bed with him. Of course when he tries to toss the strange leg out, the rest of his body follows because the "strange leg" is his own! Trying to argue with such individuals using logical reasoning is useless. Although they are perfectly lucid and intelligent in many cases, they cannot be made to grasp the simple fact that the limb they no longer feel is part of their own body and cannot be explained as being anything else.

Other examples of modularity have to do with information or knowledge stored in the brain. The brain appears to store information in groupings that are not intuitively obvious. Some damaged individuals lose their concept of tools while retaining their concept of animals, in other individuals the opposite pattern is observed. There are cases where individuals can no longer identify musical instruments from their pictures but can still identify them when they hear sounds of the instruments. Even more bizarre is evidence that abstract concepts such as size are regulated by specific locations in the brain. A woman was undergoing brain surgery for severe epilepsy, and the surgeon was probing portions of her cortex in order to establish which areas were critical and should not be tampered with. When an electrode was applied to one specific region she could no longer make judgments concerning size. When asked questions such as which is larger, a bee or a house, the subject's response was random.

Even capacities that may seem almost metaphysical in nature, such as our ability for a willful or volitional action, appear to be controlled by specific brain regions. Without the normal functioning of the prefrontal cortex, individuals are unable to make plans and carry out the behavior necessary to fulfill those plans. This deficit that results from prefrontal lobe damage was actually the basis for a surgical procedure called the prefrontal lobotomy that was popular during the 1950s and early 1960s. This procedure was originally used as a treatment for psychotic individuals who posed a danger to themselves and others. Ablating or destroying the prefrontal lobes in these individuals produced an apparent calming effect, and as a result this procedure became highly popular throughout the Western world. The prefrontal lobotomy did not improve the psychological state of these individuals. Whatever delusions or mental distortions these individuals experienced prior to the surgery were retained after the surgery. What was affected was their capacity to act on these delusional ideas and impulses. It is interesting to note that the inventor of this procedure, Egaz Moniz, died at the hands of one of his patients who had undergone the procedure and evidently retained enough will and desire to enact revenge upon the surgeon.

It is actually misleading to claim that the frontal cortex simply mediates the capacity known as will. This area of the brain is integrally involved in the higher order consciousness that is seemingly unique to the human species. Higher order consciousness, or self-reflexive consciousness, is the act of projecting a concept of self into a multitude of imagined situations. We can see ourselves interacting in a number of possible future situations, which are contingent upon certain courses of action. It is by assessing what we perceive as the likely outcome for ourselves by following a particular path of actions as opposed to another path that we reach conclusions and then act upon them. Those individuals who have lost the functional capacity of the frontal lobes can no longer maintain these elaborate mental projections, assess which courses of action are better than others, and send the messages to the motor cortex that will result in those actions being performed.

In summary, the idea that was long held in Western science that there is a command center in the brain that controls all other areas such as the sensory systems in a hierarchical fashion has been replaced by the modular brain model. In the modular brain there is no one center that monitors the activity of the rest of the brain. There is only an intricate network of modules, each of which comes to the forefront of activity when it is being used. This idea that there is no one central location for mind and intellect is an idea that has not been readily accepted by philosophers and scientists despite overwhelming empirical evidence that supports it. Not only does mind appear to be the product of a modular brain, but a series of scientific studies from the 1970s indicate that it may be possible to have more than one mind in one head.

Laterality

Humans are bilaterally symmetrical, which means that if we draw a vertical line through the center of our bodies, the right and left halves are roughly mirror images of each other. Many critical organ systems are duplicated on the right and left sides of the body. For example, we have a right and left kidney; women have a right and left ovary; men have a right and left testis. The purpose of this duplication is obvious. It provides a back-up system in case one of the critical organs is lost through injury. The separate halves of the brain system were probably derived at least in part as a back-up system. However, with ever-increasing behavioral complexity and the constraining limitations of the birth canal, it became highly adaptive to cram as much neural complexity in as small a space as possible. This ultimately resulted in the human tendency for the left hemisphere to specialize in language function and sequential information processing and the right hemisphere to be devoted more to holistic processes such as object recognition and the interpretation and display of emotional behavior. The highly lateralized nature of the human brain has been known to Western science for a long time but it was not until some fascinating experiments were done in the 1970s that the true extent of this lateralization was even guessed at (Gazzaniga, Ivry, & Mangun, 1998).

In the early 1970s a surgical procedure was developed to treat epilepsy that involved the severing of the corpus callosum. The corpus callosum is a highly myelinated (myelin is a fatty insulating material that increases the speed of the neural impulse) bundle of fibers that connects the left and right cerebral cortices of the brain. Epilepsy is caused by intense neural activity located in tiny clusters called foci. When these foci become active they generate waves of neural impulses that travel like ripples outward from the foci, eventually going to the opposite hemisphere of the brain, converging, and ricocheting back until they meet again at the starting point. The convergence of incoming and outgoing waves of neural activity results in a seizure.

The purpose of the split-brain surgery (Gazzaniga, Ivry, & Mangun, 1998) is to sever the corpus callosum, thereby disconnecting the two hemispheres of the brain. When epileptic neural activity develops, it is isolated in one hemisphere and one does not have the overload that results in a seizure. When this surgical technique was first put into use, it was observed that the operation was basically one hundred percent effective in eliminating the epileptic symptoms. Perhaps even more curious was the observation that the individuals appeared to be basically normal in other respects. It was not until these split-brain patients were studied under carefully controlled experimental conditions that a clear picture emerged of just how unusual these people actually were in their behavior.

A typical study of a split-brain patient involves seating the individual and having him stare at a dot directly in the foreground (Gazzaniga, Ivry, & Mangun, 1998). On either side of this dot, visual images are projected on screens. Because of the crossing over of the visual pathways of the brain, images in the left visual field are conveyed to the right hemisphere of the brain and images in the right visual field are conveyed to the left hemisphere. In an individual in which the corpus callosum is intact, this different information is quickly integrated by both hemispheres. However, in the split-brain patient there are two disparate hemispheres functioning in isolation. If an object is displayed in the right visual field and the subject is asked to identify this object, he will quickly and accurately respond. When the same object is displayed in the left visual field and the subject is queried as to the identity of the object, the subject will typically respond with "I don't know" or "I don't see anything." It can, however, be demonstrated that although they are unable to verbally respond to questions concerning objects displayed in the left visual field, they have nonetheless processed this information. If the subject is asked to use his left hand to feel objects behind a screen and asked to select one of the objects, he will invariably select the object that is identical to the one displayed in the left visual field. What these types of experiments suggest is that in split-brain patients there exist simultaneously two separate sites of consciousness and self-awareness.

Although the left hemisphere can be communicated with directly, via normal language, one can argue that the sense of consciousness displayed by the right hemisphere, despite its lack of verbal ability, is nonetheless real. The idea that consciousness and self-awareness is not a unitary function in each individual has profound philosophical and scientific implications. For dualistic philosophers, such as Rene Descartes of the seventeenth century, this type of information would have been profoundly disturbing. Descartes, like many philosophers before and since his time, viewed the sense of self as something at a higher level than biological function and not really a part of the physical universe. The demonstration that, through a simple neurological procedure, two separate sets of consciousness and self-identity could be produced in one person's head would seriously weaken such belief systems. Descartes, in particular, believed that the intellect was a nonphysical entity that transcended the laws of biology and physics. In the next section we will examine evidence that indicates that the mind is not a unitary phenomenon but is itself comprised of numerous modules.

The Modular Mind

The concept of the modular mind is related to, but not identical to, the concept of the modular brain. Mind is defined as the collective conscious and unconscious processes of a sentient organism that direct and influence mental and physical behavior. Moreover, these mental processes are considered to be a direct manifestation of brain activity. Although it may seem reasonable to assume that a modular mind would be the direct outcome of activity in a modular brain, this is not necessarily true. Some could argue that the activity of a multitude of modular brain components could result in a nonmodular mind. There is, however, a lot of empirical evidence that suggests that the mind itself is modular in nature.

What is meant by the term modular mind is that, instead of being a general all-purpose information processor, the mind consists of a number of specialized mechanisms designed by evolution to cope with certain recurring adaptive problems. Tooby and Cosmides (1992) have argued that the better analogy for the human mind is not that of a general all-purpose computer but rather a Swiss army knife.

Many academics have been resistant to the idea of a modular human mind despite the mass of supporting empirical evidence. Part of this resistance may arise from a basic confusion of what is exactly meant by the term modular mind. To each individual introspecting his or her own mental processes the mind appears to be a seamless whole. In response to this we should mention the stroke patients that were discussed earlier in this chapter. Oftentimes these individuals are totally unaware of the deficit they have incurred as a result of their brain damage. In a similar manner, an intact person is unaware of the limitations and innate biases that characterize his or her own mental processes. Evolutionary psychology research has demonstrated that the human mind is not a logic devise but rather a specialized mechanism for dealing with certain types of adaptive problems. In the next few sections we shall explore some prominent examples of innate predispositions and mental functionings in humans and their close relatives. The most parsimonious explanation for the particular mental biases that have been demonstrated through psychological research is that they are the result of natural selection.

Fear Learning

A phobia is an irrational fear response to an object or situation that is typically harmless. According to behaviorist theory, a phobia develops when a neutral stimulus becomes associated with an aversive experience. From the strict behaviorist view, all stimuli have equal potentiality for becoming phobic stimuli. Alternatively, preparedness theory posits that, because of certain innate predispositions, humans and other animals will acquire fear responses to certain classes of stimuli much more readily than others. In order to investigate fear learning, Susan Mineka of Northwestern University and her colleagues conducted a series of experiments on rhesus monkeys and humans during the 1980s and 1990s.

Mineka (1983) observed that rhesus monkeys born and reared in captivity evidenced no fear of snakes. Rhesus monkeys that have been captured in the wild, however, displayed a frenzied panic when confronted with a snake, even a toy rubber one. Mineka found that when naive laboratory-raised rhesus monkeys were shown motion picture films of wild captive monkeys reacting fearfully to snakes, the laboratory-reared monkeys quickly acquired the same fear of serpents. This confirmed that fear responses could quickly be developed purely through observations of other's reactions to certain stimuli. The more interesting effect from these studies was the fact that the fear responses occurred only if the subjects in the film were shown to be reacting to certain stimuli and not to others. The films were specially edited so that in some versions the snake, or rather the toy snake, which was originally inducing the agitated fear response was replaced by some other stimulus such as a flower. If the naive monkeys viewed a film displaying a fear-relevant stimulus such as a toy snake or toy crocodile then the subjects developed a fear response to the same type of object. On the other hand, if the naive subjects viewed a film displaying a toy rabbit or a flower they did not develop a fear response. To demonstrate unequivocally the same kind of hard-wired preparedness to fear certain categories of stimuli in humans would require an experiment or experiments that were parallel to those conducted on the rhesus monkeys. In other words, humans would have to be reared in a special environment that precluded their exposure to the relevant test stimuli prior to running the experiment. This of course would constitute a major breach of ethical guidelines prescribed for human subjects. However, experiments that can be legitimately conducted on human subjects provide strong support for the hypothesis that human fear learning is constrained by biological limits that are very similar to those found in rhesus macaques and other primates.

When human subjects were given mild electric shocks followed by slides of various stimuli they were more likely to form associations between electrical shock and images of snakes than between electrical shocks and images of frayed electrical cords and damaged electrical outlets (Mineka, 1983). It has been demonstrated that this sort of fallacious association will occur even in the absence of a personal history of experience with the fear-relevant stimuli suggesting its phylogenic origins. As to what sort of perceptual cues are hard-wired in the sensory processing areas of the brain that prepare us to find certain classes of stimuli more salient for fear learning than others is a question that remains yet largely unresolved.

In the studies of the rhesus monkeys it was found that only models possessing most of the features of the living animal were adequate to elicit the fear responses. Sinusoidal shapes, such as water hoses, were not adequate in and of themselves to produce the fear association. In one study of the squirrel monkey, a New World primate, it was found that these animals would only develop the fear response if they had been fed a diet of live insects but not if they had been reared on purely vegetarian fare (Masataka, 1993). These results suggest that, at least in this particular primate species, an experience with live, moving animals is necessary to prime the perceptual mechanisms upon which category-specific fear reactions are based.

Mundkur (1978) has described the universal tendency among human beings to attribute symbolic significance to certain animal species. In almost every society throughout the world, symbols of the serpent compel repugnance, reverence, or both, more so than any other animal species. Cooke (1996) has referred to this cultural phenomenon as the evolution of interest, arguing that we have evolved psychological mechanisms that make certain classes of stimuli intrinsically more interesting to us. To illustrate his point, Cooke draws attention to the prevalence of the serpent motif in art and literature throughout all of the world's cultures, going back through historical time. Even in societies where the environment is devoid of snakes, such as Ireland, the serpent is prominently depicted in the art works of the culture. What our primate relatives and we have evolved is not a hard-wired fear of snakes and other fear-relevant stimuli. Rather, these stimuli have a salience that is not present in other types of stimuli because of our inherited brain mechanisms. It is each individual's specific ontogenetic history, which of course includes the culture in which one is born, that determines whether we view creatures such as the snake with fear and repugnance, or with awe and reverence, or are even indifference. In this respect, fear learning is similar to the other types of evolved psychological mechanisms that we will discuss in this book. The final form of the behavior pattern does not depend solely on the genetically coded propensities. The individual's ontogenetic history and the proximate cues involved in each specific situation interact with the genetic predispositions to produce the myriad, complex patterns of behavior. (If you understand these last two sentences, then you have evolutionary psychology in a nutshell!)

Social Reasoning

Since 1966, one of the most widely used experimental procedures for investigating ability to reason logically has been the Wason Selection Task (Barkow, Cosmides, & Tooby). Peter Wason developed this procedure in order to see if people used scientific-hypothetico-deductive reasoning in their day-to-day problem solving. Hypothetico-deductive logic when applied to science was based on Karl Popper's idea that in order for a hypothesis to be truly scientific it had to be falsifiable. In the Wason's Selection Task, a subject has to see whether a conditional hypothesis in the form of "if p then q" has been violated by one of four instances represented by cards. The best way to understand this procedure is to work through a few of the Wason Selection Tasks. (These examples are reproduced from L. Cosmides and J. Tooby, "Cognitive adaptations for social exchange," from *The Adapted Mind*, edited by J. Barkow, L. Cosmides, and J. Tooby, © 1992 by Oxford University Press; used by permission of Oxford University Press.)

Problem 1. As part of your new clerical job at a local high school you have to make sure that student documents have been processed correctly. Your job, in part, is to make sure that the documents conform to the following rule: if a person has a D rating then his documents must be marked Code 3. You suspect that the secretary you replaced made errors in the filing system. The cards below have information about the documents of four people in the high school. Each card represents one person. One side of the card tells the person's letter rating and the other side of the card tells the person's number code. Your task is to indicate only those cards that definitely need to be turned over to see if any of these people violate this rule.

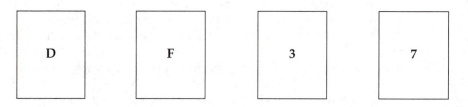

Indicate your choice or choices of the problem on a separate sheet of paper and then continue to the next problem.

Problem 2.   In the following scenario you are a bouncer in a bar, and your job requires that you prevent minors from drinking alcoholic beverages. The rule states that if a person is drinking beer then he or she must be over 20 years old. The following cards have information about four people sitting at a table in your bar. Each card represents one person. One side of the card tells the person's age and the other side of the cards tells what the person is drinking.

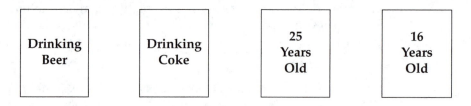

Indicate only those cards you definitely need to turn over to see if any of these people are breaking the rule. Indicate your choice or choices on a sheet of paper.

Problem 3.   Imagine a culture living on a South Sea island. In this culture, married individuals wear a tattoo on their face, and single people do not. There is a common food item called a mola nut that is readily available and can be eaten by anyone. Another food item called a cassava root is relatively rare and is forbidden to be eaten by anyone except married people. This is because the cassava root is an aphrodisiac. The rule in place here is as follows: If a man eats cassava root then he must have a tattoo on his face. The four cards, each representing a different man, would read:

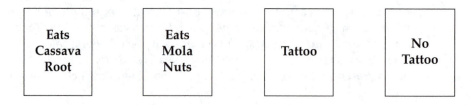

Decide which card or cards must be turned over to see if there is a violation of the rule and record your answer(s) on a sheet of paper.

Problem 4.   Imagine that an elementary-school teacher is taking her class for a field trip to a national park. The park environment is relatively benign and children can go barefooted in most of the environment with the exception of areas with tall grass. In the tall grass lurks a parasite called the fire worm. So, the following rule is in place: If the grass is tall then you must wear boots. The four cards, each representing a different child read:

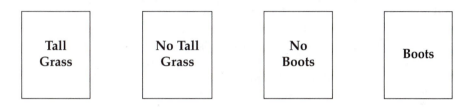

Select which cards you would have to turn over to decide if there was a violation of these rules and record your answer(s) on a sheet of paper.

In the first problem the rule stated that if a person has a D rating then his documents must be marked Code 3. The only cards with which you can falsify the hypothesis would be D and 7. In the second problem the rule stated that if a person is drinking beer then he or she must be over 20 years old. The choices here that could falsify the hypothesis or detect a rule violation would be drinking beer and 16 years old. In the third problem, if a man eats cassava root then he must have a tattoo on his face, the correct choices would be eats cassava root and no tattoo. And finally, in the fourth problem which stated that if the grass is tall then the child must wear boots, the correct choices would be tall grass and no boots. All of these problems are basically the same. There is the statement "if p then q" and to falsify the statement the correct choices are p and not q. However, unless you have had a course in formal logic you probably did much better on the last three problems than on the first one. This is the pattern observed by Tooby and Cosmides and a number of other researchers. Generally only about 25% of college students get the correct answer on the first problem, whereas 75% typically get it correct on the other problems. One of the first explanations for this variation in performance was that one involved familiar material and the other abstract and unfamiliar material. This hypothesis was tested, but did not hold up. Problems involving food and drink, for example using the rule if you eat hot chili peppers then you must drink cold milk, did not produce the high level of correct responding that you see in the second, third, and fourth problems presented here. Tooby and Cosmides hypothesized that the explanation was that we have evolved special propensities for dealing with problems involving social contracts.

Cosmides and Toobey (1992) demonstrated that it was not that social-contract content simply facilitated logical reasoning but rather that it activated a "cheater detection" mechanism. For example, a standard social contract is presented in the form "if you take the benefit, then you pay the cost." This statement corresponds to "if p then q" and the correct responses should be a choice of p and not q. P means the benefit is accepted, and q means the cost is paid. "Not q" means cost is not paid. A specific example would be "if you give me your watch, I'll give you twenty dollars." The Wason selection items that would be used to check for a rule violation would be benefit accepted: you take the watch which equals p; benefit not accepted, you do not take the watch which corresponds to not p; cost paid you pay twenty dollars which corresponds to q; and cost not paid you do not pay the twenty dollars which stands for not q. So, the correct choice here is to turn over the card saying you take the watch and the card saying you did not pay twenty dollars.

In the switch form I give you twenty dollars corresponds to cost paid which corresponds to p and I take the watch which corresponds to benefit accepted which is q, so the logical choice should be you pay twenty dollars, but you do not accept the watch which corresponds to not q. Most subjects given this switched version of the social contract chose not p, they did not pay twenty dollars, and q, they selected the watch, which is logically incorrect.

These types of results support Cosmides and Toobey's contention that what we are seeing activated is a cheater-detection mechanism. Further support for this is indicated by comparing the differential outcomes of a problem posed to detect cheaters versus the same problem posed to detect altruists (See Appendix A for a full description of these problems). Cosmides and Tooby (1992) found that when participants were asked to do the cheater-detection problem, their level of correct responses rose to 74%. Given the altruistic version of the problem their response level was around 37%. Just as we have no special evolved mechanisms allocated to finding dietary fiber, we also do not have special psychological mechanisms allocated to detecting altruists. Actually, a more correct way to put this would be to say that it is more important to detect cheaters than to detect altruists. Individuals who would gain from our actions and support of them but do not reciprocate those actions are wasting our energy and posing potential risk to us and our survival. Although it is important for us to be able to detect altruists to some degree, it is vitally important to us to be able to detect cheaters since they may jeopardize our very existence. This is also true of the other types of problems that we show a particular propensity for. Problems involving hazards like the tall grass, boots problem are similar to the cheater-detector problems in that they both potentially pose a threat to our continuing existence. Our ancestors survived and produced progeny because of their facility with problems of this kind.

Gender Differences

Since the human population is roughly equally divided into male and female, probably the quickest way to antagonize large numbers of people is to discuss differences in cognitive abilities that are the result of gender. Modern women reading Darwin's *Descent of Man*, wherein he describes what he sees as the basic differences between men and women, would probably either be amused or angered by his description. Darwin described men as being more aggressive and more intelligent than women. Women, he perceived as being the gentler and less intelligent of the sexes. While Darwin's assessment of the differences of aggression in the two sexes is still considered accurate (regarding physical aggression anyway), modern testing using standardized instruments shows no significant differences between the two genders in average cognitive level (Feingold, 1988). There is, however, a gender-based difference in the range of individual cognitive performance (Fisher, 1998). Women show much less variability in IQ than men. A proportionately higher number of men have extremely high or extremely low IQs than women. Thus in any given population, those individuals classified as either genius or mentally retarded are more likely to be men.

When we look at the sub-tests that comprise these IQ assessment instruments, we find further differences between the two sexes. Women perform at higher levels on tests of verbal fluency, reading speed, reading comprehension, and spelling (Notman & Nadelson, 1991) as well as verbal episodic memory (Ragland, Coleman, Gur, Glahn & Gur, 2000). Speech and language abilities develop earlier in girls than in boys. MRI scans of children and adolescents showed the volume of the amygdala increasing significantly more in males than females and hippocampal volume increasing significantly more in females than in males before and during puberty (Giedd, Castellanos, Rajapakse, Vaituzis & Rapoport, 1997). The amygdala is a structure involved in processing the social-emotional information associated with functioning in a dominance hierarchy, a critical aspect of male-male competition. The hippocampus is a brain structure that mediates the storage of long-term memory, especially verbal memory. The relatively accelerated hippocampal development in females compared to males may account for better performance in verbal memory by females as well as a greater reliance on landmark information when negotiating a novel environment (Sandstrom, Kaufman & Huettel, 1998).

The brains of females have 17% more neurons packed into the language centers than comparable areas in the brains of males (Fisher, 1998). Moreover, their brains are less lateralized, and they have thicker corpora callosa (the connecting fibers that allow the two hemispheres of the cortex to communicate). MRI scans comparing males and females on language tasks indicate that while the performance level is comparable, the male brains must work much harder to achieve the same level. Moreover, the scans show that females use both hemispheres of their brains in processing language information while in males that ability is largely circumscribed to the left hemisphere (Begley, 1995). It has been shown that verbal ability peaks in females during the peak of their estrogen levels which occurs during ovulation. It is also known that estrogen promotes dendritic branching (Fisher, 1998).

Males, on the other hand, outperform females in understanding and mentally manipulating spatial relations on paper-and-pencil maze tests and on standard spatial tests such as mental rotation tasks (Levy & Heller, 1992). In these tasks the participants have to match a picture of a three-dimensional object with one of four similar objects next to it that are oriented in different positions. Males are also better at perceiving underlying visuospatial relations in a confusing and conflicting context. This ability is called field independence and is highly correlated with spatial ability. Males typically do better on the Embedded Figures Test, which requires identifying a simple figure embedded in a more complex one; the Rod and Frame Test, which requires the participant to set the rod to the absolute vertical when the rod is surrounded by a tilted frame; and specifying correctly the horizontal waterline in a tilted bottle. Though positively correlated with spatial abilities, field independence has a negative correlation with many forms of social behavior.

Field-dependent people are more attentive to social forms of information, are better at expressing thoughts and feelings, and perform better in social interactions (Levy & Heller, 1992). Greater field dependency, which is typical of females, may reflect an increased use of contextual information. In a study comparing how teenage girls and boys viewed their friends, it was found that boys described their friends in terms of individual qualities, whereas for the girls, their friends were part of a greater whole including friends of their friends, their kinship relationships, and other types of connected relational information (Matthys, Cohen-Kettenis, & Berkhout, 1994). Regardless of cultural origin, females are better than males in interpreting the meaning of facial expression and other social emotional forms of information. Recent studies (Skuse et al, 1997) suggest that females may be genetically predisposed toward prosocial behavior whereas it must be predominantly acquired in human males via social learning.

The female brain is physically and functionally more symmetrical than the male brain (Levy & Heller, 1992). In the female, there is greater processing of emotional information in the right hemisphere as compared to males where the right hemisphere is little better than the left hemisphere in processing this type of information. In the male there is a significant right-hemisphere bias for processing visual-spatial information. The greater brain symmetry and thicker corpus callosum of the female allows them to have greater facility in web thinking (Fisher, 1998). Web thinking refers to the ability to synthesize and to integrate ancillary information. It may be this ability that has given rise to the folk wisdom that attributes greater intuitive powers to females. Males on the other hand, with their greater brain asymmetry, are more compartmentalized in their thinking. Their thoughts tend to be linear, goal oriented, and they are less tolerant of ambiguity.

If we characterize the female pattern as having greater verbal ability, greater emotional intelligence, and facility at web thinking, then we can characterize the male pattern as having greater spatial abilities, math abilities, and linear thinking. In females, although the average trend is toward a feminine pattern of cognition, there is a range in ability, where some females trend more toward the male pattern and some trend more toward the female pattern (Levy & Heller, 1992). The same is true within males. Some males exemplify the more extreme masculine pattern whereas other males tend toward the feminine pattern. It is only when we look at the overall mean that we can associate the feminine pattern with females and the masculine pattern with males. This is because these different patterns of cognitive ability are a product of the underlying differences in brain organization and physiology. The different patterns in brain development are in turn due to differential exposures to sex hormones in utero (Nopoulos, Flaum, O'Leary & Andreasen, 2000; Sandstrom, Kaufman & Huettel, 1998).

Prior to six weeks postconception, it is impossible to distinguish male fetuses from female fetuses without doing a microscopic examination of the sex-determining chromosomes (Carlson, 1998). We all begin life with undifferentiated primordial gonads. If we have the XX genotype, then around the seventh week following conception the outer layer of these primordial gonads develops into ovaries. The ovaries begin producing estrogens that in turn promote the development of body structures along feminine lines. If we have an XY genotype, genes on the Y chromosome code for the production of testis-determining factor (TDF) which transmutes the inner part of the primordial gonads into testes. The testes then begin producing androgens that promote the development of male sex organs and suppress the development of female sex hormones. Whether an individual develops feminine internal sex organs and external genitalia or masculine internal sex organs and external genitalia is a direct result of the sex hormones that are released into the circulatory system. The sex hormones also produce the differences in brain organization that ultimately create the behavioral differences previously discussed, as well as others. The effects of sex hormones on brain development are subtle and convoluted in their mode of action compared to their effects on the development of other body structures.

Paradoxically, the nervous system appears to be masculinized by the female hormone estradiol (Hutchinson & Beyer, 1994). This occurs through a process called aromatization. Aromatase is an enzyme present in neonatal neurons, which converts testosterone into estradiol. It is the estradiol that causes the differential growth of certain brain structures, resulting in the hemispheric asymmetry and masculine specializations discussed earlier (Hutchinson, Beyer, Hutchinson, & Wozniak). In female fetuses the plasma estradiol has no effect on neuronal differentiation because the estradiol cannot pass through the blood-brain barrier. Estradiol in the blood plasma becomes locked up with a substance called alpha fetoprotein that creates a large molecule that cannot penetrate the blood-brain barrier. Testosterone, however, is permitted to cross this barrier and because circulating levels of testosterone are going to be proportionately higher in males, once it enters the neuron there is a much greater conversion to estradiol in developing males. Thus masculinization typically occurs in male brains and not in female brains.

Within gender differences in cognition, function may be due either to the differences in plasma levels of sex hormones or to differences of aromatase levels within the neurons. It has been demonstrated experimentally that maternal stress lowers aromatase levels, and male offspring born to highly stressed mothers often times appear more feminine in their behavior patterns than male individuals born to less-stressed mothers (Carlson, 1998). The developmental physiology that makes this possible is, of course, the end product of eons of natural selection. In truth, the cognitive functioning of males and females is remarkably similar, despite major differences in their physiological and hormonal conditions. De Vries and Boyle (1998) have argued that the primary purpose of some of the sex differences in brain functioning is to compensate for the different physiologies of males and females in order to produce congruent patterns of behavior and cognition. Thus, when males and females are compared on various language tasks, their overall performance level is very similar while the brain activity underlying their performance shows marked differences (Jaeger, Lockwood, Van Valin, Kemmerer, Murphy & Wack, 1998). During such tasks, males rely almost exclusively on the language centers of the left hemisphere, while females actively recruit from both cerebral hemispheres as well as the cerebellum. Moreover, in males the percentage of grey matter (neuron cell bodies) is higher in the left hemisphere and the percentage of cerebral spinal fluid is higher in the right with a greater percentage of white matter (myelinated connecting axons) overall, but females lack this asymmetry while showing a greater volume of grey matter, overall (Gur, Turetsky, Matsui, Yan, Bilker, Hughett & Gur, 1999). Certainly, in such a highly social species as our own, there is an evolutionary necessity for highly congruent cognition and behavior between all the members of a society despite the differences that stem from different reproductive physiologies. On the other hand, while male and female cognitive function is very similar, there are subtle, yet distinct differences that are a direct outcome of different physiological patterns of development. The next question to ask is what is the adaptive significance of these different patterns.

Evolved gender differences in cognitive and other psychological functions are the direct result of differing reproductive strategies (Buss, 1994). The greater empathy and emotional intelligence characteristic of females are undoubtedly characteristics critical to the survival of dependent offspring. Another key to survival and high reproductive fitness in humans is language acquisition, which is greatly expedited by mothers and female caretakers high in verbal fluency. The verbal skills and emotional intelligence of females also contributed to their ability to form coalitions that allowed for the sharing of maternal resources. This same tendency for human females to be more affiliative and cooperative is displayed in numerous nonhuman primate societies suggesting that it is phylogenetically an extremely ancient trait (Box, 1984).

As to the male cognitive pattern, it has been suggested that the facility in spatial skills evolved to facilitate hunting. It has been shown that females typically navigate a familiar terrain by learning landmarks whereas males make use of a directional sense (Sandstrom, Kaufman & Huettel, 1998; Choi & Silverman, 1996). Proponents of the hunting hypothesis argue that in the pursuit of game, ancestral hominids would zigzag across vast stretches of terrain, but ultimately they would want to return to their home base via as direct a route as possible. Therefore, their spatial skills were finely honed in order to facilitate functioning under these conditions. The male adeptness in discerning embedded figures could be seen as another hunting adaptation that allowed the hunter to discern camouflaged animals hiding in the brush.

The male tendency toward greater spatial skills, however, has been demonstrated in various rodents as well as numerous species of nonhuman primates.

Most of these species do little if any hunting (Gaulin, Fitzgerald, & Wartell, 1990). This suggests that the ability evolved not specifically for hunting but rather to enable males to leave their natal group, travel over large expanses of countryside, and find mating partners. In actuality, both scenarios probably have truth to them. The trait probably originally arose to facilitate movement in strange surroundings in order to acquire mates. Later on, spatial abilities were co-opted for hunting. During the three to four million years in which ancestral hominids foraged, scavenged, and hunted, the trait underwent further natural selection. Other male tendencies such as aggressiveness and a lack of empathy are also due to reproductive concerns. Male-male competition for females required aggressive characteristics as well as a tendency to not feel too much empathy for the opponent. These same tendencies were probably also co-opted for hunting activities and underwent further selection during the millions of years of hominid evolution. Gender differences directly involved in mating behavior will be discussed in Chapter 5.

Summary

Encephalization (the amount of brain mass relative to body size) has reached an extreme state in the human species. Although primate species as a whole, are relatively highly encephalized, a set of selective pressures unique to human ancestors must be posited to explain human brain development. These factors include the climactic changes of the Ice Age, the development of one-arm ballistic movements, language evolutions, and intraspecific competition.

The evolutionary process has resulted in a human brain comprised of a collection of functionally specialized units or modules. The mind itself has a modular nature exhibiting strong inherent biases and specializations in areas that were critical to the survival of our forebears. These adaptive mental modules include predisposition for learning certain fear stimuli, cheater detection mechanisms in social interactions and gender typical differences in verbal skills, empathy and spatial reasoning.

Discussion Questions

1. Why is human encephalization best thought of as being the outcome of multiple interacting factors rather than one single factor?

2. What is the relationship between modular brain and modular mind in terms of gender differences in behavior? In other works, how does brain ontogeny result in gender typical behavior modules?

3. Discuss the mind as a collection of old and new modules working together. For example, the Wason Selection talk requires reading (a relatively recent cultural invention) which requires language (a relatively recent [<500,000 years ago] evolutionary development) and demonstrates some very ancient (millions of years old) cognitive biases associated with Machiavellian intelligence.

Key Terms

acromatopsia	cortical blindness	neocortex
Allen's rule	encephalization	preparedness theory
aromatization	field independence	split-brain surgery
ballistic movements	heterochrony	teleological error
Bergmann's rule	Ice Age	visual agnosia
Broca's area	laterality	Wason Selection Task
cerebellum	Machiavellian intelligence	Wernicke's area
contralateral neglect	modular brain	William's Syndrome
corpus callosum	modular mind	

Additional Reading

Evolution and Learning by Robert C. Bolles and Michael D. Beecher (Editors) (1988).

The Biology of Mind: Origins and Structures of Mind, Brain, and Consciousness by M. Deric Bownds (1999).

Human Evolution: A Neuropsychological Perspective by John L. Bradshaw (1998).

What Counts: How Every Brain Is Hardwired for Math by Brian Butterworth (1999).

The Thinking Ape: Evolutionary Origins of Intelligence by Richard Byrne (1995).

How Brains Think: Evolving Intelligence, Then and Now by William H. Calvin (1996) (Also, see his website.).

The Cerebral Code: Thinking a Thought in the Mosaics of the Mind by William H. Calvin (1998).

The Things We Do: Using the Lessons of Bernard and Darwin to Understand the What, How, and Why of Our Behavior by Gary Cziko (2000).

Cognitive Ecology: The Evolutionary Ecology of Information Processing and Decision Making by Reuven Dukas (Editor) (1998).

Origins of the Modern Mind: Three Stages in the Evolution of Culture and Cognition by Merlin Donald (1991).

The Mind's Past by Michael S. Gazzaniga (1998).

Simple Heuristics That Make Us Smart by Gerd Gigerenzer, Peter M. Todd, and the ABC Research Group (1999).

Sex Differences in Cognitive Abilities (3rd Edition) by Diane F. Halpern (2000).

Mapping the Mind: Domain Specificity in Cognition and Culture by Lawrence A. Hirschfeld, Susan A. Gelman, and Gelman Hirschfeld (Editors) (1994).

Minds, Machines & Evolution by James Patrick Hogan (1999).

Evolution, Learning and Cognition by Y. C. Lee (Editor) (1988).

The Evolution of Cognition by Cecelia Heyes and Ludwig Huber (Editors) (2000).

Defending the Cavewoman: And Other Tales of Evolutionary Neurology by Harold L. Klawans (2000).

Gender Gap in Science and Engineering: Illuminating the Differences in Career Outcomes of Ph.D.s by J. Scott Long (Editor) (2000).

How the Mind Works by Stephen Pinker (1999).

The Origin and Evolution of Intelligence by Arnold B. Scheibel and J. William Schopf (Editors) (1997).

Cognition, Evolution, and Behavior by Sara J. Shettleworth (1998).

Human Instincts, Everyday Life, and the Brain: A Paradigm for Understanding Behavior by Richard H. Wills (1998).

4

Language: Crown Jewel of Communication

Jabborwocky

'Twas brillig, and the slithy toves
Did gyre and gimble in the wabe:
All mimsy were the borogoves,
And the mome raths outgrabe.

"Beware the Jabberwock, my son!
The jaws that bite, the claws that catch!
Beware the Jubjub bird, and shun
The frumious Bandersnatch!"

He took his vorpal sword in hand:
Long time the manxome foe he sought-
So rested he by the Tumtum tree,
And stood awhile in thought.

And, as in uffish thought he stood,
The Jabberwock, with eyes of flame,
Came whiffling through the tulgey wood,
And burbled as it came!

One, two! One, two! And through and
   through
The vorpal blade went snicker-snack!
He left it dead, and with its head
He went galumphing back.

"And hast thou slain the Jabberwock?
Come to my arms, my beamish boy!
O frabjous day! Callooh! Callay!"
He chortled in his joy.

'Twas brillig, and the slithy toves
Did gyre and gimble in the wabe:
All mimsy were the borogoves,
And the mome raths outgrabe.

—*Through the Looking-Glass*, Lewis Carroll (1872)

Chapter Questions

1. Can intelligent animals reared by humans acquire languages?
2. Can humans reared by animals acquire language?
3. How can human language ability be explained as a product of biological evolution?

The Nature of Language

Of all the myriad behaviors in the human repertoire, perhaps none come closer to defining our species than language. In fact, we could succinctly describe *Homo sapiens sapiens* as "the talking animal." Communication systems abound in other living species, both plants and animals, to the point of being almost omnipresent. Human language, however, appears to sit alone, disconnected phylogenetically from the behavior of all other organisms. In this chapter we will address this seeming paradox of a huge evolutionary gap between the language abilities of our species and that of any other species on the planet.

Despite the fact that there are over 5,000 languages currently being spoken and an unknown number of dead or extinct languages (all of which are incredibly diverse in terms of their surface characteristics), there are a number of basic commonalities shared by all languages. Unlike behaviors that are largely cultural inventions, the complexity of a particular language (in terms of sentence structure and grammatical nuances) is independent of a society's political or technological complexity. Modern-day hunter-gatherers have languages that are just as complex as those of cultures with space-age technologies.

Charles Hockett (1960) called the universal characteristics of human language "design features." Some animals have communication systems that contain some of these design features. But, to our knowledge no animal communication system contains all of them. The following nine characteristics are from Hockett's original list of thirteen:

1. Mode of Communication (vocal auditory in the case of human and many animal systems);
2. Semanticity (the signals are meaningful);
3. Pragmatic Function (the communication serves a useful purpose);
4. Interchangeability (ability of individuals to both send and receive messages);
5. Cultural Transmission (specific signals are learned rather than genetically transmitted);
6. Arbitrariness (form is not logically related to meaning);
7. Discreteness (complex messages are built up out of smaller parts);
8. Displacement (ability to communicate about things not present in time or space); and
9. Productivity (ability to produce an infinite number of novel meaningful messages using a finite number of elements because individual meanings are arbitrary).

Of the nine items on this list, the first three are shared by all systems of animal communication. Items four through seven exist in some forms of animal communication. Items eight and nine appear to be unique to humans.

Animal Communication

Communication systems appear to be almost universal among living organisms. A common reproductive strategy of many plants is to attract pollinating animals, usually insects, by means of brightly colored flowers and sweet scents. Plants also communicate to animals that are instrumental in dispersing their seeds after reproduction has occurred. They advertise the presence of brightly colored edible fruit in order to attract animals that will eat these fruits and disperse the seeds when they are passed through the guts of the animals.

If we define communication as both the sending and receiving of information, then we restrict this phenomenon to the animal kingdom since plants lack a nervous system and their reception of communication is limited at best. Animal communication occurs in every sense modality. The oldest involves chemo-senses such as olfaction. It has been demonstrated that single-celled organisms such as bacteria respond to the chemical traces left by their con-specific neighbors. Olfaction plays a key role in courtship and mating in numerous species both simple and complex in terms of pheromones. Pheromones are the chemical signals emitted by animals to attract mates and to apprise them of the current reproductive potential in one's self. Olfactory signals also play a key role in the marking of territories, as is readily observed by dog owners. The urine marks that a dog leaves on various objects are signposts indicating that this area belongs to him and it is a warning to other dogs to stay clear.

In the 1950s, the ethologist Karl von Frisch discovered what has erroneously been referred to as "the language of the honeybees" (von Frisch, 1971). Through a series of elaborate experiments, von Frisch demonstrated that foraging honeybees communicate the location of new sources of nectar to their hive mates. They do this by executing what is called a "waggle dance," moving in a figure-eight pattern along the vertical surface of the honeycomb. The intensity of the waggle indicates the richness of the honey source, the inclination of the figure eight in relation to perpendicular codes for the direction of the nectar source in relation to the position of the sun. Despite its complexity, what the honeybees are doing is not really comparable to true language. The information that is being communicated is extremely limited in scope. Moreover, the symbol usage is not at all arbitrary and appears to be genetically hard-wired in the nervous systems of the honeybees. Thus honeybees are communicating, but their behavior does not meet the criteria for true language.

Complex, important behaviors such as courtship and territoriality are communicated through multiple channels. Birds sing in order to set up territories and to attract mates. This is not to imply that they are engaging in singing behavior with the intention of achieving these goals. The singing is elicited by certain proximate cues, some of them physiological and its adaptive function is to delineate teritories and attract mates. They also use visual signals such as bodily displays to communicate many of the same messages. Red-winged blackbirds, for example, use the red tufts on their wings to signal possession of a territory. If these red tufts are painted black, the animal quickly loses any territories that it possesses. In dogs, visual displays are very important in communicating many different mood states. The dog that advances toward another with fur piloerected and its front legs very stiff is displaying an aggressive posture. The dog that bows by kneeling in front of another is co-opting, a submissive gesture in order to indicate a willingness to engage in a bout of play-behavior with another. Snarling and growling among dogs and other creatures are almost universal mammalian signals of aggression and warning.

Darwin (1872) was aware that our own facial expression could be directly derived from these earlier signals of aggression and appeasement. Facial displays continue to be a primary source of nonverbal information for us humans. If we are skeptical about the veracity of what someone is telling us, we typically want to see their facial expressions and their eyes in order to determine the accuracy of the information they are giving us verbally.

The nonhuman communication systems that are generally thought to be aligned most closely to human language are those associated with vocal communication. Once again, these auditory forms of communication are found throughout the animal kingdom. The study of primates, our closest living relatives, provides a wealth of information on the evolutionary pattern toward language development. African vervet monkeys have been shown to give distinctly different vocalizations when confronted with different types of predators (Cheney & Seyfarth,1990). If the animal spots a leopard, he will give a unique call—called a "leopard call" by the biologists who study these animals—which will cause the other vervets to run for the trees. If the "eagle call" is given, it has the opposite effect—the other monkeys will dive out of the tree canopy and hug the ground. If the vervets hear the "snake call," they will stand up on their hind legs and peer intently at the grass around them. It is also clear from playback experiments that vervets can distinguish the vocalizations made by individual animals. They respond quite differently when they hear a vocalization on playback of a subordinate animal as opposed to a dominant animal, e.g., if a subordinate animal cries out, it is more likely to be ignored than if a dominant animal makes a similar cry. Vocalizations have been shown to play a subtle yet significant role in the social interactions of many other primate species. The suggestion that these animals have some incipient form of language ability led to serious attempts to train primates in language skills.

Animal Language Studies

Most investigations into the capacity of nonhuman animals for acquiring language have used great apes as subjects. There are, however, some noteworthy exceptions. A type of gestural language was successfully taught to two female California sea lions (Gisiner & Schusterman, 1992). One of the sea lions demonstrated an understanding of simple syntax (deriving meaning from word order). Another series of language studies involved a different species of marine mammal, the bottlenose dolphin. One individual dolphin was trained to respond to high-pitched sounds broadcast into the water and a second dolphin was trained in a language based on hand gestures performed by the trainer (Herman, 1987). Both animals responded correctly to commands given in their respective languages. Moreover, both dolphins could give appropriate responses to questions that were posed to them by either pressing a "no" paddle or a "yes" paddle.

One of the most remarkable examples of a language-trained nonhuman is named Alex. Alex has used his language abilities to demonstrate an understanding of abstract concepts such as same/different, bigger/smaller and quantification, as well as concrete concepts such as color and shape (Pepperberg, 1992, 1993, 1994, & 1996). For example, when presented with a collection of red keys, blue keys and toy trucks, Alex would be asked, "How many blue key?" Alex would respond vocally to these questions in clear, albeit concise English. The vocalization of human speech sounds is not unusual for members of Alex's species, the African gray parrot; however, to produce these sounds in the context of real language usage is something most animal behaviorists assumed to be highly unlikely before Alex. The common pejorative "bird-brained" is based on the typically small size of avian brains, particularly the cerebral cortex. Despite his being "cerebrally challenged," Alex's performance in the area of language competence and cognitive ability remains largely unsurpassed even by mankind's closest relative, the great apes.

During the first half of the twentieth century there were two documented attempts to teach chimpanzees to speak English (Candland, 1993). The approach involved raising a baby chimpanzee along with a newborn human infant, giving both equal attention and presumably equal opportunities to learn to speak. The outcomes of these experiments were disappointing to say the least. In the 1930s, W. N. Kellogg and L. A. Kellogg raised the infant chimpanzee, Gua, alongside their son, Donald, who was two and one-half months younger. The two were reared together under very similar conditions for a period of nine months. Despite concerted efforts to teach Gua to articulate human language, her only vocalizations consisted of species-typical grunts and cries. Moreover, her comprehension of spoken language remained extremely limited. The chimpanzee, Vickie, that was reared by Catherine and Keith Hayes never achieved more than a half-dozen words of language, and when they were produced they were barely audible. It soon became apparent that the reason chimps could not speak is because they lack the necessary vocal equipment.

Human language is made possible by the existence of a deep-set larynx that provides a large resonating chamber at the back of the nose and mouth. In addition, the deep-set larynx provides precise control and coordination of the vocal cords. Chimpanzees do not have these anatomical specializations. Therefore, in the 1960s an attempt was made to teach a chimpanzee American Sign Language (ASL) (Candland, 1993). This experiment was performed by Beatrix and Allen Gardner using a female chimpanzee named Washoe. Washoe learned over a hundred signs in ASL. However, she rarely used more than two signs together, so it is questionable if she was ever using sentences at all. Additionally, the number of novel sign combinations she produced was extremely rare. Many critics attributed the supposed sign combinations such as "water bird" which she signed after seeing a swan to mere coincidence combined with the overactive imagination of the Gardners.

The critics of ape language explain much of Washoe's behavior as a result of the "Clever Hans phenomenon" (Candland, 1993). Clever Hans was a famous horse that lived around the turn of the century. Hans was supposedly able to make any kind of arithmetical calculation. You simply asked the horse to add or subtract a sum of numbers and the horse would tap out the correct answer with his hoof. It was finally discovered how Hans was able to do this. When the math problem was whispered into the horse's ear, the horse failed to respond. It was only when the trainer was present and heard the problem that the horse would tap out the correct sum. In actuality, the horse was acutely sensitive to subtle cues being transmitted unconsciously by the trainer. The trainer knew what the correct answer was, and when the horse had tapped out the appropriate number of taps with his hoof, the trainer would unconsciously tense up. The horse would sense this tenseness, and that would be his last tap. Since the exposure of this phenomenon, investigations of animal behavior are closely watched for signs of unconscious cueing.

In the 1970s, animal language projects were begun with other primate species, notably the gorilla, Koko, and an orangutan named Chantek (Dunbar, 1996). Both of these involved ASL. Other approaches that were used involved teaching chimpanzees pictorial language. This was the approach used by David Premack (1971) to teach the chimpanzee named Sarah. With Sarah, colored plastic shapes were used to stand for words or concepts. The plastic shapes were magnetized so they could be assembled on a metal board in order to form sentences. Another study initiated by Dwayne Rumbaugh (1976) involved using a computer keyboard consisting of a large array of colored shapes rather than letters with each key representing a word. This system was taught to two chimpanzees named Austin and Sherman. The success of Austin and Sherman could be termed moderate at best. However, a young bonobo, or pygmy chimpanzee, named Kanzi spontaneously picked up language while it was being taught to his mother (Savage-Rumbaugh, Shanker, & Taylor, 1998). This in itself is somewhat remarkable as all the other ape language studies involved intensive training directed at a particular subject, whereas Kanzi seemed to acquire it without overt reinforcement.

Kanzi has since become the genius of the ape language world. Kanzi has convincingly exhibited an impressive understanding of spoken human language (Savage-Rumbaugh, Shanker, & Taylor, 1998). He has also demonstrated the ability to understand important concepts such as addition and subtraction, relationships of less than and greater than, the ability to ask for specific objects or activities, and the ability to carry out complex and novel instructions such as taking leaves from the floor and putting them in the refrigerator or taking items out of the refrigerator and carrying them outside. Kanzi can also translate from one modality to the other. English words can be spoken and conveyed to Kanzi through a headphone and he can correctly point to a corresponding symbol on a keyboard. This ability is thought to be a prerequisite to language and eventually to writing. Critics have once again pointed out that despite the extraordinary abil-ities demonstrated by Kanzi, his sentences remain simple two- and three-word af-fairs. Most importantly, Kanzi does not engage in the effortless, spontaneous talk that a typical human child engages in. Young human children are constantly com-menting on observations about the word and asking questions such as "What is that?", "What is this?", and "What are we doing?".

Symbolic reasoning has clearly been demonstrated to be one of the capabili-ties of the higher nonhuman primates. Specific language capabilities, however, do not appear to be part of their innate capabilities. The laboriousness with which they acquire language, their severely limited ability to spontaneously generate novel constructs, their lack of complex sentence structure, and the general lack of intrin-sic motivation for language production are all clear indications that a fundamental gap exists between our closest relatives and ourselves. These ape language studies have, however, provided important information in answering some questions re-garding the evolution of language. The capacity for using and understanding sym-bols may have been a capability in a common ancestor of humans and apes, as this ability is currently present in both humans and apes. However, specific language abilities, including the mental capacity for complex language use as well as the anatomical adaptations for speech articulation, are unique to humans.

Another important component of information for understanding the evolu-tion of language comes from looking at humans who do not learn language dur-ing the appropriate developmental stage. Giving intensive language training to animals that normally do not use language is one side of the coin. But, what hap-pens when a human is deprived of the early experiences involved with language acquisition? Of course, scientists cannot perform these types of studies for ethical reasons. But throughout history, events have occurred which have provided spon-taneous experiments of this sort. In the next section we will look at the outcome of these natural experiments.

Feral Children

On October 17, 1920, in the forests of northeastern India, the Christian missionary, Reverend J. A. Singh, ordered a group of workmen to begin digging out a 20-foot-high termite mound (Candland, 1993). As the workmen began digging, almost im-mediately a wolf emerged from a tunnel near the base of the mound and ran toward them. A few seconds later a second wolf appeared and followed the first. A third wolf emerged and began to ferociously harry the workmen. This wolf was a female, and the Reverend Singh guessed that it was the mother wolf defending her offspring. Before he could intervene the workmen had already killed the mother wolf. From that point on the excavation proceeded very quickly. They found inside the mound a hollow den where the cubs huddled together, clutching one another in a ball. As was expected, two of the cubs were wolves, but the other two were human children.

The canine cubs were given to the diggers, but Singh took charge of the two human children and carried them back to his mission (Candland, 1993). The wolf children were girls and the older appeared to be about eight years of age and the younger about one and a half years. Reverend Singh named the older child Kamala and the younger one Amala. Amala, the younger child was destined to die a little less than a year after her capture from a roundworm infection. Kamala would go on to live nine years under the care of the missionaries.

The remarkable case of Kamala and Amala provides evidence concerning the critical role of ontogeny in determining those behaviors we most closely associate with being uniquely human (Candland, 1993). During their first year at the mission the two wolf children generally displayed behaviors much more consistent with wolf cubs instead of human children. The two would scramble about on all fours and were not able to stand erect because of the condition of inflexibility in their joints. Their eyesight was acutely attuned to night conditions. They appeared to be able to see in darkness objects that were invisible to ordinary humans. They showed little interest or curiosity to anything other than raw meat. When they ate they would eat face down in the bowl just as a wolf would. As for human emotions such as joy or sadness, the only occurrence of such that was every displayed was shown by Kamala a few moments after her sister Amala had died. Kamala was observed to have tried frantically to awaken her sister from the sleep of death. She had to be forcibly removed from the vicinity of the coffin, and two tears were observed to drop from her eyes.

At the time of their capture Amala and Kamala displayed no language ability whatsoever (Candland, 1993). Nor do the reports suggest that Amala had acquired any before her death less than a year later. After five years in the orphanage Kamala did demonstrate some conceptual learning and some rudimentary language skills. She knew the names of many of the babies being housed in the orphanage, and she understood the concept of color. She had a vocabulary of about 30 words. The words she used were not part of the common English language that was spoken by the Singhs. The words used by Kamala were actually sounds that she had heard used by children in somewhat different contexts. Kamala used the word "who" to indicate "yes" when she was offered food. "Ha" means "yes" in Bengali, but the word "hoo" was sometimes used by the children to express "cold." An analysis of Kamala's words indicates that most of her words show a strong similarity to Bengali words. Kamala was never observed to use any of these words in a spontaneous fashion. When she was told to say what a certain object was, she would name it in a very distinct fashion. However, she would never ask for anything she wanted by naming it, but would wait for the Reverend Singh's wife to go down a list of possible items until she had named the one that Kamala wanted at which point she would nod.

Kamala would continue to live in the missionary orphanage for nine years following her discovery (Candland, 1993). During that time she continued to acquire more and more vocabulary words. But at no time did she ever begin to spontaneously use these words. Nor is there any record of her ever spontaneously producing what would be considered a proper sentence. In November of 1929 Kamala died from uremia. The uremia was probably a direct consequence of her strong preference for eating raw meat. The lupine diet was evidently beyond the physiological limits of the human body.

Although the case of Amala and Kamala is one of the best-documented accounts of humans being raised by animals, it is by no means the first of its kind (Candland, 1993). The father of modern taxonomic classification, Carolus Linnaeus, listed under the genus *Homo* the classification for *Loco ferus*. *Loco ferus* was described as four-footed, dumb (in the sense of being nonspeaking) and hairy. Linnaeus listed nine examples of these feral children. In chronological order they include a wolf boy from Hesse (1344), a Lithuanian bear boy (1661) presumably found nursing at the teats of bears, an Irish sheep boy (1672), a girl from Cranenburg (1717), a boy called Peter from Hameln, Germany (1724), and a girl from Champagne (1731). In 1799, 50 years after Linnaeus's nomenclature of animals was published, another wild child, a boy 11 or 12 years old, was found in the Caune woods of France. The outstanding commonality among these so-called feral children was their lack of any sort of human language. More importantly, none of them showed much in the way of an ability to acquire language once they were brought into civilization. One question that cannot be answered from this sort of data is whether or not the deficits in intellectual functioning were the result of their socially impoverished environment, or were these children already mentally deficient before they came to be in their strange rearing circumstances. In two of the cases that were fairly extensively studied, the experts of the time who were familiar with mentally retarded individuals declared both of these cases to be individuals of extremely low mental functioning. They attributed the failures in rehabilitation and language instruction to the inherently low capacity of these individuals for mental functioning. Of course, low mental functioning can just as readily be seen as a failure of the brain to develop properly without the appropriate environmental (social) stimulation. It seems unlikely that every single case of feral rearing involves an individual or individuals mentally defective at birth.

One of the most recent and celebrated cases of severe childhood deprivation involves the case of the individual who has been referred to as Genie (Rymer, 1993). Genie was discovered in 1970 in California when she was 13½ years old. She had been restrained to sitting on a potty seat in the basement of their home day in and day out for those entire 13 years except for the first 20 months of her life. At night she was placed in a straight jacket and caged in a crib with wire mesh sides that was completely covered over. Her mother was partially blind and her father was violent and mentally deranged. He never spoke to her with words but instead made barking sounds toward her. At the time she was discovered, Genie's speech production was limited to a few negatives such as "stopit," and "nomore." She was also unable to stand erect. After her discovery she underwent extensive rehabilitation and training over several years. During the course of her therapy she learned to walk with a jerky motion and learned to recognize many words and to speak. She had first spoken one-word utterances and then progressed to two- and sometimes three-word sequences. Unlike normal children, however, Genie continued to use sentences that were basically word salad. Her sequencing of words was random and only to people who were totally familiar with her behavior and needs were her "sentences" comprehensible. Besides never learning to understand grammar, particularly syntax (the way words are ordered to form acceptable phrases and sentences), Genie also never was able to differentiate between pronouns and between passive and active verbs.

If there is one thing the cases of the feral children tell us about language, it is that a proper socializing environment must be present during key critical periods of development. In fact the first 12 years of life up until the age of puberty is considered the critical period for language acquisition in humans. Of those 12 years or so, by far, the most critical years are between the ages of one and four. In the next section we will look at the normal developmental process through which human children acquire language.

Language Acquisition

The manner in which humans acquire various cultural traits can vary enormously from individual to individual. For example, we may acquire an interest in a certain area of knowledge or a certain activity in late adulthood, or even middle-age, and become adept and proficient at it very late in life. For example, we could acquire an interest in vegetarian cooking in our mid-forties and become very adept at it by the time we are in our late forties. Some individuals have even taken up very rigorous or skilled hobbies such as rock climbing, whitewater canoeing, painting, or piano playing late in life and become very proficient at these. However, the manner in which humans acquire language follows a very predictable pattern; a pattern which, although it can vary in some degree from individual to individual, remains relatively invariant in its sequence of unfolding. This invariant sequencing of language acquisition provides strong evidence supporting the view of language as an evolved biological adaptation.

Developmental Stages

During the first few months of life, human infants communicate through gestures and facial expressions and through what is termed "prelinguistic vocalizations." These vocalizations include crying (which is not a single vocalization, but rather a host of somewhat differentiated sounds, each having a slightly different meaning), coos (which include squealing and gurgling), and laughter. Between the ages of 3 to 6 months, there emerges what has been referred to as the babbling stage. Throughout the world regardless of the culture in which they have been brought up and even if they are deaf from birth, human infants display this babbling behavior at the same time in their development. Babbling consists of the spontaneous production of phonemes. Phonemes are the basic sounds that make up language. In the English language, there are approximately 36 phonemes. During the babbling phase, however, infants are not restricted to the phonemes that comprise their native language. Infants can and typically do produce phonemes that are not part of the native language of the child's family. Toward the end of the babbling stage the utterances become more restricted to the phonemes that comprise the language of the child's caretakers. If a child is deaf, the babbling gradually diminishes, and the production of sounds is greatly reduced after some time. Children with normal hearing, through a process of reinforcement, begin to produce expressive jargon. Expressive jargon refers to meaningful utterances that sound like sentences with pauses, inflections, and rhythms.

Between the ages of nine to 12 months, children undergo a critical period that permanently alters their ability to discriminate phonemes. At the beginning of this critical period, children can differentiate between similar phonemes that are produced outside their native language. By the end of the critical period, their phoneme discrimination abilities have been restricted to the phonemes that are present in their native language. This type of reduction in neural capacities not only occurs in language systems but is thought to be a general process that occurs in a host of behavioral categories. The terms "neural Darwinism" or "neural pruning" have been used to describe this process (Edelman, 1987). The basic theory behind this is that the brain starts with a surplus of neurons and neural connections, but only those pathways that are frequently used continue to survive and remain functional. Pathways that are not used are simply allowed to die. Thus, it is through a process of neuronal attrition that the brain shapes itself in such a way that it is optimally adapted to its environment.

By one year of age words such as "mama" and "dada" are emerging and the child is starting to demonstrate some understanding of words and simple commands. By 15 to 18 months, children have a vocabulary of about 10 to 20 words. During this time, children are using what is called the holophrase where one word is used to imply a complete concept. By 1½ to 2 years children have begun to use two words and children engage in what is called telegraphic speech where the use of short and precise words is used to communicate. By 2 years children usually have a vocabulary of about 300 words and they are beginning to use three to four word phrases. Around 2½ years of age children show their fastest increase in vocabulary. On the average they are acquiring about 50 new words per week. The sentences and phrases used by children at this time are not verbatim repetitions of what they have heard adults say. This production of entirely new sentences is referred to as the capacity for infinite generativity. In addition to this novel sentence production, children are showing a complex understanding of grammatical rules. Numerous studies have shown that children will tend to overgeneralize rules of grammar at this time. For example, a child might point to their feet and say, "Look! I have two foots."

By 3 years of age, children have a vocabulary of approximately 1,000 words and at least 80% of their utterances are intelligible to strangers. Their grammatical usage approaches that of the adult level, although mistakes occasionally occur. By 4 years of age, language is well established, and the children speak in full sentences using prepositions, pronouns, adjectives, and adverbs. By 5 years of age, children use three-syllable words and speak in whole paragraphs. Further language development after this time is more a problem of refinement rather than new development of language skills.

Critical Periods

Lenneberg (1967) proposed that language acquisition must occur before the age of puberty, for this is the time that parallels the lateralization or localization of language functions taking place in the left hemisphere of the brain. Lenneberg believed that the process of brain lateralization was complete around the age of puberty. Therefore, exposure to a linguistic environment had to occur prior to this for language functioning to be possible. The accounts of the feral children referred to earlier tend to support Lenneberg's hypothesis. The rehabilitation of these children in terms of linguistic abilities was very limited. In the case of Genie, who was able to acquire a somewhat extensive vocabulary and was able to produce word sounds, it should be noted that her isolation began at about 20 months of age (Rymer, 1993). By 20 months of age most normal children are well into the process of language acquisition.

Neurolinguistic assessments reveal that Genie used the right hemisphere of her brain to process linguistic information (Rymer, 1993). This implies that the developmental period had passed in which specialized language areas in the left hemisphere could accomplish the task of language learning with great facility. This forced the right hemisphere, which normally has little involvement in language, to take over this functioning—albeit, poorly.

Additional support for the critical-period hypothesis is supplied by studies by Newport (1986) who assessed the language capabilities of deaf adults who acquired their primary language, American Sign Language (ASL), at different age periods. If a deaf child is born into a family that used ASL, then the child is exposed to ASL from an early age. However, most deaf children are born into families where the parents have normal hearing and there is no use of ASL. For these children, their first experience of ASL does not occur until they attend a school with specific programs for teaching ASL. This first experience can occur at a variety of ages. Assessment of ASL skills indicates that the most-proficient deaf adults are those who learned ASL at an early age from signing parents. The next most-proficient ones were those who acquired ASL between the ages of 4 and 6. The least-proficient users of ASL were those who acquired sign language after the age of 12.

Johnson and Newport (1989) argued that the critical period hypothesis can take two forms:

- Version One: The Exercise Hypothesis. Early in life, humans have a superior capacity for acquiring languages. If this capacity is exercised, then language learning abilities will remain operable throughout life. If, on the other hand, the capacity is not exercised during this time, the ability to acquire languages will disappear or decline with maturation.
- Version Two: The Maturational State Hypothesis. Early in life, humans have a superior capacity for acquiring languages and this capacity disappears or declines with maturation.

To test these differing hypotheses, Johnson and Newport (1989) assessed the English language skills of native Chinese and Korean college students and faculty who had come to this country at different ages. Their data indicate that if their subjects were first immersed in English between 3 and 7 years of age, their English was equivalent to that of native U.S. speakers. After this age there was a steady decline in performance. Thus, the data from this report support the maturation state hypothesis.

Curtiss (1989) describes the case of the girl "Chelsea" who was born deaf in a remote town in northern California. She was misdiagnosed as being retarded or emotionally disturbed by a number of doctors and clinicians, and her deafness remained undiscovered. Chelsea's loving family, who did not believe that she was retarded, sheltered her. As a result she grew up shy and without language, but otherwise neurologically and emotionally normal. At the age of 31 her deafness was discovered by a neurologist who had her fitted with hearing aids that improved her hearing to near normal levels. Intensive rehabilitation therapy has since brought her to where she scores in the 10-year-old range of normal intelligence. She knows how to read and write, holds a job, and has a vocabulary of about 2,000 words. Although much more functionally normal then Genie, she nonetheless displays a use of syntax that is very similar. Some examples of Chelsea's sentence usage illustrate this point: "Orange Tim car in.", "Banana the eat.", "The boat sits water on.", "Breakfast eating girl.", "The girl is cone.", and, "The ice cream, shopping, buying the man."

In summary, the data that we have just reviewed regarding the critical-period hypothesis of language acquisition suggests that the strong version of the hypothesis can be applied to the acquisition of grammatical structure, specifically the use of syntax. The weaker version of the hypothesis applies to the acquisition of vocabulary and the production of these words. Reviewing the current empirical evidence Ruben (1997) has concluded that the critical/sensitive period of phonology (word sound production and perception) is from 6 months postconception through the twelfth month of infancy. The critical/sensitive periods for syntax (rules governing acceptable word sequencing) continues through the fourth year of life, and for semantics (word meaning) through the fifteenth or sixteenth year of life.

Language Evolution

The origin of human language has been a subject of intense interest for thousands of years (Corballis, 1991). In the mid nineteenth century Charles Darwin (1859) proposed that our linguistic abilities had arisen like our other attributes as a result of the long process of natural selection. This view of the evolutionary origins of human language was far from being universally accepted by academics. The Linguistic Society in Paris in 1866 banned any discussion on the topic of language evolution. In the century that followed, empiricists (those who argue that behavior is a result of learning) held sway over the debate concerning language origins. In the 1950s, MIT linguistics professor, Noam Chomsky, turned all of this around when he argued that the acquisition of the deep structures of language (the rules of grammar) in children could not be explained as a result of straightforward learning. Chomsky's theory regarding the innate biological basis of language generated a furor of empirical research. This research ranged across a broad span of scientific disciplines including psychology, neurophysiology, anthropology, paleoanthropology, and linguistics. The evidence that has been accumulated from these studies over the past several decades leaves little doubt that the human language capacity is a product of biological evolution.

Universals

As was pointed out at the beginning of this chapter, every human culture ever discovered possesses a complex language system. There is no such thing as a Stone-Age language. The grammatical complexity employed by the hunter-gatherer in day-to-day existence is every bit as complex as that used by the astronaut, politician, or college professor of our culture. For many researchers the universality of complex language among humans is compelling proof that language is innate. Steven Pinker (1984), however, has pointed out that not everything that is universal is innate. To give a trivial example, people always build high-rise buildings from the ground up which certainly is not a product of any innate biological predisposition but rather the laws of physics. Pinker argues that better evidence for the innateness of language comes from the causal factors that make it universal. Complex language is universal among humans not because children are generally smart, they are taught language and it is generally useful to them, but because children actually reinvent language generation after generation and they cannot help doing so. One bit of evidence for this comes from the historical record.

When run-away slaves of the New World formed communities on certain Caribbean islands, the adults had to communicate with adults from other African tribes. The result was that a pidgin dialect arose that allowed simple forms of communication between the adults. Pidgin dialects are highly variable and have little in the way of grammar. What is remarkable is that the children of these one-time slaves did not just acquire the pidgin language but created a language rich in grammatical complexity where none had existed before. This new language is called Creole. The second line of evidence comes from cases of deaf children who learned American Sign Language from parents who acquired ASL as adults and who use it very poorly. Singleton and Newport (as cited in Pinker, 1984) describe the case of the child referred to as Simon. Simon's parents did not acquire sign language until age 15 or 16 and as a result they acquired it very poorly. Simon's parents failed to use proper grammar in many cases. But, Simon himself used signing that was much better than that of his parents. Seemingly working in a vacuum, Simon was able to produce ASL that was far superior in grammatical content than that he had learned from his parents.

The other line of evidence for universality of human language comes from studies of the brain. In 1836 a medical doctor named Marc Dax presented a paper to the medical society in Montpelier, France (Corballis, 1991). Dax had observed a relationship between brain damage on the left side and a corresponding loss of speech in over forty of his patients. He could not find a single case in which there

were indications of right-side brain damage of these people with speech impairments. In the 1860s a French physician named Paul Broca made a similar observation of the relationship between language function and the left hemisphere of
the brain. One of his patients was known as Ta because that was the only articulate sound he could make. Broca predicted that an examination of Ta's brain after
death would show damage in a specific area of the left side of the frontal cortex.
This indeed was born out after Ta died and Broca did the autopsy. Today this area
of the brain in the posterior portion of the frontal lobe on the left side is called
Broca's area (see Figure 4.1).

People who have damage to Broca's area suffer from what is called Broca's
aphasia (Carlson, 1997). Aphasias are deficits in speech production or comprehension that result from brain damage (Carlson, 1997). If the damage to Broca's
area is severe, the patient may be rendered inarticulate. With less severe damage,
the individual has word-finding problems referred to as anomia (being unable to
find the names of things). Mild forms of damage to Broca's area result in what is
called agrammatism. Specifically, the agrammatism displayed is a problem in the
use of syntax. Syntax allows us to derive the meaning of a string of words based
on the word order. Thus, the string "Bob hit the ball" has a very different meaning from the same words arranged as "The ball hit Bob." A person suffering damage in Broca's area would not be able to distinguish between the previous two
sentences. In fact, one test for Broca's agrammatism is to give the patient a sentence such as "The cow kicked the horse" and to then tell the patient to pick a

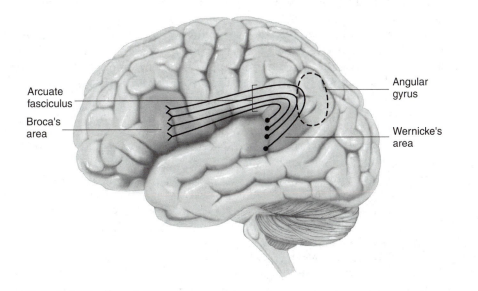

FIGURE 4.1   The language centers of the left hemisphere. The language reception
center, Wernicke's area, is connected to the language production center in Broca's area
by the arcuate fasciculus.

picture of the action described in the sentence. The patient will then have the choice of selecting between the picture of a cow kicking a horse or a horse kicking a cow. With Broca's agrammatism they are unable to make this type of discrimination. Based on this type of finding, it is suggested that the function of Broca's area is to store the motor memories that control the production of words and sentences. Speech production is a complex process involving fine coordination between the expiration of air from the lungs, the vibration of the larynx, and the movement and positioning of the mouth, the lips, and the tongue, all of which must work together to produce the proper sounds. Not only are the motor memories for the individual word sounds stored in this area, but also the proper sequencing of whole series of word sounds. Thus, the grammatical content.

Shortly after Broca's discoveries, a German neurologist named Carl Wernicke discovered another area of the brain which when damaged produced aphasias (Carlson, 1998). The aphasia associated with this area was characterized by the ability to produce seemingly fluent speech but an inability to comprehend speech that was being heard. This brain region is located in the superior temporal lobe and now bears the label Wernicke's area and the aphasia associated with it is referred to as sensory aphasia, receptive aphasia, or Wernicke's aphasia. People with Wernicke's aphasia speak fluently and with grammatically correct structure, but the content of their speech is totally meaningless. They do not appear to understand what they, themselves, are saying. Nor are they able to understand the speech that is spoken by others.

What is suggested by the deficits that occur after damage to Wernicke's area is that this area stores memories associating certain sounds (i.e., words) with their corresponding concepts. For example, when someone speaks the word "horse" this produces a certain characteristic pattern of pressure waves that travel through the air from the speaker to the ears of the receiver where it is processed and converted into a pattern of neural impulses moving through the auditory cortex. When this pattern of neural impulses is conveyed from the auditory cortex to Wernicke's area, it taps into stored memories that associate this particular pattern with a host of corresponding conceptual memories. For example, a complex visual image of a four-legged animal, an image of its movements, the sounds it makes, its odors, and various things associated with this animal. Language abilities are not synonymous with cognition. What language does is provide an interface between our cognitive world and the communication of this cognitive world, at least some aspects of it, to others who also share similar minds and language abilities.

Connecting Wernicke's area and Broca's area is a tract of fibers knows as the arcuate fasciculus (Carlson, 1998). Damage to this pathway produces a condition knows as conduction aphasia. People with conduction aphasia are unable to repeat nonsense words. However, if they are given a known word such as "horse," "cow," "house," etc., they will often be able to repeat the word. However, they are likely to produce some very uncharacteristic forms of error. For example, when the word "wolf" is given as a stimulus, they are very likely to reply "dog." If the stimulus word is "porpoise" they are likely to respond with "dolphin." This gives further credence to the idea that language and cognition are not the same thing. When the person with conduction aphasia hears a novel word that is processed in their intact Wernicke's area but the tract connecting it to Broca's area is broken, it does not allow them to convey the proper sound sequences to the motor pathways in Broca's area. However, if it is a familiar word, the sound of that word, after it is converted into a certain pattern of neural impulses, stimulates the memories associated with that pattern in Wernicke's area. Thus, when they hear the word "wolf" it calls up a visual image of a wolf, which is indiscernible from the visual image produced from the word "dog." Consequently, the patient produces that word instead of the target word.

Prosidy refers to the emotional aspects of speech, how something is said rather than what is said (Carlson, 1997). People with right hemisphere damage retain their basic language skills, but their understanding of spoken speech becomes rather computer-like. They cannot discern sarcasm, as an example, nor any other emotional connotation of what they are hearing. They cannot tell if what is spoken is said in anger, sadness, sincerity, or flippancy.

It is important to note that even when language is nonverbal, such as in the case of American Sign Language, the neurological areas that mediate it are largely the same as for spoken language. Poizner, Klima, and Bellugi (1987) have analyzed brain injury in individuals using ASL. They conclude that ASL is largely mediated by the left cerebral hemisphere and that damage to the forepart of the left hemisphere (i.e., Broca's area) produces production deficits while damage to the lower part (i.e., Wernicke's area) produces comprehension deficits.

The evidence from patients suffering brain damage supports the idea that the left side of the brain is dominant for language in the vast majority of people regardless of whether language is spoken, written, or signed. The brain is not the only physical structure of the body to show specific modifications designed to facilitate language. In order to produce the range of sounds that we are capable of special modifications have to occur in other parts of the human anatomy.

In his *Origin of Species*, Charles Darwin noted the "strange fact that every particle of food and drink which we swallow has to pass over the orifice of the trachea with some risk of falling into the lungs." The basis for this strange fact is that humans, unlike all other mammals, have their larynx placed well down their throat (Figure 4.2). The larynx is a valve-like organ that sits atop the windpipe. This structure first appeared with the evolution of the lung and served to exclude everything but air from the pulmonary tract. It was originally a band of muscles around the glottis that closed the tract preventing foreign substances from entering the lungs. For most animals, the larynx is positioned high up the neck near the base of the skull allowing animals to drink and breathe at the same time; a task impossible for adult humans. Human infants are born with their larynx placed high up in the throat. But, as the child develops, the larynx descends to its adult position. The fact that humans have evolved this high-risk anatomical position for the larynx, which allows many of our fellows to die every year as a result of choking on food objects (somewhat fewer now that the Heimlich maneuver is known to many), is one indication of the enormous pay-offs of the language adaptation. Just as larger brains increase fitness despite the greater childbirth risk incurred, so to, do language abilities offset the increased risk of dying through asphyxiation (Figure 4.2).

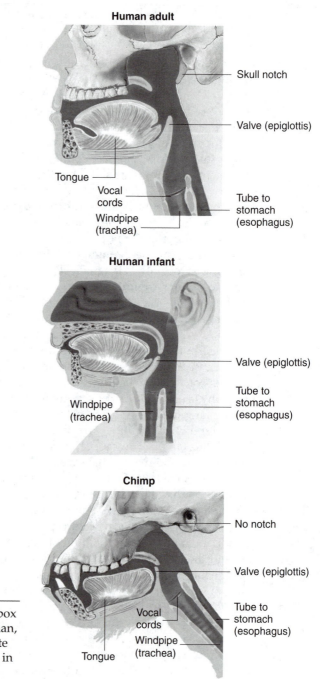

FIGURE 4.2 A comparison of the voice box relative to the windpipe in an adult human, an infant human, and a chimpanzee. Note the similar placement of these structures in the infant and the chimpanzee.

When we speak, air is forced from the lungs through the larynx's vocal cords that rapidly contract and relax in order to shape the sounds into human speech. Without the specialized adaptations of the lower larynx, human speech would be high-pitched, nasalized, and lacking the vowel tones for i, u, and a. The communication level would be reduced by as much as 30%.

Ancient Origins

Most modern European languages, and those of South Asia as far east as the Indian plains, all belong to the same group knows as Indo-European (Corballis, 1991). The ancestral tongue from which all modern Indo-European languages are derived is thought to have originated somewhere north of the Danube Basin in about 5,000–6,000 BCE. Indo-European is connected to the other language groups of Europe, Asia, and North Africa through an even more ancient precursory language known as Nostratic that probably originated around 13,000 BCE. The speakers of Nostratic appeared to have no words related to agriculture suggesting that they were hunter-gatherers. Linguists have even made attempts to connect all of the existing languages of the world as descendents of the Primordial language called proto-World. Researchers in this area claimed to have discovered about 200 words of proto-World. For example, the word "tooth" is represented in the Congo Saharian as "nigi" in the Austro-Asiatic as "gini" in the Sino-Caucasian group as "gin" and in the Nostratic group as "nigi," all from which modern words such as "nag" and '"gnaw" are thought to have derived.

When we consider the speed at which languages change, this casts some doubt as to the ultimate success of these efforts to find the common proto-language. For example, the English of Shakespeare is only 400 years removed form our own English. But for a large percentage of the English-speaking population it sounds almost like a foreign language.

The rapidity with which language changes and diverges into new dialects raises another question. Why is language so flexible and malleable? Hamilton's Theory of Inclusive Fitness may provide one possible explanation (Dunbar, 1996). So-called altruistic behavior probably arose as a mechanism for promoting the survival of our genes in the bodies of closely related kin. For example, to help close kin is not really a sacrifice because you are promoting the survival of your own genetic material. Such altruistic tendencies, however, may confer a selective deficit if we were living in extremely large social groups. When we put ourselves at risk to aid those who are not related to us and who in turn may not reciprocate the aid, we are hurting our own fitness. If we can identify individuals who have been reared in the same group as our own through their accent and dialect, then they are more likely to share genes with us and are also more likely to reciprocate our actions. Some supporting evidence for this comes from studies of language diversity in West Africa where there are more different languages per square mile in the high density populations among the equator than among the low density populations further to the north. This suggests a direct relationship between population density and the proliferation of new languages and dialects. Because of the

BOX 4.1 • *Through a Glass Darwinian*   *Wiring the Brain after the Tower of Babel*

At birth the brain has approximately one hundred billion neurons with over 50 trillion synaptic connections. Approximately one half of the known 80,000 different genes in the human gene are involved in forming and maintaining the central nervous system. In the first few months of life the number of synaptic connections in the human brain increases to more than one thousand trillion. The capacity of the brain to make new synaptic connections steadily decreases over time. Although some capacity to make new connections exists throughout life (otherwise we would not be capable of any new learning), many neural systems, especially language acquisition systems, have lost most of their plasticity by the end of certain sensitive periods in childhood. For example, an infant's auditory map for phoneme recognition appears to be almost fully completed by 12 months of age.

Human infants are capable of making a large number of categorical distinctions between phonemes during the first few months of life, in some cases from the age of one month, including distinctions not made in their native language (Jusczyc, 1997). From as early as the first month, neurons in the auditory cortex are generally sensitive to auditory stimulation and process this information according to innately determined schematic patterns. At four and one-half years of age, infants have a detailed representation of the sound patterns of their own names and will consistently show a preference for their names over control words.

At six months of age, babies can respond to every phoneme uttered in languages as diverse as Hindi and Nthlakampx, a native American language with certain consonant combinations that are impossible to distinguish for nonnative speakers (Werker & Desjardins, 1995). Six-month-old infants show a preference for words that have a prosodic organization typical of words in their native language (Jusczyc, 1997). At seven and

one-half months of age, children have the capacity to detect the sound patterns of certain words in fluent speech contexts. By the time children are nine months old, they show a preference for listening to their native language. By the time children are ten months old, they are adept at making discriminations between phonemes in their native language and begin to be insensitive to the differences between the phonemes of foreign languages. In fact, at ten months of age, they have lost nearly two-thirds of the capacity they possessed at six months (Werker & Desjardins, 1995).

As the child hears patterns of word sounds in his or her native language, certain clusters of neurons in the auditory cortex are recruited to respond to each phoneme (Jusczyc, 1997). Certain clusters only fire in response to a particular sound such as "ma." If one sound is clearly distinct from another as "row" and "low" are in English, then the neural clusters that identify one sound will lie far from those that identify the other sound. If the sounds are deemed by a particular language to be virtually identical as "row" and "low" are in Japanese, then the two sets of neurons are so physically close that the infant will have trouble distinguishing the two phonemes. After a child's auditory map is formed at 12 months he or she will be unable to pick up phonemes not heard thousands of times because no clusters of neurons have been assigned the task of responding to those particular sounds. In other words, children become functionally deaf to sounds not present in their native language. With increasing age, there are fewer and fewer uncommitted neurons available for responding to new phonemes. Consequently, with each passing year, learning a new language becomes more and more a daunting task.

The fact that the early neurological development of our auditory cortex selectively discards innate wide-ranging sensitivity in

BOX 4.1 • (Continued)

favor of a much narrower spectrum of pho-nemic sensitivity may shed some light on language evolution. Why did we develop this added twist in neurological develop-ment when it is clear that we already had the genetic programs to create an auditory sys-tem capable of parsing speech sounds into useful perceptual categories? Why is valu-able developmental energy expended to achieve the narrow, specialized capabilities of being attuned to one specific language or dialect? Why is there so much inherent plas-ticity in this type of neural organization?

The open-ended functioning of this system suggests that it has evolved to meet the exigencies of a rapidly changing auditory communication system. If auditory commu-nication (proto-language/language) evolved simply to facilitate information exchange be-tween group members the system would work more efficiently if phonemic/semantic variation were kept to a minimum. The pattern of neurological development that produces our language abilities strongly in-dicates that it is a system designed (evolved) to cope with continuously changing linguis-tic environments. A communication system where the symbols and their referents are

continuously changing makes no sense in the context of normal environmental selective pressures. This pattern makes sense only if we evoke the other form of selective pressure that Darwin noted, i.e., sexual selection. Specifically selection driven by female choice.

What sort of selection criteria might an-cestral females have been using that specifi-cally influenced language evolution? Based upon what is known about current mate se-lection criteria, they were probably verbal "displays" that evidenced intelligence, cre-ativity, kindness, devotion, and commitment. A process of runaway selection for ever-more-creative displays may have kicked in at some point. Novel pronunciations for exist-ing words would have been continuously in-troduced (look at how modern poets and singers take literary license to change the pro-nunciation of words) as well as completely new words to label new concepts. Some the-orists have suggested that these primordial courtship discourses were sung instead of re-cited. This explains the basis of another mys-terious human capacity—musical ability (see "Through a Glass Darwinian" in Chapters 5 and 6).

tendency of language to move rapidly into new dialects studies of modern lan-guages can tell us little about the ancient origins of language.

Some anthropologists have argued that language did not appear until about 50,000 years ago (Corballis, 1991). This is based on the fact that at that point in time there was an enormous surge in innovative technology. For hundreds of thou-sands of years prior to that, there was little change in the variety and complexity of stone tools. But, about 50,000 years ago there was a proliferation of a variety of implements including sewing needles, fishhooks, harpoons, buttons, and clasps. Around 30,000 years ago, numerous art objects appeared such as Venus statuettes and cave paintings as well as beads and other types of body adornments. Despite the late blooming of utilitarian and nonutilitarian technologies, the idea of a very recent origin of human language does not jibe with the anatomical evidence.

The fossil record clearly shows that humans with the anatomical specializa-tion prerequisites for producing and using language appeared by at least 250,000 years ago and possibly as far back as 500,000 years ago (Corballis, 1991). Fossil skulls from this time show evidence of brain asymmetry. In modern humans, the left hemisphere, where language function is typically located, is larger than the right hemisphere. This same pattern was shown in the fossil skulls. Examination of the postcranial remains of these specimens showed that the larynx was already located in the lowered position necessary for producing the range of sounds associated with modern speech.

Kay, Cartmill, and Balow (1998) found that the bony canal through the skull that houses the hypoglossal nerve is twice as large in humans as compared to chimpanzees after differences in overall size are compensated for. The hypoglossal is the cranial nerve that controls almost all the tongue's movements. The larger hypoglossal displayed by humans is essential to the precision tongue movements that are requisite for speech. The hypoglossal canals in the skulls of Australopithecines are small like those of modern apes, suggesting similar vocal limitations. Archaic *Homo sapiens* skulls over 400,000 years old have large, humanlike hypoglossal canals.

Early members of the genus *Homo* may have been very limited in their speaking ability. MacLarnon examined the thoracic vertebrae of a 1.5-million-year-old specimen of *Homo erectus* and found that the spinal cord was much thinner in this region than it is in modern people (Cartmill, 1998). This part of the spinal cord controls the muscles that move air in and out of the lungs. Therefore, it seems doubtful that early *Homo erectus* had the precise neural control over breathing movements necessary for speech.

As to which selective pressures pushed toward the development of language, this is an area that is still subject to speculation. One intriguing theory, which has been proposed by Robin Dunbar and which seems to tie together a number of disparate facts, has to do with group size, grooming, and the neocortex.

Dunbar (1996) showed that there was a direct correlation between the typical group size of a species and the size of the neocortex in individuals of that species, particularly in primate groups. The neocortex comprises most of the forebrain by volume. It has expanded considerably in the course of human evolution and comprises 80% of the human brain. The human neocortex has an area up to 2,500 square centimeters, but a thickness of only 1.5 to 3.0 millimeters. The surface of the cortex is highly wrinkled as a result of cramming a very large area of material into a relatively small space, the limits of which have been set by the birth canal.

Dunbar (1996) has argued that the neocortex expands with the increase in group size because the primary function of the neocortex is to handle social information. In a social group, each individual animal has to keep track of friends and enemies as well as friends of friends and enemies of friends, etc. With each increase in group size these calculations become increasingly complex. There is an ever-increasing demand for Machiavellian intelligence and for a more and more complex theory of mind type processing. Theory of mind refers to the type of conceptual understanding an individual must possess in order to modify behavior in accordance with the assumption that other individuals have similar minds. In nonhuman primate societies, alliances and coalitions are maintained through the process of grooming. Grooming originally evolved as a mechanism for ensuring good hygiene. One animal will sit and pluck parasites and detritus from the fur of another, who in return may or may not reciprocate the action. Grooming was co-opted for another function in social primates. Namely, it became a kind of social cement creating a bond between the grooming partners.

Dunbar (1996) has shown that as group size increases, more and more time must be devoted to the grooming behavior. In open areas such as the African savanna, larger group sizes are needed to protect against predation. Unfortunately, grooming, being a one-on-one process sets a limit on how much grooming can be accomplished and, therefore, sets an upper limit on group size. Language provides a way to circumvent the limiting aspects of grooming by allowing several alliances to be forged simultaneously.

Studies have shown that groups of two, three, and four individuals comprise the optimal numbers for conversation units (Dunbar, 1996). This has to do with our range of hearing and with our ability to take turns in conversation. If we consider that one human can engage in conversation with three others, but a nonhuman primate can only groom one other at a time, then the capacity for coalition building is tripled through the use of language. Nonhuman primates engage in vocalizations called contact calls during the process of grooming. Moreover, as in the vervet monkeys, it has been demonstrated that these animals already have the capacity to associate specific meanings with specific sounds. These pre-existing tendencies could readily be modified into vocalizations that could serve as substitutes for the grooming process.

Some theories of language origins suggest that language evolved as a means to facilitate hunting. For example, telling other members the location of prey animals that have been spotted and directing them to that location. Dunbar (1997), however, suggests that language originated as a means to maintain coalitions in increasingly larger groups. Part of the evidence he presents to support this has to do with the content of most human conversations. Rather than being devoted to technical issues, most casual conversations fall under the rubric of what we would call gossip. The primary content of gossip is observations of other individuals in the social group. A small group of individuals engaging in gossip are emphasizing their common views and exaggerating the differences between themselves and other individuals in the social group. Often times the gossip emphasizes his or her moral superiority over those about whom they are speaking. This all supports the idea that this mechanism exists for coalition building. It probably serves as the source of the in-group, out-group phenomena where members of the in-group emphasize their solidarity and similarity and at the same time emphasize the differences the out-group members exhibit.

Calvin and Bickerton (1998) also emphasize social cognition as the critical selective force for the deep structures of language. They propose that the ability to conceptualize complex patterns of social obligations formed the basis for syntax. They also suggest that the ability to use symbols arose as a consequence of interpreting signs in the natural world. For example, footprints of a certain size and shape are referents for a certain type of animal.

Corballis (1999) contends that gesture was the first form of language and that it was from here that grammatical structure developed. Observational evidence supporting this theory has been obtained on Taiwanese and American deaf children (Goldin-Meadow & Mylander, 1998). It was noted that deaf children spontaneously introduce language-like structure into their gestures. The two cultures had a number of similarities in sign structure that parallel the semantic and syntactic organization of true language. The children's gestures were structured at both sentence and word levels.

In most nonhuman primate social groups, matrilines (lines of descent as traced through the maternal side of a family) form the stable nucleus of these groups. It is the females who do the predominant amount of grooming, and it is the females who form the core nucleus of the group. In humans, females appear to have the edge in language skills; they develop language earlier and in more complexity. The greater the numbers of hominid and human infants, the greater the necessity for increased support networks among the females involved in childrearing.

Once language ability started to be selected for to promote coalition building, other selective pressures probably began to operate. One of these was probably runaway sexual selection. In runaway sexual selection, the females would come to select males on the basis of their language ability. Language ability, because of its interfacing nature, allows one individual to readily make some assessment of certain cognitive abilities in the other. Through this mechanism, females can not only select for mates with good language abilities but also those who have somewhat higher intelligence. Males, in turn, with good language skills could use these abilities to exploit tendencies of females to be enamoured of males with high language abilities. With the advent of language, linguistic deception, or lying, was almost certainly soon to follow. Males could conceivably promise commitment and resources and not necessarily follow through with these. This would have set up an arms race in which females would have had to develop better and better detection skills for spotting male deception. This, no doubt, set up a runaway arms race for even greater language abilities and for even greater mental abilities. The adaptive advantages of language are so numerous that once it began there was probably enormous selective pressure for better and better language abilities. At some point, the hypothesis regarding hunting probably became true; language was selected for because hunters were better able to communicate. Intergroup conflict, i.e., warfare, was undoubtedly a source of language selection, with those who were better able to communicate and coordinate their movements having an edge over those who could not. Of course, the single greatest boon of language was that it made possible the transmission of information across time—from generation to generation. In other words, language potentiated the rise of culture.

Conceptual Domains

In modern humans the information that is expressed in overt language is but a tiny, highly select fraction of the information that is being processed subjectively, the so-called "language of thought" or "mentalese" (Pinker, 1994). Philosophers and psychologists have long wondered to what extent language influences our mental organization of reality. There has been much debate regarding the quality, quantity or even the existence of mentalese in nonhuman, non-language-using species. The studies of language-trained animals have confirmed that they possess many conceptual patterns similar to our own, albeit simpler in scope. Moreover, numerous species incapable of language acquisition have been demonstrated to have conceptual abilities. For example, macaque monkeys can conceptualize num-bers up to nine (Brannon & Terrace, 1998), faces (Rolls, 1984), their species (Yoshikubo, 1985), and mother-infant relationships (Dasser, 1988).

Cross-cultural language studies have identified many conceptual primitives, the innate species-typical building blocks that give rise to conceptual structure (Wierzbicka, 1992, 1996; Jones,1999). These conceptual primitives can be sorted into broad, general domains such as (1) objects, space, and time, (2) quantity, (3) causality, (4) folkbiology, (5) social relationships, (6) language, and (7) theory of mind. As noted above, many of these conceptual primitives exist in animals without language. Some are also present in human infants (see **A Priori Mind** in Chapter 6). More complex concepts such as theory of mind do not fully develop in humans until long after they have acquired language (Mitchell, 1997), and among nonhuman species, theory of mind has been demonstrated only in an in-cipient form in chimpanzees (Premack & Woodruff, 1978; Povinelli & Eddy, 1996) (see **Consciousness and the Symbolic Universe** in Chapter 9).

Fundamentally similar belief systems about plants and animals are shared by all human societies (Atran, 1999). The term for belief systems of this type is folk-biology. Folkbiology shares certain critical ideas with modern biological science. These ideas include (1) the classification of plants and animals into species, (2) a belief that each species has its own particular, underlying essence, (3) further clas-sification of species as groups nested within other groups (taxonomic classifica-tion), and (4) the use of these taxonomic groupings to provide an inductive framework for making inferences about the organisms within these groupings. For example, whenever a new species of bird is encountered it will be assumed that it propagates by laying eggs. Such patterns of hierarchical classification and con-comitant inferential reasoning are rare in categories of nonliving things. People tend to believe that membership in animal categories is an absolute matter whereas membership in artifact categories is graded depending upon its typical-ity (Diesendruck & Gelman, 1999).

Caramazza (2000) argues that our conceptual knowledge is organized into broad domains of knowledge representing evolutionary adaptations. Selective pressures shaped specialized neural mechanisms for quick, accurate perception and classification of certain stimulus objects. Improved facility to rapidly identify and react to certain stimulus categories enhanced survival and reproductive fit-ness. Evidence supporting this hypothesis comes from studies of patients with neurological damage who exhibit specific deficits or selective sparing of certain categories. For example, some neurological patients have selectively lost the ability to process the category, animals while other patients show significant impairments in all categories tested *except* animals. In addition to animals, these categories include fruits and vegetables, body parts and artifacts (tools). The basic core conceptual organization of the human mind appears to reflect evolved cognitive domains (bottom-up processing) rather than arbitrary linguistic/cultural (top-down) influences.

Summary

Although communication systems abound in nature, human language appears unique in that it allows for communication about things not present in time or space and has the capacity to produce a practically limitless number of novel meaningful messages. Attempts to train nonhuman animals in language demonstrate that symbolic reasoning is a capability of many neurally complex species. However, specific language abilities, including the mental capacity for complex language use are found only in humans.

Human children that are deprived of normal language experience in early childhood experience permanent linguistic deficits regardless of rehabilitation attempts. All human children follow a similar developmental timetable for language acquisition. Different aspects of language have different critical/sensitive periods ending at different times: phonology (1 year), syntax (4 years), and semantics (16 years).

The nativist perspective that there is an innate biological basis for human language is supported by the fact that every human society ever identified possessed a complex language. When people from disparate cultures are pooled together and forced to rely on simple pidgin dialects their children spontaneously invent Creole languages, rich in grammatical complexity. The brain structures used in language function are roughly identical in people everywhere, even the users of American Sign Language (ASL).

The fossil record indicates that the brain asymmetry associated with language capabilities appeared 500,000 to 250,000 years ago. Robin Dunbar has proposed that language originally evolved as a mechanism for building coalitions in groups that had become too large for ordinary primate grooming behavior to achieve this purpose.

The greater language facility evidenced by females supports the idea that language arose to facilitate coalition building. In most nonhuman primate social groups, it is the females who form the core nucleus of the group and who have the greatest need for support networks to aid in childrearing. Because of the multiple adaptive functions conveyed by language abilities, once such abilities had emerged in a rudimentary form, a host of selective pressures promoted the development of these abilities to a highly complex level. Runaway sexual selection may also have played a role in language evolution. It is language that makes human cultural development possible. The basic core conceptual organization of the human mind appears to reflect evolved cognitive domains (bottom-up processing) rather than arbitrary linguistic/cultural (top-down) influences.

Discussion Questions

1. What do nonhuman animal language training studies tell us about human language abilities?

2. How can it be argued that language ability is a universal biological predisposition in humans when there are so many different languages?

3. Since language facilitates cultural evolution, how could language have evolved hundreds of thousand of years (as evidenced by the fossil record) before the appearance of significant cultural innovations?

Key Terms

agrammatism
American Sign Language
  (ASL)
anomia
babbling stage
Broca's aphasia
Clever Hans phenomenon
communication
conduction aphasia
Creole

critical period hypothesis
empiricist
holophrase
in-group phenomena
hypoglossal nerve
language
larynx
nativist
neural Darwinism
out-group phenomena

phonemes
phonology
prosidy
semantics
syntax
symbolic reasoning
Wernicke's aphasia
Wernicke's area

Additional Reading

The Seeds of Speech: Language Origin and Evolution by Jean Aitchison (2000).

The Symbolic Species: The Co-Evolution of Language and the Brain by Terrence W. Deacon (1998).

The Origins of Complex Language: An Inquiry into the Evolutionary Origins of Sentences, Syllables and Truth by Andrew Carstairs-McCarthy (2000).

Genes, Peoples and Languages by Luigi Luca Cavalli-Sforza (2000).

The Lopsided Ape: Evolution of the Generative Mind by Michael C. Corballis (1993).

Grooming, Gossip, and the Evolution of Language by Robin Dunbar (1998).

The Design of Animal Communication by Marc D. Hauser and Mark Konishi (Editors) (2000).

Eve Spoke: Human Language and Human Evolution by Philip Lieberman (1998).

Language Behaviour: Acquisition and Evolutionary History by Rangaswamy Narasimhan (1998).

Human Evolution, Language and Mind: A Psychological and Archaeological Inquiry by William Noble and Iain Davidson (1996).

The Emergence of the Speech Capacity by D. Kimbrough Oller (2000).

The Alex Studies: Cognitive and Communicative Abilities of Grey Parrots by Irene M. Pepperberg (2000).

Language Learnability and Language Development by Steven Pinker (1996).

The Language Instinct by Steven Pinker (1995).

Words and Rule: The Ingredients of Language by Steven Pinker (1999).

Apes, Language, and the Human Mind by Sue Savage-Rumbaugh, Stuart Shanker, and TalbotTaylor, (1998).

5

Mating and Reproduction

Do you want me to tell you something really subversive? Love is everything it's cracked up to be. That's why people are so cynical about it. . . . It really is worth fighting for, being brave for, risking everything for. And the trouble is, if you don't risk anything, you risk even more.

—*How to Save Your Own Life*, by Erica Jong (1977)

Chapter Questions

1. Why are women more discriminating than men are when assessing a prospective romantic partner?
2. What qualities do men typically prefer in women and why?
3. What qualities do women typically prefer in men and why?
4. Why is an "hour-glass" figure considered attractive in a woman but not in a man?
5. How could homosexual behavior evolve?
6. Why should "falling in love" be considered a dangerous thing?

Of all the complex patterns of behavior in the human repertoire, none captivate and intrigue us like those relating to courtship and reproduction. Every aspect of our social environment is permeated and even driven by this complex of behaviors. The vast majority of songs broadcast by popular radio stations are about "love" relationships. Fictional entertainment in books, movies, and TV series almost invariably contains central thematic threads related to sex and pair-bonding. Soap operas focus on these themes almost to the exclusion of anything else. Tabloid newspapers make sizable profits, not because of their space-alien stories, but because of their romance stories (of course stories about alien breeding experiments with humans are always popular). Mainstream newspapers are also quick to exploit the selling power of sex scandals. In fact, just the sex aspect, with little or no reference to pair-bonding, forms the basis of a multi-trillion dollar industry. This is, of course the pornography industry.

The topic of this chapter spans the ethical value range of human intentions and behaviors from the most prosaic to the most sublime. Carnal lust devoid of higher emotional involvement is often considered one of the lowest of human inclinations. Conversely, love, which may have developed (at least partially) from the evolutionary necessities of pair bonding and childrearing, is considered to be the noblest of all human attributes.

Sexual Selection

One of Charles Darwin's most brilliant and original insights was the idea of sexual selection. Unfortunately, this concept was readily criticized and largely forgotten for over a century. In the last few decades a resurgence of interest has occurred in the concept of sexual selection and with it studies amassing an overwhelming amount of evidence in support of this idea.

Darwin realized that many of the characteristics he observed in animals could not be explained as evolved adaptations to environmental conditions. For example, the elaborate plumage of certain male birds such as the peacock was clearly maladaptive, making the possessors of such plumage more vulnerable to predation and requiring the consumption of larger amounts of nutrients to support the elaborate displays. Darwin understood that evolution was a matter of differential reproduction rather than differential survival. Any heritable traits that help in competing for mates will tend to increase in frequency and diffuse through the populations even if they compromise individual survival.

Darwin distinguished between two broad categories of sexual selection. One was male competition for female mates, sometimes referred to as male-male competition. Male-male competition promotes the evolution of any characteristics that help a male out-compete other males. These include weapons, such as antlers and horns, larger muscles, and more cunning brains. The other form of sexual selection was female mate choice. Under female mate choice, characteristics preferred in a mate would become more pronounced over evolutionary time. For example, a preference of female birds for gaudy plumage in males would lead to the evolution of extravagant plumage displays in males of that species. Female choice could also select for behavioral potentials such as intelligence or a proclivity for nurturance on the part of males (see Figure 5.1).

Darwin saw that the preferences of female animals for certain characteristics in males were directly parallel to what humans do in the selective breeding of animals. Darwin (1871) made the following comments: "All animals present individual differences, and as man can modify his domesticated birds by selecting the individuals which appear to him the most beautiful, so the habitual or even occasional preference by the female of the more attractive males would almost cer-

FIGURE 5.1 Examples of strongly sexually dimorphic species that have been shaped by sexual selection, adapted from *The Descent of Man*, 1871. Clockwise from top left: (1) *Spathura underwoodi*, left, female; right, male. (2) *Chamaeleo owenii*, upper figure, male; lower figure, female. (3) Head of male Mandrill. (4) *Triton cristatus*, upper figure, male; lower figure, female. (5) *Paradisea papuana*, male bird of paradise.

tainly lead to their modification; and such modification might, in the course of time, be augmented to almost any extent, compatible with the existence of the species" (pp. 750–751).

The male dominated Victorian society in which Darwin lived was not at all open to the idea of female mate choice. This idea placed the role of females in a very powerful position to direct evolution. The idea of male-male competition was readily accepted, but female choice was not and was ignored by most scholars until fairly recently.

The biologist and statistician R. A. Fisher (1930) was one of the few biologists to accept Darwin's idea of sexual selection. He accepted the idea of female mate choice and elaborated on this concept with his own idea of runaway sexual selection. Runaway sexual selection is a process in which a positive feedback loop becomes established between female preference for certain male traits and the male traits themselves, causing the trait to develop in an unchecked fashion. Thus, peacock tail fans would continue to evolve until they reach a level of exorbitance beyond which survival was severely compromised. Zahavi (1975) developed a hypothesis called the *handicapping principle* to explain why female animals would choose to select for such exaggerated characteristics. He argued that females selected males with extravagant and costly physical displays because they were reliable indicators of genetic quality (e.g., only very healthy peacocks could maintain such huge handicapping tails).

In 1972, Robert Trivers explained why males court and females choose by pointing out that the higher levels of necessary parental investment by females of most species make females a limited resource over which males must compete. Trivers theory of parental investment emphasizes that it is not maleness and femaleness per se that is important, but rather it is the relative amounts of investment and which sex does more in a particular situation. Intersexual selection driven by mate choice is predicted to operate most strongly in the high investing sex compelling it to be highly selective in making a partner of the less investing sex. Intrasexual competition is predicted to be strongest among the sex that invests less in offspring. This is why human females are highly selective choosers and males compete with other males for the right to be chosen. This explains why there is a greater tendency toward aggressive behavior in human males and a greater proclivity for traits such as nurturance in human females. In species where the parental investment is mainly performed by the males, such as the seahorse who carries the eggs of its offspring in a brood chamber, the females are aggressive competitors with each other and the males are choosy, nurturant selectors of females.

The Evolutionary Basis of Sex Differences in Human Behavior

Men and women are, of course, much more similar to each other than they are to members of other species. Human beings as a whole are mentalistic, language-using beings boot-strapped by culture. However, there are certain domains that

At the end of Chapter 4 we suggested that human language abilities evolved very quickly as a result of runaway sexual selection where females came to select males on the basis of their language ability. Language allows one individual to assess certain cognitive abilities in the other. Through this mechanism, females who select mates with good language abilities are also, in general, selecting mates with high levels of intelligence. In Chapter 7 an argument is made with respect to creative/artistic abilities because they conferred the possessors of such abilities with novel methods for attracting a mate. Evolutionary psychologist, Geoffrey Miller, takes this argument of runaway sexual selection in humans to a new level, saying that it is the basis of virtually all unique qualities of the human mind.

Basically, Miller (2000) argues that the plodding pace of natural selection cannot account for the rapid brain evolution and behavioral sophistication seen in our species. It is his contention that our huge brains and our amazing cognitive capabilities are the result of female mate choice. In other words, females preferred and probably still prefer to mate with males who are cerebrally endowed rather than cerebrally challenged. If this is true then male brains should have evolved to be bigger than those of females just as the tails of peacocks greatly exceed those of peahens. In fact, after adjusting for differences in body size, males have about 100 grams more grey matter than females, a difference of about 8 per cent. This difference does not appear to produce much of a difference in overall cognitive ability between the two sexes. Although men are generally better at women on spatial reasoning tasks, women are generally better than men on verbal tasks. The area where big differences are manifested is in the male penchant for creative display. In almost every activity, from science to performing arts to writing to architecture males do it more, and more competitively, than females. Moreover, this "creative display" reaches a peak between the ages of 20 and 30 years, a time of life when sexual competition and courtship activities are at their most intense.

There is a simple reason there is not a huge size disparity between the brains of men and women like the size disparity between peacock tails and peahen tails. It is because assessing cognitive traits requires cognitive ability. As we pointed out in Chapter 4, language provides a window into another person's behavioral tendencies and abilities. Unfortunately, language also provides a means of signaling false intentions and making false claims. Females would have had to develop better and better detection skills for spotting male deception. Unlike, selection for a simple physical trait like fancy tailfeathers or a large rack of antlers, selection for mental complexity necessitated an arms race between the sexes for greater and greater neural complexity.

When we consider the complexity and sophistication of the human brain, it is hard to argue that it is the product of the selective forces of the environment. Even the pressures exerted by the social environment seem inadequate in accounting for human brain evolution. There are many species living in complex social environments but none approach humans in neural complexity. Miller's female mate-choice hypothesis provides a viable explanation for phenomena that are difficult to explain, otherwise. Without doubt, female mate choice has played a significant role in human evolution. On the other hand, women choose on the basis of a multitude of criteria and to say that women are simply selecting for better cognitive abilities is grossly simplistic and reductionistic. The full extent of the role of female mate choice in humans has yet to be determined. Throughout our evolutionary history, female choice was one factor in a very complex and constantly changing system. The other form of sexual selection that Darwin described must have also played some part. Male-male competition in humans was not carried out with horns or antlers or slashing canine teeth but with cunning.

evolutionary theory predicts will produce different patterns of behavior in men and women. These are the domains that relate to parental investment. In most sexually reproducing species, including humans, there is a huge disparity between the two sexes in terms of the minimum effort or investment required for reproduction. The bare minimum investment for a woman to reproduce is nine months, the length of human gestation. Realistically, under the conditions in which our ancestors lived, a woman would have to devote much more than nine months to insure the viability of her offspring. Under primitive conditions several years of nursing followed by many more years of dependency would be typical in the rearing of offspring. In contrast, the minimum investment time for a human male could be merely a matter of minutes or even seconds. Male reproduction in essence requires nothing more than the ejaculation of sperm into the vagina of a fertile female. Although human evolution has favored males that do show some parental investment, there is still a huge disparity in the reproductive costs and benefits between the two sexes.

Mate Selection Criteria

The selection of certain individuals over others as mating partners is a consequence of an individual acting upon mate preferences. Miller (1998) describes the basis of mate preferences: "These preferences are usually 'mental adaptations' implemented as complex neural circuits, and constructed through the interaction of many genes and environmental conditions, which bias mating in favor of individuals with certain perceivable traits" (p. 92).

Buss (1998) has argued that the mate preferences and mating strategies will vary depending on whether an individual is pursuing a short-term mate or a long-term mate. Both men and women engage in these two types of mating strategies, but for somewhat different reasons. Ultimately both short-term and long-term mating strategies increased the reproductive fitness of our ancestors.

The Preferences of Men.   Because of the basic nature of male reproductive physiology, men can potentially greatly enhance their reproductive fitness by impregnating as many different women as possible. The best method for achieving this end is the short-term mating strategy. For a short-term mating strategy to be successful, a man must be able to identify potentially fertile women and also minimize the time invested in securing mating opportunities with them. The other corollary of this theory of short-term mating as a strategy is that a man's standards regarding mate choice should be greatly relaxed. These predictions of evolutionary theory have been supported by empirical research. Men are willing to accept lower levels on a number of mate characteristics such as intelligence, kindness, dependability, and emotional stability (Buss & Schmitt, 1993; Kenrick, Sadalla, Groth, & Trost, 1990). Studies by independent investigators also show that men value physical attractiveness more in a short-term mate than in a long-term mate (Buss & Schmitt, 1993; Kenrick et al., 1990).

Because human young were unlikely to survive without a high level of paternal as well as maternal investment, there has been strong selective pressure for males to seek long-term pair bonding relationships with females. One of the most important criteria in selecting a female as a long-term mate was her degree of fidelity. Until the development of sophisticated DNA testing, the paternity of any particular child was largely an uncertainty. In other words, throughout history men could never be certain that a child was their own offspring, whereas for women it was never a question. Thus, the only solution to this problem was for men to find women who displayed indicators of faithfulness and possibly low or moderate levels of previous sexual activity. In this regard their long-term mating preferences are a complete reversal of their short-term preferences where highly promiscuous women are favored. It is important that a potential long-term mate display indicators of good parenting skills or high levels of nurturance. Finally, they needed to show indicators of health, fertility, and overall genetic quality. Once again the predictions of evolutionary theory have been supported by empirical research.

In a study of 37 cultures (Buss, 1989) it was found that men rated kindness, understanding, intelligence, and physical attractiveness as the top qualities they valued in a potential long-term mate. They also rated exciting personality, good health, and adaptability high on the list. This list was very close to the list compiled by long-term mate preferences of women with the exception of two qualities that men universally desired more. These two qualities were a partner younger than them and physical attractiveness. None of the 37 cultures studied showed a reversal of this trend (Table 5.1).

The Preferences of Women   The reproductive physiology of women is vastly different than that of men. Whereas men can generate sperm at a rate of 12,000,000 per hour, producing trillions over the course of their lifetime, the number of reproductive cells that can be produced by a women is fixed and unreplenished and numbers around 400 ova (Buss, 1994). The limited number of gametes produced by women is a direct consequence of the fact that fertilization and gestation occur within the female's body. When we factor in postnatal lactation and prolonged childrearing, it is clear that reproduction in women is a highly costly investment compared to that of men. Considering the high level of dependency of human children it might seem logical to assume that women would benefit primarily from a long-term mating strategy (if we define long-term as three to four years). Having a male partner committed to giving resources, aid, and protection could make the difference in survival of any offspring. However, women, just like men, follow both short-term and long-term mating strategies; albeit, for very different reasons.

Short-term mating in women can be viewed as a sort of "shopping around" behavior. It allows her to assess a number of potential male mates and to clarify more precisely which traits are more important to her in a long-term mate. Furthermore, in the process she is able to hone her own skills for acquiring and keeping a long-term mate. A second reason for pursuing a short-term mating strategy would be that a woman could obtain immediate resources in exchange for short-term matings. Another reason for short-term mating would be to improve the genetic quality of her offspring. By mating with someone other than her long-term

TABLE 5.1   *Top 13 Characteristics Desirable in a Long-Term Mate or Marriage Partner*

Men and women in 37 cultures rated the desirability of a list of mate characteristics.

Rank	Characteristics Preferred by Males	Characteristics Preferred by Females
1	Kindness and understanding	Kindness and understanding
2	Intelligence	Intelligence
3	Physical attractiveness	Exciting personality
4	Exciting personality	Good health
5	Good health	Adaptability
6	Adaptability	Physical attractiveness
7	Creativity	Creativity
8	Desire for children	Good earning capacity
9	College graduate	College graduate
10	Good heredity	Desire for children
11	Good earning capacity	Good heredity
12	Good housekeeper	Good housekeeper
13	Religious orientation	Religious orientation

(Table contents reprinted from "The Psychology of Human Mate Selection: Exploring the Complexity of the Strategic Repertoire" by D. M. Buss, in *Handbook of Evolutionary Psychology,* © 1998 by Lawrence Erlbaum Assoc., Inc.; used by permission of Lawrence Erlbaum Assoc., Inc.)

mate (termed an EPC, or extra pair copulation) a woman could potentially produce children with better genetics. Short-term mating could also provide the first step in a mate-switching process or a sort of back up in case the long-term mate left or was killed. The empirical data on short-term mating in women is generally supportive of the above speculations.

A study by Bereczkei, Voros, Gal, and Bernath (1997) found that women were twice as likely as men to demand long-term pair bonds including marriage, which they preferred to men by a factor of four. Women weigh status and wealth in short-term mates much more than in long-term mates. Buss and Schmitt (1993) also found that women elevate the importance they attach to immediate resources in short-term mating contexts over long-term mating. In short-term mating they have a strong preference for extravagance and strongly dislike men who are perceived as being stingy.

Nisa, a bushman woman living in the Kalahari Dessert, was interviewed by an anthropologist in 1970. Nisa was married to her fifth husband, but she also had a large number of extramarital relationships. When asked why she had taken on so many paramours, Nisa replied, "There are many kinds of work a woman has to do, and she should have lovers wherever she goes. If she goes somewhere to visit and is alone, then someone there will give her beads, someone else will give her meat, and someone else will give her other food. When she returns to her village, she will have been well taken care of" (Fisher, 1992). The extra resources acquired in this manner would have given ancestral women obvious fitness advantages. The hypothesis that women are seeking to improve the genetics of their offspring through short-term mating is supported by the finding that women place a greater premium on physical attractiveness in short-term mating relationships (Buss & Schmitt, 1993; Gangestad & Simpson, 1990; Kenrick et al., 1990).

Evolution theory predicts that the long-term mating choices of females will be based on criteria that will facilitate the survival of their offspring. Women should prefer men who can provide them with food and other resources and protect them from predators and aggressive humans and provide some degree of social status. Furthermore, prospective long-term mates should demonstrate a potential for good parenting skills and quality genetics. Moreover, the mere possession of these qualities is not enough in a prospective mate. He must also demonstrate a willingness to commit these resources to his partner. Therefore, women should possess a keen interest in assessing the commitment a potential partner has toward her.

As indicated in the section on male preferences, many of the characteristics preferred by a female in a mate are identical to those preferred by males (see Table 5.1). Kindness, understanding, intelligence, exciting personality, good health, and adaptability are all similar in their rankings to those of males. Women gave physical attractiveness a significantly lower ranking compared to men, but earning capacity was ranked significantly higher as a preference by women (Buss, 1998). Buss's (1989) study of 37 cultures indicated that women not only prefer men with resources but also show a preference for characteristics indirectly related to resources. These include social status, ambitiousness, and industriousness, and a preference for men older than themselves.

Hrdy (1997) has argued that the universal preference of women for wealthy husbands is a product of the monopolization of resources by men in all current cultures. Some mixed support for this came from a study by Bereczkeki, Voros, Gal and Bernath (1997) who found that Hungarian women placed greater emphasis on traits associated with family commitment rather than those associated with wealth. These authors point out that wealth is fairly evenly distributed among males in Hungary, although it is not as uniform as it was under the Communist regimes. However, in the same study it was found that women having higher physical attractiveness demanded higher standards in social status and wealth in the men they were looking for. They also found that socially and financially successful women demanded even higher levels of status and wealth in perspective mates. This appears to contradict the hypothesis that a preference for resources in men is dictated by their monopolization of resources.

Regan (1998) found that women's minimum mating criteria were significantly associated not with their self-perceived attractiveness but rather with their self-perceived social status. The higher a woman's self-appraised ranking on ambition, education, earning capacity, wealth, and social status, the more exacting were her standards on the same attributes in a prospective partner.

The Aesthetics of Attraction

Physical attractiveness was listed as one of the most important characteristics in mate selection for men and women, although men ranked it significantly higher than women did. This finding raises the question of exactly what constitutes physical attractiveness. A long-held belief among Western social scientists is that aesthetic judgments, particularly those having to do with fellow humans, are based on cultural influences and arbitrary individual tastes. Evolutionary psychology, on the other hand, predicts that aesthetic judgments form the basis of decisions that relate directly to survival and reproduction. Empirical findings show that although there is individual and cultural variation in aesthetic judgments, the underlying core—aesthetic sense—is a product of eons of natural selection.

Symmetry

Mate choice in a variety of species including scorpion flies, fruit flies, swallows, and humans, appears to be based in part upon assessments of body symmetry (Gangestad, Thornhill, & Yeo, 1994). All vertebrate animals are bilaterally symmetrical, meaning that the right and left sides of their body comprise mirror images of each other. Although there are some exceptions, such as the fighting claw in lobsters, most of the body parts on one side are roughly proportional in size to their counterparts on the other side. High levels of symmetry are thought to be indicative of high levels of developmental precision. Consequently, an organism that displays high symmetry can be inferred to possess good genes that are resistant to parasites and to other sources of developmental perturbations. Conversely, an organism displaying low levels of symmetry may be unhealthy and/or have poor quality genes.

One method of assessing the relative symmetry of an organism is to measure fluctuating asymmetry (FA). FA is computed by measuring a number of traits such as ankle breadth, wrist breadth, elbow breadth, and ear length and computing the difference between the right and left sides and in summing a composite score for all the measurements. Thus, FA is a measure of the lack of symmetry. Thornhill and Gangestad (1993) and Gangestad, Thornhill, and Yeo (1994) found that FA measures based on nonfacial body traits correlated significantly and negatively with ratings of attractiveness for the faces of those individuals. This finding is consistent with that of Langlois and Roggman (1990) who found that composite faces were judged to be more attractive than individual faces. The composite faces that were produced by computer averaging of hundreds of individual faces may have been perceived as more attractive because they were more symmetrical. In a study by Grammer and Thornhill (1994), opposite-sex attractiveness ratings of facial photographs of men and women were found to correlate positively with the combined measures of bilateral symmetry of the faces of each sex. Thornhill and Gangestad (1994) found that nonfacial fluctuating asymmetry correlated negatively with the number of self-reported lifetime sex partners and positively with self-reported age of first intercourse of college students of both sexes.

One of the most surprising findings coming from studies of fluctuating asymmetry and human behavior is the correlation with female orgasm. Thornhill, Gangestad, and Comer (1995) found a significant negative correlation between the self-reports of orgasms on the part of the female subjects and the measures of fluctuating asymmetry of their partners. A study by Bellis and Baker (1990) suggests that one function of the female orgasm is to selectively take up sperm into the cervix via the spasmodic contractions that occur. Female orgasm is also associated with the release of oxytocin from the posterior pituitary gland. It has been demonstrated that oxytocin plays a key role in the pair-bonding of prairie voles (Carter, 1992) and, by implication, it may play a role in human pair-bonding. Morris (1967) and Eibl-Eibesfeldt (1989) considered the female orgasm to be an adaptive mechanism evolved to facilitate pair-bonding. However, the study by Thornhill and Gangestad (1996) was not supportive of this hypothesis. In their study, orgasm frequency in women was unrelated to the three measures of relationship investment by men: men's love, men's socioeconomic status, and men's perceived future earnings. Fluctuating asymmetry of the men was significantly and negatively correlated with the frequency of orgasms in their female partners. Factors associated with fluctuating asymmetry, such as men's weight and physical attractiveness, also predicted female orgasm.

A study by Baker and Bellis (1993) showed that women engaged in extramarital affairs (extra pair copulations, EPCs) were more likely to have affairs with more attractive partners than their long-term mate. They were also more likely to have EPCs around the time of their ovulation, and they reported more orgasms during the EPCs than when copulating with their regular partner. Taken as a whole, these findings suggest that human females, like the females of many other species, tend to select males that are more symmetrical and are also more likely to experience orgasm when copulating with these males. Female orgasm can be viewed as a physiological mechanism to promote fertilization from some mating partners over others (i.e., symmetrical males).

The human female may have very different mating strategies that work in parallel to each other. On the one hand, she may have a strong preference to find a male who is very committed and can invest a great deal in terms of time and resources in her future offspring. On the other hand, she may be motivated by mechanisms that facilitate her becoming impregnated by males of high genetic quality. This sort of mixed reproductive strategy in women may be a consequence of the fact that highly symmetrical males have greater mating opportunities with large numbers of women and may be less likely to invest in one particular female.

Waist-Hip Ratio

Evolutionary psychologist Devendra Singh reasoned that men, like the males of many other species, should display an evolved preference for women who possess physical traits associated with high fecundity (1993). One highly reliable indicator of a woman's health and fertility is her waist-hip ratio (WHR). The WHR is computed by measuring the waist at the narrowest portion between the ribs and the iliac crest and the hip at the level of the greatest protrusion of the buttocks and comparing the circumferences of each measurement to produce a WHR. Biomedical studies indicate that WHR reliably signals female reproductive status, reproductive capability, and health status in women. The typical range of WHR is from 0.67–0.80 for women and 0.80–0.95 for men (Singh, 1995). The reason the WHR is such a good predictor of a woman's health and fertility is also the reason why there is such a marked difference between the WHR of men and that of women.

Prior to puberty, the waist-hip ratios of boys and girls are very similar. After puberty, the flood of sex hormones into the body creates differences in the deposition of fat deposits between males and females (Singh, 1993; Singh & Luis, 1995). In men, testosterone stimulates fat deposits in the abdominal region and inhibits fat deposition in the thighs and buttocks. In women, estrogen inhibits fat deposits in the abdominal region and stimulates fat deposition in the region of the thighs and buttocks. The male type of fat, termed "android fat," is readily mobilized for energy and can be readily depleted through a regimen of physical exercise. The feminine type of fat, termed "gynoid fat," is highly resistant to mobilization (thus fueling the modern proliferation of diet and exercise fads for women). Gynoid fat has evolved as an energy reserve for pregnancy and one year of lactation following birth. Because a developing human must have an almost constant supply of nutrients for the first two years following conception and because our ancestors typically experienced a pattern of feast-famine, the gynoid fat supply evolved as an emergency reservoir of energy to cope with this problem. In fact, human females will not enter puberty until they have accumulated approximately 35 pounds of gynoid fat. Moreover, as adults, if their reserve of gynoid fat drops below this 35 pounds they will stop ovulating.

In a series of studies, Singh found strong support for his prediction that men would have a consistent preference for women whose WHR fell within a certain range. Data for Miss America winners from 1923–1987 show a range in WHR from 0.72–0.69 over those years (Singh, 1993). Data for *Playboy* centerfolds between 1955–1965 and 1976–1990 showed an increase in WHR from 0.68–0.71 over the years examined. For both the centerfolds and the beauty contest winners, there was a trend toward greater slimness over the years, but the WHR remained virtually the same. Even the fashion model Twiggy, who was the epitome of tubular thinness, had a WHR of 0.73.

In studies where men were asked to rate the attractiveness of a series of line drawing of women (Figure 5.2), they consistently chose the normal weight figure with a 0.70 WHR as their favorite (Singh, 1993). These findings were true not only for college-aged men but also true for men with ages ranging from 25–83 and encompassing a wide range of professions, income levels, and life experiences. African-American and Indonesian men exposed to the same set of line drawings showed similar preferences (Singh, 1994; Singh & Luis, 1995). In almost all studies, the average preferred choice is the normal weight figure with the WHR of 0.70, and the 0.70 WHR is the preference falling within both the female overweight and underweight figure categories.

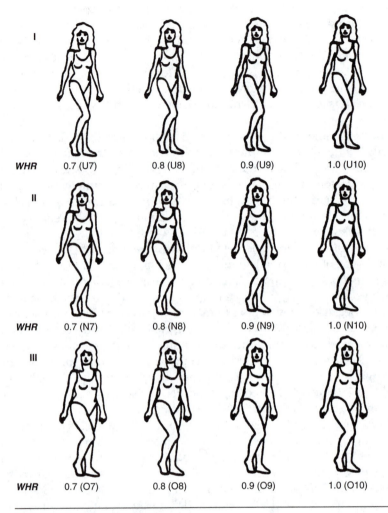

I

| WHR | 0.7 (U7) | 0.8 (U8) | 0.9 (U9) | 1.0 (U10) |

II

| WHR | 0.7 (N7) | 0.8 (N8) | 0.9 (N9) | 1.0 (N10) |

III

| WHR | 0.7 (O7) | 0.8 (O8) | 0.9 (O9) | 1.0 (O10) |

FIGURE 5.2 Stimulus figures representing three body-weight categories: underweight (I), normal weight (II), and overweight (III). Waist-to-hip ratios (WHR) are shown under each figure and each category, along with a letter and a number in parenthesis identifying body-weight category.

(Reprinted from "The adaptive significance of female physical attractiveness: Role of waist-to-hip ratio" by D. Singh, from *Journal of Personality and Social Psychology*, 65, Fig. 2, p. 298, © 1993 by American Psychological Association; used by permission of American Psychological Association.)

Evidently, in a few remote cultural groups where food supplies are generally scarce and unpredictable at best, the heaviest female forms are preferred and WHR is generally ignored. This was found to be true of the Matsigenka, of Peru, who practice swidden agriculture (Yu & Shepard, 1998) and the Hadza, a foraging population, living in Tanzania (Wetsman & Marlowe, 1999). These findings reinforce the idea that figure preferences, like other evolved human predispositions, are modified under certain contingencies. Under conditions of food scarcity, the fertility advantage that a 0.7 WHR might signal over a 0.9 WHR is trumped by the information conveyed by weight. When starvation is a chronic threat, the heaviest woman of reproductive age should always be preferred. When moderate food supplies are consistently available and there is no threat of scarcity, female form assessments should begin to take into account WHR as well as body weight. The general reliance on WHR for assessing female figures demonstrated by the vast majority of men tested may reflect the general abundance of food. When food scarcity is not a concern, the most reliable fertility cue (at a distance) is the WHR. Of course, more cross-cultural research is needed to test these hypotheses and sort out the complex mix of evolved predispositions, ontogeny, and individual/cultural experience.

Singh (1995) also looked at the WHR preferences of women. He found that women generally preferred men to have a WHR of 0.90 and to be within the normal weight range. In order to compare the relative importance of resources to physical attractiveness in women's mate selection, the line drawings of the male figures were presented with information regarding income and occupation (Singh, 1995). When the interaction between physical attractiveness and financial status was examined, it was found in this particular study that these two factors were roughly equal in importance. Women may prefer men with a WHR between 0.90 and 1.00 because it is an indicator of good health. Women want mates who not only have resources but who also have indicators of good health because they want their children to inherit a predisposition toward good heath, and they want a provider who will continue to provide and who will not fall ill or die.

The Masculine Ideal

Based on the research cited above, we can construct the hypothetical ideal man who would have universal appeal as a mate choice for the average woman. The ideal man is kind and understanding, suggesting that he will tend to meet the needs of his mate and children above his own selfish needs and willingly channel his resources and energy into them. He is intelligent, creative, and adaptable. These are traits that have an obvious adaptive payoff in the competitive, rapidly changing environment of human society. He has good health and an overall good physical package. He has good bilateral symmetry but not perfect symmetry because it has been somewhat compromised by the effects of androgens. The production of androgens, such as testosterone, in utero, causes a slight perturbation in the general development of symmetry. However, since testosterone produces functional adaptations in men, women tend to weigh these effects against perfect symmetry in assessing masculine beauty. A large jaw, heavy brow, broad shoulders, and above-average upper-body musculature are some of the androgen-related characteristics that women look for in males. The ideal man also has a WHR of about 0.9, and he is above average in height.

The ideal man displays indicators that he either has resources or is capable of obtaining resources. Consequently, he is industrious, well educated, and ambitious.

Resource holdings can also be thought of in terms of prestige and power, and thus the ideal man is one who is high in status. This ideal man is a few years older than his prospective mate, which probably relates indirectly to status and the ability to acquire resources.

Finally, the ideal man demonstrates dependability and stability. He is willing to commit himself, his resources, and his energy to his mate and to the children he fathers. He demonstrates fidelity to his spouse, and he is a devoted parent to his children. In sum, he is a protector, a supporter, and a nurturer of his spouse and children. He is not only willing to do these things but, most importantly, is capable of doing them.

The Feminine Ideal

The ideal woman is also kind and understanding as well as intelligent. With regard to her physical package, she also displays high levels of symmetry in body and face. She has a delicate jaw, full lips, and a body that is softly curving rather than angular, all good indicators of appropriate estrogen levels. She has a WHR around .70 indicating that her hips are wide enough to successfully bear children, while her smaller waistline indicates that she is not currently pregnant. Her overall soft curvaciousness and rounded feminine breasts indicate that she has good levels of circulating estrogens and that she carries the requisite amount of gynoid fat to insure a successful gestation period and a year of lactation. Her clear, unblemished skin is an additional indicator of good health. She has an exciting personality and nurturing qualities indicating that she would be a good parent. She also has qualities indicating commitment and loyalty, and she can be relied upon to be a faithful spouse. The mate of this ideal woman will be assured that any children she bears will be his, that they will have good genes, and that she will provide excellent parenting for them.

Human Pheromones

In the nineteenth century the French naturalist, Jean Henri Fabre, discovered that the female emperor moth was capable of attracting scores of male moths as a result of an excretion from her extended abdomen. Biochemicals such as this, produced by members of a species to influence the behavior of other members of that species, are termed pheromones. Since the time of Fabre's discovery hundreds of different animal species have been demonstrated to use pheromonal communication. Pheromones can have a variety of functions from territoriality to mother-infant bonding, but the focus of this section will be on their effect upon courtship and reproduction.

Despite the long history of pheromonal research, it is only in recent years that a significant amount of research has been directed toward the study of human pheromones. One reason for this was the pervasive belief among researches that pheromones had little influence upon the behavior of humans or other higher primates. In fact, there was a certain amount of truth to this idea because in the lineage's leading to the old-world primates, which include the old-world monkeys, the great apes, and man, the olfactory system had been gradually supplanted over evolutionary time by greater emphasis on the visual system. The early primates, such as purgatorious of 70,000,000 years ago, were creatures with highly developed olfactory systems. Large portions of their brains were devoted to processing olfactory information. Although we have clearly evolved away from having a primary reliance on olfaction, the physiological structures mediating chemical communication have not been entirely lost. For many years scientists believed that an accessory olfactory system, involving a structure called the vomeronasal organ, was vestigial and nonfunctional in humans. However, recent research has revealed that this vomeronasal organ is indeed active in humans and sensitive to certain pheromones (Garcia-Velasco & Mondragon, 1991).

In a number of studies that involved sniffing T-shirts that had been previously worn by other people, it has been demonstrated that based on olfactory cues sex can be discriminated (Russel, 1976), siblings could be distinguished from strangers (Porter & Moore, 1981), infants belonging to a family could be distinguished from infants belonging to other families (Porter, Cernoch & Balogh, 1985), and ovulating women preferred T-shirts that had been worn by symmetrical men (Gangestad & Thornhill, 1998). The strength of the scent preference exhibited by women for symmetrical men is greatest during their peak monthly fertility (Thornhill & Gangestad, 1999) (see Figure 5.3).

Menstrual Synchronicity

When a number of female mice are introduced to the odor of a pheromone in the urine of a male, all of these females quickly adjust their estrous cycles so that they go into estrous simultaneously (Whitten, 1959). As a result of this Whitten effect, many of the females give birth at approximately the same time. This is a very adaptive pattern because mice typically nurse their offspring communally. If a mother dies or fails to lactate, other mothers in the group will be able to nurse and protect her offspring. The evolution of this behavior can be explained in terms of inclusive fitness because females in a group are typically close relatives. A similar pheromonally mediated pattern of behavior has been demonstrated in humans.

Researchers extracted male pheromonal essence by having donor males wear pads under their armpits several days a week. This male essence was then extracted from these pads in alcohol and later dabbed on the upper lip of female subjects. Whether the women were exposed to the experimental swab containing the male essence or to the control swab containing pure alcohol, they always reported smelling nothing except alcohol. However, after twelve to fourteen weeks of treatment, women with irregular menstrual cycles at the onset reported that their estrous cycles had become highly regular. It was concluded that some unknown male pheromonal factor stimulates normal cycling in women which, of course, enhances their reproductive potential (Cutler et al., 1986).

Menstrual synchronicity in women is also influenced by pheromonal secretions produced by other women. A number of studies have demonstrated that

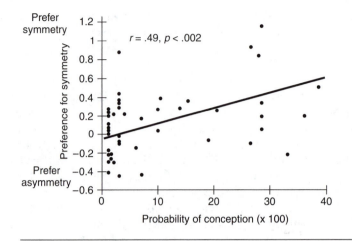

FIGURE 5.3 Normally ovulating (non-pill-using) women's preference for the scent of symmetry as a function of their probability of conception, with men's fragrance use and shower-taking controlled. Men who said they used fragrance were eliminated. Number of showers by men was partialed out of the regression of each woman's scent ratings on male FA.

(From "The scent of symmetry: A human pheromone" by R. Thornhill & S. Gangestad, from *Evolution & Human Behavior*, 20, Fig. 2, pp. 175–201, © 1999 by Elsevier Science; used by permission of Elsevier Science.)

women who live in close proximity to each other, for example in college dormitories, begin to show menstrual synchrony (McClintock, 1971; Graham & McGrew, 1980; Quadagno, Shubeita, Deck, & Francoeur, 1981). To determine whether pheromones were responsible for this synchronization effect, researchers exposed young, volunteer women to the underarm secretions of donor women (Preti, Cutler, Garcia, Huggins, & Lawley, 1986; Russell, Switz, & Thompson, 1980). In these studies most of the women exposed to these odors became synchronized to the menstrual cycle of the donor women. It required approximately ten to thirteen weeks for this synchronicity to take place, which may correspond to the 85 days required for an ovarian follicle to mature. The adaptive function of menstrual synchronization may be similar to the adaptive function of the mice displaying the Whitten effect. Menstrual synchrony would result in the birth of infants around the same time period. Consequently, if something happened to an infant's mother, another lactating female could then possibly adopt the infant. During the Pleistocene Era, if a nursing infant lost its mother and there was not another lactating female available, then that infant would certainly have died.

Major Histocompatibility Complex Preferences

It appears that human females may be able to use odor cues to access prospective mates on the basis of whether they will produce offspring with good immune systems. One group of genes having a major impact upon the immune system is called the major histocompatibility complex (MHC). When a pathogen such as a virus or bacteria invades a body cell, certain transport molecules within the cell attach themselves to proteins on the surface of the invader, called antigens, and transport these antigens to the surface of the cell. By carrying these antigens to the surface of the cell, they present them to certain specialized white blood cells, called lymphocytes, which can target and destroy the pathogens associated with these displayed antigens. It is the function of the MHC genes to make these transport molecules, which are critical to the immune process. When the MHC genes are in a heterozygous condition (different MHC genes on each allele of the different chromosomes), the organism that possesses this genotype has a much broader range of antigens that it can identify and transport; therefore, a much better immune system. It was hypothesized that humans could use odor to select mates that would potentially produce MHC heterozygous offspring.

Wedekind and Furi (1997) asked 121 men and women to score the odors of T-shirts worn by two women and four men. They found that the reported level of pleasantness of the T-shirt odor correlated negatively with the degree of MHC similarity between the smeller and the T-shirt wearer in both men and women. In women using contraceptive pills, however, this relationship was reversed; they showed a positive correlation between their degree of MHC similarity and the reported pleasantness of the T-shirt odor. This finding can be explained as a tendency for nonpregnant women to be attracted to males who are not close kin and who will potentially produce offspring with strong immune systems. When women become pregnant, however, it may be more adaptive for them to remain within proximity of their close kin for support and protection. It is still uncertain at this time if the preference for the odor for people with dissimilar MHC is directly linked to our detection of the MHC gene itself, or is it merely correlated with a general preference for genotypes that are dissimilar to some degree from our own.

Male Pheromones

Androstenone is a steroid compound found in the sweat and urine of adult male mammals. It has been demonstrated to act as a male pheromone to many species. For example, when a sow in estrous is exposed to androstenone she will immediately arch her back and assume a spread-legged mating posture. This hard-wired response occurs only if the sow is ovulating. Otherwise, she is indifferent to the odor.

Androstenone is probably the chemical agent (male essence) that shortens and normalizes the menstrual cycles of women with irregular periods who are exposed to this compound (Cutler et al., 1986). Grammer and Jutte (1997) showed that androstenone is invariably perceived as an unpleasant and even repellant odor by male subjects. Women who sniffed this compound expressed a similar reaction with one important exception. When women are in mid-cycle (near the time of their ovulation) they evaluate the odor positively.

Cutler, Friedmann, and McCoy (1998) evaluated the effect of a synthetic form of androstenone on the social-sexual behavior of men. They collected data on 38 heterosexual men during a two-week baseline period and then for six weeks using placebo-controlled double-blind trials of a synthetic pheromone. It was found that the pheromone users showed a significant increase in sexual intercourse and sleeping with a romantic partner. Pheromone users also showed a significant increase in rates of petting, affection, kissing, and informal dates. But, there was no change in rates of masturbation. Thus, the synthetic pheromone appears to increase sexual behavior of a social kind but not sexual behavior that is solitary in nature.

Female Pheromones

Copulins are a mixture of vaginal acids and are maximally secreted by women at the time of ovulation. Copulins may be one of the substances responsible, in part, for the menstrual synchronicity effect discussed earlier. Grammer and Jutte (1997) showed that when men were exposed to copulins, they exhibited a surge in testosterone levels. These researchers also found that copulins could produce an unusual perceptual change in men exposed to it. When men were asked to rate photographs of different women in terms of attractiveness, they had no trouble doing so. However, after these same subjects were exposed to copulins, their ability to make fine discriminations in the attractiveness levels of the different females was severely compromised. The adaptive function of this phenomenon remains unclear.

Copulins may provide a means for individual women to assess their own cycle status. Grammer (1996) found a significant correlation between cycle state and the amount of exposed skin women displayed while visiting discotheques. Specifically, women in mid-cycle who were not using birth control pills displayed much more bare skin and wore tighter clothing and shorter skirts when attending discotheques and bars.

Jealousy and Mate-Guarding

The sociologist, Davis (1948) defined jealousy as a fear and rage reaction fitted to protect, maintain, and prolong the intimate association of love. In a pair-bonding species like our own that lives in social groups, jealousy is a logical prediction from evolutionary theory. In fact, if jealousy did not exist as a universal human characteristic, it would represent an oddity that demanded scientific explanation.

The function of jealousy is somewhat different between the two sexes. In males, jealousy revolves around the issue of uncertainty of paternity. Whereas women have always known if an infant is hers or not, until the advent of modern DNA testing techniques men could never be certain that a child was the product of their loins.

Although paternal uncertainty is a problem in all primate species, true jealousy may be unique to the evolution of the human line. The fossil record indicates that our Australopithecine ancestors were probably polygynous based on the fact that adult males were much larger than adult females. Polygamy is a general term referring to one individual with many mating partners. Polygyny refers to one male with many female mating partners, and polyandry refers to one female with many male partners. Monogamy refers to a one-to-one mate pairing of male and female. In a polygynous species, where one male monopolizes the reproduction of many females, the males are typically much larger than the females (Alexander, Howard, Noonan, & Sherman, 1979). This is because males compete directly with other males for control of a harem of females. For example, a male silverback gorilla may weigh about 450 pounds while the adult females in his harem weigh an average of about 200 pounds. The monogamous gibbon species are virtually identical in body size between male and female. In these animals the pair-bonded adults and their offspring vigorously defend their territory against the intrusion of any other members of their species. Male and female chimpanzees are also very similar in body size, but their mating system is of a promiscuous nature. When a female chimpanzee goes into estrous, she is mated with by numerous male partners. Male chimpanzees do not appear to display any kind of behavior resembling human sexual jealousy. Male chimps do compete with each other but mainly for dominance status, not directly for access to females. In chimpanzees mating competition occurs at the level of the sperm, which will be discussed in the next section.

Jealousy probably arose from other drives involving the proprietary defense of resources. Three factors that lead to the evolution of jealousy in the human line were: (1) group living, (2) pair-bonding, and (3) gender-based division of labor. Living in social groups is a trait that we share with our closest living relatives, the chimpanzees. Therefore, it was probably displayed by our common ancestor 5 to 7 million years ago. Group living serves a protective function and helps facilitate the procurement of resources. Because of the prolonged dependency and vulnerability of hominid infants, and possibly because of the harsh conditions of the Ice Ages, pair-bonding became increasingly important to the survival of our ancestors. Infant survival may have been highly tenuous without the provisioning provided by a pair-bonded male. A pair-bonding system meant that males were investing a great deal of energy into one particular female. Because the pair-bonded male lived in a social group there was always the possibility that the child or children that he was investing in were not his own. This problem is further exacerbated by a gender-based division of labor. For tens of thousands, if not hundreds of thousands, of years humans have followed a hunter-gatherer lifestyle. Gathering is typically done by females within a fairly close proximity of the base camp; whereas hunting is a male activity that may involve great distances and days or weeks of being away. The chronic separation between pair-bonded males and females necessitated by this division of labor provided ample opportunity for infidelity. Any hominid males lacking a tendency toward jealousy may have spent all of their time rearing the offspring of other males and genes coding for such tendencies were long ago eliminated. Similarly, female hominids who failed to show a jealous response to their pair-bonded male being involved with other females, were likely to lose that pair bond and consequently their offspring were at risk for perishing.

Based on evolutionary logic, it was predicted that male jealousy would be more concerned with sexual infidelity and female jealousy would be more concerned with emotional infidelity. Buss, Larson, Westen, and Semmelroth (1992) used a series of forced choice experiments to demonstrate that men indicated greater distress to a partner's sexual, rather than emotional infidelity, whereas women showed the reverse response displaying greater distress to a partner's emotional infidelity rather than their sexual infidelity. Physiological measures of autonomic arousal corroborate the subject's self-reported weighting of these different conditions of fidelity. For example, when men were asked to imagine either the scenario of their significant other being engaged sexually with another partner, or emotionally with another partner, their heart rate and galvonic skin responses were greatly elevated by the idea of sexual infidelity much more so than the idea of emotional infidelity. In interviews with men and women, sexual involvement with another party was the most mentioned situation evoking jealousy among men. But in women, their partner spending time socially with another was the most frequently mentioned cause of jealousy (Francis, 1997). A cross-cultural comparison of The Netherlands, Germany, and the United States made the same finding: men find sexual infidelity a more salient trigger for jealousy and women find emotional infidelity a stronger trigger (Buunk, Angleitner, Oubaid, & Buss, 1996).

Once the emotion of jealousy has been triggered in an individual, it elicits any of a number of behaviors that can be classified under the category of mate-guarding or mate retention. The most overt forms of mate-guarding include physical intimidation and violence directed toward the perceived rival or toward the mate. Much more subtle forms of mate-guarding would be tactics such as simply making oneself more attractive to the mate or acting in a subordinate fashion to the mate and promising to do better in the future. Buss and Shackelford (1997) investigated a number of mate-retention tactics used by married couples. They found that for men, the number of acts of mate retention was positively correlated with their partner's youth and physical attractiveness. In fact, the peak levels of mate retention also correlated to the peak reproductive years for women in general. Partner's age and physical attractiveness did not effect women's mate retention; for women, their partner's income and level of ambition was positively correlated with their level of mate-guarding. Women responded to perceived competition for their mate by striving to enhance their physical appearance and by telling others that their man was committed to them in a long-term relationship. Men were likely to respond to the perceived threat posed by a rival by increasing their display of resources. Men were also more likely than women to use submission to their partner as a mate retention tactic. Men were much more likely than women to use threats or physical violence to deal with perceived rivals, and the likelihood of this was highly correlated with the attractiveness and youthfulness of their mates.

Sperm Wars

As was noted in the previous section, although a dominant chimpanzee may try to monopolize time with a female in estrous, most of the competition in this species is carried out at the level of the sperm. The reproductive tract inside a female chimpanzee becomes the battleground for a sperm war that takes place over the course of several days. Only one sperm among all of the billions within her vaginal tract and uterus can win the prize of fertilizing the egg. In fact, only a very small percentage of sperm, possibly as little as 1%, are even capable of fertilization; the rest of the sperm have an entirely different function. This other 99% of sperm consists of what are called blockers, or kamikaze sperm. Their function is to prevent the sperm of other males from reaching the egg. There appear to be at least two types of kamikaze sperm (Baker, 1996). Type A sperm block the passage of sperm that enter the female after they do. Type B sperm actually attack sperm that have been delivered prior to themselves. This sperm competition in chimpanzees has necessitated the evolution of testicles large enough to produce adequate amounts of sperm. This is why the testicles of chimpanzees are much larger than those of men.

The testicles of gorillas are relatively tiny compared to those of chimpanzees. This is because of the sexual monopoly that is obtained by a single silverback male gorilla over his harem of females. In this type of mating system, sperm competition is almost nonexistent. Human testicle size is somewhat proportionally larger than that of the gorilla. Nevertheless, the general similarity suggests that early hominid mating systems were of a polygynous nature similar to that of the gorilla, where you have a single sexually active male (Hrdy, 1988). Conversely, humans display a greatly reduced sexual dimorphism for body size as compared to the gorilla, suggesting that humans trended toward a greater degree of monogamy in the latter stages of our evolution. Because this shift toward monogamy occurred within the context of a larger social group, evolved behavior and physiology aimed at combating infidelity is part of our legacy as modern humans.

Baker (1996) discovered evidence that human male sexual psychology has evolved to respond to the prospect that his mate has been inseminated by another man during his absence. He found that the volume of sperm a man ejaculates while having sex with his partner is unrelated to how long it has been since he last had an ejaculation; the important variable is the length of time that has passed since he last had sex with his wife. The volume of sperm may be as much as three times that of normal if the man has been separated from his wife for a long period of time. If the men were in proximity of their wives during a similar period and were sexually abstinent, their subsequent ejaculate did not show the same rise in volume. Baker and Bellis (1993, 1995) also found that female orgasm plays a role in sperm competition. When a woman has an orgasm, the uterus starts to contract rhythmically, causing sperm to be drawn into the cervix—a kind of vacuuming effect. If a woman has had intercourse with several men within a short period of time, the sperm of the man associated with her orgasm has a much higher probability of fertilizing her ovum than that of men whose copulation did not result in orgasm. When we couple this finding with Thornhill's data, showing that women have more orgasms with symmetrical men than with less symmetrical men, and with the findings of Gangestad and Thornhill (1998), showing that women during the time of their ovulation show a preference for the scent from symmetrical men, we can see a connection between sperm competition and female mate choice.

Both sperm competition and female mate choice have been evoked to explain the unique anatomical distinction of the human species. Although chimpanzees have the largest testicles among our closest living primate relatives, humans have the largest penis in terms of length and thickness (see Figure 5.4). Diamond (1992) provides the following anatomical data: In the gorilla the length of the erect penis measures 1¼ inches; in the orangutan it averages 1½ inches; in the chimpanzee it averages 3 inches; and in man it averages 5 inches. Advocates of the sperm competition theory argue that a longer penis provides sperm delivery closer to the cervix and gives sperm a head start in their competition with rivals. Advocates of the female choice theory would argue that ancestral hominid females, at least in part, selected males who could provide more vaginal and clitoral stimulation. In

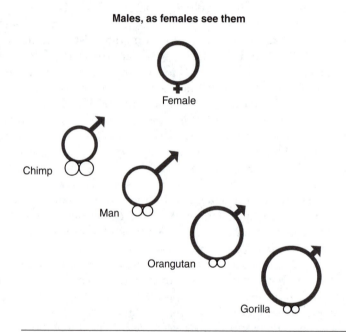

Males, as females see them

Female

Chimp

Man

Orangutan

Gorilla

FIGURE 5.4   Males, as females see them: Humans and great apes differ with respect to the relative body size of males and females, penis length, and testes size. The main circles represent the body size of the male of each species relative to that of the female of the same species. Female body size is arbitrarily shown as the same for all species at upper right. Thus, chimps of both sexes weigh about the same; men are slightly larger than women; but male orangutans and gorillas are much bigger than females. The arrows on the male symbols are proportional to the length of the erect penis, while the twin circles represent testes weight relative to that of the body. Men have the longest penises, chimps the largest testes, and orangutans and gorillas the shortest penises and smallest testes.

(Reprinted from *The Third Chimpanzee* by Jared Diamond, © 1992 by Harper Collins; used by permission of Harper Collins.)

all probability, there is some interaction between both of these processes such that a thicker penis provides more clitoral stimulation and, hence, increases the likelihood of an orgasm that would facilitate delivery of sperm into the cervix. Post coital uterine examinations of women show that sperm retention is positively correlated with the women's self-reported sexual satisfaction (Graham-Rowe, 1998). Phylogenetic comparisons also suggest that the breasts of human females have evolved as a result of sexual selection pressures (see Figure 5.5).

Sexual Orientation

Perhaps the most obvious behavioral difference between the genders has to do with sexual orientation. In other words, heterosexual women are attracted to men and heterosexual men are attracted to women. Because we are a sexually reproducing species, it is necessary for us to be attracted to a member of the opposite sex to reproduce. Because of the biological necessity of an opposite-sex sexual orientation, we might expect this to be as unvaried in its manifestation as say the number of digits on the hand. Except for an extremely small and rare number of

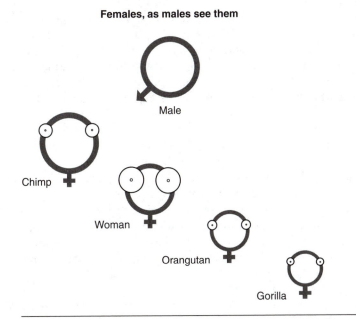

FIGURE 5.5 Females, as males see them: Human females are unique in their breasts, which are considerably larger than those of apes even before the first pregnancy. The main circles represent female body size relative to male body size of the same species.

(Reprinted from *The Third Chimpanzee* by Jared Diamond, © 1992 by Harper Collins; used by permission of Harper Collins.)

individuals, every human on the planet has five digits on each hand. However, the incidence of heterosexual sexual orientation may be only as much as 95%. Behavioral genetics research on human sexual orientation indicates that at least half of the variance in sexual orientation is genetically influenced (Pillard & Bailey, 1998). This raises a logical conundrum. How could a behavior that produces zero fitness be maintained in a species over evolutionary time?

To understand this phenomenon, we must understand the ontogenesis of sexual behavior and physiology. All individuals, whether they are genetic males or genetic females, begin life with identical structures including their reproductive anatomy. Prior to five weeks postconception, males and females are indistinguishable phenotypically. It is only after the primordial gonads differentiate either into ovaries and testes and their respective hormones are being produced that we start to see the differentiation into male and female. Much of the development involves differentiation of male and female reproductive anatomy. But a much more subtle aspect of it involves the differentiation of the brain. The female brain, with its greater symmetry between the right and left hemispheres and its thicker corpus callosum, represents the default pattern. In male fetuses, the testes release testosterone, which is carried across the blood-brain barrier and there converted by an enzyme called aromatase into estradiol, a female hormone. Paradoxically, it is estradiol that causes the masculinization effect upon the brain. Some of the cognitive differences resulting from the masculinization of the brain are discussed in Chapter 2. This prenatal pattern of brain development determines many other aspects of feminine and masculine behavior, including sexual orientation.

What is probably being inherited are not genes coding specifically for homosexual behavior but rather genes that predispose the individual to a vulnerability to perturbations in prenatal brain development. Maternal stress during pregnancy in particular has been identified as a critical factor affecting subtle aspects of brain development in utero. Ward (1977), Ward and Reed (1985), Ward, Ward, Winn, and Bielawski (1994), and Ward and Ward (1985) stressed pregnant rats by placing them in a transparent plexiglass tube under a bright light. As a consequence, endorphins were released into the mother's blood stream, some of which crossed the placenta and reached relevant brain structures in the hypothalamus. The endorphins, as well as maternal stress hormones, interrupt the synthesis and release of testosterone (Ward, Monaghan, & Ward, 1986). The male offspring born to such stressed mothers exhibit a variety of behaviors that could be construed as a model for homosexual behavior. These males are attracted to other males instead of females and will present themselves in a feminine mating posture to these other males.

Data suggesting a similar pattern in human sexual orientation was collected by Ellis, Ames, Peckham, and Burke (1988). These researchers surveyed 283 mothers of homosexual and heterosexual men without letting them know why and how they had been chosen. The survey made no mention of sexual orientation, but it asked a variety of questions concerning illnesses and stressors that the women may have experienced before, during, and after pregnancy. They found that mothers who recalled having had at least one severe stressful experience during the second trimester were significantly more likely to have borne a homosexual son than were mothers who did not recall having a severe stressful experience during the second trimester. A later survey study by Bailey, Willerman, and Parks (1991) found no significant correlation between homosexuality and prenatal maternal stress. This study did, however, find a significantly higher rate of childhood effeminacy in those boys whose mothers had reported the highest levels of stress during their pregnancy. Clearly, a great deal more research is needed before we have a complete understanding of the phenomenon of sexual orientation.

There is also evidence that the brains of homosexual men differ from those of heterosexual men. The anterior commissure, which like the corpus callosum provides for communication between both hemispheres, is on average larger in women than in heterosexual men. In homosexual men it is as large as that of women and even larger (Allen & Gorski, 1992). A structure in the anterior hypothalamus known as the interstitial nucleus-3 is generally twice as large in heterosexual men as in women. This structure, in homosexual men, was roughly the same volume as that of women (LeVay, 1991, 1993). In other parts of the hypothalamus known to differ between the sexes, homosexual men resemble heterosexual men and not heterosexual women (Swaab & Hofman, 1990). This further supports the idea that sexual differentiation is a continuum and not a dichotomy.

Prenatal hormonal perturbations are also implicated in the sexual orientation of women. In the 1950s and early 1960s a number of women took the synthetic estrogen, diethylstilbestrol (DES), to prevent miscarriages. DES produces masculinizing effects comparable to testosterone. Ehrnhardt et al. (1985) reports that of 30 adult women whose mothers had taken DES during their pregnancy, seven had reported having a homosexual or bisexual orientation. In contrast, of 30 women not prenatally exposed to DES only one reported any homosexual or bisexual responsiveness. Women who are exposed to high levels of prenatal testosterone because of a medical condition known as congenital adrenal hyperplasia (CAH) are more likely to report bisexual or lesbian orientations (Dittmann, Kappes, & Kappes, 1992; Money, Schwartz, & Lewis, 1984).

In summary, the seeming paradox of homosexual behavior is largely resolved when we look at sexual orientation as the product of a developmental continuum, much like sexual anatomy and physiology. There are also, undoubtedly, postnatal influences that contribute to sexual orientation. In particular, there is probably an imprinting-like stage for sexual orientation that accompanies an individual's initial sexual experience. In many avian species, the sexually maturing bird must be in proximity to members of its own species to develop a normal sexual orientation. For example, if the bird is exposed to humans rather than to members of its own species, it will develop a sexual orientation toward humans. Similarly, this process could explain, in part, why many humans opt for a homosexual orientation and also the development of fettishism. In fettishism, individuals develop a neurotic attraction for unusual objects. Fettish objects include items such as women's shoes and underwear, but may include items as bizarre as an exhaust pipe on an automobile. Objects probably become fettishes by being present incidentally during a person's initial sexual experience. If sexual imprinting does occur in humans, this random association could become a permanent part of the person's sexual behavior. Initial sexual experiences undoubtedly play some role in determining sexual orientation. However, most homosexuals report a leaning toward this orientation in their early childhood years long before reaching puberty or having any sort of overt sexual encounter.

Pair-Bonding Strategies

Limerence: Short-Term Pair Bonding

Everything about her delighted him. The lines of her body were athletic, lean, young, and hard. She laughed at all of his jokes and shared his twisted sense of humor and egocentric world-view. She seemed to understand everything about him, and he thought he understood everything about her. He looked into her eyes and saw an innocent, playful child smiling back. He craved her presence and eagerly looked forward to every tryst. It didn't matter to him that she was not a good mother to her young child, that she treated her husband poorly and cheated on him frequently, and that she had a habit of lying and drinking too much. In spite of her glaring flaws, he thought about her constantly when they were apart, and his obsession of her caused him to get behind in his work and to cheat on his beloved wife. But he didn't care. He was willing to give up everything for her—his successful career, his beautiful and faithful wife of many years, his dear children. He had only known her for a few weeks, but he believed he was the most special being alive in her young eyes, something that seemed vitally important to him in his middle age.

Three months later, he had an entirely different view of her—she was totally disgusting and contemptible in his eyes. Her body appeared haggard, bony, and far too masculine to him. He noticed the long, beard-like hairs on her chin and the varicose veins on her skinny, knobby legs. She looked repulsive and ugly. Even worse, he was appalled at her selfishness and her degraded world, her lack of morality, her spiritual bankruptcy. He was disgusted at the terrible way she treated her husband and child. She was empty and understood little about anything of importance—she had been a mere parrot and mirror, with no real substance. There was nothing innocent or child-like about her, she was simply vacuous, immature, and not very bright. He was humiliated and angry to find out that he was only one of many in her long line of shallow sexual relationships and that he wasn't special to her after all. He lost all interest in her—his sexual desire for her was completely dead, and she was a horrible, embarrassing memory that he wanted to forget forever. What had he ever seen in her? He was deeply chagrined and ashamed at the near loss of his career and family. His wife, whom he loved very deeply, had been devastated by his betrayal and had suffered an emotional breakdown. On top of this, he had alienated his children. He was far behind in his career activities, so much so that it would take years to regain what had been lost. What had he been thinking? It had been absolute insanity to risk so much for so very little . . .

The above is not just the stuff of soap operas. Shakespeare wrote of it, the ancient Greeks incorporated it into their tragedies, and the phenomenon is known worldwide. Many (if not most) humans have gone through a similar experience, although the duration may have been longer, and the outcome may have been more pleasant. We commonly call it "being in love."

What does it mean to be "in love?" Like the song by Tina Turner, you might ask, "What's love got to do with it?", for most of us are aware that being in love is not the same thing as loving someone. Although we may develop deep or abiding love for someone with whom we are in love, being in love is more akin to infatuation, obsession—and some would say madness—than it is to real love. As Tennov writes: "It is not love. It is the force of evolution expressed as the compulsion for the particular, this particular one above all others. Often, it is called love. . . ." (Tennov, 1979; p. xii). But as most of us know, it is not truly love.

Dorothy Tennov (1979), in her groundbreaking book, *Love and Limerence*, coined the word "limerence" to describe the state of what is commonly known as being in love. She lists a number of characteristics of limerence. Some of the more salient mental processes that the person who is limerent (i.e., in love) is likely to experience include:

- intrusive thinking about the limerent object (the LO, or the object of one's desire)
- acute longing for the LO to reciprocate affection
- euphoria or buoyancy of mood when reciprocation occurs
- feelings, thoughts, and actions focus on the LO to the extent that other concerns—even very important ones—are ignored or neglected
- a strong, delusional-like bias that distorts the limerent person's perception of the LO: this bias magnifies the appearance and importance of the LO's admirable qualities while simultaneously minimizing the LO's negative traits, rendering them either neutral or even positive
- sexual desire for the LO

Being in love, limerence, is a physiological phenomenon that may have evolved to facilitate pair bonding for the purpose of conceiving children and nurturing them in the first few months or years of life. The purpose of limerence appears to be to draw two people together into a bonded relationship to order to ensure their mating—the conception and care of young. Tennov (1979) reports that limerence, when reciprocated, seems to be most commonly directed, not just toward sexual intercourse alone, but toward the creation of a love-nest in which to enjoy making love and producing and raising offspring. Although limerence is more than simple sexual attraction, Tennov makes the point that if sexual desire is lacking, then it is not true limerence.

If two individuals are limerent towards each other, the limerence can last for a long time. However, in most cases, limerent feelings fade within a few months to a few years, rarely lasting more than two or three years. The obsessiveness and euphoric episodes subside, and the LOs negative traits become more prominently noticeable, as shown in the real-life scenario described above. The individuals may find that the previously minimized negative traits are too disturbing, and they will break up—often with much arguing, bickering, and hatred. Even when limerence is reciprocated, it usually does not last longer than two to four years. A deeper, more abiding bond may develop between the two individuals, and the relationship may continue to deepen through the years. But in these cases, the limerence appears to be replaced by a different type of bond.

The most common time for divorce is in the fourth year after marriage, and this is congruent with limerent theory (see Figure 5.6) (Fisher, 1992). Children by the age of two or three years are walking, talking, feeding themselves, and have gained a modicum of independence. Two parents are no longer as critical as they were earlier. Of course, two parents are usually better than one throughout the life of the child. But from a bare-survival point of view, two parents are far more necessary to the baby than to the older child. As a mechanism evolved to give an advantage to the young developing child, limerence would not be expected to last more than the time needed to court, marry or form a home together, conceive, bear a child, and perhaps nurture it until it is walking and possibly talking. This would take approximately four years, and it is in the fourth year that most divorces occur, presumably when limerence fades and a more enduring love does not replace it.

Limerence is a strong force, and Tennov (1979) discusses its uncontrollable aspect. Her massive amount of data, collected with interviews and surveys, sug-

**The four-year itch: divorce peaks, 62 societies,
all available years, 1947–1989 (188 cases)**

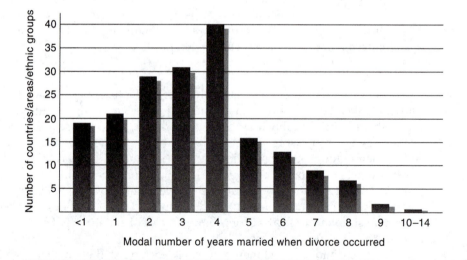

Modal number of years married when divorce occurred

FIGURE 5.6   The four-year itch: Divorce peaks of 62 societies from years 1947–1989 (188 cases). This demonstrates that humans in a variety of a societies tend to divorce between the second and fourth years of marriage, with a divorce peak during the fourth year.

(From "The Natural History of Monogamy Adultery, and Divorce" by H. E. Fisher, in *The Anatomy of Love,* Fig. 2, p. 360, © 1992 by W. W. Norton; used by permission of W. W. Norton.)

gests that limerence is preventable primarily in two ways. First, if an individual has a psychological or cognitive barrier against falling in love, he or she will be unlikely to fall prey to it. For example, if a married man has firmly decided that he will be monogamous, he will be far less likely to fall in love with someone outside of his marriage than would be someone who had not made such a conscious decision to be committed to one person only. The second "window" of preventability occurs early on in the relationship. At this point, if the individual begins to feel that special brand of "in love" attraction and does not want it, he or she can cut off all contact with the potential LO and nip the limerence in the bud.

The difficulty with which limerence is controlled or prevented attests to its hard-wired quality. Being in love is akin to a drug-induced state and can even be addictive for some persons. Many individuals who are sex addicts are actually limerence addicts—addicted to the euphoria of being in love. These individuals fall in love with one person after another in a never-ending succession of romantic affairs, each lasting a few months or years. These limerence addicts may be married to one person for a number of years while having a series of affairs or romances outside of the marriage, or they may have a long series of relationships, one after another, with none lasting more than a year or two. Limerence addiction can be as pernicious as cocaine addiction and as damaging to the family unit as alcoholism.

Tennov (1979) discusses three ways for limerent individuals to end their feelings of limerence. They can stop all contact with the LO. In this way, the feelings will eventually subside and die out in most normal people—although going "cold turkey" can be somewhat painful. The second way for limerence to die is for the relationship to be consummated. Once the two individuals are spending time together, the idealistic patina wears off, and the couple either develops a more enduring love or they break up. Thirdly, the limerence for one LO can be transferred to a different LO.

Long-Term Pair Bonding

There may be a somewhat less intense and longer-term form of pair bonding that is qualitatively different from limerence. A long-term pair bond is congruent with some of the information gathered in Tennov's (1979) interviews with couples. Marriages that last for decades or lifetimes are indicative of a long-term form of pair bonding, whereas marriages that approximate a four-year span are indicative of a short-term form of pair bonding.

The two forms of pair bonding are thus differentiated:

1. Limerence is the more intense, shorter-term pair bond, congruent with those types of people who tend to form short-lasting relationships of either serial monogamy or polygamy and congruent with the fourth year divorce mode. Adolescents and young adults appear to be more likely to form short-term pair bonds than are mature and older adults. There may be a gender difference with men tending to be somewhat more likely to form short-term

bonds. Limerence is more akin to infatuation, obsession, and delusion than it is to love. Limerence affords the opportunity for two people to bond for the purpose of conceiving, giving birth, and perhaps raising a child up to the age of walking and talking (approximately 1–2 years of age).

2. A less intense, longer-term pair bond also occurs, congruent with those types of people who tend to form longer-lasting, monogamous relationships. More mature and older adults are more likely to form long-term pair bonds than are younger and more immature adults. This type of pair bond is more akin to abiding love than limerence is. It is not infatuational, obsessive, and delusional, as limerence is. However, it does involve feelings of intense loyalty and affection, the tendency to see the other in more positive than negative light, and strong possessiveness, protectiveness, and jealousy of the other's affections. This longer-term type of bonding affords the opportunity to conceive, give birth, and raise children until they are sexually mature or older (approximately age 13–15 years or older). Both types of pair bonding involve the desire to create a home or nest and engage in continual sexual intercourse, and the tendency to give birth to young and nurture them.

There appears to be a developmental progression, with younger people more predisposed to form short-term pair bonding, and more mature adults more predisposed to form a long-term pair bond. The two strategies may also be preferred by different types of people. The type of person who might opt for short-term pair bonding might be more impulsive and more likely to have experienced a tumultuous, unstable childhood, perhaps receiving low levels of nurturance. The type of person who might opt for the long-term pair bonding would have a less impulsive personality and would be more likely to have experienced a calmer, more stable, more nurtured childhood. The two types of pair bonding may correspond with monogamous versus polygamous strategies of mating, each conferring a different type of evolutionary advantage.

Summary

Darwin understood that evolution was a matter of differential reproduction contingent not only upon individual survival but also upon sexual selection. The sex that invests most heavily in nurturing the offspring (typically female) tends to be highly selective choosers of mating partners. The sex that invests less in offspring (typically male) tends to compete with members of the same sex for access to the opposite sex.

Cross culturally, both men and women rate kindness, understanding, and intelligence as desirable in a mating partner. Men differ from women in placing more importance on physical appearance and prefer younger partners. Women differ from men in placing more importance on status and resource holding and preferring an older partner.

Aesthetic judgments of the opposite sex are strongly influenced by perceptions of symmetry, which is associated with good health and good genetics. Aesthetic judgments are also unconsciously influenced by appraisals of the secondary effects of androgens and estrogens in men and women respectively. Men show a preference for waist-hip ratios in women around .7. The fact that the waist-hip ratio is a highly reliable indicator of a woman's health and fertility suggests the male prefers for .7 is an evolved adaptation.

Although olfactory communication has been deemphasized in the evolution of higher primates, pheromones can still have a major influence on the course of human life. It has been demonstrated that menstrual synchronicity in women is mediated by pheromones. Other studies show that both male and female pheromones can significantly effect patterns of sexual behavior in men and women.

Jealousy arose as an adaptive response in men to help insure certainty of paternity. In women jealousy functions to help insure continued investment from a mating partner. The triggering of jealousy often results in a pattern of behaviors referred to as mate-guarding which range in expression from physical intimidation to submission.

The adaptive problem, i.e., certainty of paternity that jealousy addresses at the behavioral level is addressed at the physiological level by sperm competition. In species where insemination by a rival is a possibility there is a large volume of ejaculate produced. Moreover, a high percentage of the sperm in this ejaculate is infertile, its primary function being to block or destroy sperm that has been injected by a rival. Human sperm has these general characteristics. Women also show a capacity for mate choice at the physiological level. When a woman has an orgasm the uterus starts to contract rhythmically causing sperm to be drawn into the cervix, greatly enhancing the possibility of impregnation. Moreover, it has been demonstrated that women have more orgasms with symmetrical men than less symmetrical men.

The logical conundrum posed by homosexual behavior in the context of evolution is unraveled when one examines sexual ontogeny. Sexual differentiation into male or female is the result of different hormonal milieus in utero. Sexual differentiation of the brain differs from sexual differentiations of the rest of the body because of the blood-brain barrier. Maternal stress during pregnancy can alter different aspects of brain differentiation, including sexual orientation.

In humans, some degree of pair bonding greatly facilitates offspring survival. The "falling in love" phenomenon referred to as limerence by Tennov is an evolved psychological mechanism that promotes a temporary pair bond. This limerent pair bond typically lasts long enough to insure that a child is born and that that child reaches an age where he or she is somewhat independent. Limerent states can be highly disruptive and even devastating phenomena with strong behavioral and physiological parallels to drug addiction. Long-term pair bonds are a very different sort or phenomena that insure stability and lasting, high quality rearing experiences for offspring.

Discussion Questions _____

1. Discuss the idea of runaway sexual selection. Do humans exhibit any characteristics analogous to the tail fans of peacocks? If so, develop a scenario that would explain how such a trait or traits became part of ancestral hominid females mate choice criteria.

2. Discuss the adaptive significance of those traits that both men and women share in their mate selection criteria. Now discuss the adaptive significance of those traits in which men and women show significant differences in their mate selection criteria. What is the reason for those differences?

3. Discuss the respective functions of android and gynoid fat deposits and evolved preferences for certain waist-hip ratios. What are the implications of this information with regard to the diet and exercise industry?

4. In American society, being "in love" is typically regarded as the single most important reason for marriage. In light of what is know about limerence, described the potential pitfalls inherent in this perspective.

5. How can a trait like homosexuality be strongly influenced by heredity and yet not be the direct outcome of natural selection?

Key Terms _____

android fat	intersexual selection	oxytocin
androstenone	kamikaze sperm	pair bond
copulins	limerence	pheromones
extra pair copulation (EPC)	major histocompatibility	polyandry
female mate choice	complex (MHC)	polygamy
fluctuating asymmetry (FA)	male-male competition	polygyny
gynoid fat	mate-guarding	runaway sexual selection
handicapping principle	menstrual synchronicity	sexual selection
intrasexual competition	monogamy	waist-hip ratio (WHR)

Additional Reading _____

Sexual Selection by M. B. Andersson (1994).

Sex in the Future: Ancient Urges Meet Future Technology by Robin Baker (2000).

Sperm Wars: The Science of Sex by Robin Baker (1995).

Making Sense of Sex: How Genes and Gender Influence Our Relationships by David Philip Barash and Judith E. Lipton (1997).

Human Sperm Competition: Copulation, Masturbation and Infidelity by Mark A. Bellis and R. Robin Baker (1995).

Promiscuity: An Evolutionary History of Sperm Competition by Tim R. Birkhead (2000).

Sperm Competition and Sexual Selection by Tim R. Birkhead and Anders Pape Moller (1998).

The Dangerous Passion: Why Jealousy is as Necessary as Love and Sex by David M. Buss (2000).

The Evolution of Desire: Strategies of Human Mating by David M. Buss (1995).

As Nature Made Him: The Boy Who Was Raised As a Girl by John Colapinto (2000).

Heroes, Rogues, and Lovers: Testosterone and Behavior by James McBride Dabbs and Mary Godwin Dabbs (2000).

The Descent of Man and Selection in Relation to Sex by Charles Darwin (1990).

Why Is Sex Fun?: The Evolution of Human Sexuality by Jared M. Diamond (1998).

Primate Sexuality: Comparative Studies of the Prosimians, Monkeys, Apes, and Humans by Alan F. Dixson (1999).

Survival of the Prettiest: The Science of Beauty by Nancy L. Etcoff (1999).

Anatomy of Love: A Natural History of Mating, Marriage, and Why We Stray by Helen E. Fisher (1995).

Sexual Selection: Mate Choice and Courtship in Nature by James L. Gould and Carol Grant Gould (1996).

Physical Attractiveness and the Theory of Sexual Selection: Results from Five Populations by Doug Jones (1996).

Sex and Cognition by Doreen Kimura (1999).

The Scent of Eros: Mysteries of Odor in Human Sexuality by James Kohl (1995).

A General Theory of Love by Thomas Lewis, Fari Amini, and Richard Lannon (2000).

Why Sex Matters; A Darwinian Look at Human Behavior by Bobbi S. Low (2000).

Straight Science: Homosexuality, Evolution and Adaptation by Jim McKnight (1997).

Sex Differences: Development and Evolutionary Strategies by Linda R. Mealey (2000).

The Mating Mind: How Sexual Choice Shaped the Evolution of Human Nature by Geoffrey F. Miller (2000).

Evolutionary Perspectives on Human Reproductive Behavior by Dori Lecroy and Peter Moller (Editors) (2000).

Ever Since Adam and Eve: The Evolution of Human Sexuality by Malcolm Potts and Roger Short (1999).

Love and Limerence: The Experience of Being in Love, 2nd Ed. by Dorothy Tennov (1999).

A Natural History of Rape: Biological Bases of Sexual Coercion by Randy Thornhill and Craig T. Palmer (2000).

What Women Want–What Men Want: Why the Sexes Still See Love and Commitment So Differently by John Marshall Townsend (1998).

Reproduction in Context: Social and Environmental Influences on Reproductive Physiology and Behavior by Kim Wallen and Jill E. Schneider (Editors) (2000).

The Handicap Principle: A Missing Piece of Darwin's Puzzle by Amots Zehavi and Avishag Zahavi (1997).

6

Ontogeny

> *Childhood lasts all through life. It returns to animate broad sections of adult life. . . . Poets will help us to find this living childhood within us, this permanent, durable immobile world.*
>
> —Gaston Bachelard, *The Poetics of Reverie* (1960)

Chapter Questions

1. What is meant by "ontogeny recapitulates phylogeny" and does it really do so?
2. Are mothers engaged in an arms race with their unborn children?
3. How is our personality, including the patterns of our love life shaped by our childhood experiences?
4. Why are women the only primates to experience menopause?

As was pointed out in Chapter 3, slight modifications in the activity of various genes during the developmental process are typical of evolutionary changes in complex organisms. Once a certain level of complexity is achieved (i.e., multicellular organization) changes at a more fundamental level such as radically different gene structures are usually disastrous. Thus the avenue most readily open to evolutionary change is in the control of the expression of existing genes, which is accomplished through slight modifications in the regulator genes. It is during the unfolding of ontogeny that the regulator genes work their magic. Many key events in the developmental trajectory occur prior to birth but the process continues through adulthood and into later life. It appears that in humans certain adaptations appear even during the postreproductive years of the life cycle. This chapter will explore the synergistic unfolding of the human organism from conception through old age that is the product of the complex calculus of eons of gene selection.

Prenatal Development

Why Ontogeny Seems to Recapitulate Phylogeny

During the early part of the nineteenth century, the science of comparative embryology was established by a German named Karl von Baer. Among his many discoveries, he is credited with discovering the mammalian ovum, thereby establishing that mammals, including human beings, develop from eggs. Later in the nineteenth century another German, zoologist Ernst Haeckel, took the embryological concepts developed by von Baer and fused them with his concepts of Darwinian evolution. Haeckel's Biogenetic Law was the result of this merger of embryology and Darwinism and is epitomized by the famous phrase, "ontogeny recapitulates phylogeny." In simple terms, Haeckel's Biogenetic Law posits the theory that as an individual organism passes through its early embryonic and fetal stages of development it replays or recapitulates the evolutionary history of its species. For example, a human embryo passes through various stages during its nine months in the womb, going from an invertebrate, to a fish, to amphibian, to reptile, mammal, primate, hominid, and human being. The sweeping generalizations of this law have been largely discredited by modern biologists.

Karl von Baer proposed the idea that embryos of one species pass through stages comparable to adults of other species. His idea, referred to as von Baer's Law, emphasized that embryos of one species could resemble embryos but not adults of another species; and that the younger the embryo the greater the resemblance. Von Baer's Law represents a more accurate model of biological reality than Haeckel's Recapitulation or Biogenetic Law. Von Baer's Law suggests that evolutionary change happens most often in the later stages of development and that early stages must be evolutionarily more conservative. The explanation for this is that any mutation that affects early development is more likely to have greater phenotypic effects than one that influences development beginning at a later stage. Because development is continuous and cumulative, changes in early stages will have increasingly greater and greater consequences than changes during later development. The most probable outcome of any mutation happening at an early stage is that it will be deleterious and often lethal. A mutation that acts relatively late in the developmental sequence has a much better chance of not having deleterious effects and in some circumstances may even improve adaptation through the fine-tuning of some small phenotypic effect. This phenomenon can be illustrated through the analogy of constructing a skyscraper. If changes are made to the structural design of the walls on the ground floor, there is a high probability that every floor that is laid after that will be affected, possibly adversely. Any changes made to the top-most floor of the skyscraper will not influence any of the floors below, and there is a much greater range of possible variability that can exist without compromising the entire structure.

Von Baer's Law is more likely to be true of organisms that are brooded inside their mother, such as mammals, than organisms where the larval stages are such that the organisms must fend for themselves. When an organism is being brooded inside its mother, there is little or no selective pressure from the external environment for it to change. However, a larval organism that must fend for itself is under constant pressure from natural selection. This explains why the early stages of mammalian development are so similar across species, but in organisms such as insects the larval stages are very different from the adults.

Regulator Genes

The sequences of DNA that orchestrate the turning on and turning off of other sequences of DNA are referred to as regulator genes. Surprisingly, many of these regulator genes are comprised of identical nucleotide base pair sequences, in species as disparate as the mouse and the housefly (McGinnis & Kuziora, 1994). In all animal embryos, similar aspects of body differentiation are controlled by an interrelated group of genes called HOM genes in invertebrates and HOX genes in vertebrates. In fact, in some experiments the regulator genes have been transplanted between the two species and, remarkably, the developmental sequences occur without ill effect. In other experiments, manipulation of these regulator genes has resulted in monstrous phenotypic effects. For example, insects growing legs where antennae would normally develop. In totality, these types of genetic manipulations demonstrate the profound power of the regulator genes as well as their extremely ancient phylogenetic origins. Vertebrates have 13 HOX subgroups that have remained distinctive for hundreds of millions of years (Sharkey, Graba, & Scott, 1997). Many regulator genes were undoubtedly present in the common ancestor of the arthropods and the vertebrates, presumably some simple metazoan creature living over one-half billion years ago.

The Adaptive Function of Morning Sickness

In mammals successful development from conception to birth is contingent upon the physiology of the mother. Any comprehensive discussion of mammalian ontogeny must look at the evolution of maternal modifications. Profet (1992) has hypothesized that morning sickness, rather than being a pathology or an aberration, is actually an evolved adaptation designed to protect the developing embryo or fetus from the ingestion of toxic substances by the mother. The symptoms of morning sickness are most intense between six and 18 weeks postconception when embryonic organ formation is most vulnerable to chemical disruption. Women who experience morning sickness are significantly less likely to miscarry than women who do not, and women who vomit suffer fewer miscarriages than those who experience nausea alone (Flaxman & Sherman, 2000).

In Western societies references to morning sickness date back to ancient times. It is also present in many traditional societies but not all. Minturn and Weiher (1984) examined the cross-cultural prevalence of morning sickness and found that it occurred in 22 cultures but was absent in 8 others. Interestingly, seven

BOX 6.1 • *Through a Glass Darwinian*   *Digit Length and the Masculinized Brain (Fingers as Windows to the Masculinized Brain)*

In vertebrates the differentiation of both the urinogenital system and the appendicular skeleton is controlled by Homeobox (Hox) genes (Manning, Scutt, Wilson, & Lewis, 1998). The common control of digit and gonad differentiation is reflected in the relationship between relative digit length and indicators of prenatal masculinization. The differentiation of the testes during the eighth week following conception results in an increase in fetal testosterone that effects both digit formation and the differentiation of the central nervous system. The ratio of the second digit (index finger or 2D) and the fourth digit (ring finger or 4D) shows a pattern of sexual dimorphism. Manning et al. (1998) found a mean 2D:4D ratio of 0.98 for males and 1.00 for females. In other words, in men the fourth digit tended to be longer than the second but in women the two digits tended to be identical in length. This dimorphic pattern is present in young children and is probably established before birth. Testosterone levels and sperm production in men is negatively correlated with 2D:4D ratios. Thus, a longer fourth digit in relation to the second digit is associated with higher testosterone levels and greater spermatogenesis.

These findings suggest that 2D:4D ratio may be a marker for prenatal testosterone levels. Consequently, many behavioral tendencies associated with highly masculinized brains should correlate with 2D:4D ratios and relative digit length. Exposure to high concentrations of testosterone in utero may have the effect of slowing left-hemisphere growth while accelerating growth in certain right-hemisphere areas. Such a pattern of neural development might be manifested in impaired verbal abilities but enhanced spatial,

mathematical and musical abilities. High testosterone levels have also been associated with immunosuppression and vulnerability to depression. Martin, Manning and Dowrick (1999) found a significant correlation between digit length divided by height and depression for all five digits in 52 male participants. The strongest correlation was with the fourth digit. In 50 women participants no correlations were found with any digits divided by height and depression.

Sluming and Manning (2000) found that 54 male musicians had significantly lower 2D:4D ratios than 86 controls. Furthermore, among the musicians, 2D:4D ratios predicted rank with low 2D:4D ratios being associated with high rank. This may reflect either differences in musical talent or differences resulting from testosterone-mediated competitiveness. Differences in 2D:4D ratio were not found among instrument groups, suggesting that 2D:4D was not related to mechanical advantages in playing particular instruments. Concert audiences showed evidence of a female-biased sex ratio in seats close to the orchestra. Sluming and Manning contend that this data supports the thesis that music is a sexually selected trait in men that provides honest signal of fertilizing capacity and perhaps good genes. Musical ability is an honest signal because high prenatal levels of testosterone are associated with a number of deleterious effects such as immunosuppression, dyslexia and stammering. The presence of musical ability without these negative aspects indicates male virility and good genes. In males who had high prenatal testosterone levels but did not become musicians their fertility might be advertised in other ways, athletic prowess, for example.

of the eight cultures that lacked pregnancy sickness—in contrast to the 22 that possessed it—had diets based on maize. Profet has suggested that nutritional deficiencies typically associated with diets based primarily on maize may disrupt the physiological processes that normally produce pregnancy sickness. This physiological disruption would be the result of a niacin deficiency that typically develops in people whose diet depends primarily on maize that has not been treated with alkali or limestone. Niacin deficiency is associated with disturbances to the central nervous system, with gastrointestinal disorders, and with vasodilation. However, there is a more straightforward explanation for the variation in the occurrence of morning sickness across cultures.

Flaxman and Sherman (2000) found that the traditional societies where morning sickness had never been observed were significantly less likely to have animal products as dietary staples and significantly more likely to have only plants (primarily corn) as staples than the traditional societies in which morning sickness occurred. Moreover, they found that many pregnant women, especially in the first trimester, experience aversions to alcoholic and caffeinated drinks as well as strong-tasting vegetables, but the greatest aversions are to meats, fish, poultry, and eggs. Animal products may be particularly dangerous to pregnant women and their embryos because they often contain parasites and are rich breeding grounds for pathogenic microorganisms. The inherent risks associated with meat eating are exponentially increased in pregnant women because their immune systems are suppressed in order to reduce the chances of rejecting the proteins of their own offspring.

Little and Hook (1979) showed that women who smoked cigarettes regularly during or prior to early pregnancy suffered much lower rates of pregnancy sickness than did nonsmokers (52% compared with 79%). This suggests that pregnancy sickness is triggered by olfactory and gustatory cues because both olfaction and chemoreception have been demonstrated to be interfered with by smoking (Ahlstrom, Berglund, Engen, & Lindvall, 1987).

Profet (1992) views the pregnancy sickness adaptation as functioning to prevent the ingestion of toxins that were typical of the Pleistocene Age rather than the avoidance of modern toxins. Most plants, in order to protect themselves from consumption, produce alkaloid compounds that are bitter to the taste. Studies show that pregnancy sickness deters the drinking of coffee, which is a bitter plant alkaloid, yet only slightly deters alcohol consumption and does not affect cigarette smoking at all (Hook, 1976; Little & Hook, 1979). The quantities of alcohol required to produce the mental retardation and birth defects associated with fetal alcohol syndrome have been available to pregnant women only since the advent of agriculture (Tanaka, 1980).

Profet (1992) suggests that our human ancestors were under more intense selective pressure to evolve pregnancy sickness than any other mammal because they exploited a vast array of different plants and animals in their diet. During the early stages of pregnancy, women's sense of smell becomes more acute, foods remain in the stomach for a longer period before being absorbed as if being assessed for toxicity, and the area postrema, the part of the brain that triggers vomiting, is made more sensitive. Women store a much higher percentage of their body weight in the form of gynoid fat before pregnancy than almost any other mammal and thus require a proportionately lower daily intake of food during their pregnancy (Prentice & Whitehead, 1987). From the point of view of the developing fetus, it may have been better for the mother to eat nothing at all during the pregnancy and to simply live off the energy reserves within the mother's body. This way the fetus would have been safeguarded from any potential dietary hazards especially foods like meat that, prior to widespread refrigeration, were likely to be heavily laden with microorganisms and their toxins.

Mother–Fetus Competition

The intimate connection between a human mother and a fetus developing in her womb has traditionally been viewed as the ultimate example of cooperative effort and even self-sacrifice on the part of the mother. However, Haig (1993) has pointed out that the genetic interests of the fetus are not in total alignment with the genetic interests of the mother. This is because the fetus carries only one-half of the genes carried by its mother. The mother–fetus situation can be thought of in terms of three separate genes with somewhat different interests. The genes of the mother constitute one set. The genes of the fetus that are derived from the mother (maternal) constitute a second set. And the genes of the fetus that are derived from the father (paternal) constitute a third set.

From the perspective of the mother's genes, investment in the current fetus must be weighed against investment in existing children or in future children. If conditions are such that investment in the current fetus will severely compromise the probability of survival of existing children or future offspring, then it is in the mother's interest not to invest in the fetus. However, even if the situation is such that future offspring are more likely to survive than the current fetus, from the perspective of the maternal genes in the fetus a greater weight is given to the fetus than to future offspring. This is because only a certain percentage of the genes present in the fetus that are derived from the mother will also be present in future offspring. The genetic interests of the genes derived from the father are even more divergent from those of the mother. Because the paternal genes could come from different fathers in future offspring, there could potentially be even less representation of the paternal genes in future offspring. The maternal and paternal sets of genes in the fetus can exert their respective self-interests because of a phenomenon called gene imprinting. Imprinted genes have different expressions depending on whether they are inherited via an egg or a sperm.

The differing interests of these different sets of genes have led to a process of constantly evolving escalation. This sort of evolved arms race is sometimes referred to as the Red Queen Hypothesis. The Red Queen of Lewis Carroll's fantasy runs in place all day long but never gets anywhere. Similarly, in evolutionary competition, predators get faster and their prey also gets faster, with the net result that the balance remains the same. Examples of the mother–fetus arms race range from the basic issue of sustaining the pregnancy to the struggle for fuel resources if the pregnancy is maintained. One consequence of placental gestation is that the fetus is able to release substances into a mother's blood that have distinct effects on her physiology (Haig, 1993). Among these substances are placental hormones that act on maternal receptors. One example of a placental hormone is human chorionic gonadotropin (hCG). One action of the placental hCG is to usurp the role of the mother's pituitary in the production of hCG. This makes it much more difficult for the mother to spontaneously abort the fetus if it is of genetically low quality or if there is a shortage of nutrients in the current situation or some other stressful factor. Human chorionic gonadotropin indirectly results in the stimulation of the release of progesterone that is essential to maintaining the pregnancy. After the eighth week following conception, the placenta starts to manufacture its own supply of progesterone making it impossible for the mother to spontaneously abort through this particular physiological mechanism.

Maternal blood sugar levels typically drop during the early pregnancy and stabilize at a consistently low level throughout gestation (Haig, 1993). The early drop in blood sugar level is not a result of the fetal utilization of glucose because the demands of the fetus in these very early stages are relatively minor. The lowered glucose levels in the mother's blood appear to be an adaptation that has resulted in her resetting her homeostatic controls during pregnancy, as if in anticipation of off-setting the future demands of the fetus. The mother initially reduces her blood sugar levels to limit fetal uptake throughout the pregnancy.

Prior to the pregnancy, when the mother ingested a carbohydrate meal, her blood glucose levels would rise but then quickly return to normal levels in response to the release of insulin from the pancreas. When the mother eats the same type of meal in the advanced stages of pregnancy, her blood glucose levels and her insulin levels both go to higher levels and they remain elevated for much longer periods of time. These phenomena make sense from the perspective of an evolved arms race motivated by the conflicting genetic interests of the fetus and the genetic interests of the mother. The mother and her fetus are in competition for nutrients following every meal. The longer the mother has elevated levels of blood sugar the greater the amount of glucose that can be gained by the fetus. It appears that the maternal insulin resistance displayed in late pregnancy is caused by the placental release of human placental lactogen (hPL). Human placental lactogen is the most abundant peptide hormone produced by primates and its concentrations rise throughout the pregnancy. The human secretions of hPL are largely independent of maternal regulation or maternal levels of glucose or amino acids. Interestingly, the absence of hPL does not appear to have any effect on the pregnancy. Babies born from pregnancies where there has been a total lack of hPL fall within the normal range of expected birth weights. The placenta also produces enzymes that rapidly break down insulin and thus may counter the maternal insulin production. The pancreatic cells that produce insulin become greatly enlarged during pregnancy and women who experience impaired glucose tolerance during pregnancy have a greatly increased risk of developing gestational diabetes.

Postnatal Development

A Priori Mind

In the late eighteenth century, the philosopher, Immanuel Kant proposed that certain active organizing principles exist in the human mind, which function to organize perceptions of the physical world (Kant, 1927). He called these organizing principles "categories" and believed that they were a priori in nature (existing prior to experience). Kant believed that although we commonly think that we are passively and directly experiencing sensations external to ourselves we are really actively organizing these sensations into humanly acceptable categories. Thus, when we think we are experiencing the outer world, we are in a reality experiencing the categories of our own minds.

In the twentieth century some behavioral scientists adopted theories that had a somewhat Kantian perspective. The psychologist Carl Jung (1969) proposed ideas that on a basic level were similar to Kant's. He believed that every individual inherited preformed patterns of apperception (archetypes), which were of indefinite form until crystallized into a particular pattern as a result of the individual's personal experience. The ethologist, Konrad Lorenz (1965) also considered categories and forms of perception to be genetically determined as a result of evolution, in the same manner as morphological characteristics.

Unfortunately for ardent nativists like Lorenz, it was not until the latter decades of the twentieth century that substantial corroborative evidence emerged supporting the idea of a priori mental structures (Gregory, 1987). This was the result in a dramatic shift in theoretical thinking as well as the development of new research techniques to accurately measure infant behavior. For example, infants will habituate (become bored with) with certain stimuli and seek more novel stimuli. Thus, infants demonstrate longer looking times for novel or unexpected phenomena than for expected ones.

Film analysis of newborn infants shows complex coordination between tracking objects with their eyes and making reaching-grasping movements with arms and hands (Gregory, 1987). Newborns will also turn in the direction of a voice, orienting eyes and ears toward the sound. In addition to built in sensory-motor coordination, there is spontaneous transfer of information from one sense modality to another. For example, one-month-old infants can recognize objects visually that they have only felt in their mouths (Meltzoff & Borton 1979).

Long before they can actively explore the world, infants have a good perceptual understanding of what they can see. Minutes-old infants show a marked preference for pictures of faces over pictures of blank ovals or faces with scrambled features (Slater & Johnson, 1998). Moreover, by three to four months of age, infants show a preference for more-attractive faces (as judged by adults) over less-attractive faces (Samuels, Butterworth, Roberts, Graupner, & Hole, 1994). This early ability to perceive fine details of the facial and head region, specifically, the internal features of the face and the external contour of the head, also allows three-month-old infants to categorically distinguish between perceptually similar natural animal species such as cats and dogs (Quinn & Eimas, 1996).

Using the habituation technique, Spelke (1988) demonstrated that infants have expectations regarding the movement of physical objects long before they have the experience of manipulating or moving around objects. The infants anticipated the position of objects that had moved out of their sight and made inferences about where the objects should be when they came into view again. Three-month-old infants can use the relative motion of moving and stationary objects to develop a sense of object boundaries (Kellman & Spelke, 1983). Four-month-old infants expect objects to be solid (objects can not move through other objects) and permanent, even when out of sight (Spelke, 1988).

The infant mind can also make judgments concerning quantity. Five-month-old infants who watched one, two or three dolls disappear behind a screen, expressed surprise, as indicated by a longer gaze interval, when an incorrect number of dolls reappeared (Wynn, 1994). Six-month-old infants can discriminate between large sets of objects provided that the sets to be discriminated differ by a large ratio, such as 8 versus 16 (Xu & Spelke, 2000). This ability to make numerosity judgments without counting has been demonstrated in many animal species, as well as prelinguistic human infants (Jones, 1999). Counting ability depends on linguistic competence but without the proper functioning of the bilateral areas of the parietal lobes, involved in visuospatial processing, there is no capacity to understand numerical magnitudes (Dehaene, Spelke, & Pinel, 1999). Considering the phylogentically ancient origins of the brain's visuospatial capacities, the early appearance in human development of certain attendant abilities, such as facility in anticipating object motion and assessing quantities, is not surprising.

One phenomenon that in particular, demonstrates the early emergence of complex perceptual/sensory-motor abilities, and social-emotional communication is infant imitation. Newborns, just minutes old, will protrude their tongues and open their mouths wide in imitation of their mother (Trevarthen, Kokkinaki, & Fiamenghi, 1999). Complex facial expressions, indicative of happiness, sadness, fear and surprise are also imitated. Within a few weeks, simple vocalizations and finger gestures are part of the infant's imitation repertoire. Imitation may be one element of an infant's inborn capacity for complex give and take interaction with the mother.

Human infants intently focus on their mother's facial expression, her vocalizations and her gestures (Reddy, Hay, Murray, & Trevarthen, 1997). They respond in kind. Warm soothing maternal displays evoke smiles and cooing sounds in the infant. Impatient tones and threatening facial expressions in the mother evoke expressions of fear or sadness in the infant. Film analysis of mother-infant interaction reveals a rhythmic, conversation-like, back-and-forth exchange. During these exchanges infants emit facial expressions, gestures, cooing sounds, and lip and tongue movements. This prelinguistic communication is part of a developing behavioral template that will eventually become true language.

At birth, a baby demonstrates a preference for hearing his/her mother's voice, the identifying vocal characteristics having been learned in utero. In fact, infants not only have a preference for hearing the voice they most often heard prenatally, they also demonstrate a preference for listening to long, complex vocalizations (specific stories read out loud by the mothers) that they first heard in the warm, watery darkness of the womb. This early ability to parse the elements of spoken sound is a necessary prerequisite for language acquisition. Babies less than four months old can discriminate all of the 150 phonemes (basic word sounds) that make up human speech (Kuhl, 2001). Although human infants spontaneously parse human speech into phonetic categories, monkeys appear to lack this ability (Kuhl, 1991).

Another necessary prerequisite for normal language acquisition is the ability to spontaneously articulate a word that has been heard for the first time. The ease with which ordinary toddlers do this leads many people to take this phenomenon for granted when in reality it is quite extraordinary. The physiological mechanisms that process the sensory perception of spoken words are totally different from the physiological mechanisms that produce spoken words. Articulation is a complex process requiring the fine coordination of the muscles of the face, the lips, the tongue, the larynx and the diaphragm. Kuhl and Meltzoff's (1982) study of 18- to 20-week-old infants provided some insight into the developmental precursors for word parroting. When infants were shown two different video recordings, side-by-side, of the same individual articulating, in synchrony, two different vowel sounds they were able to correctly match the auditory stimulus they were being presented with its video component. This auditory-visual matching ability undoubtedly makes maternal/social interaction more effective for the infant as well as facilitating their eventual mastery of speech. The neurological basis of auditory communication is a complex hierarchy of specialized forebrain areas in which motor and auditory centers interact closely. Certain songbird species, as a result of convergent evolution, have similar brain structures (Doupe & Kuhl, 1999). Like humans, these species learn complex vocalizations during early critical periods, with a strong dependence on hearing adults they will eventually imitate. Unlike humans, birds (with the possible exception of a few avian savants like Alex the Parrot) never come to associate abstract meanings with the vocalizations they produce.

The famous Swiss psychologist, Jean Piaget, devoted his life to trying to understand how humans develop cognitively. He believed that infants lacked internal (mental) representations and simply responded reflexively to environmental stimuli. He further believed that extensive physical (sensory-motor) interaction with the environment was essential to constructing the foundations of conceptual representations. One reason Piaget believed that infants do not possess concepts was the universal difficulty displayed by infants in finding hidden objects. This phenomenon was attributed to the absence of an object permanence concept in the young child. For Piaget, the inability of a child to recover an object that had been occluded from view indicated an absence of a mental representation of that object, thus "out of sight" equated with "out of mind." However, as noted above, it has been demonstrated that four-month-old infants do conceptualize objects as permanent in nature (Spelke, 1988). The difficulties displayed by infants in the object permanence task are probably due to the undeveloped state of the frontal cortex. Without the inhibitory control exerted by a developed frontal cortex, the infant is unable to reign in errant motor impulses.

Furthermore, while there is no question that interaction with the environment is essential to the development of full, rich, concepts, it is also clear that the core, platforms for cognitive development are encoded in the human genome. The cognitive building blocks of concept formation are termed conceptual primitives (Jones, 1999). As noted above, infants have an innate understanding of temporal patterns, and object motion. They can make judgments concerning magnitude and quantity (Wynn, 1994; Xu & Spelke, 2000). They are able to spontaneously parse out the elements of spoken language. They have an inborn grasp of the fine nuances of emotional communication and interpersonal give and take. Very young infants and can organize perceptual information in their environment into discreet objects (Kellman & Spelke, 1983) including faces (Johnson, 1989).

Additionally, three-month-old infants can differentiate biological motion from nonbiological motion (Bertenthal, Proffitt, Kramer, & Spetner, 1987) and, by one year of age, the concept of animal is present (Mandler & Bauer, 1988). By three years of age, children attribute an underlying essence to animals but not to artifacts (Diesendruck, Gelman, & Lebowitz, 1998). Young children not only attribute an unalterable essence to members of a species (Atran, 1998) but also make inferences about an animal's behavior and physiology if it has a species label (Gelman & Markman, 1987) regardless of radical changes in its external appearance (Keil, 1989). The pre-Darwinian notion that species are enduring, unchangeable types may reflect an innate, essentialist view of biological organisms (Fiddick, 1999).

Essentialist thinking is also reflected in the early formation of concepts for gender, kinship and race (Hirschfeld, 1996). Moreover, children appear to spontaneously think of organisms and their behaviors as either good or bad (Gelman, Coley, & Gottfried, 1994). The coupling of essentialist thinking with good/bad dichotomizing may, in part, explain the ubiquity of group stereotyping in human cultures.

Parent–Infant Conflicts of Interest

Following birth, the parent-infant conflicts of interest continue. Investment in a child who is unlikely to survive may compromise all prospects of future reproduction in the mother. Infanticide has been documented in traditional hunter-gatherer societies throughout the world. But it also occurs in modern Western societies when the mothers are young, poor, and unwed (Daly & Wilson, 1998). The commonalities surrounding maternal infanticide throughout the world's cultures are that the odds of survival for the infant are very low, that the child is fatherless, that the mother is young, and that she lacks social support. She may also be overburdened with previous offspring, or food and other essential resources may be in extremely low supply.

In many mammalian species there is a critical period shortly following birth during which the mother and infant must be in close physical proximity for a strong attachment or bond to be established. Klaus and Kennel (1976) found that mothers who had extended contact with their infants shortly following birth demonstrated a much stronger attachment for their infants during the next several years than mothers and their babies who followed the usual hospital routine and were kept apart for long periods of time. Subsequent attempts to replicate the demonstration of a critical period for bonding in humans have been largely unsuccessful (Chess & Thomas, 1982). This may be due to the fact that the original study by Klaus and Kennel used unwed teenage mothers as its subject pool.

According to parent–infant conflict theory, these would be the mothers who would be most at risk for deciding against the interests of their infants. Critical-period bonding in humans may represent a phylogenetic vestige that has been supplanted by more-sophisticated forms of maternal assessment.

As Steven Pinker (1997) has pointed out, the only weapon at the disposal of the infant in this struggle for survival is "cuteness." Of course, if the characteristics that constitute cuteness were purely arbitrary and the result of culture and individual experience, there would be no hope for the infant. However, because of the shared genetic interests of parents and offspring, humans and other species that invest heavily in the rearing of their young are predisposed to find infantile characteristics very appealing. The developmental process proceeds in what is called the cephalocaudal pattern, meaning that the head and eyes develop first and the rest of the body catches up. Konrad Lorens noted that a disproportionately large head and large eyes coupled with pudgy cheeks and short limbs typically elicits feelings of affection and tenderness. These essential characteristics appear again and again in the products of industries that market cuteness.

While all healthy infants invariably possess the physical qualities that tend to elicit affection, they are by no means passive in their struggle for survival. Some particularly effective weapons in an infant's cuteness arsenal are smiling and laughing.

Smiling and laughing probably evolved from appeasement signals used in hierarchical interactions (Dunbar, 1996). When a lower-ranking chimpanzee signals submission to a chimpanzee of a higher rank, it uses facial signals that are structurally very similar to both smiles and laughter. Smiling and laughing, no doubt, are still used as appeasement signals in our species. A study of doctors in a hospital showed that junior doctors were much more likely to smile at their seniors and to laugh at their jokes than vice versa. As human societies evolved into more egalitarian groups the role of smiling and laughing came to be more concerned with social bonding than pure appeasement, although both processes are closely related.

Human infants begin smiling shortly after birth as a result of spontaneous central nervous system activity (Stroufe & Waters, 1976). This smile is purely a reflex and often occurs when the infant is in a sleeping state. This smiling reflex is undoubtedly an evolved adaptation functioning to enhance the infant's appeal to the mother in the hours immediately following birth. In the second week after birth, infants often smile drowsily after feeding. By one month of age, the infant's smiles become more frequent and more in response to environmental cues. The relevant environmental cues are typically social cues from the primary caregiver. By the end of the second month, babies smile more at the people they know, particularly those who provide a majority of their nurturance. By four months of age, infants typically laugh out loud, especially when they are being tickled or stimulated by an adult (Stroufe & Wunsch, 1972). By seven months of age, children laugh frequently when the expectations of a situation are violated. By laughing at the unexpected, a child shows that they know what is to be expected, providing insight into their cognitive development. The child's laughter in these situations not only strengthens the parent-child bond, but it also provides the parent with information regarding the increasing competency of the child.

Not all of the techniques employed by the child to manipulate his or her mother are as benign as the smile. One pattern of behavior human children share with young chimpanzees is the temper tantrum (Trivers, 1985). Human children who engage in temper tantrums show a remarkably similar pattern of behavior, despite the fact that in most cases they have never witnessed such a display by others. A temper tantrum is elicited in the child by some sort of frustration, and typically the child will stamp his feet, throw himself upon the ground while kicking their legs, crying, and screaming. Similarly, when a young chimpanzee is frustrated it will leap into the air screaming loudly, throw itself upon the ground and while writhing about, strike and flail its arms and hands against surrounding objects. In chimpanzees, temper tantrums are often provoked during the weaning process. As in human temper tantrums, when the young chimpanzee is engaged in a tantrum it is often observed to glance covertly at its mother or caretaker presumably to determine if its action is attracting attention. As disturbing as the idea may be to some, conflict theory predicts that brattiness should evolve as one adaptive strategy. Many of the endearing qualities, as well as the not-so-endearing qualities of children, are probably direct results of the inherent conflict of interests between the parent and child.

Incest Avoidance

In animal species that are naturally inbred, matings between close relatives, such as brother-sister mating or parent-offspring matings, do not produce harmful consequences. For example, all of the thousands of pet shop hamsters alive today are all descended from a single pair of wild hamsters captured in Syria back in the 1920s. For outbreeding species, however, the consequences of matings between close kin are usually harmful and often disastrous. This is because in outbred populations a sizable number of recessive genes can accumulate over time as a result of periodic mutations. In inbred species these harmful mutated genes are quickly selected out, but in outbred organisms the harmful effects of the recessives are typically masked by normal genes occupying the corresponding loci. From a selfish gene perspective there is some benefit from an incestual mating. The offspring of mating between close family members contains 75% of each parent's genes instead of the usual 50%. However, in outbred species like ourselves the genetic gains are far outweighed by the genetic costs that accrue from the expression of recessive genes. Because of the weighting of this genetic balance sheet, we should expect the existence of an evolved mechanism for incest avoidance in humans.

In the latter part of the nineteenth century, a Finnish anthropologist, Edward Westermark, taking a Darwinian perspective proposed a mechanism for the prevention of incest in humans (Westermark, 1891). Westermark hypothesized that growing up in close proximity to individuals of the opposite sex produced a form of indifference or repugnance to the idea of sexual relations with that person.

These incest avoidance algorithms would be based on eons of natural selection in situations in which children who are raised together are biological siblings. Largely because the views of cultural relativism and environmental determinism held sway during the first half of the twentieth century, it was not until the 1950s that anyone made a serious attempt to empirically validate Westermark's hypothesis. The logical test of the Westermark hypothesis would be to see if children who are not biologically related and who are reared together show the same indifference or repugnance to the prospect of sexual relationships between themselves as biological siblings do.

The Israeli kibbutzim provided a real-world social experiment for investigating the validity of Westermark's hypothesis. The kibbutzim were communal villages founded in the early part of the twentieth century where there was a deliberate attempt to break down the nuclear family. Boys and girls of similar ages were raised together in peer groups of six to eight children and shared common living quarters from infancy to adolescence. Although there were no cultural prohibitions on children from the same kibbutz marrying each other, Spiro (1958) could not find a single case of this happening nor even a single incidence of sexual intercourse occurring in children who had been raised together from childhood in the same kibbutz.

The Simpua marriages that are practiced in some parts of China provide another natural test of Westermark's hypothesis. In this type of marriage a family adopts a young girl for the purpose of becoming their son's future bride. The children who grow up in this type of situation invariably detest the idea of marrying or mating with each other (Wolf & Huang, 1980). In humans, incest avoidance is a universal biological strategy and a frequent cultural strategy. In the case of the Simpua marriages the cultural strategy is at odds with the biological strategy which may be one reason that this particular cultural practice is on the decline. The cultural prohibition of incest is a phenomenon unique to humans, but incest avoidance as a result of ontogenetically acquired inhibition seems to be a widespread phenomenon in other outbred species.

Evolved Contingency Mechanisms

Evolution has shaped our physiologies such that our bodies constantly fine-tune themselves to adjust to the environment. One extreme example of this type of phenotypic adjustment is displayed by a type of coral fish called the blue-headed wrasse. These fish live in polygynous groups of one adult male and many adult females. If the male in the group dies, the largest female becomes the new male. We can think of this sort of phenomenon as an evolved contingency mechanism. The sex of an adult female blue-headed wrasse is contingent upon the information that is processed by her piscine brain. If she is not the alpha female in the group, or if she is the alpha female and there is an adult male present, then she remains female. On the other hand, if she is the alpha female and there is no male present, her perception of these facts sets into motion a cascade of physiological events that ultimately transform her into a fully functioning adult male.

We humans also adjust our physical phenotype according to environmental contingencies, albeit in somewhat less-spectacular fashion than the blue-headed wrasse. These adjustments can occur at a proximate or day-by-day level. The melanization of our skin is contingent upon the amount of sunlight that it is exposed to. Calluses are determined by the degree of chafing or friction that the surface of our skin encounters. And the strength of our skeletal muscles is contingent upon the degree of exercise to which they are exposed. As is clear from these examples, proximate adjustments can come and go throughout our lifetime. More permanent changes fall under the rubric of evolved ontogenetic contingency mechanisms. One such ontogenetic change relates to the cardiovascular system. People who grow up living in high altitudes develop permanently enlarged lungs and barrel chests (Moran, 1982). This condition allows them to pump a greater volume of blood to the lungs for oxygenation. In humans, much of our fine-tuning to our environment involves our behavioral phenotype.

Childhood Experience and Adult Reproductive Strategy.   Traditionally, pubertal timing has been viewed as the product of genetic and nutritional factors. Belsky, Steinberg, and Draper (1991), however, have proposed that menarche (the first menstrual cycle) is determined to some degree by social cues that are experienced by individuals during childhood. They contend that pubertal onset and patterns of adult sexual behavior reflect reproductive strategies that are contingent upon the social milieu in which an individual develops. Young girls who are reared by mothers with no single long-term partner tend to enter puberty earlier, become sexually active earlier, and have more sexual partners than girls coming from households having both mother and father. According to Belsky et al. (1991), the ability of these individuals to form lasting and strong pair bonds and their earlier sexual maturation reflect evolutionary strategies designed to cope with environments where resources are inadequate or unreliable and adult pair bonds are not enduring. Thus, growing up in a fatherless home during the first five to seven years of life triggers a kind of quantitative reproductive strategy. A quantitative strategy pays off by producing more offspring to offset the disadvantages posed by a lack of male provisioning for the young.

Ellis, McFadyen-Ketchum, Dodge, Pettit, and Bates (1999) conducted a longitudinal study to test Belsky's evolutionary model of menarcheal timing. These researchers observed 173 girls and their families for eight years to determine if more negative-coercive family relationships in early childhood provoke earlier reproductive development in adolescence. It was found that the quality of a fathers' investment in the family was the most important aspect of the proximal family environment relative to influencing a daughter's pubertal timing. Girls reared in father-absent homes reached menarche several months earlier than their peers in father-present homes. The longer the paternal absence, the earlier was the onset of puberty. However, if the father was present but had an abusive relationship with their daughter, then the daughter's menarche was also earlier. The greater the time spent by fathers in child care and the greater the level of father-daughter affection, the more delayed was the onset of menarche.

The proximate mechanism for delaying the onset of menarche is probably the chronic release of stress hormones. Extremely high levels of stress delay pubertal onset, but chronically moderate levels such as those associated with the experience of a fatherless household produce the opposite effect. Mothers can affect their daughter's pubertal timing by creating a stressful home environment. In a short-term longitudinal study of 87 adolescent girls (aged 11–13 years), it was found that a history of mood disorders in mothers predicted earlier pubertal timing in daughters (Ellis & Garber, 2000). In families where the mother was involved with a male who was not the biological father, interpersonal stress accounted for almost half of the variation in daughters' pubertal timing.

Ellis and Garber (2000) have proposed that in addition to family stress, a second path to early pubertal maturation in girls is the presence of a stepfather. They hypothesize that pheromones emitted by adult men other than the biological father, such as stepfathers or the mother's boyfriends, activate physiological mechanisms that accelerate pubertal onset in young girls. Their research showed that stepfather presence, rather than biological father absence, best accounted for earlier pubertal maturation in girls living apart from their biological fathers.

In addition to entering puberty earlier, girls who are reared by mothers with no single long-term partner become sexually active earlier and have more sexual partners than girls coming from households having both mother and father (Belsky et al., 1991). The inability to form lasting pair bonds in these individuals may in part be due to the typically impaired orgasmic potential characteristic of many women reared in father-absent households (Thornhill & Gangestad, 1996).

Individuals who grew up in a two-parent household with a reliably investing and nurturing father during their first five to seven years of life develop a very different set of social expectations about the nature of other people. Their pubertal timing is delayed, thus insuring that they remain in the nest for a longer period of time. And when they reach sexual maturity, their patterns of mating are oriented toward a more qualitative reproductive strategy. They are involved with a fairly limited number of sexual partners throughout their lifetime and in young adulthood most become strongly pair bonded to one other individual. Thus they display a reproductive strategy oriented toward producing a limited number of offspring with maximal investment from both parents.

Childhood Experience and Adult Personality.   Studies of rhesus macaques by Mehlman et al. (1994) have shown that impulsivity and aggression are also linked with low serotonin (a neurotransmitter associated with mood state) levels in this species. Their research indicates that although the degree to which individuals are predisposed toward impulsivity is genetically determined, ontogenetic and proximate factors play a greater role. The research of Higley, Suomi, and Linnoila (1996) suggests that ontogeny plays a greater role in producing long-term dysfunctional impulsivity than proximate factors. Their findings indicate that an impoverished rearing environment (i.e., peer-reared) produces individual rhesus monkeys with chronically low serotonin levels and tendencies toward excessive aggression and impulsivity.

Research into the etiology of impulsivity in humans suggests causal mechanisms congruent with those indicated in studies of Old World monkeys. Like other Old World primates studied in this regard, individual humans may be predisposed toward impulsivity by their genetics (Eysenck, 1983; Plomin, 1976), but developmental history probably plays a larger role in determining the degree to which they manifest this characteristic. Borderline personality disorder (BPD) has been linked to a history of child abuse or neglect. The rate of childhood physical abuse and sexual abuse reported in patients with BPD is above 70% (Ludolph et al., 1990; Ogata et al., 1990). BPD and a number of other disorders associated with compromised impulse control such as eating disorders, obsessionality, and pathological aggression have been shown to be at least in part to be due to hyposerotonergic activity and consequently amenable to treatment with serotonin reuptake inhibitors (SRIs) (Markovitz, 1995).

In Old World primates including humans, the level of individual impulse control appears to be contingent upon that individual's perception of the social environment. Although genetic, ontogenetic and proximate effects all play a role, it is the ontogenetic effects that have the greatest impact. It is suggested that what has evolved is an ontogenetic contingency mechanism that causes low ranking individuals to fail to develop adequate inhibitory control of spontaneous impulses. Inhibitory control is a necessary capability for organisms living in tightly knit hierarchical groups. Inhibitory control makes it possible for a low-status individual to defer to a higher-status individual when a limited resource is sought by both. Without this arrangement (the essential feature of any dominance hierarchy) constant strife would quickly result in the destruction of the group members. However, deferment to higher-ranking individuals by lower-ranking individuals is adaptive only up to a point. If an individual is extremely low ranking, or if resources are in very-limited supply, or these two factors interact at some critical level, then absolute obsequiousness by the low-ranking individual can result in zero fitness. Impetuously snatching a morsel of food from a higher-ranking group member or, even more hazardously, copulating with a female "belonging" to a higher-ranking male, may raise a low-ranking individual's fitness level. Individuals of middle rank improve their fitness via a moderate level of impulsiveness, with their behavior being a mix of socially acceptable patterns and rash actions.

An individual that experiences extremely low status throughout its early development will manifest extremely poor impulse control as a juvenile or young adult. Consistent failure by an individual to control impulses makes it unlikely that the individual can remain integrated in the group. The fissioning of a very-low-ranking individual from the group may increase the potential fitness of that individual via alternative social strategies (e.g., clandestine copulations, forming or joining different groups).

Birth Order and Adult Personality.   Charles Darwin often speculated as to why certain men and not others made new discoveries. Specifically, he wondered why men who are very intelligent, much more intelligent than the discoverers, never originate anything in their lives. Darwin considered himself to be a man of very modest intellectual gifts and yet he made outstanding contributions to a very wide range of scientific disciplines throughout his lifetime. Darwin contributed greatly to the fields of geology and natural history during his twenties and early thirties. In his forties he became a world-class expert on invertebrate zoology, writing several definitive monographs on barnacles. After publishing *The Origin of Species* at the age of fifty Darwin turned his attention to botany, a field in which he had very little knowledge. Within a short period the professional botanists at this time were astounded at the numerous discoveries that Darwin made in the field in which they had practiced for their entire lifetimes. In his sixties and seventies Darwin laid down the foundation for modern evolutionary psychology, writing *The Descent of Man* and *The Expression of Emotion in Man and Animals*. Before his death at the age of 73 Darwin opened up yet another field with numerous new discoveries relating to the earthworm. Darwin's ability to make these original discoveries where no one else could was due, in part, to his particular personality. Many of his methods were so revolutionary that other scientists had never even conceived of them, and if they had been they would undoubtedly have been shunned for being far too unorthodox. For example, Darwin loved to carry out what he called "fools' experiments" to test ideas that were so implausible that other people would have never have thought to have considered them at all. Darwin had so many inspired insights into so many diverse areas that we may speculate that he may have had some insight into his query regarding the discoverers of new facts and ideas. If he did, he did not write about it so we may never know for sure. Part of the explanation relates to birth order and sibling competition.

Sulloway (1996) has amassed data to support the idea that birth order plays a critical role in shaping individual personalities. The first dominance hierarchy into which individuals are placed is that of the nuclear family. Because of the obvious advantages of size and experience conferred on the firstborn, they are invariably at the top of this mini social hierarchy. Consequently, firstborns tend to identify strongly with power and authority. Contrasted with their younger siblings, firstborns are more assertive, ambitious, and jealous of their status and ready to defend it. Conversely, younger siblings who are basically disenfranchised by the status quo are inclined to question everything having to do with it and in some instances tend to embrace revolutionary perspectives. Concepts of equality and fairness are foremost in the minds of latter-born siblings, whereas established order supercedes equality in the minds of the firstborns. In a study investigating the reception of liberal theories by scientists who were sibling of one another, it was found that latter-born siblings were 7.3 times more likely to support scientific innovations than were their own eldest siblings. Firstborns tend to reject new ideas especially when the innovation has the potential of disrupting long-accepted principles. These firstborns typically welcome conservative doctrines that may serve to protect against radical changes. The nineteenth century naturalists, Georges Cuvier and Charles Lyell, who were also firstborns, extol the balance of nature which works to keep all creatures in their intended place including the different racial varieties of human beings. In summary, the majority of the pivotal innovators in the history of science were latter-borns, including Copernicus and Darwin.

Optimizing Cognitive Potential

For any given trait, each individual has a genetic recipe that codes for a range of possible outcomes. For example, an individual's reaction range for physical height might be anywhere from four feet to seven feet. A combination of illness, starvation, and endocrine shut-down might result in the individual being only four feet tall as an adult. Conversely, a diet copious in nutrients and hyperactive endocrine glands might produce a height of seven feet in an individual with the same genotype. Developing under more "normal" conditions, individuals with this genotype would be more likely to reach a height of around six feet.

Behavioral traits, such as intelligence, also show a range of potential outcomes for each particular genotype. Many of the factors that influence traits such as height also effect traits such as intelligence. A lifetime of poor nutrition and near starvation not only stunts the body but, of course, stunts brain development as well and, consequently, the cognitive complexity of the individual. The factors that influence adult cognitive potential have the greatest impact during the earliest stages of the individual's life. One simple decision that can have far reaching effects on the part of the parents is whether or not to breast-feed their children. These effects are manifested not only in terms of overall health, but also in terms of cognitive potential. A study by Lucas, Morley, and Cole (1998) showed that preterm infants who were either randomly assigned to an infant formula group, an enriched formula group, or a breast-feeding group showed marked differences in their IQs when they were tested at seven to eight years of age. The group with the highest cognitive performance was that which had received the breast milk. The next highest group was the group that had received the enriched formula, and the poorest outcome was displayed in the group that had received the standard formula. Males, in particular, seemed to be the most vulnerable to the effects of the dietary differences. There appear to be special fatty acids present only in mother's milk that facilitate neurological development.

The IQ of boys is also more effected by maternal nurturance levels than are girls (Andersson, Sommerfelt, Sonnander, & Ahlsten, 1996). Conversely, girls' IQs are vulnerable to maternal harsh discipline in a context of low maternal warmth (Smith & Brooks-Gunn, 1997). Girls who experienced harsh maternal discipline and low nurturance showed IQ scores that were 12 points lower than the IQ scores of girls who received low punishment and high maternal warmth.

Studies of animals show that by varying the rearing environment, marked differences in brain development and intelligence can be produced in adults (Diamond, 1988). In one study, rats were taken after weaning and placed in either an enriched environment or an impoverished environment. The impoverished environment consisted of a small steel cage with food and water. The enriched environment consisted of a large box with climbing toys and a varied terrain, but most importantly, it contained other rats with which to interact with. Upon completion of the study it was found that rats in the enriched environment had brains that were notably heavier and at the microscopic level they contained many more dendritic connections than did the brains of the impoverished group. The brain size and complexity of the enriched animals were also manifested in faster learning rates and greater intelligence.

An impoverished rearing environment (childhood neglect and abuse) has also been demonstrated to produce permanent changes in both brain function and structure in humans (Teicher, 2000). Brain scans of adults who were abused as children indicate underdevelopment of the left hemisphere, which may be associated with memory deficits and depression. There is also a reduction in the size of the corpus callosum, the bundle of myelinated fibers that connects the two cerebral hemispheres and makes communication possible between the right and left sides of the brain. As expected, behavioral tests of these individuals showed that they did not integrate the function of the left and right sides of their brain as well as those who had not been abused. It was also found that neglect and abuse produced different developmental outcome depending upon the sex of the childhood victim. Neglect was associated with a reduction in the size of the corpus callosum in boys but sexual abuse had no effect. Conversely, in girls, sexual abuse was associated with a decrease in the size of the corpus callosum, but neglect had no effect. Note how this pattern is similar to the differential outcomes of male and female IQ as a result of neglect or harsh discipline discussed earlier in this section (Andersson, Sommerfelt, Sonnander, & Ahlsten, 1996; Smith & Brooks-Gunn, 1997).

For a human infant, the most enriching environment is one in which he or she has close contact with a highly involved adult caregiver. No computer or learning tool can approach the complexity of an adult human being for providing complex stimulation and interaction with a developing infant. This idea is supported by the fact that firstborn and only children are more likely to score higher on IQ tests, to be national merit scholars, to acquire Ph.D.s and to appear in Who's Who than are later-born children (Belmont & Marolla, 1973; Helmreich, 1968; Sutton-Smith, 1982).

Intelligence, like many other positive potentials, can be stimulated by parents who are nurturing and caring. However, it should be kept in mind that to a large extent intelligence is a product of genes. In a study that compared IQ scores of adopted children with those of their adopted siblings and parents and with the educational level of their biological mothers, it was found that young siblings scored similarly whether they were related by blood or adoption. However, when they reached adolescence their scores had zero correlation with their adoptive siblings and high correlations with their biological mothers' level of schooling (Scarr & Weinberg, 1983). Another study that compared the IQs of adopted children with the IQs of their adoptive parents and their biological mothers found that the children resembled their biological mothers twice as much as their adoptive mothers despite the fact that they had been with their biological mothers less than one week after their birth (Horn, 1983). In a longitudinal study of 500 pairs of identical and fraternal twins from infancy to adolescence, it was found that identical twins became increasingly similar in IQ while fraternal twins showed lower and lower similarity with age (Wilson, 1983). Cohen (1999) has summarized a number of similar studies, all of which show that variations in parenting style within the normal range have very modest effects on IQ outcomes as compared to genetics.

The Adaptive Function of Menopause

Human males and most females of other species remain fertile until they die. For human females the situation is very different. Most women experience a sharp decline in fertility beginning around the age of 40 and within a decade or so are no longer ovulating. Without special hormonal intervention, conception by a woman over 50 years of age is practically unknown. Since evolutionary theory is based on the idea that everything revolves around increasing capacities for leaving genetic replicates, human menopause presents a conundrum. Diamond (1996) explained this paradox by saying that as a woman ages she can do more to increase the number of people carrying her genes by investing her energy into her existing children, grandchildren, and other relatives rather than by directly producing another child of her own.

The reason this behavior appears to be unique among primates and very, very rare among other species of animals (among nonhuman animals, only the short-finned pilot whale is known to have menopause) is that human children have such a prolonged period of dependency. In most human societies humans do not become capable of economic independence until their teens or twenties. In a hunter-gatherer society, a mother who has several children risks losing her genetic investment in them if she does not survive until her youngest is at least a teenager. With the birth of each successive child, a mother's previous children are placed in greater and greater risk due to the inherent dangers of pregnancy and childbirth. Other children are also placed at risk even if both mother and newborn infant survive because there is less energy to be invested in them. Studies of existing hunter-gatherers show that postmenopausal women put in more hours of foraging and bring in more food per day than women in the fertile age range bring in. These postmenopausal women were sharing this gathered food with close relatives and were also investing a great deal of time and energy into their children and grandchildren. The complex calculus of natural selection has weighed out the potential benefits and risks associated with human females continuing to bear children throughout life. Evidently, the benefits gained from improved survival from ones grandchildren, prior children, and more distant relatives appear to outweigh potential benefits incurred from having one's own children late in life due to the risks that are involved.

Summary

In complex organisms, most evolved adaptations are orchestrated by regulator genes during the process of developmental unfolding (ontogeny). The developmental stages of different mammalian species tend to resemble each other in the early stages because evolutionary modifications are usually manifested in later stages and the earlier stages are relatively unaffected by environmental selection because of internal brooding.

Evolutionary changes occur maternally in mammals both to facilitate the success of the unborn offspring and to defend against the selfish needs of these offspring. The morning sickness phenomena of pregnancy may be an example of the former. It has been hypothesized that morning sickness evolved to protect the developing embryo of fetus from the ingestion of food toxins. Many maternal physiological changes that occur during pregnancy may be defensive reactions to fetal responses designed to overly exploit the mother. For example, the placental release of human placental lactogen (hPL) appears to make the mother's cells resistant to her own insulin thereby elevating her blood glucose levels and making more glucose available to the fetus. The maternal defensive response is a down regulation of blood glucose levels early in pregnancy. High levels of hPL are directly implicated in the onset of gestational diabetes.

Mother-infant conflicts of interest continue after birth with the arsenal of infant behavioral strategies ranging from cute to bratty. Infanticide can be viewed as an adaptive strategy in mothers who are pushed to the limits of survival.

Patterns of mating behavior (phenotypes) are effected by early rearing experiences. An adaptive need for incest avoidance has resulted in a mechanism that produces sexual indifference or repugnance between opposite sex individuals reared together in typical sibling fashion. The timing of pubertal onset and patterns of adult sexual behavior in girls is to some degree contingent upon the social milieu in which the individual develops. The differing patterns may reflect different reproductive strategies.

Adult personality is also contingent upon early rearing experiences. Rearing experiences characterized by low level of nuturance, neglect or even abuse typically produce individuals predisposed towards impulsive behaviors. Impulsivity may be an adaptive response to low social rank in a dominance hierarchy. The presence of siblings is an important factor in the rearing environment. In general, first borns tend to be conservative, authoritarian defenders of the status quo. Later borns tend to be more innovative, liberal minded, and concerned with equality and fairness.

Early experience also plays a critical role in the degree to which one's cognitive potential is realized. Good nutrition is key both before and after birth. Breast milk contains certain essential fatty acids that are difficult to obtain from other sources and breast-feeding has been shown to have a significant impact on IQ. Environmental stimulation is absolutely essential to cognitive development. For a human infant, the greatest environmental stimulation is provided by a highly involved, highly nurturing and intelligent adult caregiver.

Maternal caregiving is probably the functional adaptation achieved by menopause. Unlike the females of other primate species who remain fertile throughout their lives, women typically become infertile (stop ovulating) by age 50 or 60. Menopause is explained by the prolonged dependency period of human children. With the birth of each successive child, a mother's previous children are placed in greater and greater risk due to the inherent dangers of pregnancy and childbirth. As a woman ages she can do more to increase the number of people carrying her genes, i.e., increase her fitness, by investing her energy into her existing children, grandchildren, and other relatives than by giving birth to another child.

Discussion Questions

1. Explain the differences between Haeckel's Biogenetic Law and von Baer's Law. Why is von Baer's Law considered to be a more accurate model of reality?

2. Discuss the concept of mother–fetus genetic conflicts of interest. Describe the action of human chorionic gonadotropin (hCG). Explain the relationship between the release of human placental lactogen (hPL) and the onset of gestational diabetes.

3. Discuss the idea that our genes code for certain adaptive behavioral phenotypes that are triggered by particular rearing experiences (evolved ontogenetic contingency mechanisms). Discuss empirical evidence that supports this theoretical perspective over simple social learning theory, for example, Belsky's finding of altered pubertal timing.

4. You are given the task at raising the child who will become the greatest innovative genius of the twenty-first century (the genes for genius are already included). How do you optimize the child's genetic potential for high cognitive ability? How do you insure that this child will realize his/her potential for innovative thinking and creativity?

Key Terms

gene imprinting
gestational diabetes
Haeckel's Biogenetic Law
HOM genes
HOX genes
human chorionic
   gonadotropin (hCG)

human placental lactogen
   (hPL)
insulin
kibbutzim
menarche
menopause
ontogeny

parent-infant conflict theory
phylogeny
Red Queen Hypothesis
regulator genes
Simpua marriages
von Baer's Law
Westermark's hypothesis

Additional Reading

Cycles of Contingency: Developmental Systems and Evolution by Susan Oyama, Paul E. Griffiths, and Russell D. Gray (Editors) (2000).

The Relationship Code: Deciphering Genetic and Social Influences on Adolescent Development by David Reiss, Jenae M. Neiderhiser, E. Mavis Hetherington, and R. Plomin (2000).

Necessary but Not Sufficient: The Respective Roles of Single and Multiple Influences on Individual Development by Theodore D. Wachs (2000).

Play and Exploration in Children and Animals by Thomas G. Power (1999).

Evolutionary Principles of Human Adolescence by Glenn Weisfeld (1999).

Stranger in the Nest: Do Parents Really Shape Their Child's Personality, Intelligence, or Character? by David B. Cohen (1999).

Piaget, Evolution, and Development by Jonas Langer and Melanie Killen (Editors) (1998).

Uniting Psychology and Biology: Integrative Perspectives on Human Development by Nancy L. Segal, Glenn E. Weisfeld, and Carol C. Weisfeld (Editors) (1997).

Rethinking Innateness: A Connectionist Perspective on Development by Jeffrey L. Elman, Elizabeth A. Bates, Mark H. Johnson, and Karmiloff-sm (1998).

Are We Hardwired: The Role of Genes in Human Behavior by William R. Clark and Michael Grunstein (2000).

Nonverbal Communication: Where Nature Meets Culture by Ullica Segerstrale and Peter Molnar (Editors) 1996.

DNA and Destiny: Nature and Nurture in Human Behavior by R. Grant Steen (1996).

Living With Our Genes: Why They Matter More Than You Think by Dean H. Hamer and Peter Copeland (1998).

Twins: And What They Tell Us About Who We Are by Lawrence Wright (1997).

Born That Way: Genes, Behavior, Personality by William Wright (1998).

Synthesizing Nature-Nurture: Prenatal Roots of Instinctive Behavior by Gilbert Gottlieb (1997).

Phenotypes: Their Epigenetics, Ecology and Evolution by C. David Rollo (1995).

Baby Wars: Parenthood and Family Strife by Robin Baker and Elizabeth Oram (1999).

The Truth About Cinderella: A Darwinian View of Parental Love by Martin Daly and Margo Wilson (1999).

Mother Nature: A History of Mothers, Infants, and Natural Selection by Sarah Blaffer Hrdy (1999).

Our Babies, Ourselves: How Biology and Culture Shape the Way We Parent by Meredith F. Small (1998).

Born to Rebel: Birth Order, Family Dynamics, and Creative Lives by Frank J. Sulloway (1997).

The Evolution of Sibling Rivalry by Douglas W. Mock and Geoffrey A. Parker (1998).

Human Birth: An Evolutionary Perspective by Wenda R. Trevathna (1987).

The Evolution of Parental Care by T. H. Clutton-Brock (1991).

7

Social Order and Disorder

The strongest and most effective [force] in guaranteeing the long-term maintenance of . . . power is not violence in all the forms deployed by the dominant to control the dominated, but consent in all the forms in which the dominated acquiesce in their own domination.

—Maurice Godelier, *The Mental and the Material: Thought, Economy and Society*, Preface (1986)

Chapter Questions

1. Does human society resemble a "pecking order?" Why and why not?
2. Who do "number twos" try so hard. In other words, why is a striving for improved social status such a prevalent pattern of behavior?
3. Does Prozac make "losers" feel like winners?
4. If stress responses are so harmful how did they evolve?
5. How can some of the highest of human virtues, such as compassion be traced to our animal origins?

One striking feature of our species is the fact that groups of humans, whether they number in dozens or hundreds or millions, can coexist in a productive and reasonably harmonious fashion. Although customs and laws exist within any human society to help maintain this order, it is clear that these explicit and implicit rules could not solely in themselves accomplish this end. Although violations, of course, exist they are invariably viewed as aberrations. No matter how high the crime rate of a given area, the vast majority of social interactions are of a peaceful, mutually advantageous sort. Even among subgroups that are considered outlaws by the society as a whole, there is an internal system that maintains order and trust among its members. A classic illustration of this idea of "honor among thieves" is the ethical code strictly followed by Mafia hit men. Although the hit men probably perceive their ethical system as perfectly congruent, most outsiders find it highly ironic. This is because the taking of a human life by a fellow human being is considered the most heinous of social violations. The greater irony, however, is the fact that the proportion of deaths that result from murder is miniscule compared to the wholesale slaughter of war. The achievement of this level of carnage is made possible by the mobilization of whole societies focused upon the destruction of other societies. The cooperative effort that make this possible is truly remarkable. What is also remarkable is the sense of righteousness possessed by each and every society engaged in conflict regardless of the side they are on. Even societies openly bent on the genocidal destruction of the opposing peoples feel they hold the ethical high ground. It is this facility we possess for both cooperation and conflict and our ability to simultaneously possess any number of seemingly inconsistent ethical beliefs that will be explored in this chapter.

Dominance Hierarchies: The Coordination of Affiliation and Aggression

If one were to casually observe a group of Old World monkeys such as rhesus macaques under wild conditions or free-ranging captive conditions, the following observations would almost certainly be made. First, the observer would notice that the group had a definite organization or structure to it. Within the overall group there would be subgroups. One of these subgroups would consist of adult females and their dependent offspring. Among the adult females, certain individuals would appear to be given more respect and deference than others. This deference would also be afforded to the offspring of these individuals. Among the male animals, one individual in particular would seem to stand out from the group. This male would walk about the group maintaining erect posture with head and tail up, slow deliberate body movements, and unhesitating, measured appraisal of any other monkeys that happened to cross his path. If the human observer wanted to wax anthropomorphic in her description of this animal, she might describe him as having an almost regal carriage. In human society we often use the term "highly regarded" when speaking of someone considered of high status. In the rhesus macaque group this term "highly regarded" takes on a very literal meaning. The before-mentioned alpha male is the animal that is most looked at of any individual in the group by the other group members. Objective measures of gaze clearly indicate that the alpha animal is disproportionately the object of scrutiny by the other group members.

As observations continued it would become apparent that the alpha animal had first access to whatever resources became available. This would include everything from choice sleeping spots, to food, to mating opportunities. Any animal that was presumptuous enough to usurp the alpha in a resource opportunity would instantly become the target of a vicious aggressive attack. Such challenges would occur fairly infrequently and usually, when they did occur, they would be direct attempts by other animals to depose the alpha from his position. For the most part, lower-ranking or subordinate animals would go out of their way to indicate their acquiescence to the wishes of the higher-ranking animal. This communication would be in the form of facial expressions, body postures, and certain other behavioral displays. Typical subordinate displays would include averting the eyes, lowering the head, crouching, or baring the teeth in a frightened, grimacing display. Displays performed by a higher-ranking or dominant animal would include a nonwavering stare, fully erect body posture, and, occasionally, a short lunge toward a potential interloper. With the exception of the top-ranking or alpha animal and the very bottom-ranking or omega animal, each individual in the group would have at least one animal that it dominated and one or more that it was submissive to. These relationships would form a hierarchical structure called the status hierarchy or dominance hierarchy. The dominance hierarchy can be defined as the set of sustained aggressive-submissive relations among a group of animals (Wilson, 1975).

Dominance hierarchies have an irregular distribution throughout the animal kingdom. Not all species that live in social groups have a hierarchical social organization based on aggressive interactions. Invertebrate species, including social insects with primitive levels of organizations such as bumble bees and paper wasps, display dominance hierarchies (Wilson, 1975). Other invertebrate species with this form of social structure include the crab spider, the pagurid crab, and certain crayfish. Fish and amphibians have also been observed to form dominance hierarchies, although some researchers would contest categorizing these species in terms of forming true dominance relationships. Bernstein (1981) has defined dominance relations as constituting a learned relationship between two individuals in a social group based on a previous aggressive encounter. According to this type of criteria, mainly avian species and mammals form true dominance hierarchies where the relationships remain relatively stable, and they are based at least in part on the memory that individuals have of previous aggressive encounters with group members.

In fact, it was with an avian species, the domestic fowl or chicken, that the idea of a dominance hierarchy or pecking order was first introduced to the literature (Schjelderup-Ebbe, 1922). The pecking orders in chickens described by Schjelderup-Ebbe were for the most part linear hierarchies. In other words, there was a top or alpha animal that pecked all other animals. The animal directly below it was pecked only by the alpha, and so on down the chain. This type of linear hierarchy has been documented in many mammalian species and even some groups of primates. However, when one starts to observe more complex primate species, it is very unusual to find a strict linear hierarchy. For example, animal A may be dominant to animal B, and B dominant to C, but C may be dominant to A. A further complicating factor is the tendency for more complex animals to form alliances. They actively recruit allies for the purpose of having this coalitional support when they go against a higher-ranking animal.

Dominance hierarchies can be viewed as an evolutionary compromise between the benefits accrued to organisms by living in social groups versus the costs associated with the increased competition for food, mates, nesting sites, and other limited resources (Alcock, 1984). The benefits for living in a social group are numerous. They include reduction in predator pressure by improved protection and defense from would-be predators. Foraging becomes more efficient in a group compared to an individual because there is more likelihood that one of the many individuals in the group will discover a rich source of food or something else of value to all group members. In the case of hunting behavior, it is clear that cooperative hunting greatly improves the individual's probability of obtaining food. In a study of Serengeti lions it was found that capture rates for solitary lions were 15 percent, but for groups of lions over five, capture rates were around 40 percent (Curaco and Wolf, 1975). Individual lions have a much higher probability of starving to death.

Each individual within a group, though benefiting by being in the group, must compete with other group members for many of these benefits. In more primitive organisms, the right of access to resources is simply a matter of physical size and strength. As organisms become more complex, they are able to remember interactions with different individuals and do not have to engage in fighting after their initial encounter. Any social organisms that did not develop this system in the past would continually engage in aggressive episodes any time any new resource became available. This constant aggression would invariable weaken all members of the group, and, as a consequence, it is unlikely that genes coding for such behavior would have persisted.

The gains associated with a rise in hierarchical status are considerable. Higher-ranking primates are much less likely to die during periods of low resource availability (Cheney & Sefarth, 1990). In most species, high dominance rank is intimately related to reproductive success (Clutton-Brock, 1988; Dewsbury, 1982). In many primate species, this relationship between dominance rank and reproductive success is not always immediately obvious. However, studies of baboons (Hausfater, 1975) show that, although lower-ranking males may mate with females, higher-ranking males typically monopolize the females on the day that they ovulate. Higher-ranking chimpanzees have also been observed to have greater access to females in estrous (De Waal, 1982). In the first six civilizations (ancient Mesopotamia, Egypt, Aztec Mexico, Inca Peru, imperial India, and ancient China) kings and noblemen had the privilege of mating with hundreds of women and siring hundreds of offspring (Betzig, 1993).

The evolution of dominance hierarchies may be intimately linked to the evolution of intelligence (Cummins, 1991). In Chapter Two, the evolution of Machiavellian intelligence was discussed. This is the idea that there was intense selection for individuals who could infer the behavior of other individuals and manipulate such behavior. This would, of course, result in an arms race for greater and greater manipulative social intelligence. The ideal milieu to facilitate such an arms race for social intelligence was, of course, the dominance hierarchy. Despite, the obvious advantages conferred by intelligence it is apparent that humans, like most other species still attend to primitive physical attributes in the creation of social hierarchies (see Figure 7.1). In the United States, eighty-two percent of the presidential

BOX 7.1 • *Through a Glass Darwinian* *The Evolutionary Origins of Pride and Shame*

The signals associated with dominant status and subordinate status show numerous, structural similarities across diverse species. The function of submissive appeasement signals is to turn off the aggressive behavior of a threatening conspecific. In terms of maintaining social order it can be argued that the submissive display is the most important of all signals. When encountering a higher-ranking individual, subordinates avert their gaze and lower their heads and bodies. Dominant individuals display an erect posture and threaten subordinates with an unrelenting stare. Moreover, the dominants have a relaxed nonchalance and confidence in their bearing, in marked contrast to the subordinates, who appear nervous and fidgety. These patterns hold true for great apes, Old World monkeys and wolves. Darwin (1872) noted that expressions of pride and shame in humans parallel the signals for dominance and submission displayed by other species. The behavioral concomitants associated with a subjective experience of pride can be viewed as spontaneous and largely unconscious signals indicating high rank. Conversely, the subjective experience of shame results in spontaneous, involuntary signals of submission which function to deescalate conflict.

Weisfeld (1999) makes a compelling argument that the terms shame and pride can be used to subsume a plethora of divergent psychological constructs such as self-esteem, guilt, prestige striving, success striving, social comparison, approval motivation, prosocial behavior and a multitude of others. These constructs differ from each other mainly in the particulars of the situations in which they are manifested but all are part of essentially the same behavioral system. The failure of psychology to incorporate these patterns of behavior into a comprehensive biologically meaningful system has led to innumerable erroneous judgments. For example, pride and shame were considered by many psychologists to be "learned motives," which is equivalent to saying that hunger is a "learned motive."

The types of evidence needed to demonstrate that a particular behavior is an evolved adaptation, as proposed by Darwin (1872), clearly exist for pride and shame. The behaviors exist throughout the species. The emotions of pride and shame are present in every human culture (Edelmann, 1990). They have an invariant developmental timetable, developing around the ages of two or three (Weisfeld, 1999). Pride and shame have distinct stereotypical display structures. An erect, expansive, relaxed carriage characterizes pride. Proud people make direct eye contact in conversation. Shameful individuals avert their gaze and lower their heads. They may also display a nervous smile or display facial blushing. Pride and shame appear to be mediated at the proximate physiological level by an area of the brain called the orbitofrontal cortex (Carlson, 1998). Damage to this area appears to remove a person's capacity for pride and shame. Levels of the neurotransmitter, serotonin and the hormone, testosterone are positively correlated with feelings of pride (dominance) and negatively correlated with feelings of shame (submission) (Masters & McGuire, 1994; Mazur, 1983). Finally, similar patterns of behavior and similar adaptive outcomes occur in other species. This phylogenetic evidence is particularly compelling in making a case for pride and shame being evolved adaptations.

In humans, the old hierarchical system underlies recently evolved propensities for reciprocal altruism and an even more recently evolved language capacity that allows social exchange to occur in a very abstract and symbolic fashion. Verbal threats, apologies, and promises are used to maintain equity in a system of reciprocal altruism (Trivers, 1971). The basic drives that give impetus to this complex social system are pro-

BOX 7.1 • (Continued)

vided by emotional states derived from hierarchical evolution. Dominance (pride) is experienced as a pleasant emotion we seek to obtain (positive reinforcement) and submission (shame) is experienced as aversive state we seek to avoid (negative reinforcement).

Thus when we succeed in obtaining material resources or win a prized mating partner we experience pride. Conversely, when we lose out in a competition for resources or are rejected by someone we value as a mating partner we experience shame.

elections of the twentieth century were won by the taller candidate and, for every inch above the mean height of 5 feet, 8 inches, men earn six hundred dollars more per year (Gillis, 1982).

Dunbar (1982, 1992) has shown that neocortical brain volume correlates with the mean group sizes among primate species. One interpretation of this finding is that primates cannot maintain the cohesion of groups that are larger than the size fixed by their cognitive capacity to keep track of the relationships within the group. In other words, a bigger group requires a greater memory capacity and a greater capacity for inferential reasoning. The animal living in a dominance hierarchy often has to infer the proper relationship between itself and another animal with whom it has never had a direct agonistic encounter. The first animal must make its inference by comparing the second animal's known rank to other group members with whom the first animal has an established dominance relationship. To give an example of this transitive reasoning in a social hierarchy: If one knows that A is dominant to B and B is dominant to C, then one can infer the relationship between A and C without ever observing an encounter between the two.

The modular mental capacities for hierarchical mental reasoning appear to be far older than the Plio-Pleistocene evolution of our species. In fact, this type of specialized transitive reasoning has been demonstrated in numerous social primate species. Squirrel monkeys and chimpanzees can form transitive inference tasks on objects only after a considerable drilling of paired stimuli (Gillan, 1981; McGonigle & Chalmers, 1971). Yet they readily make transitive inferences when making discriminations about rank and kinship among individuals in their social groups (Dasser, 1985; Cheney & Seyfarth, 1990).

Human children also show a similar type of dissociation between transitive reasoning about objects and transitive reasoning about fellow humans. Three-year-old children have a rather poor ability to do transitive reasoning concerning nonsocial stimuli, yet they can readily infer transitive dominance relations (Smith, 1988). General transitive reasoning ability does not consistently appear until about six years of age.

The dominance hierarchy also provides an ideal situation for the evolution of reciprocal altruism as Trivers (1971) described it. In order to maintain high status or to rise in status primates must possess strong alliances (De Waal, 1982; Goodall, 1986). Individuals that can form alliances among non-kin have a much-improved

FIGURE 7.1   Striving for social status is a trait shared by numerous species that live in hierarchical societies.

advantage over individuals who can only form alliances among near kin. To maintain these alliances among non-kin, the individuals depend on the formation of reciprocal obligations. A vervet monkey, for example, is more likely to respond to calls from non-kin during an aggressive episode if the caller has groomed him recently. In fact, in the vervets, Cheney and Seyfarth (1990) observed that the strongest alliances were between individuals that frequently groomed each other. Studies on coalition and alliance formation among nonhuman primates show a great capacity for reasoning about obligations and in particular reciprocal obligations (Cummins, 1996). Chimpanzees in particular show the marked capacity for cheater detection. For example, if animal B has consistently spent time grooming animal C, and animal B finds itself in a confrontation with animal A, and it invokes aid from animal C but is ignored by animal C, then animal B will demonstrate intense distress and anger. This type of interaction has been observed repeatedly among groups of chimpanzees (De Waal, 1982).

In summary, stable dominance hierarchies based on stable relationships have been observed in numerous avian and mammalian species as well as some reptilian species. In more complex species such as higher primates the hierarchies are not strictly linear, and coalitions and alliances are formed to facilitate upward mobility of the individuals in these hierarchies. One consequence of high-status rank is greater access to resources, particularly mating opportunities. The importance of social rank for reproductive success has resulted in organisms that simultaneously strive for their status but who often have alternative strategies for reproduction if they happen to be of lower rank. These strategies include clandestine mating and generally impulsive behavior. More will be said about these alternative strategies and the ontogenetic priming that creates them later in this chapter.

Studies based on ethological observations of human preschool children, human adolescents, and adults in prison have confirmed that humans, like other primate species, form stable dominance hierarchies (Austin & Bates, 1974; Savin-Williams, 1976; Strayer, 1975). In these studies, the hierarchies were derived by looking at the outcomes of agonistic encounters between the individuals in the groups. It was found that not only were such structures formed, but the dominant individuals had greater access to whatever resources were available. Clearly an examination of the dominance concept has implications for understanding human social behavior and human cognition. There is, however, a paradox that must be addressed.

Modern-day hunter-gatherers, although not a perfect model of our ancestors during the Pleistocene Era, are nevertheless, a much more relevant model than groups of humans living today who employ advanced technology, or even agriculture or domesticated animals—none of which are thought to have existed during the Pleistocene Era. In these hunter-gatherer groups, the society is basically egalitarian. In other words, there is no clear-cut dominance structure (Erdal & Whiten, 1994). In such groups outstanding hunters are often listened to in terms of directing the groups on a hunt. But, if these leading individuals attempt to achieve personal dominance, the other group members quickly bring them down.

The same tendencies apply to their food-sharing customs. When one individual is seen as trying to monopolize food the other group members quickly sanction him. The central feeling in such groups is that "No one is going to get away with more than me." The necessity of such a system in a hunting society is obvious. Hunting is a high-risk activity where the cooperation of several individuals is more likely to produce a payoff than the efforts of one person alone. Moreover, when a large animal is killed the hunter that brings it down can only utilize a small percentage of the meat, even including his family members and kin. Most of the carcass will spoil and go to waste if it is not shared with the overall group. Self-interest is still a factor at work within these "egalitarian" groups. Those who have a surplus of meat sometimes try to avoid sharing, and those who have no meat sometimes try to steal (Turnbull, 1965). Erdal and Whiten (1994) proposed the term "vigilant sharing" to describe the complex food-sharing behavior. The individuals within these groups have a strong desire to get enough for themselves as well as a strong desire to make sure that no one else gets more than they do.

Although there is some debate among physical anthropologists concerning the exact duration, it is clear that the hunter-gatherer phase of human existence comprised a long period of time. Estimates range from tens of thousands of years to hundreds of thousands of years. In some cases it is argued that the entire Pleistocene (over two million years) was occupied by hunting bands of ancestral hominids. Even if we opt for the more conservative estimates, it is very likely that hunting has existed for at least one hundred thousand years or so. Because this hunter-gather egalitarian phase comprised a significant portion of human evolutionary history, Erdal and Whiten (1994) have argued that it has become part of our repertoire of innate behavioral predispositions. It was only with the advent of agriculture or the domestication of grazing animals that the hunter-gatherer egalitarian system no longer worked as a social strategy. When it became possible for individuals to monopolize resources and to centralize power, a new type of dominance system emerged (Betzig, 1993). Concerning the reemergence of dominance hierarchies in humans, Erdal and Whiten (1994) make the following comment, "Such hierarchies are not merely reborn ape hierarchies, but uniquely human in both their behavioral detail and their cultural recognition" (p. 178). With the new dominance systems that emerged in human social structures each individual was not part of a dominance hierarchy, but rather played a role in multiple hierarchies. To use a modern-day example, one individual might be highly dominant in their career setting, for example, a bank president. At their sports club they may be a middle-of-the-road tennis player. At home they may occupy the bottom rung of a hierarchy with their wife and daughters at the top, and so forth. In summary, the Stone Age minds that we carry around with us contain not only the tendency for hierarchical living but also a strong urge for an egalitarian way of life. When this ancient genotype is expressed in the complex, social, and technological milieu of the twenty-first century, it is not surprising that many individuals find themselves suffering major problems. In the next section we will examine the biochemical and psychological states that are directly related to living in a status hierarchy.

The Biochemistry of Status and the Function of Mood States

Serotonin

An essential characteristic of organisms living in a social hierarchy is the ability to control individual impulses. Inhibitory control makes it possible for a low-status individual to defer to a higher-status individual when a limited resource is sought by both. Without this arrangement, the social structure would quickly collapse into chaos. In the higher primate species the ability to assess the status of other individuals and to modify one's own behavior accordingly is in large part mediated by the developed frontal cortex. This development of the frontal cortex has reached its highest pinnacle in humans, who are capable of making very complex assessments of very intricate situations and modifying their behavior in very complex ways to accommodate. Although the frontal cortex is of undoubted importance in complex primates, many animal species are quite capable of maintaining social hierarchies with very little cortical development. A much more primitive physiological mechanism is involved in the regulation of dominance behavior.

The extremely primitive nature of this physiological mechanism is indicated by the fact that it is found in an extremely wide diversity of species from the phyla Annelida, Arthropopa, Mollusca, Platyhelmenthese, and Chordata (Turlejski, 1996). Although this system varies in its particulars from species to species, it is always involved in the modulation of motor behavior, varying its tempo or inhibiting it altogether. The neurons, or nerve cells, in this system use a neurotransmitter called serotonin. Neurotransmitters are chemical messengers released from the ends of nerve cells in order to facilitate the transmission of an electrical signal to the adjacent nerve cell. The remote Metazoan ancestor that we have in common with flatworms, leeches, crayfish, and all sorts of other creatures must have had this type of serotonergic system. In primitive solitary organisms, increases in serotonin activity would lead to increases in motor activity. Conversely, decreases in serotonin activity would lower motor behavior or inhibit completely. If an organism happened upon a rich foraging opportunity the firing rate of its serotonin neurons would increase, and, as a result, the animal would have more energy to take advantage of the abundant resources it had found. If, however, this same animal sensed the presence of a predator, there would be a lowering of serotonin activity and a corresponding inhibition of its motor behavior. Immobility is a primary defense against predation as long as the predator has not spotted the prey animal. As animals evolved to live in a hierarchically organized social group, these primitive serotonergic motor systems were co-opted and modified to facilitate the new behavioral demands.

McGuire and Raleigh (1975) demonstrated that serotonin level covaries with changes of status in vervet monkeys. Moreover, artificially raising the serotonin levels in subordinate vervet monkeys with fluoxetine (Prozac) results in these individuals rising in status, in some cases to alpha rank (Raleigh, 1991). Dominant animals display an air of calm self-assurance, self-control, and self-directed behavior.

Subordinates, on the other hand, appear fidgety, easily perturbed, and their be-havior seems to be largely controlled by external stimuli rather than being self-directed. Subordinates are also prone to impulsive behavior including impulsive aggression. The higher serotonin levels and correspondingly higher levels of motor activity in the dominant animals provides them with the means to take advantage of their relatively better resource opportunities. In the subordinates, lowered serotonin levels are adaptive in that motor activity is lessened thus con-serving energy in the face of diminished access to food. Moreover, their behavioral inhibition helps to reduce potential conflict with higher-ranking animals. Low serotonin is also associated with the hypervigilant state, which, of course, allows the subordinate to keep track of potentially dangerous higher-ranking animals.

Impulsive behavior is another characteristic associated with lowered sero-tonin in the low-status individual. A direct association between low serontonin production and impulsive aggression has been demonstrated in numerous species including humans (Roy & Linnoila, 1988; Kalat, 1997). The adaptive significance of impulsivity in the low-ranking individual may not be immediately apparent. Keep in mind, however, that deferment to higher-ranking individuals by lower-ranking individuals is adaptive only up to a point. If an individual is extremely low ranking, or if resources are in very limited supply, or these two factors inter-act at some critical level, then absolute obsequiousness by the low-ranking indi-vidual can result in zero fitness. Impetuously snatching a morsel of food from a higher-ranking group member or, even more hazardously copulating with a fe-male "belonging" to a higher-ranking male may raise a low-ranking individual's fitness level. Individuals of middle rank improve their fitness via a moderate level of impulsiveness, with their behavior being a mix of socially acceptable patterns and rash actions.

Consistent failure by an individual to control impulses makes it unlikely that the individual can remain integrated in the group. The fissioning of a very-low-ranking individual from the group may increase the potential fitness of that indi-vidual via alternative social strategies (e.g., clandestine copulations, forming or joining different groups).

Research into the etiology of low serotonin levels and impulsivity suggests, that like other Old World primates, individual humans may be predisposed to-ward this condition by their genetics (Eysenck, 1983; Plomin, 1976). To explain why genes for strong impulsivity and chronically low serotonergic activity are maintained in populations resulting in a small percentage of inherently impulsive individuals, one has to look at selective pressures in the totality of time. High im-pulsivity generally lowers fitness in an established stable group. However, during times of group upheaval (e.g., internecine conflict or invasion by outsiders) the highly impulsive individuals would have increased fitness relative those group members who continued to behave as though the status quo relations still applied. These periods of group upheaval, though relatively rare, would be sufficient to maintain impulsivity genes despite their reduced fitness during stable periods.

Individual developmental history probably plays a larger role in determin-ing the degree to which impulsive tendencies are manifested. Research by Higley,

Suomi and Linnoila (1996) indicates that an impoverished rearing environment (i.e., peer-reared) produces individual rhesus monkeys with chronically low serotonin levels and tendencies toward excessive aggression and impulsivity. In humans the rate of childhood physical abuse and sexual abuse reported from patients with borderline personality disorder (BPD) is above 70% (Ludolph et al., 1990; Ogata et al., 1990). BPD and a number of other disorders associated with compromised impulse control such as eating disorders, obsessionality, and pathological aggression have been shown to be at least in part due to hyposerotonergic activity and consequently amenable to treatment with serotonin reuptake inhibitors (SRIs) (Markovitz, 1995).

The nuclear family is the first social group into which people are fully integrated. Studies by Palmer, McCown, and Kerby (1997) and Palmer, McCown, and Thornburgh (1998) demonstrate that childhood environments high in parental nurturance produce individuals predisposed to high-status functioning as adults (e.g., they are highly sociable, responsible, self-controlled and low in impulsivity). Conversely, childhood environments low in parental nurturance and high in family discord produce individuals predisposed to low-status functioning as adults (e.g., they have low levels of sociality, responsibility, self-control and high levels of impulsivity).

Genetic, ontogenetic, and proximate factors all play a role in determining an individual's level of serotonergic functioning and concomitant behavioral tendencies. Because higher status is associated with greater fitness, we have evolved motivational tendencies that push us toward achieving higher social rank. An improvement in status and a corresponding elevation in serotonergic activity is experienced as an elevation in mood state. Common terms used to refer to a highly elevated mood state include joy, happiness, and euphoria. This subjective state is analogous to the pleasure we feel when eating a sumptuous meal when we are really hungry. We experience pleasure when eating because the pleasure insures that we will continue to engage in the survival-promoting behavior of eating. By the same token, we try to avoid the unpleasant sensations of hunger because it signals a threat to our survival. Mood states function in a similar manner to direct us toward survival-enhancing patterns of behavior.

If an individual suddenly discovers that they possess the winning lottery ticket and that they are now in possession of a huge sum of money, they will immediately experience a surge in serotonergic activity and a flood of stress hormones. Their subjective state will be one of euphoria, and they will have extremely high levels of energy. This will be partly due to the serotonin, but also a result of the stress hormones, which they experience as a state of elated excitement. This elevation in energy will enable them to utilize this sudden flood of resources. Whereas before, a simple trip to the local grocery store would have been perceived as tiring, the same individual now can shop twenty hours of the day without experiencing any fatigue. Compare this behavior with that of the individual who has just experienced a traumatic loss. For example, they have just been fired from their job. This individual will experience a sudden decrease in serotonergic activity and their system will also be flooded with stress hormones. In the case of this individual, the stress hormones will not cause them to feel elation and excitement, but rather anxiety, apprehension, and nervousness. The low serotonin activity will be subjectively experienced as a state of depression. Once the initial rush of stress hormones has diminished, the individual will experience a general state of depression. They will feel lethargic and possess very low levels of energy. In the ancestral hominids such a depressed state may have had an adaptive function. The individual who found his or herself at the fringe of the group, with very low social rank, would have benefited from conserving energy as much as possible since they would have been last in line for any food resources that came available. They also would have been less likely to challenge higher-ranking individuals in the group and thus would have avoided potentially harmful conflict. This depressive state may no longer have such an adaptive role in the modern world in which we live. A state of profound lethargy may prevent the individual who has just lost a job from actively seeking another job. (Of course, it should be noted that depression has a complex etiology, and the evolutionary explanation is only one part of the etiology.)

Special pharmaceutical drugs, which work by blocking the re-uptake of serotonin, were discovered to have a mood elevating effect on individuals suffering from severe depression. Selective serotonin re-uptake inhibitors (SSRIs), such as the brands Prozac, Zoloft, and Paxil, became very popular in therapeutic usage many years before the function of serotonin was well understood. Early popular books about such drugs such as *Listening to Prozac* (Kramer, 1993) advocated the use of these drugs for people who were shy and felt intimidated in the work place. In light of the evidence for the role of serotonin and status functioning, this advice seems particularly credible. However, analogous to drugs that numb our sensitivity to physical pain and therefore make us more vulnerable to injury, the SSRIs may have hidden dangers. The use of Prozac and similar drugs may induce a subjective state that mimics that of a high-status individual. Being highly self-directed and fairly oblivious to other people may work well for a truly high-ranking individual, but for a low-ranking individual to feel and act this way may prove problematic if not disastrous. For example, the SSRI-using employee that habitually ignores his or her boss and to modify work activities according to whim may become unemployed.

Psychiatrist Russell Gardner described a patient of his who was able to advance her career presumably because of her treatment regimen of Prozac (1998). While this is the case with some individuals, Gardner pointed out that human beings as a whole do not rise in status automatically as a result of using SSRIs. The vervet monkeys studied by Raleigh and McGuire did rise in social rank as a result of this type of pharmaceutical intervention, but in humans the interaction appears to be more complex. A host of biochemical factors including numerous neurotransmitters, reproductive hormones, and stress hormones are all effected by changes in social status. Of these biochemical factors, serotonin is probably the one that is most central in its relation to status functioning. However, it seems doubtful that even in great apes could the manipulation of serotonin effect dominant status. In chimpanzees, for example, the cognitive complexities are already on a scale that probably precludes simple manipulation of dominance rank through a single neurotransmitter.

Testosterone

The male reproductive hormone testosterone has also been shown to be intimately linked to dominance rank (Mazur & Lamb 1980; Pusey, Williams, & Goodall 1997). In chickens exogenous manipulation of testosterone levels via injection can result in the elevation in rank of the injected animals (Allee, Collias & Lutherman 1939). In primates, despite the fact that testosterone levels are positively correlated with dominance rank, active manipulation of testosterone levels does not result in change of social rank. In a study by Gordon, Rose, Grady, and Berstein (1979), injections of testosterone in a free-ranging group of rhesus monkeys failed to produce changes of rank in the dominance hierarchy. The testosterone injections did result in an increase of general levels of activity. Therefore, animals that typically engaged in fighting did more fighting, animals that habitually engaged in grooming did more grooming, and animals typically engaged in mating did more mating. The relationship between testosterone and dominance rank is more indirect than the serotonin relationship discussed earlier. When an individual acquires high dominance rank, it is presented more mating opportunities which in turn seem to produce the greater production of testosterone. Studies of nonhuman primates support this idea that testosterone rise is situational and only indirectly related to dominance rank. One primary function of testosterone is to elevate spermatogenesis, clearly a necessary function for successful mating and reproduction. The secondary effects of testosterone are to increase muscle mass and possibly prime adult males for successful aggressive encounters. Nonhuman primate studies have also shown that aggressive encounters tend to elevate testosterone levels. Investigations into the link between testosterone and aggression have shown that the relationship is very indirect.

A study by Ehrenkranz, Bliss, and Sheard (1974) measured testosterone levels in a group of prison inmates. While it was found that criminals convicted of violent crimes had high testosterone levels, another group with comparable testosterone levels consisted of nonviolent, socially dominant criminals. The prisoners with the lowest testosterone levels were the nonviolent, nondominant individuals. When testosterone levels were measured in humans prior to and after athletic competition (tennis matches and college wrestling bouts), it was found that evenly matched competitors would experience a surge in testosterone just before the match. Following the match, the loser would experience a drop in testosterone level and the winner would experience a surge in testosterone level (Elias, 1981; Mazur & Lamb, 1980). When victory was by a very slim margin and neither contestant experienced a clear triumph then both parties experienced a drop in testosterone level. This same effect has also been documented in sports fans observing their favorite team in an athletic competition. If their team wins they experience a surge in testosterone level, and if their team loses they experience a drop in testosterone level (Ellis, 1993). Among a group of medical school seniors, a study showed that when they passed their final exam they also experienced a surge in testosterone level. A simple adaptationist explanation of these results would be that testosterone facilitates the aggressive physical tendencies necessary to compete for higher status, or upon achieving high status to maintain that position against potential usurpers. The other role of testosterone is to facilitate the reproductive behavior that is associated with the greater mating opportunities made available to the dominant males in the group.

The role of testosterone in females is not as well studied. Although young women have a much lower percentage of testosterone in their blood plasma than men of comparable age, they are proportionately more sensitive to its effects (Hoyenga, 1993). Presumably, the role of testosterone in women may be similar to its role in men. Testosterone may prime an individual for upward mobility in the social strata. Studies of both human and nonhuman primates indicate that female dominance hierarchies display much more cooperation between individuals and much less conflict and competition than do male hierarchies (Cronin, 1980).

Stress Hormones

Social status is also directly linked to levels of stress hormones. Studies of nonhuman primates consistently show that low-status animals have elevated levels of stress hormones such as adrenocorticotropic hormone (ACTH) and cortisol compared to higher-ranking animals (Botchin, Kaplan, Manuck, Mann, 1994; Suomi, Scanlan, Rasmussen, Davidson, Boinski, Higley, Marriott, 1989). A study by Gust, Gordon, Hambright, and Wilson (1993) showed that stress-hormone levels were negatively correlated with instances of affiliative behavior.

A function of stress hormones is to mobilize energy reserves in the body for a fight-flight situation. When this response kicks in, heart rate increases, blood pressure goes up, and blood is selectively pumped to the large muscle groups of the body. At the same time, the blood supply decreases to the reproductive organs, the digestive tract, and other noncritical (in terms of fight-flight functioning) organs in the body. Systems such as digestion and reproduction, although critical to individual and genetic survival, are put on hold until the emergency has passed. Those organisms that continued to invest energy into the digestion of food during an emergency were less likely to survive than those who selectively diverted their energies to coping with the physical emergency. Seen from this perspective we can understand why the effects of chronic stress are so devastating. The sole function of the stress response is to help you overcome a physical emergency. Natural selection can be seen as a very short-sided or actually sightless process. The animal that does not successfully fight or flee does not contribute to the subsequent generation.

One system that is turned off by the fight or flight response is the immune system. This is fine if the emergencies are few and far between. But, as Selye (1956) observed, if the stress is chronic and persistent the results can be fatal. In a study by Bower (1997) it was shown that rhesus monkeys that were of low status exhibited lower body weights, higher rises in stress hormones, and significant reductions in immune cell function.

Sapolsky (1997) found a similar pattern in wild olive baboons. Many of the negative effects of chronic stress are due to the hormone cortisol. In the short term, cortisol mobilizes stored energy reserves into available fuel but its long-term over-production leads to muscle atrophy, hypertension and compromised immune and reproductive systems. For the fight-flight response to be maximally effective, cortisol secretion should be low except when a highly threatening situation occurs. Sapolsky found this to be true of the dominant male baboons. The dominant animals had lower baseline levels of cortisol than subordinates but a larger and faster rise in cortisol when confronted with a stressor. Moreover, Sapolsky found that this difference in physiology was primarily a function of dominance rank. As long as an animal occupied a top position in the hierarchy it displayed a healthy, efficient pattern of physiological responses. However, if the same animal fell significantly in dominance rank its physiological profile came to resemble the impaired pattern typical of low-ranking baboons.

Among humans individuals of lower social economic status are more prone to a variety of health problems and have shorter life expectancies than those of higher social economic status (Brunner, 1997; Stronks, van de Mheen, Looman, & Mackenbach, 1998). Moreover, higher-ranking individuals, including humans, are generally better able to cope with stressful situations than lower-status individuals. In a study by Rejeski, Gagne, Parker, and Koritnik (1989) human subjects were assessed on their dominance status and then subjected to a debate with a trained technician in order to provide a stressor. It was found that the subordinate subjects experienced greater heart rate activity and lower testosterone levels compared with those who were assessed as higher in dominance. With the evolution of dominance hierarchies, it would appear that natural selection has stacked the deck for "the rich to get richer and the poor to get poorer." Dominant individuals are happier, healthier, and typically live longer than their subordinate counterparts. Non-human primates not only inherit genes that facilitate the acquisition of dominant status, but they also inherit status as a result of the families into which they are born. In most groups of rhesus monkeys, for example, the alpha male happens to be born to the alpha female in the matriarchy. In humans the direct inheritance of status is, of course, even more probable. Bequeathing titles, lands, and other material possessions has long been a part of our codified legal system. Humans not only inherit high status as a consequence of their cultural birthright, they also typically inherit many of the traits that promote the acquisition of high status. Moreover, such individuals are primed by their early experiences (ontogeny) to develop behavioral tendencies consistent with a high-status mode of functioning.

When ancient humans abandoned the hunter-gatherer life, they also abandoned the natural checks and balances that prevented any one individual from gaining too much power. Once it becomes possible for individuals to stockpile resources such as land and livestock, the uniquely human cultural characteristic of material inheritance comes into play. Wealth and power are not limited to what one individual can acquire in a lifetime but can, through bequeathal to younger kin, snowball across an unlimited number of generations. Left unchecked, human societies may tend to spontaneously produce despotic rulers who produce large-scale suffering for their people. The first six civilizations provide an illustration of this (Betzig, 1993), as do most civilizations that have followed. Fortunately, evolution acting in a social context has also produced some countervailing tendencies. These tendencies, in fact, form the basis for some of our highest and noblest human ideals.

The Evolution of Compassion

On August 16, 1996, at the Brookfield Zoo in Brookfield, Illinois, a three-year-old boy somehow got over a three-foot stone and bamboo barrier and fell 24 feet to the cement floor of the gorilla enclosure. The compound contained six gorillas. One of them, a female named Binti-Jua, approached the boy and picked him up in her arms. Zoo visitors looked on with trepidation, but Binti protected the toddler as if he were her own child. Keeping other gorillas at bay, she gently carried him across the compound and laid him in front of the entrance where paramedics and zoo officials were waiting. The child suffered a broken hand, some abrasions, and a concussion, but would eventually completely recover from these injuries. The story was carried by news media throughout the world. A theme that was commonly repeated in many of the stories was to describe the actions of Binti as amazingly human. The irony of calling Binti's behavior amazingly human was not lost on primatologists or other scientists investigating animal behavior. Given the fact that Binti had been socialized to the presence of humans during her entire life, and that she was the mother of a 17-month-old daughter, her actions were what one would have predicted. Even without human socialization, it would not have been that unusual for Binti to respond as she did. Maternal nurturance is elicited by similar cues across many different mammalian species. This similarity of the cues is of course increased within the different primate species. When we consider the fact that Binti's ancestors diverged from our own a mere seven to nine million years ago, her actions appear even less strange than the media would have had us believe. In the following sections we will explore the thesis that human virtues such as compassion are derived from our animal nature.

Kin Selection and Altruism

When one individual performs a seemingly selfless service for another individual for no benefit and sometimes at risk to itself, altruism is said to have occurred. The paradox that altruism can be found in almost all animal societies was resolved by Hamilton's (1963) theory of kin selection, which was described in Chapter 1. Kin selection or inclusive fitness shows that individuals within a species can best enhance their own reproductive success by aiding their close relatives, so long as the gain conferred on the recipient is much greater than the cost to the donor. This idea is formalized mathematically in the equation $K > 1/r$. For selection of altruistic genes to occur, K must be greater than the reciprocal of r, where r equals the coefficient of relationship of the recipient to the altruist. Because full siblings have

$r = \frac{1}{2}$, an animal will suffer no loss in reproductive fitness if it sacrifices its own life to save the lives of two of its siblings.

One puzzle in biology that was resolved by Hamilton's formulation was why hymenopterons (bees, wasps, and ants) comprise 11 of the 12 groups that evolved true sociality in insects (Wilson, 1975). Truly social or eusocial insects are characterized by three traits: (1) conspecific individuals cooperate in caring for the young; (2) nonreproductive individuals work on the behalf of reproductive nest-mates; (3) offspring assist parents during some period of their life cycle. The reason hymenopteron insects (bees, wasps, and ants) have a near monopoly on eusociality is because of their peculiar reproductive genetics. In the hymenoptera, unfertilized eggs develop into males, hence they have only one set of chromosomes which is termed haploid. Fertilized eggs develop into females, thus they have two sets of chromosomes (diploid). Haplodiploidy is a fairly rare mode of reproduction and is found in only a few arthropod groups, other than the hymenoptera.

It is this unusual form of reproduction that primed the hymenopteras to evolve complex social systems (Wilson, 1975). In the hymenoptera, the coefficient of a relationship among sisters is three-quarters, whereas between mother and daughter, it is one-half. This is because the sisters received all of the paternal genes, but only, on average, one-half of the maternal genes that were contributed by their parents. Because of this pattern of a relatedness, a female's genetic self-interest is best served by helping her mother rear her younger sisters, rather than investing in the rearing of her own offspring. The haplodiploidy reproductive pattern also predicts that hymenopteron males should behave in a very selfish fashion. This is exactly the behavior displayed by the drones in bee colonies, which perform no work and are highly competitive with other males during mating times.

The only non-hymenopteron eusocial insects are termites. Termites follow the more common diploid pattern of reproduction. In diploid species, males and females have the same patterns of relatedness. Inclusive fitness theory predicts that termite males should be workers rather than drones. This is indeed the case. Termite males constitute approximately one-half of the worker force and are just as altruistic as their sisters (Wilson, 1975). As to why the termites were the only diploid insects to develop eusociality, the answer probably lies in their unusual feeding and digestive behavior. Termites depend on symbiotic intestinal protozoans to enable them to digest the wood that they consume. The protozoans are passed from older termites to younger individuals by anal feeding, an arrangement that necessitates a low level of social behavior. This pattern of behavior can be considered a form of nurturance.

In vertebrate species, cooperative and altruistic forms of behavior probably evolved from basic patterns of parental nurturance. In vertebrate species as a whole, the level of social organization is generally directly related to the level of parental investment. In reptiles, for example, parental care is generally poorly developed or nonexistent, and the same can be said of their social behavior. The crocodilian species, however, form an exception to this general reptilian pattern

(Ross & Garnett, 1989). Alligators and crocodiles build nests for their eggs and fiercely guard them until the time of their hatching. They then assist the hatchlings down to the water, sometimes carrying them in their steel-trap jaws, and they remain with their young ones until they have grown to sufficient size to be relatively safe from predators. Social development is also correspondingly complex in these animals. They have a complex system of vocal and postural communication and form dominance hierarchies where individuals recognize other individuals.

In birds, parental investment is an absolute necessity among all species, and most bird species display fairly complex forms of social development (Wilson, 1975). Individual birds in many species will cooperate to drive away predators, in a behavior called mobbing. Numerous species also nest together in a communal fashion, which serves to lower predation rates. Many of the earlier studies of territorial communication and dominance behavior were done on avian species. One of the better examples of animal altruistic behavior is avian cooperative breeding, in which more than one pair of adults join at the same nest to rear young together. In many bird species, certain kin of nesting individuals will assist in raising the young of others, without laying eggs of their own.

In mammals, parental investment reaches a new level of involvement. By definition, mammals are creatures whose young must feed on the body secretions (milk) of their maternal parent. This necessitates a pattern of intimate physical contact between infant and mother that does not exist in nonmammalian species. When your pet dog licks your hand, he is conveying a message of affection. This signal has been co-opted from the association between early oral behavior involved in nursing and mother-infant affiliation.

In mammals, the altruism that was directed from parents to offspring could easily evolve to be directed at other related individuals. Hamilton's inclusive fitness theory predicts that altruism among animals will correspond directly to the degree of relatedness among these animals. Studies of ground squirrels (Sherman, 1977, 1980) have shown that the degree of altruism displayed between individual ground squirrels is structured along a gradient of relatedness. Studies conducted by Rushton (1989) suggest that humans have the ability to detect and choose individuals genetically similar to themselves, even among nonrelatives. A study by Judge and Hrdy (1992) showed that the inheritance of accumulated resources among kin was directly related to the degree of genetic relatedness. Inclusive fitness, or kin selection theory, also explains the occurrence of avuncular relationships in some societies. In these societies, the maternal uncle plays a greater role in raising a child than the husband of the mother. The biological father has 50% of his genes in common with his biological child, whereas the uncle has only about 25% in common with a niece or nephew. If paternity is certain, then inclusive fitness theory predicts it should be the father investing in the child, not the uncle. The avuncular relationship should only occur in societies where there is a high incidence of adultery, and as a result, paternity is a very uncertain issue. This is exactly the pattern that is found empirically (Alexander, 1974; Hartung, 1985).

Reciprocal Altruism.   Although kin selection theory answered a number of questions, it did not explain all cases of altruistic behavior. Humans and many other species have been observed to perform selfless and oftentimes risky services for totally unrelated individuals. Darwin, in his book *The Descent of Man,* argued that altruism would develop when reasoning and foresight had evolved to the point that individuals understood that their benevolent acts for others could work to their advantage when the assisted individuals returned the favor. Williams (1966) pointed out that a system of mutual reciprocation would evolve as long as it was favored by natural selection, and that conscious reasoning ability was not a necessary factor. Wright (1994) makes Williams' basic point in the following statement, "Animals, including people, often execute evolutionary logic, not via conscious calculation, but by following their feelings, which were designed as logic executers." The theory of reciprocal altruism was formally developed by Trivers in a paper titled the "Evolution of Reciprocal Altruism" (1971). In this paper, Trivers argued that friendship, moralistic aggression, gratitude, sympathy, trust, suspicion, guilt, dishonesty and hypocrisy can all be explained as adaptations that facilitate the functioning of the highly evolved altruistic system of humans.

To support the logic of his premise, Trivers used a decision-making game called Prisoner's Dilemma. In this game, two partners in crime have been arrested and taken to separate cells for interrogation. The state lacks the evidence to convict them of the major offense, but does have enough evidence to convict them on a lesser charge, for a prison term of one year. The prosecutor, wanting a conviction for the major crime, makes the following offer to each prisoner. He says to each of them in turn, "If you confess, but your partner doesn't, I'll let you go scot-free, and use your testimony to put your partner away for ten years. If you don't confess, but your partner does, you go to prison for ten years. If you confess, and your partner also confesses, I'll put both of you in prison for three years." For the players, the game poses the dilemma of selfish individual gain (betraying your fellow prisoner) versus altruistic action (cooperating with your fellow prisoner and not confessing). If one player betrays the other, his prison time can be zero years or three years depending on the action of the other player. Betrayal yields an average payoff of one and one-half years. If the player cooperates by not confessing he gets either one year of prison time or 10 years. Cooperation yields an average payoff of five and one-half years. Clearly betrayal is the best strategy for maximizing self-interest, at least for a one-time only situation. However, optimal strategies change dramatically when the game is played several times with one player. This version is called the Iterated Prisoner's Dilemma.

In the 1970s, Axelrod created a computer program based on the Iterated Prisoner's Dilemma. This program simulated a small society, with several dozen regularly interacting individuals. Axelrod invited experts in game theory to submit computer programs embodying specific strategies for the prisoner's dilemma. He then allowed these programs to intermingle in cyberspace, and see which one had the advantage. The winning program was called TIT FOR TAT. On the first encounter with another program, it would invariably cooperate. Thereafter, however, it would do whatever the other program had done on the previous encounter, hence the name TIT FOR TAT. Not only was TIT FOR TAT the winning program, it was also, by far, the simplest, in terms of lines of the computer code of any of the programs submitted. If TIT FOR TAT does represent a real-world behavior strategy for living organisms, its simplicity suggests that it could have been readily cobbled together by random mutation and natural selection. The TIT FOR TAT strategy suggests that the reciprocal altruism can be highly adaptive, provided that adequate policing mechanisms are in place. Trivers (1991) mentioned some of the forms these policing mechanisms might take. They include moralistic aggression against noncooperative behavior, a sense of justice, and a capacity for detecting deceit. As discussed in Chapter 3, Cosmides and Tooby (1992) amassed empirical evidence for the existence of specialized cognitive mechanisms to detect violations of social contracts. These mechanisms they call cheater detectors. Mealy (1993) found evidence for the existence of selective memory for faces of cheaters.

Nonhuman primates exhibit extremely sophisticated abilities to display emotions and to respond to the emotional displays of other individuals. Neurological studies show that there are specialized brain regions in primates (e.g., inferior temporal lobe, amygdala) that specialize in the recognition of faces. (Brothers, 1990). Studies looking at the social behavior of these animals, indicate that monkeys and apes are very adept at interpreting social signals in order to assess the motivations of others. Brothers (1989) suggests that the emotional communication in primates reached such a state of sophistication that it provided the basis for empathy. Empathic ability would greatly facilitate some forms of altruistic behavior.

Once the evolutionary threshold for reciprocal altruism had been crossed, the complex forms of cognition necessary for establishing and maintaining it became extremely vital to survival. These cognitive specializations for reciprocal altruism include the ability to predict the behavior of others, to manipulate it, and to detect attempts by others to manipulate oneself. Empirical evidence has shown that chimpanzees and some of the other great ape species probably engage in a form of mental state attribution, sometimes referred to as theory of mind. (Heyes, 1994). Theory of mind refers to the idea that one individual sees another individual as experiencing a mental state, and, as a consequence, can make accurate predictions about the other individual's behavior, given information regarding the other individual's experiences.

Altruistic behavior directed toward near kin undoubtedly provided the springboard for reciprocal altruism to develop within social species. For most of the period of hominid evolution, group sizes undoubtedly remained relatively small. Each individual could keep track of whether an unrelated or distantly related individual reciprocated favors that were given. Over the last 10,000 years, however, human group sizes have grown increasingly large. It is possible that there has been some selective pressure for the evolution of an unconscious ability to assess the probability of a stranger reciprocating a favor. Thompson (1980) has presented an equation that expresses the benefits and costs of altruistic behavior in terms of relative reproductive rates, which are then multiplied by probabilities of reciprocation between donors and recipients of altruism. According to Thompson, his mathematical model predicts that as the probability of reciprocation decreases, the probability of the performance of an altruistic act also decreases. To support the validity of his theory, he cites evidence of the covariance of crime rate with size of urban place. In other words, the increase in crime in larger urban populations is explained as a result of the low probability of a situation reversal occurring between donors of altruistic behavior and their recipients. This low benefit-cost ratio of altruistic behavior reduces the cost of crime to criminals, and so increases the crime rates.

The concept of crime itself is a uniquely human idea made possible by our use of language and existence of culture. As humans, we have taken our natural behavioral tendencies toward altruism, reciprocal altruism, and the policing of reciprocal altruism, and have structured rules, laws and moral codes around them.

Universal Morality and Ethics.   Studies of nonhuman primates, particularly of chimpanzees, suggest that complex systems of reciprocal altruism developed in our ancestors long before the emergence of language and culture. In fact, reciprocal altruism may have played an important role in the evolution of language and cultural capacities. There was probably a long period of synergistic coevolution between all of these capacities. It may be impossible for us to ever fully understand the evolutionary process that has resulted in our present day complexity. We do know, however, that language and culture allow us to take these evolved adaptations that promote cooperation as well as the detection and punishment of noncooperation and give them an abstract reality that has never existed previously. What were once simply individual impulses to certain actions became laws and codes of conduct that were passed from generation to generation via oral traditions. As soon as these codes of conduct were subject to cultural transmission, a new level of natural selection could begin operating. Cultural beliefs that fostered maladaptive consequences could be replaced by more adaptive cultural beliefs extremely quickly. Genetic mutations cannot be called forth on demand, nor are they likely to be useful once they appear. The vast majority of them are very maladaptive. On the other hand, ideas are tailor made to address specific problems and they can be generated and transmitted (through language) in a matter of seconds.

The quantum difference in rates of cultural evolution compared to biological evolution often results in a large schism between the two. Throughout human history and prehistory, various societies have served as large-scale laboratories for the testing of new ideas. Some of the more radical attempts to revise the codes of conduct (i.e., morals, laws and ethical concerns of a society) were totally divorced from any considerations of human nature. For example, communist ideology has traditionally had a strong intellectual appeal, but the application of this ideology to human societies has been, generally, spectacularly unsuccessful. Communism is an ideal form of government but only for social insects not human primates. The failure and collapse of unfit social systems is illustrative of cultural evolution proceeding via a process of natural selection. Unfortunately, natural selection can be a highly wasteful and even horrible (when viewed from a human perspective) process. For this reason, many scientists, philosophers and other academics have advocated that we construct new codes of conduct for our society based on the scientific understanding of the biological nature of human beings.

A quick perusal of books that have appeared on this topic in recent years and their authors give an indication of the interest this topic has produced in individuals from a diversity of disciplines. From the field of philosophy, come the following works: *Darwin's Dangerous Idea: Evolution and the Meaning of Life* (Dennett, 1995), *The Secret Chain: Evolution and Ethics* (Brandie, 1994), *The Biology and Psychology of Moral Agency* (Rottschaefer, 1998) and *From a Biological Point of View: Essays on Evolutionary Philosophy* (Sober, 1994). Representing the field of law is *Law and the Mind: Biological Origins of Human Behavior* (Gruter, 1991). From psychology comes *A New Morality from Science: Beyondism* (Cattell, 1972). Biologists have made the following contributions: *The Biology of Moral Systems* (Alexander, 1987), *The Origins of Virtue* (Ridley, 1996), *On Human Nature* (Wilson, 1978), and *Consilience: The Unity of Knowledge* (Wilson, 1998). From anthropology come: *The Imperial Animal* (Tiger & Fox, 1971), *Optimism: The Biology of Hope* (Tiger, 1979) and *Manufacture of Evil: Ethics, Evolution in the Industrial System* (Tiger, 1991). There are also books that compile the essays of authors from a swath of disciplines such as *Investigating the Biological Foundations of Human Morality* (Hurd, 1996).

To a greater or lesser extent, the authors in all of these works not only explain human behavior in terms of evolutionary adaptations, they also attempt to devise new systems of moral and ethical conduct for modern human society. Devising codes of conduct that mesh with our biological nature is a logically sound and appropriate enterprise. Unfortunately, many of these authors have unnecessarily created an underlying weakness in their arguments. They have made basic assumptions about evolution and the nature of the universe that go beyond the scientific evidence. Those assumptions go something like this: There's nothing beyond the physical universe, everything that happens is the result of basic physical laws, and evolution is a result of the interaction between these physical laws and random events; therefore the existence of life, mind, and consciousness are merely accidents with no higher meaning or purpose. This basic assumption of meaninglessness creates the paradox of a creature who has no real higher purpose striving to create a meaningful code of conduct for his fellow purposeless humans. As Cartmill (1998) points out, beliefs of this type are nothing but beliefs and they go beyond the scope of what can be determined by science. Many evolutionary psychology writers take the neurobiological view described by Crick (1994):

> A modern neurobiologist sees no need for the religious concept of a soul to explain the behavior of humans and other animals. One is reminded of the question Napoleon asked after Pierre-Simons Laplace had explained to him the workings of the solar system: Where does God come into all this? To which Laplace replied, "Sire, I have no need of that hypothesis." Not all neuroscientists believe that the idea of the soul is a myth—Sir John Eccles is the most notable exception—but certainly the majority do. It is not that they can yet prove the idea to be false. Rather, as things stand at the moment, they see no need for that hypothesis. (Crick, 1994; p. 6–7)

Crick makes the important point that the ideas have not been proven false. In short, lack of proof does not constitute proof of lack. However, many scientists appear to proceed as though it does, maintaining that there is nothing but the physical universe and the physical laws operating in it. While this may seem to be an apparent truth to many, there are those who disagree and who can offer their own evidence to the contrary. An important point to remember is that neither side has definitive proof of their argument. The hard-line, atheistic stance of many neuroscientists and evolutionary psychologists is basically a belief system.

If we can develop codes of conduct that take into account both the strengths and shortcomings of our biological nature we may be able to lessen or even eliminate many of the problems that currently plague our societies. However, most people will find it difficult to accept these new codes of conduct if they are tied to a belief system that argues that life is a meaningless accident without purpose. If proponents of evolution based moral/ethical systems stay within the bounds of what can be supported by science and leave their personal beliefs aside, their ideas will be much more palatable to the general public and more likely to be adopted.

Summary

Dominance hierarchies arise in group living organisms to minimize the aggression that occurs between individuals competing for limited resources. Because high social rank confers ready access to available resources, a tendency toward upward social striving has been strongly selected for. Primates, in particular, have also evolved high levels of social intelligence to facilitate this upward mobility.

The evolution of humans is complicated by the fact that our remote ancestors lived in dominance hierarchies but during the Pleistocene Era, the social structure was egalitarian to facilitate a hunter-gatherer existence. With the advent of agriculture it became possible for individuals to monopolize resources and centralize power allowing the emergence of a new type of dominance hierarchy.

At a proximate physiological level, functioning within a dominance hierarchy is mediated by the neurotransmitter, serotonin. When an individual primate moves up in social rank, there is an increase in serotonin activity raising motor tempo and creating an upbeat mood state. When there is a drop in social rank, serotonin activity decreases along with motor tempo facilitating the conservation of resources. Selective serotonin re-uptake inhibitors (SSRIs) treat depressive mood states by raising serotonin levels.

The male reproductive hormone, testosterone, also covaries with changes in social status. Higher-ranking individuals need higher levels of testosterone to facilitate increased mating opportunities and to make them better able to defend against challenges to their social ranks.

The stress hormones that mediate the fight-flight response are also integrally involved in the physiology of an organism living in dominance hierarchies. In high-ranking individuals, the release of stress hormones during critical situations generally enhances functioning. Conversely, in lower-ranking individuals, chronic stress appears to compromise physiological efficiency of the stress response and leads to health problems and shorter life expectancy. In human societies, cultural factors, such as the inheritance of material wealth often make it more difficult for low ranking individuals to ascend greatly in social rank.

Affiliative behaviors probably evolved in vertebrate, from basic patterns of parental nurturance. Kin selection theory suggests that the altruism that was directed from parents to offspring could easily evolve to be directed at other related individuals. Once groups living organisms had reached a certain level of complexity altruistic acts could be directed toward non-kin with the understanding that the assisted individuals would return to favor. Gratitude, sympathy, trust, suspicion, and guilt can be viewed as adaptation that facilitate the functioning of the highly evolved reciprocal altruism system of humans.

It has been suggested that we should develop codes of conduct that take into account our evolved psychologies in order to create a better society. However, many of the proponents of these biologically congruent systems of moral conduct have taken the scientifically unwarranted position that life and consciousness are mearly meaningless accidents with no higher purpose. As a result, the arguments for better moral systems are undermined at the onset and generally unpalatable to the public at large.

Discussion Questions _____

1. Dominance hierarchies have evolved independently in many unrelated groups of animals. This suggests that this type of social structure is one of the simplest and best solutions to a certain set of problems imposed by group living. Describe these problems, then try to think of an alternative social system that would also solve these problems. Would your system work with human societies? Could your system evolve in organisms that lacked culture?

2. How is an egalitarian society, like that of foraging humans, different from a communistic society like that of honey bees? How is it different from a human communistic society like Red China?

3. Discuss some of the biochemical events that typically occur in the physiology of a primate that moves up in social rank. Discuss the biochemical events that typically occur when a primate drops to a lower social rank.

4. In light of the fact that evolution must invariably select for genetic self-interest, how do you explain the often observed human behavior of risking one's life to go to the aid of complete strangers? Give an explanation that is encompassed by evolutionary theory.

Key Terms _____

adrenocorticotropic hormone (ACTH)	altruism	chromosomes (diploid)
alpha	avuncular relationships	conspecific
	biological evolution	cortisol

cultural evolution
dominant animal
dominance hierarchy
egalitarian
eusocial
fight-flight response
haploid
haplodiploidy
hormone

hymenoptera
inclusive fitness
kin selection
matriarchy
neurotransmitter
Prisoner's Dilemma
reciprocal altruism
selective serotonin re-uptake
   inhibitors (SSRIs)

serotonin
stress hormones
subordinate
testosterone
theory of mind
TIT FOR TAT
transitive reasoning

Additional Reading

A Darwinian Left: Politics, Evolution, and Cooperation by Peter Singer (2000).

Hierarchy in the Forest: The Evolution of Egalitarian Behavior by Christopher Boehm (2000).

Social Darwinism: Linking Evolutionary Thought to Social Theory by Peter Dickens (2000).

Natural Conflict Resolution by Filippo Aureli and Frans B. M. De Waal (Editors) (2000).

Primate Males: Causes and Consequences of Variation in Group Composition by Peter M. Kappler (Editor) (2000).

Cheating Monkeys and Citizen Bees: The Nature of Cooperation in Animals and Humans by Lee Dugatkin (1999).

Ethnic Conflicts Explained by Ethnic Nepotism by Tatu Vanhanen (1999).

Individual Strategy and Social Structure: An Evolutionary Theory of Institutions by H. Peyton Young (1998).

Foundations of Social Evolution (Monographs in Behavior & Ecology) by Steven A. Frank (1998).

Evolutionary Games and Population Dynamics by Josef Hofbauer, Karl Sigmund (1998).

Indoctrinability, Ideology and Warfare: Evolutionary Perspectives by Irenaus Eibl-Eibesfeldt and Frank K. Salter (Editors) (1998).

Grooming, Gossip, and the Evolution of Language by Robin Dunbar (1998).

Evolutionary Games and Equilibrium Selection by Larry Samuelson (1998).

Homicide by Martin Daly and Margo Wilson (1988).

Guns, Germs, and Steel: The Fates of Human Societies by Jared Diamond (1997).

The Complexity of Cooperation: Agent-Based Models of Competition and Collaboration by Robert Axelrod (1997).

Aggression and Violence: Genetic, Neurobiological, and Biosocial Perspectives by David M. Stoff and Robert B. Cairns (Editors) (1996).

The Winner-Take-All Society: Why the Few at the Top Get So Much More Than the Rest of Us by Robert H. Frank, Philip J. Cook (1996).

Beloved Enemies: Our Need for Opponents by David Philip Barash (1994).

Coalitions and Alliances in Humans and Other Animals by Alexander H. Harcourt and Frans B. M. De Waal (1992).

Human Territorial Functioning: Empirical, Evolutionary Perspective on Individual and Small Group Territorial Cognitions, Behaviors, and Consequences by Ralph B. Taylor (1988).

Sociobiology and Conflict: Evolutionary Perspectives on Competition, Cooperation, Violence and Warfare by Johan M. G. Van Der Dennen and V. Falger (1990).

Evolutionary Politics by Glendon Schubert (1989).

Territorial Cognitions, Behaviors, and Consequences by Ralph B. Taylor (1988).

Deception: Perspectives on Human and Nonhuman Deceit (Suny Series in Animal Behavior) by Robert W. Mitchell and Nicholas S. Thompson (1986).

Evolution and the Theory of Games by John Maynard Smith (1982).

Biology and Freedom: An Essay on the Implications of Human Ethology by Samuel Anthony Barnett (1989).

Toward a New Philosophy of Biology: Observations of an Evolutionist by Ernst W. Mayr (1989).

The Search for Society: Quest for a Biosocial Science and Morality by Robin Fox (1989).

On Human Nature by Edward O. Wilson (1988).

The Biology of Moral Systems by Richard D. Alexander (1987).

Ideas of Human Nature: From the Ghagavad Gita to Sociobiology by David P. Barash (1998).

Unto Others: The Evolution and Psychology of Unselfish Behavior by Elliott Sober and David Sloan Wilson (1998).

Biology and the Foundation of Ethics by Jane Maien-schein and Michael Ruse (Editors) (1999).

Sex and Death: An Introduction to Philosophy of Biology by Kim Sterelny and Paul E. Griffiths (1999).

Death, Hope, and Sex: Steps to an Evolutionary Ecology of Mind and Morality by James S. Chisholm (1999).

The Biology and Psychology of Moral Agency by William A. Rottschaefer (1998).

The Origins of Virtue: Human Instincts and the Evolution of Cooperation by Matt Ridley (1998).

8

Personality and Psychopathology

In the Timaeus, the creating God bestows the essential of the Soul, but it is the
divinities moving in the kosmos [the stars] that infuse the powerful affections
holding from Necessity our impulse and our desire, our sense of pleasure and
of pain, and that lower phase of the Soul in which such experiences originate.
By this statement our personality is bound up with the stars, whence our
Soul [as total of Principle and affections] takes shape; and we are set under
necessity at our very entrance into the world: our temperament will be of the
stars' ordering, and so, therefore, the actions which derive from temperament,
and all the experiences of a nature shaped to impressions.

—Plotinus (204–270), *Six Enneads*

Chapter Questions _____

1. What does personality mean to a psychologist and how is it studied?
2. How can the majority of personality traits be reduced to three factors or five
   factors?
3. How can many patterns of abnormal behavior including many personality
   disorders be explained in terms of adaptive evolution?

Personality can be roughly defined as a particular pattern of behaviors prevailing
across time and situations that differentiates one person from another. Psychologists who study personality are interested not only in describing the phenomena
of human similarities and differences, but also in understanding how much
change in personality is possible and how such change should be undertaken.

Evolutionary psychologists are interested in understanding personality as a quality that has influenced reproductive fitness. From this perspective, individual personality traits can be viewed in terms of their adaptive significance.

Personality is clearly a complex and abstract area. It is not an objective and definable substance, in the physical sense of the word, but instead is an empirical construct. It cannot be directly seen, only indirectly measured. While this problem is common in psychology, it is more problematic in personality research. Behaviors can be observed. Personality is abstracted from similarities in behaviors, introducing not only a level of vagueness but also an additional degree of abstraction. Assessing the adaptive significance of particular personality traits or even whole suites of personality traits is consequently highly problematic.

Early Personality Theorists

Psychology has a long and intertwined history that is closely linked with attempts at laying a foundation that is adequate for subsequent personality research. Perhaps the most famous theorist regarding the structure of personality is presently the psychiatrist Sigmund Freud (1856–1939) who wrote extensively on the development of abnormal behaviors (Boring, 1950). Freud and his adherents today use a clinical method of case study to determine what the functions and structure of normal personality are. This method is discussed in greater detail below. Many other theorists have used the case study method to illuminate the functions of normal personality. This tradition of uncritical observations, largely based on unsystematic observation of clinical cases, influenced the elaborate work of Freud and his followers (Prochaska & Norcross, 1994). It was also reflected in the work and clinical practices of descendents of this tradition who took a diverse path. These include Alfred Adler, Karl Jung, Karen Horney, and many of the existentialist and Gestaltist therapists and personality theorists.

The first empirical research program investigating personality probably should be credited to Darwin's cousin, Sir Francis Galton (1822–1911). Galton was a rare individual. He was a pioneer in statistics, genetics, meteorology, and in several areas of psychology (Boring, 1950). Among his contributions to the study of human behavior was an attempt to link physical attributes, such as body type, to different personality traits. Galton is credited with beginning an empirical approach to personality theory known as the London school (Eysenck, 1997). This influence, and the subsequent influence of the London school, continue to be important today. Moreover, he was among the first researchers to systematically attempt to measure behavioral and psychological variables, such as memory, intelligence, and performance (Boring, 1950). He was perhaps one of the first empirically oriented evolutionary psychologists.

At the heart of Galton's beliefs was the notion that individual differences in behavior were partly or largely inherited. This was a radical idea for nineteenth century scientists, who tended to believe that all complex human behavior was voluntary and influenced more by theological, i.e., moralistic, concerns. Galton also rejected the popular economic determinism that arose during his lifetime. This latter theory stated that people's behavior was largely shaped by their social class and other economic factors. The major proponent of this philosophy was the economist Karl Marx (Hergenhahn, 1997).

Galton's research strategy was cumbersome by present standards. He essentially believed that a large number of physical and mental measurements should be obtained and then correlated together (Hergenhahn, 1997). In fact, the early versions of the correlation coefficient, a common statistical tool, were pioneered by this many talented individual. Galton believed that traits or attributes that correlate highly probably have a common source or cause. This belief laid the ground for the statistical procedure known as factor analysis, which is a major tool of contemporary personality theory.

Galton also believed that most special abilities were most likely to be inherited (Hergenhahn, 1997). He was particularly concerned with intelligence. He developed a method for rating the genius or eminence of people and conversely developed a measure of the capacity of speakers to bore their audiences! Based on his studies he found a high relationship between biological closeness and intellectual functioning. Galton was also the first scientist to systematically investigate the study of twins and siblings. His research methodology was very similar to the modern psychological research laboratory. He used questionnaires to measure attitudes and ratings to measure an individual's view of herself and others' view of that person. His consistent emphasis was on individual differences, measurement, and heredity. This work was carried on through his student Karl Pearson (1857–1936), who refined Galton's methodology into what today is known as the Pearson product moment correlation. Galton's work on intelligence was further undertaken by British psychologist Charles Spearman (1863–1945), who postulated a theory of general intelligence that is not unlike the theory held by many present-day researchers (Sheehy, Chapman, & Conroy, 1997).

Contemporary Approaches to Personality Theory

Presently, there are a number of different paradigms or theory building methods in personality inquiry. Each has its strengths and weaknesses. Each has its lengthy history and strong adherents. Not all approaches, however, are of equal value to the scientifically oriented student of human behavior.

The Case-Study Research Paradigm: The Clinical Approach to Personality

Clinical or case-study approaches to personality were popularized in psychiatry and psychology by Freud and his followers. They involve the in-depth and systematic study of individuals. Findings from specific people are often extrapolated and general principles of personality are then hypothesized. The clinical method can often be useful in suggesting theories. A beneficial way to test theories may be to see if they have explanatory power with the clinical cases that generate the most interest. However, the clinical approach has its scientific limits. It may exaggerate the importance of statistical outliers, or people with personality traits that are far from the average. Often, it artificially separates extremes of personality, which are assumed pathological or impaired, from normal personality functioning. Because it is developed in regard to clinical cases, it usually ignores normal functioning. Too often, it gives us very little testable theory. However, many contemporary scientific personality theorists recognize some value in the clinical/case-study approach. They use this approach to illuminate and strengthen their current theories, rather than to build specific bodies of theories. They may even use exceptions or clinical cases to suggest successful grounds for new theories.

Trait Theory

Francis Galton's influence is most pronounced in what is known as the nomothetic method of personality research (Hergenhahn, 1997). This is also known as trait theory, since the aim is to identify the underlying traits and link them with learning, physiological, and even processes. Here, researchers attempt to use statistical procedures to detect underlying traits of personality. Much of correlational research concerns itself with trait theory. Largely, much of the research also focuses on the statistical method that is intellectually a descendent from Galton's approach, that of *factor analysis,* which is described below.

A goal of trait theory is to *describe as much of personality as is possible with as few traits as is possible.* This is an example of the principle of scientific parsimoniousness that we have seen elsewhere (Cattell, 1965). It is important to realize that trait theorists do not believe that broad traits are sufficient to describe the complexities of human behavior (Eysenck, 1999). Trait theorists usually believe that broad traits, often referred to as types, exist as common factors in human personality. However, unique or less common factors of personality also exist and are important (Cattell, 1972). They combine with the common "super" factors to shape our behavior and furnish an adequate description of much, but not all, of personality (Eysenck, 1999). Some people are adequately described by their position on common traits, while other people often warrant description with unique personality descriptors (Costa & McCrae, 1998). As an example, most everyone knows someone who is obsessed with television. Broad personality traits would not likely include a description for this person, whose behaviors are centered on the quest for more TV watching.

Factor Analysis: A Major Tool of Correlational Research

This statistical method attempts to identify mathematical constructs that account for the relationship (or correlation) between the almost infinite number of personality traits. For example, a factor analysis might be performed on self-report ratings of personality from a group of several thousand. The procedure would indicate that people who believe that their personality is cheerful are also likely to report that they are talkative and somewhat impulsive. Factor analysis would mathematically relate these concepts and show how close they are in the population being sampled. The researcher then attempts to identify the most parsimonious, or briefest, explanation for the correlations that he finds. Items that correlate highly are assumed to have a common cause (Loehlin, 1992).

Technically, factor analysis is a set of procedures employing matrix algebra that maximizes description and variance explanation while reducing variable numbers. For our purposes, factor analysis can be best thought of as a procedure that gives us the structure of relationships between various pieces of data. We are able to "look inside" a single set of variables and attempt to assess the structure of the variables independently of any relationships they have outside of the data set. Factor analysis is a method of data reduction.

In a typical, contemporary, factor-analytic study, personality traits, such as talkativeness, assertiveness, and cheerfulness are correlated until they produce a first-order factor. These are mathematical constructs that are not statistically independent. In factor-analytic terms, they lack *orthogonality*. These first-order factors are then factor analyzed themselves, with the accompanying presupposition that they produce results that do not correlate. These second-order factors are called orthogonal, meaning they are statistically independent. The exact relationship between factors may be further clarified by a statistical procedure known as factor rotation, which often works to reduce ambiguity.

Not every factor-analytic theorist uses this identical procedure. Raymond Cattell (1905–1998), a well-known trait theorist, believed that it was theoretically proper to have factors correlate, since he believed that imposing orthogonality was an artificial constraint on the real world. For the most part, however, factor theorists attempt to maintain orthogonal factors. There is also some disagreement about types of factor rotations. Fortunately, most rotations produce approximately the same results, also known as factor loading.

Factor analysis has been severely criticized in the past. One complaint is that the results are limited by what goes into the study. This is a criticism of any scientific research. It is somewhat muted by developments in factor analysis which enable most thorough hypothesis testing. Initially, factor analysis was largely a method to generate hypotheses, which capitalized on chance relationships. Now, through what is called confirmatory factor analysis, we can specify what factors we expect to find and what their relationship will be. We can then test our model to see whether it is the best fitting for the data.

A second criticism is that the results may be more subjective than proponents wish to think. This may be one reason that the proponents of this method disagree regarding the number of factors that optimally represent human behavior. More current methodology, such as the use of confirmatory factor analysis, has reduced the subjectivity. There may also be more subjectivity than scientists wish to admit in our choices of rotational methods. Some of the disputes between personality theorists regarding factor structure are very technical and rely on different interpretations of some fairly sophisticated mathematical theorems. Perhaps because of these and other reasons, factor analytic theorists differ somewhat in the numbers and positions of the factors that they find.

The Three-Factor Model of Personality

Perhaps the most influential trait and factor analytic personality theorist is H. J. Eysenck (1916–1997), a controversial German immigrant to Britain. Eysenck, who not unlike Galton, made contributions to many areas, received training that was very much in the Spearman/Galton tradition. He performed some very early factor-analytic studies when the only tools available were a hand calculator. (What would take six or more months of difficult calculations can now be done in a matter of seconds with common computers and readily available programs!) He determined that much of the intercorrelation of the behavior of psychiatric patients could be explained by two "superfactors," or orthogonal second-order **neuroticism** and **extraversion.** This was a radical finding that allowed him to run afoul (one of many times) with the psychiatric establishment of his day.

Five years later, he added a third, more controversial factor, that of **psychoticism,** also known as insensitivity or tough mindedness. While the first two traits or factors emerge from almost every modern, factor-analytic study of personality, the third, psychoticism, is more controversial (Eysenck & Eysenck, 1985). It is the source of serious disagreement among factor-analytic personality theorists.

Regarding neuroticism or N, as it is called, people who score high on a test of N tend to be emotionally changeable. They are predisposed to anxiety and worry, to bodily aches, depression, and strong emotional reactions (Eysenck, 1999). It is postulated that differences in the limbic system, which are partly heritable, are responsible for differences on the dimension of N. Persons who are low on N have higher self esteem, are less tense, and less likely to feel guilt and moodiness. Most of us are in the middle of this normally distributed trait.

The trait of introversion extraversion (E) relates to differences in sociability and to aspects of impulsivity. Introverts tend to be more reserved, reflective, and quiet. More extraverted people tend to be more lively active, assertive, carefree, dominant and venturesome. These differences are hypothesized to be due to biological processes, specifically the ascending reticular activating system and the prefrontal areas of the brain (Eysenck & Eysenck, 1985). There is also evidence that introverts are more influenced by punishment where extraverts are more likely to be influenced by rewards. More than half of the variation in behavior due to this trait appears related to genetic factors.

Eysenck's dimension of psychoticism was the last to arrive and has proven the most problematic (Eysenck, 1999). It is proposed to be an underlying trait related to the susceptibility of being vulnerable to schizophrenia or other psychotic disorders. People who score high on it tend to be aggressive, cold, egocentric, impulsive and tough minded. They are also very creative. People who score low on this trait have the reverse characteristics, again, with most of us in the middle. This trait is believed to be highly inherited, primarily through serotonergic and dopaminergic systems (Zuckerman, 1999).

The Five-Factor Model of Personality

Most factor-analytically-oriented personality researchers believe that neuroticism and extraversion are broad factors that have important genetic and explanatory aspects. Researchers disagree on the rest of the variance in personality. During the past fifteen years the five-factor model (FFM) of personality has become immensely popular. This model concurs with Eysenck's that neuroticism and extraversion are important and separate constructs (Costa & McCrae, 1992). The model adds a new dimension: **openness to experience,** which relates to fantasy, aesthetics, feelings, and ideas. Furthermore, it splits the variance of psychoticism into two statistically independent factors of **conscientiousness,** which is a trait measuring organization, self discipline, and punctualness, and **agreeableness,** which measures trust and good naturedness as compared to cynicalness, suspiciousness and ruthlessness. Although there is some elaborate disagreement (Eysenck, 1999), many researchers now believes that it is more fruitful to adopt the working hypotheses that the five-factor model of personality represents a good picture of the structure of human personality traits. Evidence supporting this is that the five factors of personality show good agreement across diverse cultures (John, 1990).

Is there any way to determine which of the two conceptualizations, the three-factor or five-factor model, is "right"? Unfortunately, at this time, the answer is a hesitant no. The five-factor model may have more usefulness in describing some of the subtleties of human behavior. The three-factor model seems to have more biological and laboratory findings emphasizing its predictive accuracy. Future research will probably arbitrate the differences between these models.

Regardless, evidence also suggests that people are relatively stable on their positions on traits. There is good evidence for the longitudinal stability of traits from either the three- or five-factor models. This is true even if the traits are measured years apart (Costa & McCrae, 1998).

The correlational approach has a number of strengths. It is able to study a large number of variables and reduce them to meaningful smaller numbers. It is also able to specify the relationship of these variables and why correlations or patterns of association seem to emerge and are consistent. Yet, this approach has some serious problems. Among them is the fact that relationships are often only associational and not causal. Although this has been mediated somewhat by advances in the relatively new field of structural equation modeling, a procedure similar to confirmatory factor analysis, the criticism is a strong one and still holds.

Evolutionary Theory and Personality

In order for evolutionary theory to have some relevance or usefulness to the scientific study of personality and to psychopathology, discussed later, a number of facts may have to be true. Evolutionary psychology may be relevant if genetics are important in personality or psychopathology. Hereditability refers to the proportion of variance of a particular trait that is due to the contributions of multiple genes. The degree of hereditability seems to vary from trait to trait. Yet for both Eysenck's three factors and the big five factors it is approximately one-quarter to one-half. This means that genetics play a substantial, though not overwhelming role in the formation of a person's position on a particular trait.

Evolutionary psychology may also be important if it can be shown that our environment today is different from the ones in which inherited personality traits were shaped by natural selection. This latter finding may help explain behavioral problems. Finally, evolution may help explain some anomalies or quirks in personality functioning that are not otherwise explained by any of the other research methods or theories that are present.

The Adaptive Significance of Personality Traits

It is clear that in order for a trait to have survived, it must have had some degree of functionality. This suggests that shifting environmental pressures, particularly social ones, encouraged a range of variation on a number of traits (Buss, 1991). Furthermore, traits that were at one time adaptive, may be maladaptive in the present environment. We shall now examine the three- and five-factor models to discuss how they might have been adaptive.

Neuroticism is associated with the ability to perceive and respond to environmental warnings associated with impending punishment. Being elevated on this trait makes people more vulnerable to spurious and inappropriate contingencies associated with being too sensitive to future punishment. A person who scores high on this trait, for example, might be more likely to develop a phobia.

In some situations persons who score high on this trait would have a reproductive advantage. They might be more likely to avoid dangers. On the other hand, persons who scored low might be more likely to engage in reproductive behaviors that were accompanied by a risk. Males low in neuroticism could also gain reproductive advantage by engaging in high risk behaviors that increased their social status and consequently their level of attractiveness to females.

Extraversion or surgency is related to the need for cortical stimulation (Eysenck, 1997). People who are extraverted become more bored more quickly. They also demonstrate faster habituation to a stimulus, especially intense stimuli. Being extraverted might be reproductively advantageous in males by motivating them to mate with many different partners, a quantitative strategy. On the other hand, more introverted males may be likely to develop and sustain more material resources and invest these resources in a single mate which may confer a reproductive advantage by producing high-status offspring, a qualitative strategy.

Similarly, psychoticism is related to interpersonal aggressiveness, which conveys a reproductive advantage in adverse social situations and perhaps during war (Zuckerman, 1999). Persons who score high on the measure of psychoticism are more likely to be aggressive with other humans. Their sexual behavior is more likely to be nondiscriminatory, promiscuous, and perhaps forceful (Eysenck, 1976). Their capacity to grab resources, often to the exclusion of others, may give them a reproductive advantage. During war, they may be more likely to benefit from the plunders of an enemy's resources. They may aggress against others in order to mate.

There are many circumstances in which psychoticism might also be a reproductive disadvantage. Psychoticism (P) is associated with increasing criminality (Zuckerman, 1999). Being incarcerated for criminal behavior or ostracized by society probably limits reproductive advantages. P is also associated with bizarre and cold behaviors that make a person less attractive as a sexual partner than someone whose P is in a more typical range. Presumably, people with elevated psychoticism are less nurturing parents, which may reduce their reproductive advantage. Depending upon the specific circumstances, different levels of P produce different reproductive payoffs. Continuous fluctuations in social stability over time probably maintain a wide distribution of P scores throughout any given population.

Openness to experience may be widely distributed within a population because of the labile nature of social groups. As long as conditions remain constant there is an advantage in being conservative and closed to newness and outside influences, i.e., low openness. When conditions radically change, holding on to old customs and being closed to new ideas becomes a liability. Under rapidly changing conditions, the individual high in openness has the advantage. There is evidence that traits related to openness, such as novelty seeking, may be more prevalent in migratory societies or societies with a migratory history (Chen, Burton, Greenberger, & Dmitrieva, 1999). The long allele for dopamine D4 receptors (DRD4) has been linked to the trait of novelty seeking as well as hyperactivity. In a genetics study of 2,320 subjects from 39 populations, it was found that compared to sedentary populations, migratory populations showed a higher proportion of long alleles for DRD4. The correlation between long-distance group migration and the proportion of long alleles of DRD4 was .85 (see Figure 8.1).

The optimum level for conscientiousness and agreeableness probably depends upon the social environment. When social conditions are relatively stable, individuals high in these traits will be the ones most sought after as viable long-term mates. As we saw in the chapter on courtship and reproduction, both men and women rate these qualities very high in terms of what they are looking for in a long-term partner. These traits may be essential in maintaining a long-term pair bond. Relatively high conscientiousness and agreeableness may also be necessary for the kind of strongly nurturing parental investment required in rearing high quality offspring.

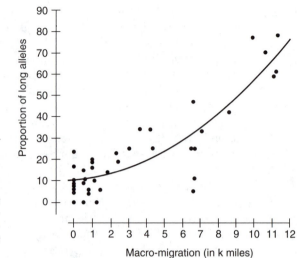

FIGURE 8.1 Scatter plot of proportion of long alleles for 39 populations by the distance of their macro-migration.

(Reprinted from "Population Migration and the Variation of Dopamine D4 Recept" by Chen, Burton, Greeberger, and Dmitieva, in *Evolution & Human Behavior*, 20(5), Fig. 1, p. 316, © 1999 by Elsevier Science; used by permission of Elsevier Science.)

Ashton, Paunonen, Helmes, and Jackson (1998) hypothesized that traits such as empathy and attachment mainly facilitate kin altruism, and traits such as forgiveness and nonretaliation mainly facilitate reciprocal altruism. In a study of 118 participants, it was found that the empathy/attachment factor (kin-based altruism) was related positively to agreeableness and negatively to emotional stability whereas the forgiveness/nonretaliation factor (reciprocal altruism) was positively correlated with both agreeableness and emotional stability.

Phylogeny and Ontogeny of Personality

What makes personality such an interesting area of research is not the fact that there is stability and consistency in behavior persisting across time and situations but rather the fact that these patterns vary from individual to individual. This variation between individuals within a species, in terms of behavior, may be at its peak within our own species but it exists throughout much of the animal kingdom. It may be that with the evolution of relatively complex behavior, consistent individual differences in behavior emerge as a corollary. A number of animal studies have demonstrated variation along the single dimension of a shy-bold continuum (Wilson, Clark, Coleman, & Dearstyne, 1994). This approach, however, may be too simplistic to capture the richness in individual variability present in many species, including some invertebrate species.

Mather and Anderson (1993) tested individual differences in adult octopuses (*Octopus rubescens*) under conditions of alerting, threat and feeding. A factor analysis of the resulting behaviors showed that these animals vary on three orthogonal dimensions—activity, reactivity, and avoidance. A study of stable individual behavior in stickleback fish (Huntingtonford, 1976) found the factors of curiosity and activity. In a study of personality in spotted hyenas (*Crocuta crocuta*) Gosling (1998)

BOX 8.1 • *Through a Glass Darwinian*   *The Authoritarian Personality:*
The Quintessential Xenophobic,
Hierarchically Motivated Primate

In a number of nonhuman primate societies, many individuals (particularly males) are preoccupied with concerns related to dominance status, group affiliation, and group integrity. Anything that is perceived as a threat to their place in the group is a powerful source of fear and trepidation. Extreme xenophobia (fear of the strange) is manifested when other groups of conspecifics are encountered. Studies of proto-cultural transmission in Japanese macaques show that the females and their young acquire new innovations but hierarchically enmeshed adult males are virtually closed to new experience. This xenophobic, closed-minded, control-driven individual, ready to submit to dominants and equally ready to oppress subordinates certainly continues to exist in our species as well.

Altemeyer (1988) conceptualized the authoritarian as a person highly dependent upon a strong group, demanding high ideological conformity. The right-wing authoritarianism scale was developed by Altemeyer (1988) to measure the three reliable facets of authoritarianism: *conventionalism*, i.e., rigid conformity to group norms; *submission* to higher status individuals; and *aggression* toward out-groups and unconventional group members. The emergence of an authoritarian personality appears to be unrelated to intellectual ability or socioeconomic status. Altemeyer believed this personality type was the product of a development history of harsh parental discipline acquired through social learning. However, a study of 39 pairs of monozygotic (identical) and 38 pairs of dizygotic (fraternal) adult twins reared apart and 423 pairs of monzygotic and 434 pairs of dizygotic adult twins reared together indicates that genetic factors account for at least 50% of the phenotypic variance and unshared environment for 35% (McCourt, Bouchard, Lykken, Tellegen, & Keyes, 1999). The hypothesis that authoritarianism derives from aspects of the rearing environment was not supported by this study. Nor was the right-wing authoritarianism trait related to general cognitive ability. It appears to be primarily influenced by genetic factors as well as by unique environmental factors. The superficial perspective, that the family environment is an important influence is due to its confounding with genetic relationships.

Eigenberger (1998) hypothesized that authoritarian behavior results from fears associated with social exclusion and group dissolution, which were genuine threats to survival during much of our evolutionary past. To test this hypothesis 522 participants were give the right-wing authoritarian scale and the fear perception index. It was found that individuals with higher scores on the right-wing authoritarian scale also had greater fears associated with social acceptability and the perceived deviant behavior of others. A fear of out-groups perceived as powerful was clearly indicated. For example, the fear item with the highest correlation with the right-wing authoritarian scale was "People associated with a cult." Certainly, the components of authoritarianism—conformity, submission and aggression—had an important function in our remote evolutionary past, *i.e.*, adapting to the social hierarchy and defending the integrity of the group. However, the antidemocratic ideology and personally intolerant views of authoritarians are highly problematic in a modern, global society.

found five broad dimensions—assertiveness, excitability, human-directed agree-ableness, sociability, and curiosity. Stevenson-Hinde and Zunz (1978) found three main factors in rhesus monkeys (*Macaca mullato*)—confident, excitable and socia-ble. Gold and Maple (1994) assessed personality in gorillas (*Gorilla gorilla*) and found four main factors—extraverted, dominant, fearful and understanding.

From an adaptive perspective, the range of variation in individual personal-ity types can be explained as the result of shifting selective pressures or variabil-ity in available ecological and social niches. As we saw in Chapter 6, differences in birth order can produce differences in the social environment resulting in per-sonality differences. For animals living in social groups, reproductive fitness is en-hanced when there is a goodness-of-fit between the individual animal's general pattern of behavior and its social niche. Individual members of more-complex an-imal species, such as those listed above, are active participants in creating their particular social niches as a result of their innate proclivities. The emergence of personality is the result of the dynamic interaction of genetic predispositions with the social and ecological environment.

The fact that nonhuman and human personality traits vary almost infinitely in small details but in a broad sense can be reduced to a few distinct patterns sug-gests that there are constraining influences. If personality development were a purely open-ended process there would be no clustering of traits into a limited number of distinct factors. The limited number of personality factors may stem from the fact that, in a given species, there are only a limited number of behavioral types or precursor personalities that an individual can be born with. The behav-ioral types produce stable individual differences in patterns of emotional re-sponding. This early emerging, stable pattern of behavior in is referred to as temperament. It is temperament that forms the scaffolding for the more complex stable patterns of behavior, referred to as personality.

Thomas and Chess (1977) isolated nine dimensions of temperament using detailed descriptions of infants and children's behavior obtained from parental in-terviews. They then used these nine dimensions to rate the behavior of children in their longitudinal of study of 141 individuals. Factor analysis of their data indi-cated that the characteristics studied tended to cluster together into three distinct types of temperament. About 40 percent of their sample were classified in the **easy child** category. The easy child quickly adapts to regular routines in infancy, is tol-erant of new experiences, and is generally cheerful. About 10 percent of their sam-ples were classified in the **difficult child** category. The difficult child does not conform to daily routines and tends to cry a great deal and react negatively to new experiences. About 15 percent of the samples were placed in the **slow-to-warm-up child** category. The slow-to-warm-up child is fairly inactive and exhibits mild or slightly negative reactions to environmental stimuli. The remaining 35 percent of the sample showed diverse mixtures of traits that were not easily classified. By school age, 70 percent of the difficult children had developed behavior problems, compared to 18 percent of the children classified as easy (Thomas, Chess, & Birch, 1968). Among the slow-to-warm-up children, 50 percent developed adjustment problems during the school years (Chess & Thomas, 1984).

Other researchers have described temperament somewhat differently. Three factors—emotionality (arousal), activity (movement), and sociability (preference for companionship)—were derived by Buss and Plomin (1986) to describe temperament. Many developmental psychologists theorize four main dimensions of temperament—activity, reactivity, emotionality and sociability (Goldsmith et. al., 1987). Digman and Shmelyov (1996), in a study of 480 Russian schoolchildren, found four components of temperament: sociability, anger, impulsivity, and fear. These four components were found to correlate highly with the big five personality factors supporting the idea that temperament not only is a major component of personality but may be the foundation of personality

Svrakic, Svrakic, and Cloninger, (1996) posit four somewhat different temperament dimensions (harm avoidance, novelty seeking, reward dependence, and persistence) that are moderately heritable, moderately stable throughout life, and invariant despite sociocultural influences. Extremes on these dimensions are correlated with a number of mental disorders (Battaglia, Przybeck, Bellodi, & Cloninger, 1996). High novelty seeking characterizes subjects with eating disorders, alcohol abuse, or substance abuse. High harm avoidance characterizes subjects with mood or anxiety disorders.

John Bowlby (1969) was a psychoanalyst (Freudian psychologist) who recognized the process of human mother–infant attachment as an elaborate evolutionary adaptation essential to survival. Bowlby believed that early-childhood experiences often affect adult patterns of behavior because they influence some psychological structure with a biological substrate, thus, a person's ability to develop affectional relationships in later life is dependent on the proper development of selective attachments in the first few years of life. Bowlby's ethologically-based perspective has proven very useful in explaining a host of behavioral phenomena, and it accounts for the general pattern of children's early social behavior better than any other theories that have been proposed (Rutter & Rutter, 1993).

There are two features of Bowlby's attachment theory that should be noted (Rutter & Rutter, 1993). Attachment still develops in situations of neglect and severe abuse. Young children and the young of other mammalian species are most likely to cling to an adult when they are disturbed or frightened. If the only adult available is the perpetrator of abuse they will cling to this individual. Ethological theory suggests that attachment is an innate predisposition in social animals. Its adaptive function is to provide security and develops without need of selective reinforcement. Attachment develops in extremely harsh unpropitious circumstances and is highly resistant to extinction. Attachment is clearly not the same as a dependency trait. Infants with secure attachments at twelve to eighteen months are much less likely than insecurely attached infants to show high dependency at four or five years of age (Stroufe, Fox, & Pancake, 1983). Insecure attachments foster dependency. Secure attachments promote autonomy. More so than any other species, human infants must have a secure nurturing relationship with an adult caregiver (preferably both mother and father) in order to adequately develop cognitively and socially. Early deficits in parental care and nurturance inevitably produce deficits and abnormalities in social behavior and mental capacities.

As strange as it may seem, some of the persistent patterns of strange or abnormal behavior that emerge in individuals that have been neglected or abused as children may actually be the product of adaptive evolution. This is supported by the fact that remarkably similar personality disorders appear in diverse adults who have little in common except a deficit in parental nurturance. A number of specific examples of this phenomenon are described in the section below on Axis II Personality Disorders. Refer to the concept of the Evolved Ontogenetic Contingency Mechanism in Chapter 6 for a more thorough discussion of this idea.

Personality and Abnormal Behavior

For most people, personality factors are not usually the direct cause of abnormal behaviors. Yet, personality can cause abnormal behavior in several ways. People with specific traits, such as being high on neuroticism or psychoticism, may be more likely to develop specific problems. For example, people who score high on neuroticism are more likely to acquire depression and anxiety. Neurotic disorders represent a process of learning maladaptive responses. Therapeutic techniques involve the unlearning or extenuation of these responses.

Second, elevations in specific traits may be best conceptualized by the concept of personality disorders. The descriptive approach advocated in the five-factor model may be able to explain personality disorders. Personality disorders can be conceptualized as extremes in factor analytic scales and may be largely sufficient for characterizing both normal and abnormal personality functioning and processes (Costa & McCrae, 1998).

Third, extreme manifestations of a particular trait may result in faulty coping processes. For example, people who are excessively disagreeable may not develop social supports, which are apparently very important for stress coping. Furthermore, people who are excessively extraverted may rely on their friends, to the exclusion of developing skills necessary for problem solving.

Many researchers now believe that one important area of abnormal behavior, the personality disorders, can be largely explained by the dimensional approach to personality. Personality disorders are enduring ways of dysfunctional coping that exist in the individual across situations. They are extremes of inflexible behavior, resulting in negative consequences. As many as 13% of the population have a personality disorder (United States Surgeon General's Office, 1999). Many researchers now believe that the personality disorders are simply combinations of extremes of normal personality.

This approach suggests that for most of us, personality is sufficiently flexible so that our personality factors do not result in recurring behavioral problems. However, for people with extreme personality functioning, inflexibility is likely to result in maladaptiveness, anxiety, and feelings of distress, unhappiness, and behavioral inefficiency. The point at which a personality style becomes a personality disorder is unclear and is certainly related to environmental vectors acting to support or impair an individual's efforts.

Axis I Psychiatric Diagnoses

Clinical disorders with the exception of personality disorders and mental retardation are classified as Axis I disorders. These include the reporting of most of the diagnosable disorders in the current Fourth Edition *Diagnostic and Statistical Manual, DSM IV* (American Psychiatric Association, 1994). There are 16 classes of Axis I disorders, which make a detailed discussion out of the range of the present volume. However, some of the more common Axis I disorders may lend themselves to a behavioral evolutionary interpretation and explanation and are included below.

Schizophrenia.   Schizophrenia is one of the most perplexing psychiatric conditions known. It is categorized by a number of disparate and often poorly connected symptoms that often correlate poorly across different people. These include the "positive symptoms" of disorganized speech, thought, ideas of reference, hallucination, and delusions, thought insertions and several other well-known symptoms. They also include the "negative symptoms" of apathy and withdrawal, which progress when the disease progresses. The negative symptoms also include a poverty of thought processes, content, flat affect, and a lack of directedness. Schizophrenia is so heterogeneous that it is likely that it is several different diseases, leading some investigators to call it "the schizophrenias."

At the proximate level, the positive symptoms appear to be the result of a neurotransmitter imbalance, particularly excessive dopamine activity in the reinforcement centers of the brain. Two lines of evidence suggest this. The positive symptoms are amenable to treatment with drugs that block dopamine activity such as chlorpromazine (thorazine). Secondly, acute psychotic episodes involving hallucinations and delusions can be induced by sustained usage of drugs that elevate dopamine activity such as cocaine or amphetamines.

The proximate cause for the negative symptoms is probably a neurological deficiency. CAT scans and MRI images reveal that the cerebral ventricles (the fluid filled spaces in the brain) are significantly larger in the brains of schizophrenics. Consequently, the brains of chronic schizophrenics typically contain significantly fewer neurons than similar non-schizophrenic individuals. Currently there is no real treatment for the negative symptoms associated with chronic schizophrenia. Unlike acute schizophrenia, which is characterized by positive symptoms that can appear suddenly and also disappear suddenly either spontaneously or with drug treatment, chronic schizophrenia with its negative symptoms progressively worsens over time.

While the more distal causes of schizophrenia are not clear, it is most likely that it is due to genetic vulnerability superimposed on a number of risk factors of environmental stresses. The chances of a monozygotic twin sharing the disorder are 50%, suggesting that genes play a major role but must interact with some environmental trigger for the disorder to manifest (United States Surgeon General's Office, 1999). The environmental risk factors may include exposure to a virus in utero, trauma at birth, specific family styles, poverty, and social ostracism.

Over 200 studies show that individuals born between the months of December and March are at significantly higher risk for schizophrenia than individuals born at other times of the year (Carlson, 1998). Other studies show that the cerebral spinal fluid of schizophrenics contains viral antibodies whereas the cerebral spinal fluid of non-schizophrenic control subjects is free of such antibodies. The "season of birth" effect coupled with antibody studies suggests that at some point in the early development of some schizophrenics, a viral pathogen crossed the blood-brain barrier and inflicted permanent neurological damage. The damage may not have been sufficient to noticeably alter the individual's behavior as long as they remained in the relatively constant, sheltered home environment. However, when first confronted with the stresses and demands of young adulthood such an individual would have lacked the neurological reserves available to most people and would have started to exhibit the first signs of behavioral degeneration associated with schizophrenia. This scenario explains the long-standing observation that in many individuals the first schizophrenic episodes do not occur until early adulthood and are often associated with stress.

The neurological damage accounts for not only the negative symptoms but the positive symptoms as well (Grace, 1991). Damage to the frontal cortex alters the nature of feedback signals sent to the dopaminergic reinforcement centers such as the nucleus accumbens. As a result of this defective feedback dopamine levels are chronically low. Consequently, there is a compensatory increase in the sensitivity of the postsynaptic dopamine receptors. When the dopaminergic neurons of the reinforcement centers are activated by environmental events (particularly events of a stressful nature) there is an overreaction leading to the positive symptoms of schizophrenia.

If a large percentage of schizophrenia is caused by the neurological damage of an early viral infection, the question that is raised is why susceptibility does not vary greatly across populations. In fact, schizophrenia occurs in about one percent of any given human population, regardless of geographic location or ethnicity. Given the apparently negative impact this disorder has on reproductive fitness, it would seem that that natural selection should have largely eliminated genes that predispose the individual to such vulnerability.

One theory is that schizophrenia affords some type of reproductive advantage in its less-dominant or nonthreshold forms. For example, the properties of schizophrenia associated with divergent thinking may hold a reproductive advantage for some people under some circumstances. Schizophrenia is associated with being able to generate novel associations to new problems. This can be demonstrated on neuropsychological tests and also on tests for creativity. For schizophrenics, too often the associations are irrelevant or tangential. However, for someone with a tendency towards schizophrenia, this may be a propensity for socially adaptable creativity (Eysenck, 1997). In some of its milder forms, schizophrenia may occasionally provide a large evolutionary (fitness) payoff. Typically, the bizarre behavior and magical, irrational thinking exhibited by the schizophrenic individual puts them at marked disadvantage in terms of mating success. However, during conditions of social upheaval, when general levels of uncertainty and anxiety are extremely high, the unusual individual with a "different approach" may come to be viewed as a potential savior. Without question, during the course of human history, many of these "messiahs" led their followers down paths that were even more disastrous than whatever they were trying to leave behind. On the other hand, radical innovations do not spring from stable people living under stable conditions. Innovations arise when environments become unstable or individuals become unstable or both. The first individual to try to manipulate fire was undoubtedly regarded as disturbing and strange by other group members. Population migrations can also be viewed as innovations. When the ancestral Polynesians launched their outrigger canoes into the vastness of the Pacific Ocean only a small percentage reached the "Promised Land," a habitable island. Exactly what these people were promised by their leaders to undertake such a perilous voyage, we will never know. What we do know is that the genetic underpinnings for generally high-risk patterns of behavior can be maintained as long as a certain percentage of the risk takers achieve a high level of reproductive success.

Depression.   Depression has been a recurrent phenomena throughout recorded history. It is amply evident in Homeric accounts and also in the Old Testament. According to the *DSM IV,* the diagnosis of major depression requires evidence of either a depressed mood or marked loss of pleasure or interest in daily activities for at least two weeks. At least five of the following symptoms are also required for diagnosis: agitation or retarded movement, weight gain or loss, sleep disturbances, fatigue or loss of energy, guilt or sense of worthlessness, slowed or disrupted thinking or indecisiveness and suicidal ideation. Peak occurrence is in the 20-to-45 age range. Predisposing factors include a family history of depression, a depressive episode in childhood, alcohol abuse, high negative stress, recent losses, low self-esteem, chronic illness or anxiety (Meyer & Deitsch, 1996). One out of seven people with major depression will attempt suicide and one in three will develop a drug or alcohol problem (United States Surgeon General's Office, 1999). Unfortunately, depression appears to be on the increase. Of Americans born before 1905, only one percent had major depression by age 30. After 1955, this number increased by six-fold (Meyer & Deitsch, 1996). Similar data exists regarding the prevalence and increasing frequency of depression for other diverse countries and cultures, including Taiwan and Lebanon.

     In a slightly less-severe form, dysthymic disorder involves similar symptoms that are long lasting, though not of as long duration. Dysthymia can be chronic. Both depression and dysthymia respond to psychotherapy, or talk therapies, particularly cognitively-oriented and socially-related approaches that emphasize changing depressive thoughts and increasing social contacts. Depression, but probably not dysthymia, often responds to medications as well. The most popular medications are the selective serotonin re-uptake inhibitors (SSRIs), which work by blocking the re-uptake or reabsorption of serotonin. At least four other major classes of antidepressants exist, with over 60 pharmaceutical agents now available. Depression is very common and, fortunately, is imminently treatable, and no one should be stigmatized for seeking help for this disorder.

What possible evolutionary basis could depression have that was at one time functional? Superficially, it appears that many of the symptoms of depression are similar to those experienced by people who are forced to conserve food, for example in cold conditions or in a famine. Seasonal affective disorder occurs most frequently in winter, where it is presumably a response to fewer hours of sunlight. It is usually characterized by somatic symptoms, such as overeating, carbohydrate craving, and sleeping more than usual. The prominent French psychiatrist Jean Esquirol (1772–1840) reportedly advised a patient whose depression appeared when the days grew shorter to move from Belgium to Italy during the winter (Sheehy, Chapman, & Conroy, 1997). Today, seasonal affective disorder is often treated by exposing the patient to bright, artificial light for an extended period of time each day.

As was pointed out in Chapter 7, the serontonergic systems in the raphe nuclei of the brain evolved to regulate motor tempo and are quite ancient. They served to increase motor tempo when resources were plentiful and to decrease tempo when resources were scarce or excessive activity would make one a target for predators. When animals began living in social hierachies, the raphe serotonergic system was co-opted to regulate dominance interactions (McGuire & Troisi, 1998). High social status increases resource entitlement and the concomitantly higher serotonergic activity of the raphe increases motor tempo and allows one to take advantage of the higher resource availability. The accompanying mood state is one of joy or euphoria. The mood state can be thought of as the motivating influence. Conversely, with low social status one is entitled to fewer resources and excessive activity may attract the unwanted attention of dominant individuals. Consequently when there is a perception of low social standing, the activity of the raphe is reduced, resulting in a reduction of motor activity. Thus, energy is conserved, and one does not become a target for aggression from more dominant individuals. A reduction in raphe activity can also occur when there are environmental necessities for conserving energy, such as the limited food supplies and cold climate of the winter months. The mood state that motivates this energy-conserving pattern of motor activity is referred to as depression. Moreover, the social withdrawal generally associated with depression may give the individual time to reevaluate failed social strategies and devise new ones. A capacity for depression may be just as critical to survival as a capacity for pain.

Anxiety.   Anxiety is a diffuse and vague feeling of unpleasantness often associated with fear and apprehension. Anxious people worry a great deal and appear hypersensitive to environmental signals of future harm (Gray, 1987). Fear differs from anxiety not only in its intensity, but also in its clarity of cause. Anxiety disorders include psychiatric conditions where the individual experiences inappropriate anxiety.

There are five major classes of anxiety disorders. Generalized anxiety involves anxious feelings occurring much of the time and not connected to appropriate stimuli. Panic disorder involves the sensation of acute anxiety in inappropriate situations. Posttraumatic stress disorder involves a cluster of symptoms of anxiety that occur following a psychological or physical trauma that is out of the range of normal human experience. Phobias involve irrational anxiety towards a specific object, event, or occurrence. Obsessive-compulsive disorder involves a preoccupation with specific thoughts and subsequent behaviors that if interfered with produce profound anxiety.

Since natural selection acts in a probabilistic manner, erring on the side of caution generally represented a viable selective payoff with regard to responding to possible dangers. For example, numerous false positives (perceiving danger and reacting fearfully when no real threat existed) exacted a relatively small loss compared to even one false negative (failing to perceive a real danger and react to it) which could prove fatal. The serotonergic systems of the raphe that control depression are also involved in anxiety (McGuire & Troisi, 1998). Low seroternergic activity promotes vigilance and feelings of anxiety, very adaptive when there is a prospect that you will be attacked by a higher-ranking group member or a coalition of group members.

As was pointed out in the section on Fear Learning in Chapter 3, humans are predisposed to readily acquire fear associations with certain stimulus categories (e.g., heights, snakes, spiders) that consistently represented a danger during our evolutionary past. The development of phobias simply represents the extreme end of the development of fear associations. Obsessive-compulsive disorder also represents the extreme end of a pattern of behavioral tendencies that served a protective function, such as the avoidance of infection and other environmental hazards. In the case of posttraumatic stress disorder, the super sensitivity that develops to the cluster of stimuli associated with a traumatic, near fatal occurrence, has an obvious adaptive function. The hair trigger responses that develop in posttraumatic stress disorder greatly increase the probability that the individual will survive if a similar life-threatening episode occurs in the future.

Currently, millions of people, the world over, experience intense psychological suffering as a result of these clinical disorders. The fact that the statistical likelihood of successfully producing viable offspring was improved by maintaining the capacity for these tendencies in our ancestors may be of little comfort to the afflicted. On the other hand, viewing the etiology of psychological disorders from an evolutionary perspective may be of vital importance to those who seek to develop more effective treatments.

Axis II Personality Disorders

A personality disorder is defined as an enduring pattern of inner experience and behavior that deviates markedly from the expectations of the individual's culture, is rigid and pervasive, is stable over time and leads to distress or impairment. The etiology of many personality disorders makes them prime candidates for being the proximate outcomes of evolved contingency mechanisms. For example, many of the people diagnosed as having a particular personality disorder share similar deficits in their early rearing. Moreover, many aspects of their apparently maladaptive personalities can be explained as alternative fitness strategies that have been triggered by their early social/familial experiences. In some cases these fitness strategies are so effective that a small percentage of a given population can benefit from them regardless of their family background. In other words, some individuals are born with a powerful innate predisposition to manifest a pattern of behavior which, if it occurred more frequently, would lose its adaptive advantage. The pattern can only have an adaptive advantage as long as it occurs below a certain critical threshold in frequency, hence it is called a frequency-dependent adaptive strategy.

Antisocial and Histrionic Personality Disorders.   Antisocial personality disorder, also referred to as sociopathy or psychopathy, is characterized by a pervasive pattern of disregard for the rights of others, lying, deception, impulsivity, aggressive behavior, lack of empathy, and lack of remorse. The typical sociopath views his (males outnumber females 20 to 1) fellow humans as mere objects to be manipulated for personal gain (Stevens & Price, 1996). Sociopaths represent the "cheaters" that evolutionary theorists have argued would subvert the spread of genes for altruism. Basically, the sociopathic strategy is to take advantage of the altruistic leanings in other people by pretending to have similar altruistic motives themselves.

Linda Mealy (1995) has argued that the sociopathic strategy is maintained by frequency-dependent selection. She summarizes her argument as follows

> (1) there is a genetic predisposition underlying sociopathy which is normally distributed in the population; (2) as the result of selection to fill a small, frequency-dependent, evolutionary niche, a small, fixed percentage of individuals—those at the extreme of this continuum—will be deemed "morally insane" in any culture; (3) a variable percentage of individuals who are less extreme on the continuum will sometimes, in response to environmental conditions during their early development, pursue a life-history strategy that is similar to that of their "morally insane" colleagues; and (4) a subclinical manifestation of this underlying genetic continuum is evident in many of us, becoming apparent only at those times when immediate environmental circumstances make an antisocial strategy more profitable than a prosocial one. p. 526.

In other words, some individuals are born to be sociopaths as a result of their genetics, others are made to be sociopaths as a result of a harsh developmental history interacting with some predisposing genetic factors, and many individuals are capable of a temporary pattern of antisocial behavior in response to proximate environmental factors. Sociopathy can be maintained in human society only if it is limited in scope, either in the percentage of the population effected or in the length of time a large segment is engaged in antisocial behavior. During relatively stable (e.g., peacetime) conditions, sociopathic individuals who follow a cheating strategy and prey upon the larger prosocial segment of the population can not exceed a certain percentage because their success is dependent upon the naiveté of their victims. During times of chaotic social upheaval and violence (e.g., war) the proximate conditions may make a temporary pattern of antisocial behavior adaptive for a much larger percentage of individuals. However, even during the worst of times, antisocial behavior produces an adaptive payoff only in certain situations and over very limited periods of time.

The early environmental conditions that appear to trigger sociopathy in those with the requisite genetic predispositions include physical or sexual abuse as children and a history of parental separation and loss (Stevens & Price, 1996). Oftentimes, much of their early life was in an orphanage or foster home. Presumably, roughly equal numbers of males and females are subjected to such degraded rearing experiences, but males are much more likely to become sociopaths whereas females are much more likely to develop histrionic personality disorders.

Histrionic personality disorder is characterized by exaggerated attention seeking behavior, sexually inappropriate, seductive or provocative behavior, a tendency to be easily influenced by others and to perceive relationships to be more intimate than they actually are. Harpending and Sobus (1987) have argued that histrionic females are employing a cheating strategy that is equivalent to that of sociopathic males. Because the reproductive strategies of males and females differ, the cheating strategies of males and females must differ accordingly. A male sociopath should be adept at seducing females and deceiving them about his degree of commitment. A histrionic female should be adept at exaggerating her need for the male and her vulnerability in order to induce him to lavish love and attention upon her. The histrionic female should also show a readiness to abandon her offspring opportunistically (former mating partners or their close kin typically take care of the abandoned offspring).

This indeed, is the pattern displayed by these two clinical groupings. Sociopathic males are typically charming, charismatic, promiscuous, and deceitful. Histrionic females are skilled at exaggerating their needs to desired males while masking their true promiscuous nature. They often seek to control their partner through emotional manipulation. Histrionic females manipulate others to gain nurturance whereas sociopathic males manipulate others for material gain.

Borderline Personality Disorder. The borderline personality disorder is characterized by a pattern of unstable interpersonal relationships, where significant others are alternatively unrealistically idealized and then just as a unrealistically devalued. These individuals have a very poorly developed, unstable sense of self. They often regard themselves as evil and sometimes nonexistent. They engage in reckless self-destructive behavior, such as unsafe sex, gambling or binging on food or drugs. They have an intense fear of abandonment and become angry and frantic when faced with even brief periods of separation. Borderlines typically have a history of insecure parental attachments from childhood. Stevens and Price (1996) give the following apt summary of the condition:

> People with this disorder may be understood as having embarked on a lifelong
> quest for reliable figures (or parent substitutes) to provide the love, care, stability,
> and security that their own family failed to provide. With each new encounter they
> feel they may have found what they are looking for, and gross over-idealization of

the new acquaintance may occur as early as the first or second meeting. But as soon as it is realized that the new person is unable to lavish all the loving care that is longed for, the initial feelings of love and admiration rapidly turn into anger, resentment, and despair as well as an indulgence in self damaging behavior. (p. 125.)

On the whole, borderlines harbor a great deal of misery and destruction for themselves and the people around them. It is difficult to think of this pattern of behavior as an adaptive response but the reproductive outcomes may be similar to those of the histrionic personality, which it resembles in many respects. Borderlines are distinguished from histrionics by the chronic feelings of loneliness and deep emptiness in the former.

The Other Axis II Personality Disorders.   **Narcissistic personality disorder** may represent yet another form of the "cheating strategy." Narcissists have a grandiose sense of entitlement from others but are very poor reciprocators. The *DSM-IV* states "They often usurp special privileges and extra resources that they believe they deserve because they are so special" (p. 659). Like the sociopath, they are unempathic and exploitative of others. But unlike the sociopath, the narcissist needs the recognition and admiration of others. Their grandiose sense of self-importance, and haughty condescending manner defends a very fragile sense of self-esteem.

   Paranoid personality disorder is characterized by a pattern of pervasive distrust and suspicion for others and the unwarranted assumption that other people will exploit, harm or deceive them. Paranoids hold grudges and are quick to counterattack or even make a preemptive attack upon a perceived enemy. Lower-ranking animals living in hierarchical groups often display this pattern of behavior. Vigilance and aggression can also be adaptive when neighboring groups pose a threat. The "in-group/out-group" thinking that exaggerates minor differences and creates negative stereotypes is manifested in the extreme in paranoids. The ontogenetic trigger for this disorder appears to be strong authoritarian parenting, where harsh criticism and punishment are used to enforce discipline and there is very little nurturance.

   Paranoid personality disorder is grouped with **schizoid personality disorder** and **avoidant personality disorder** by the psychiatrists Anthony Stevens and John Price (1996) under the rubric "spacing disorders" because the people with these disorders all have difficulties with personal relationships and functioning as members of a social group. The common strategy adopted is social withdrawal, either physically or psychologically or both. The pervasive characteristic of people with schizoid personality disorder is their extreme social and emotional detachment. These people have no desire for close relationships with others, and they appear indifferent to how they are regarded by other people. Schizoid individuals typically have an ontogenetic history of prolonged separation from or permanent loss of their mother in early childhood. Unlike the schizoid individuals who prefer their social isolation, people with avoidant personality have a strong desire for relationships. The avoidant individual is inhibited in forming social relationships because of their feelings of inadequacy and inferiority. They are preoccupied with a fear of being criticized or rejected in social situations. Avoidant individuals often have a history of parenting and peer relations conducive to low self-esteem (i.e., low dominance rank).

Dependent personality disorder may represent an alternative adaptive strategy adopted by individuals who have experienced unreliable, negligent parenting leading to an insecure pattern of mother-infant attachment (Stevens & Price, 1996). The individual with dependent personality disorder displays a pattern of submissive behavior and an overriding need to be taken care of by others. These individuals go to extreme lengths to obtain and maintain nurturance and support from others by always playing the role of subordinate group member.

Schizotypal personality disorder is described by the *DSM-IV* as a pervasive pattern of social and interpersonal deficits marked by acute discomfort with, and reduced capacity for, close relationships as well as by cognitive perceptual distortions and eccentricities of behavior, including magical thinking, bizarre fantasies and unusual perceptual experiences. Individuals with this disorder also display paranoid ideation, excessive social anxiety, and a lack of close friends. According to the *DSM-IV*, schizotypal personality disorder appears to aggregate familially and is more prevalent among the first-degree biological relatives of individuals with schizophrenia than among the general population. Unlike schizophrenics, schizotypal individuals do not experience persistent psychotic symptoms such as delusions and hallucinations. The coping strategy of schizotypal individuals is to avoid social interaction by withdrawing into their own mental world. However, under certain conditions, e.g., social discontent, schizotypal individuals may develop an ideology at variance with that of the parent group which attracts a following thus facilitating group splitting (Price & Stevens, 1998).

Obsessive-compulsive personality disorder is characterized by a preoccupation with orderliness, perfectionism, and mental and interpersonal control, at the expense of flexibility, openness, and efficiency. Individuals with this disorder are often excessively concerned about their relative status in dominance-submissive relationships and may show extreme deference to a person in authority that they respect and extreme resistance to authority figures that they do not respect (American Psychiatric Association, 1994). Stevens and Price (1996) describe people with this disorder as being motivated by a fear of losing control and attracting criticism from authority figures in the social hierarchy. In a fascist society, individuals with obsessive-compulsive personality disorder might function as highly valued bureaucrats. Fascist societies were made possible by agriculture, which stabilized and centralized resources allowing hierarchically organized dictatorships to emerge five to ten thousand years ago. Prior to that, human populations lived in egalitarian bands of hunter-gatherers. This suggests that obsessive-compulsive personality disorder might be a relatively new pattern of behavior. Genes for this general tendency may have existed as a legacy from the millions of years that our early forebears lived in primate dominance hierarchies. Natural selection, operating during the period when our ancestors were hunter-gatherers might have largely eliminated the expression of such genes. If these genes atavistically reappeared in one of the newly formed agrarian dictatorships, a new set of selective pressures may have acted to promote and refine them.

Resurrected dominance hierarchies were not the only factors to alter selective pressures. Civilization brought with it a whole host of changes in what influenced reproductive fitness. Civilization largely eliminated predation and starvation as major selective forces in human evolution. At about the same time that humans began to shape the genetic destiny of animals such as dogs, cattle, and horses they began to shape their own genetic destiny. The method used was selective breeding.

Although sexual selection had, no doubt, been operating in our line for millions of years, the sexual selection process had, prior to civilization, been greatly constrained by the exigencies of the natural environment. Once those exigencies had been largely removed, mate selection could be based on arbitrary criteria, e.g., cultural fads. For example, people of "royal blood" could bear royal offspring only by marrying other royalty. Just as hip dysplasia is part of the heritage of purebred dogs, hemophilia is part of the heritage of human royalty. A casual reading of history quickly reveals numerous records of bizarre behavior exhibited in royal families. This is not to suggest that abnormal behavior is purely the legacy of inbred kings, queens, and their descendants.

The entire human species has been part of this great, unconscious experiment. Many of the clinical disorders and personality disorders detailed above may be the result of a new sort of freedom that our ancestors discovered centuries ago, a freedom from the sometimes cruel, yet ultimately balancing forces of nature and natural selection. In other words, arbitrary trends in human assortative mating without many of the natural checks and balances that constrain the survival of nonhuman species may have resulted in an increase in the frequency of genes predisposing personality disorders and psychopathologies.

Summary

The concept of personality (enduring patterns of behavior that distinguish one individual from another) is very ancient, but the first scientific research on personality began in the nineteenth century. The most effective empirical method for investigating personality has proven to be an approach called factor analysis. This is a set of statistical techniques that reduces large numbers of traits to a few broad factors. From this approach, the three-factor model of personality arose with neuroticism, extraversion, and psychoticism as factors. Later, psychoticism was split into two independent factors, conscientiousness and agreeableness and the dimension of openness to experience was added to create the five-factor model of personality.

Personality is a phylogenetically ancient phenomenon. It exists throughout the animal kingdom particularly in complex species. Personality may emerge as a corollary of the evolution of complex behavior. The range of variation in individual personality types can be explained as a result of shifting selective processes or variability in available ecological and social niches.

All of the five factors have a high degree of hereditability. Natural selection appears to have produced relatively large phenotypic reaction ranges with regard to most personality traits. Thus, traits are fine-tuned by the physical and social environment to increase the "adaptive fitness" of the individual. Harsh early rearing experiences often produce "disordered" personalities that may be adaptive alternative reproductive strategies. Examples of such alternative reproductive strategies may include antisocial personality disorder, histrionic personality disorder, and borderline personality disorder. The development of civilization in humans may have removed many of the checks and balances imposed by the natural environment on behavioral phenotypes. The result has been an increased frequency in the occurrence of psychopathology and personality disorders in our species.

Discussion Questions

1. Discuss the five-factor model of human personality in terms of evolution for adaptive behavioral phenotypes.

2. Explain why "personality" is a recurrent phenomenon throughout the animal kingdom, at least in the more behaviorally complex species.

3. Discuss the idea of frequency-dependent adaptive strategies that take the form of certain personality disorders.

4. Discuss the idea that the emergence of civilization may have permitted patterns of mate selection and reproduction that increased the frequency of abnormal behavior.

Key Terms

agreeableness
antisocial personality
 disorder
anxiety
avoidant personality disorder
borderline personality
 disorder
conscientiousness
correlational research
clinical or case-study
 approaches
dependent personality
 disorder
depression

dysthymia
dopamine
extraversion
factor analysis
histrionic personality
 disorder
narcissistic personality
 disorder
neuroticism
obsessive-compulsive
 personality disorder
openness to experience
paranoid personality disorder
personality

psychoticism
reinforcement centers
schizoid personality disorder
schizophrenia
schizotypal personality
 disorder
season-of-birth effect
temperament
The five-factor model of
 personality
The three-factor model of
 personality
trait theory

Additional Reading

Personality: Evolutionary Heritage and Human Distinctiveness by Arnold H. Buss (1998).

Social and Personality Development: An Evolutionary Synthesis by Kevin B. MacDonald (1998).

Shame: Interpersonal Behavior, Psychopathology, and Culture by Paul Gilbert and Bernice Andrews (Editors) (1998).

Toward a New Personology: An Evolutionary Model by Theodore Millon (1990).

Human Paleopsychology: Applications to Aggression and Pathological Processes by Kent G. Bailey (1986).

Mean Genes: From Sex to Money to Food: Taming Our Primal Instincts by Terry Burnham and Jay Phelan (2000).

Subordination and Defeat: An Evolutionary Approach to Mood Disorders and Their Therapy by Leon Sloman and Paul Gilbert (Editors) (2000).

Darwinian Psychiatry by Michael T. McGuire, Alfredo Troisi and Alfonso Troisi (1998).

Evolutionary Psychiatry: A New Beginning, by Anthony Stevens and John Price (1996).

The Maladapted Mind: Classic Readings in Evolutionary Psychopathology by Simon Baron-Cohen (1997).

Exiles from Eden: Psychotherapy from an Evolutionary Perspective by Kalman Glantz and John K. Pearce (1989).

9

The Creative Impulse: The Origins of Technology and Art

Space-ships and time machines are no escape from the human condition. Let Othello subject Desdemona to a lie-detector test; his jealousy will still blind him to the evidence. Let Oedipus triumph over gravity; he won't triumph over his fate.

—Arthur Koestler, *The Trail of the Dinosaur* (1953)

Art is the objectification of feeling.

—Suzanne K. Langer, *Mind, An Essay on Human Feeling* (1967)

What is art,
But life upon the larger scale, the higher,
When, graduating up in a spiral line
Of still expanding and ascending gyres,
It pushes toward the intense significance
Of all things, hungry for the Infinite?
Art's life,—and where we live, we suffer and toil.

—Elizabeth Barrett Browning, *Aurora Leigh* (1857)

Religion and art spring from the same root and are close kin. Economics and art are strangers.

—Willa Cather, *Four Letters:* Escapism (1949)

Chapter Questions _____

1. Why is tool using behavior not always an indication of intelligence?
2. When did our ancestors first use tools?
3. How can art be explained as a product of Natural Selection?

The success of our species can be attributed, to a large degree, to our mastery of the external environment. Although all living organisms alter the world around them to some extent, the human influence impacts on nearly every ecological niche on this planet and even extends outward to the other worlds in this solar system. The means by which we are able to control and alter the material world to suit our whims is technology. The most dazzling technological innovations have all occurred in the last century. A perusal of these technological marvels (e.g., electronic communication, space flight, deep-sea submersibles, computers) suggests an enormous schism between our species and every other life form. A similar schism was noted when we compared language abilities across species. This is not surprising since language makes complex technology possible. Language and the cultural transmission of information that it potentiates are essential to technological development. The rate at which new technological innovations are produced has been slowly picking up speed for tens of thousands of years. The stone hand-axe represented the "cutting edge" of technology for over 1,200,000 years with scarcely any alteration in basic design. A mere 66 years separates the flight of the Wright brothers at Kitty Hawk and Neil Armstrong's stepping on to the surface of the moon. The rate of technological change is currently increasing exponentially and, barring the collapse of civilization, it will only continue to accelerate.

Technology used to master the physical environment can be classified as utilitarian technology. Technology that has no practical function can be classified as nonutilitarian technology. The more familiar term for nonutilitarian technology is art. The goal of utilitarian technology is to make the external environment conform to certain aspirations e.g., making an expanse of wilderness into a wheat field or fruit orchard, such that survival and reproductive success is directly enhanced (at least potentially). The goal of art is to manifest something internal and subjective as some sort of concrete representation that can be perceived and possibly appreciated by others. Art does not directly enhance survival. By defining art as something that does not directly contribute to survival, the argument that art is the product of natural selection seems problematic. Nevertheless, art is part of our behavioral repertoire because it does enhance survival and reproductive success but in a manner that is far less obvious than that of utilitarian technology.

Tool-Use

Although very different in terms of final goals, the requisite precursor of art was utilitarian technology. A certain level of technological sophistication had to be obtained before the production of artwork became possible. Technology had its' origins in simple tool-use, which is manifested in many other species including our prehuman ancestors.

In Nonhuman Animals

Tool-use was once considered an exclusively human attribute, and for many it constituted one of the defining characteristics of man. Tool-use was thought to be a direct indicator of cognitive ability and the capacity for culture. The discovery that many nonhuman species, including numerous invertebrate species, construct and use tools had the effect of forcing humans to reappraise the uniqueness of their abilities and also, to reappraise what could be inferred from tool-using behavior.

Although the notion of tool-use may seem clear enough, a variety of different definitions have been given by many researchers from 1963 through 1980. For the purpose of this discussion, we will use Beck's (1980) definition of tool use. Beck required the following criteria for behavior to qualify as tool-use:

> Tool-use is the external employment of an unattached environmental object to alter more efficiently the form, position, or condition of another object, another organism, or the user itself when the user holds or carries the tool during or just prior to use and is responsible for the proper and effective orientation of the tool. (p. 10)

Since our interest in tool-using behavior does have to do with inferring something about the cognitive abilities of the user, Beck's definition is not flawless. Beck (1986) has pointed out that many high-level cognitive manipulative behavior patterns displayed by animals are not tool-use by his definition. One illustration of this is Beck's (1981) field study of predatory shell dropping by herring gulls at Cape Cod, Massachusetts. He found that the gulls usually drop the same shell repeatedly, orient directly toward the dropping sites that are not in sight at the point of prey capture, show appropriate selection for dropping sites, and make appropriate adjustments for height and wind when dropping. Beck argues that proficiency in this behavior is acquired through learning and that shell dropping in gulls may be comparable in its' cognitive complexity to termite fishing in chimpanzees.

As we saw in our discussion of language, complex behavior may not necessarily imply complex cognitive abilities. "Honeybee language" is certainly a complex form of symbolic communication, but it is based on hard-wired genetic propensities rather than high levels of cognitive plasticity. Similarly, the most sophisticated nonhuman tool-use is displayed by invertebrates. For example, the neotropical assassin bug imploys a tool that captures termites. First, it locates a termite nest that has been disturbed and has a breach that is being repaired by colony members. The invading insect then proceeds to glue fragments of the nest onto its' body, thereby enabling it to approach the breach without alarming the termites. The assassin bug then grabs a termite worker, which is held in front of the breach with its forelegs, bait fashion. When other workers approach the captured worker to investigate they are captured and eaten by the assassin bug (Beck, 1986). The imported fire ant is another insect that has evidenced tool-use by using debris to mop up bits of honey (Barber, 1989). Along with insects, the invertebrate classes that have demonstrated tool-use include arachnids, crustaceans, cephalopods, and gastropods (Henschell, 1995; Beck 1986).

If a tool-using animal is morphologically and physiologically similar to ourselves, we tend to correlate learning, the understanding of cause and effect, and sometimes the mysterious quality called "insight learning" with tool-using ability.

On the other hand, when tool-use is displayed by an insect, or some other animal low on Aristotle's *Scala Natura*, we tend to think of it as a genetically programmed automaton. This is not to deny that these views are fairly valid in certain instances but rather to suggest that "learned tool-use" and "programmed tool-use" represent the extremes of a continuum. Learning may be a necessary part of even the most "hard-wired" tool-using program, and, conversely, innate behavior patterns may constitute the basic motor components for tool-use that is presumably highly cognitive in aspect.

Schiller (1952, 1957) studied the acquisition of tool-using behavior in a large group of captive chimpanzees. He found that the chimpanzees' level of tool-using capabilities appear to depend upon the individual's age rather than the amount of relevant experience. Moreover, he found that most or all of the motor behavior patterns displayed in "spontaneous" tool-use by these apes appeared in free play, unreinforced situations where manipulative objects were provided. It was found that despite radical differences in the physical properties of the manipulative objects (boxes, sticks, pieces of cloth, and string), they were used in very similar ways. Three general patterns of behavior usually occurred which seemed to correspond to aggressive display, grooming/probing, and nest building. When given sticks, there was a strong tendency for the chimpanzees to use the sticks to probe any available holes or crevices, draw the implement out, and lick off any detritus and moisture adhering to the implement (these observations were made decades before the reports of termite fishing and ant dipping emerged from Africa). A stick can also be waved aggressively at a human or another cage-mate, or broken into small pieces which could be stacked in a particular area of the cage and lain upon by the chimpanzee. When given two sticks, one of which had a hole in one end; the chimpanzee almost invariably inserted one stick into the hole of the other. Schiller concluded that the occurrence of this innate motor tendency provides the basis of the "two-stick" reaching problem. The two-stick reaching behavior was first described by Wolfgang Kohler in 1927. He observed that when a chimpanzee was confronted with the problem of a desired object being beyond his reach, he could solve this problem by inserting one stick into another and using this longer stick to pull this object within reach. Although the motor tendency to push a stick into a hole appears to be innate and maturationally determined in a chimpanzee, it does not in itself account for the appearance of tool-using behavior. When Schiller provided food that could only be obtained by the double stick, the animals often joined the sticks together without comprehending that it constituted a solution to the food problem. This understanding seems to depend upon associative learning acquired through fortuitous manipulation of the implement.

Kohler's (1927) interpretation of a chimpanzee solving of the two-stick problem was that it was due to "insight learning." It is possible both Kohler and Schiller are correct in their assessment. Certain hard-wired motor sequences may predispose the chimpanzee to certain tool-using behaviors, but to actually employ these behaviors to solve problems related to survival, higher cognitive functioning is required.

The tool-use displayed by many species of birds may represent a sort of middle ground between genetically programmed and learned tool-use. In the geospizine finches of the Galapagos Islands, tool-use constitutes a major ecological adaptation. These birds pick up twigs or cactus spines and use them to probe holes and crevices in trees and under bark. When an insect is encountered, the twig or cactus spine is used to impale or pry out the insect. Without their tool-using behavior, these finches might have as much difficulty procuring food as a woodpecker suddenly divested of its' specialized bill. It's likely that these finches are strongly predisposed by heredity to develop their tool-using behavior (Beck, 1980).

The tool-use displayed by some other bird species may fall closer to the cognitive end of the continuum. Hunt (1996) compared the tool-using behavior of New Caledonian crows to the stone and bone tool-using cultures of humans from the lower Paleolithic period. The crows were observed to manufacture and use two different types of hook tools to assist in capturing prey. The tool-use observed by Hunt in these crows had a high degree of standardization, distinctly discrete tool types and the use of hooks. According to Hunt, these features had never before been demonstrated in free-living nonhumans, and they only appear in human cultures after the lower Paleolithic period.

Among nonprimate species of mammals, only four have been reported to repeatedly use tools in different instances. These are the African elephant, the Asian elephant, the polar bear, and the sea otter (Chevalier-Skolnikoff & Liska, 1993). All of these animals are deemed to be highly intelligent. Among the polar bears and sea otters, the tool-using behavior is primarily for the purpose of obtaining food. Among the elephants, which use tools with the highest frequency and diversity among nonprimate mammals, the tool-using behavior is primarily in the context of body care, e.g., parasite control and body cooling. This demonstrates the multiple adaptive functions and multiple origins of tool-using behavior among animal species.

In light of the fact that humans are the paragon of tool-using animals, one would expect the other species of primates to display a relatively high level of competence in this behavior as well. In truth, the appearance of free-ranging tool-using behavior is very limited or nonexistent among most of the higher primate species. Of 175 species of primates, only six species have been reported to use tools on a regular basis (Chevalier-Skolnikoff & Liska, 1993). These include three species of the New World capuchin monkey (Cebus species) and the three great apes (the common chimpanzee, the gorilla, and the orangutan). Among these six species, only the common chimpanzee consistently and regularly uses tools in the wild.

Even among chimpanzees, the form of tool-use and its frequency varies considerably from population to population. Some chimpanzee populations practice termite fishing, and others use hammer stones to crack coula nuts, while many populations have never been observed to use tools. All this suggests that tool-using among our closest phylogenetic relatives is very cognitive in nature and closely associated to the phenomenon we refer to as culture.

Goodall (1968) observed the process by which termite fishing was transmitted to a new generation. Infants under the age of two attend to their mother and her actions while she is fishing at a termite mound. They manipulate discarded tools and play at poking holes in the mound. They also imitate some gestures used in the gathering of the insects, such a mopping. Moreover, there is a great deal of direct learning by the individual prior to the successful integration of the component parts, typically accomplished around five years of age. Different populations of chimpanzees show particular variations in termite fishing techniques (when the behavior occurs at all) and this has been attributed to different traditions. It has been suggested that ecological variations are responsible for the variations in technique (McBeath & McGrew, 1982; Collins & McGrew, 1987).

Variation in ecological determinants does not explain many features of chimpanzee tool-use. Boesch and Boesch (1981) studied the use of natural hammers in a population of wild chimpanzees at the Tai National Park, Ivory Coast, West Africa. They claim that there is a gradient in difficulty in the tool techniques of chimpanzees ranging from termite fishing, to coula-nut cracking on the ground, to coula-nut cracking in a tree, and panda-nut cracking. In termite fishing, the tools are picked up at a shorter distance from the working site than in coula-nut cracking. Of the fishing tools, 85 to 94 percent are collected within arms' reach, whereas only 75 percent of the hammers for cracking nuts are found on the anvil or at arms length. Efficient nut cracking requires greater coordination and control of movements than does termiting. A stroke that is too forceful can smash the nut, leaving scarcely anything edible. Even greater difficulties are met in cracking coula-nuts in a tree because the use of a hammer must be anticipated before climbing the tree. It also requires careful transfers of hammer and nuts between the mouth, hands, and feet between phases of the task. Panda-nut cracking appears more difficult than coula-nut cracking on the ground since it requires exact positioning of the panda-nut at least three times during the opening process, as well as a precise dosage of strength. This gradient of difficulty in chimpanzee tool-use corresponds to a sex bias in tool-using. The two most difficult techniques were employed almost exclusively by females. The researchers noted that the females produced flaked stone by pounding the hard panda-nut. Boesch and Boesch speculated that the first human toolmakers were women who produced stone artifacts when they used stone hammers in their gathering activity.

Kortlandt (1986) argued that the stone "artifacts" produced by modern chimpanzees are not at all similar to the stone tools left by early hominids. With chimpanzees, the direction of the blow of the hammer stone on the nut follows the perpendicular to a flat surface of the hammer through its gravity center. In contrast, nearly all early hominid stone tools were used as cutting, cleaving, and chopping implements. The hominid tools show wear patterns over the entire length of their edges, indicating that the users were continuously adjusting the tools so as to use the best available cutting surface. Kortlandt indicates that the stone tools used by chimpanzees and the earliest hominids show no indications of homology, functional equivalence, or similarity of motor patterns.

Modern great apes can be trained to make and use simple stone tools (Wright, 1972; Schick & Toth, 1993). For example, the bonobo, Kanzi, can make sharp-edged flakes through hard-hammer percussion or by throwing the stones against a hard floor (Schick & Toth, 1993). He then uses the flakes to cut through a cord binding a box containing food treats. The stone tools that Kanzi produces do not resemble the earliest hominid artifacts. The stone tools produced over two million years ago indicate they were made with great precision and an understanding of flaking angles. Kanzi's technique can be characterized as "random bashing," which produces flaked stones that resemble natural eoliths created by geological forces. This suggests that the earliest stone tools, dating back to over 2.5 million years ago, are likely to be overlooked because they closely resemble stones shaped by climactic and geological forces.

The Hominid Archaeological Record

Undoubtedly, the first tool-use of our hominid ancestors was of an opportunistic nature closely resembling that of modern chimpanzees. Whatever twigs, leaves, sticks, or stones happened to be on hand at the time were employed as tools with little or minimal modification. It is doubtful that we will ever find evidence that will unequivocally identify such implements. As we saw in the previous section, it will also be very difficult to identify the earliest stages of stone tools because they so closely resemble stones shaped by natural processes. Despite these methodological limitations, the incredible antiquity of hominid tool-use has been well established.

Thousands of sharp-edged stone flakes, flake fragments, and stone-tool cores, dating to over 2.5 million years in age, have been found in a dry riverbed in Ethiopia (Schuster, 1997). This earliest stone-tool industry is referred to as the Oldowan because the first artifacts from this assemblage were found in the oldest beds of the Olduvai Gorge in Tanzania (Tattersall, Delson, & Couvering, 1988). The Oldowan tools, sometimes referred to as pebble tools, consist of choppers and scrapers modified by simple stone on stone percussion. One use of the Oldowan chopper tools is evidenced by the broken limb bones of animals; these bones were probably broken open to obtain the rich marrow inside. It is also highly likely the cutting tools were used to dismember the carcasses of animals. The Oldowan technology persisted with almost no change for over 1.5 million years. Most archeologists believe *Homo habilis* was the creator and user of the Oldowan tools, although there is no definitive evidence for this.

The appearance and dispersal of the next stone-tool industry, called the Acheulean, corresponds to the emergence and migratory dispersal of a new hominid species, *Homo erectus,* over 1 million years ago (Schick & Toth, 1993). The Acheulean industry is named after St. Acheul in France where a Paleolithic site was discovered in the nineteenth century containing tools of this type. Acheulean artifacts have been found throughout Africa, Europe, and Asia and date from a period of 1.7 million to 200,000 years ago. The production of the Acheulean tools is thought to have required a shift from using a hard-stoned hammer when napping flakes from a stone core to "soft" hammers, such as bone or antler. An Acheulean tool kit consists of large, generally bifacial forms, such as hand axes, picks, and cleavers. Bifacial refers to the fact that the stone has been chipped from both sides to produce a symmetrical cutting edge. The quintessential Acheulean tool is the hand axe. The hand axe is a large teardrop-shaped tool with very sharp thinly flaked edges and a tip but with a thick base that makes it comfortable for being held in the hand. The hand axe was probably an all-purpose tool. Microscopic analysis of wear patterns on hand axes show that they were employed in butchery activities as well as working wood, hide, and bone. The Acheulean artifacts demonstrate a very powerful cultural tradition that was maintained over hundreds of thousands of years and over vast geographic distances. The hand axes did undergo some refinement over these vast periods of time. The earliest Acheulean hand axes were very thick across their midsection with one face flatter than the other, whereas toward the end of the Acheulean period the hand axes were highly symmetrical and very thin. As such, the Acheulean industry demonstrates the existence of a cultural tradition yet it also shows that this tradition is so conservative that the rate of new innovations was even slower than that of biological evolution.

The next tool industry to emerge is called the Mousterian for the type site at Le Moustier, Dordogne, France (Tattersall et al., 1988). The tool forms of the Mousterian consist of side scrapers, back knives, hand axes, serrated blades, and points. The Mousterian industry appeared nearly 200,000 years ago and persisted until about 40,000 years ago in the same regions in the Old World where the Acheulean tools had been found. Most Mousterian tools are associated with Neanderthals, but in some sites *Archaic Homo sapiens* is found in association with these tools. The Mousterian technologies involve a careful preparation of the stone core before the actual flaking process begins. Sometimes the core is shaped as a long prism of stone and other times it is shaped into a rounded surface from which shaped flakes are struck from it. The appearance of points suggests stone tipped spears, a significant advance over the simple wooden spears that were used previously.

The most sophisticated stone-tool industries coincide with the emergence of *Homo sapiens sapiens* possibly as early as 100,000 years ago but clearly prominent from 40,000 years ago (see Figure 9.1). These late Paleolithic technologies are characterized by tools produced by blade industries. A blade is a flake that is generally twice a long as it is wide, typically with straight parallel sides and struck from a prepared stone core (Tattersall et al., 1988). The blade-tool industries often involved the use of a punch or indirect percussion technique. Blades can be used without modifications, or they may be the precursors for tools such as scrapers, burins (a type of stone chisel), bagblades, and awls. Paleolithic technologies also produce bifacial points and a range of bone and antler tool forms. A variety of stone-working techniques were employed including hard, soft, and indirect percussion as well as pressure faking. Between 22,000 and 19,000 years ago another stone-working innovation was discovered involving the heating and cooling of flint to shatter it in a very controlled manner. Between 18,000 and 12,000 years ago, harpoon points were developed as well as spear throwers. The earliest conclusive

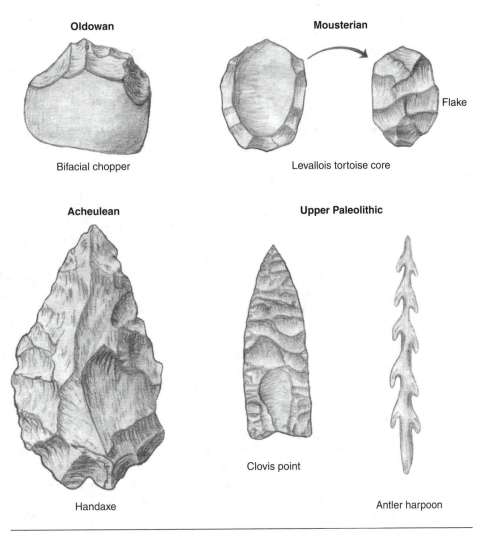

FIGURE 9.1   Examples of stone tools spanning a period of 2.5 million years.
(Printed with permission of Nani Faye Palmer.)

evidence of use of the bow and arrow comes from Stillmore, Germany in the form of arrow shafts dated to about 10,500 years ago.

Tool-Use as a Selective Force in Human Evolution

Although as our closest living relatives, the chimpanzees demonstrate a fair number of tool-using behaviors; our species may be unique among the primate order in having evolved an anatomy and behavioral propensities specific to tool using

(Wynn, 1994). The human hand for example has the same muscles, bones, and tendons as that of the chimpanzee, however, it shows at least five anatomical features that allow for the maintenance of an effective grip and stabilization of the palm for accommodating great external and internal forces (Marzke and Shackley, 1986). These features are: 1) a long thumb relative to the fingers, 2) structures in the center of the palm that promotes stability, 3) positioning of the muscles of the palm to allow optimal gripping, 4) the thumb and first two fingers are relatively robust and function as a unit, and 5) the tips of the fingers are flattened and have broad pads. Fossil hands dating back to 2 million years demonstrate many of these distinctive features indicating even at this early date the hominid lineage was being shaped by tool-using behavior.

In modern human populations, about 90% of all people are dominantly right-handed with the remaining 10% being left-handed (Schick & Todd, 1994). This right-handed bias is not a product of the constraints of modern civilization, but appears to be universal among all humans alive today. Ecological studies of preliterate cultures show that the tendency toward right-handed dominance is less extreme than that of literate cultures (Marchant, McGrew, & Eibl-Eibesfeldt, 1995). However, tool-use, specifically tool-use that requires precision gripping, was performed exclusively with the right hand during observations of the San of Botswana, the Himba of Namibia, and the Yanomamo of Venezuela. Naturalistic studies of chimpanzees indicate that the animals employ either the right or left hand when engaged in nut-cracking behavior, however, there is no significant bias in the proportions of left-hand versus right-hand users (Sugiyama, Fushimi, Sakura, & Matsuzawa, 1993). Because right-handed stone napping produces a different pattern of flaking than left-handed stone napping, it is possible by examining artifacts to infer how far back a bias toward right-handedness extends. Schick and Todd's (1994) study of artifacts suggests that the bias in right-handedness extends back to 1.9 million years. This of course raises the question as to why this bias toward right-handedness has evolved in our species. Handedness is a consequence of the existence of distinct neural structures, particularly brain asymmetries, with the slight enlargement of the left occipital and right frontal lobes in humans (Holloway, 1981). Stone napping requires very specific and very different neural functions for the two hands. One hand holds the stone stable while the other hand applies precise blows in order to remove flakes. Because brain tissue is a costly investment for a number of reasons, it is more economical for each respective hemisphere of the brain to develop its' own specializations. It is for the same reason, i.e., economy of function, that the language centers are found predominately in one hemisphere. Some theorists have suggested a strong link between the evolution of language and the evolution of tool-use. Both behaviors require complex sequencing. The archaeological fossil record however, suggests that tool-use preceded the development of complex language ability by millions of years. Although brain asymmetry is directly predicted as a consequence of specialized complex abilities, such as toolmaking and language, it does not explain why there would be predominance in right-handedness among our populations. We do know that toolmaking technologies persisted for hundreds of thousands of years as a consequence of cultural transmission. During these long stretches of time, the toolmaking behaviors display an astonishing level of conservatism with tens of thousands of years passing with virtually no change. It is possible that learning the toolmaking procedures from a mentor was greatly facilitated by both mentor and apprentice being right-handed.

Assessment of Hominid Cognitive Ability

Wynn (1979, 1981) has argued that the cognitive level of the Oldowan tool users differs from that of the latter Acheulean Period. Wynn believes that the tools produced by the Oldowan culture could have been made by a process of trial and error and required only that the maker have an internal representation of the kind of task the tool was intended for. This would place the Oldowan tool users at the preoperational level of intelligence in Jean Piaget's system of cognitive development. Piaget said that children between two and seven years of age had preoperational intelligence, meaning that they could use symbols, think, and use language, but they did not reason logically. Wynn believes the stone tools from the Acheulean period of Ismila, Tanzania, which date back about 300,000 years, indicate an operational level of intelligence. He bases this belief primarily of the bifacial hand axe. The cross-sectional and bilateral symmetry inherent in this object must be envisioned prior to the construction of the object in order to precorrect for errors. Piaget argued that symmetry is never passively perceived but must be actively constructed by means of the operational relation of reversibility. Since bilateral symmetry results from the reversal of a shape across its midline, the ability to perform such a task is not achieved until the operational stage because it requires the simultaneous conception of the shape and its inverse. Wynn's argument is valid if each stone artifact is considered to be an isolated invention by the maker. However, this is clearly not the case. Cultural practices can undergo a process of selective shaping just as gene frequencies do under the process of natural selection. It is known that stone toolmaking traditions were a part of hominid culture, or preculture, for at least 2 million years prior to the making of the late Acheulean hand axe. This constitutes an enormous time period for cultural evolution to operate. In such a span of time, it is likely that symmetrical artifacts could have been produced by chance alone, and if they were favored by the makers, at least some components of the procedure by which it was made could be incorporated into the learned traditions of the artisans. In time, all the components of making perfectly symmetrical stone tools could be incorporated into tribal tradition. An Acheulean artisan may have been no more able to visualize the symmetry of a hand axe prior to its construction than a modern physicist can visualize time and space curving in on itself.

Aesthetic Manipulation

Unlike utilitarian technology that has developed over millions of years, consistent, solid evidence of aesthetic manipulation of art does not appear until relatively recently, i.e., 30,000 to 50,000 years ago. Moreover, unlike utilitarian technology, art seems to have been almost full-blown in its development at the very onset. The utilitarian technology that was available during the peak of the last Ice Age is vastly different from the technology of the twentieth and twenty-first centuries, but the cave paintings produced then are as fully expressive as art produced today.

Pleistocene Art

Our aesthetic sense may simply be a refined version of the Gestalt perception that we share with many other species. Depending on their particular adaptations, different species have specific preferences regarding their sensory environment. Some may prefer dense foliage, others open savanna; some feel a sense of rightness in bright sunlight, others feel comfort only in the darkest gloom of evening. In each respective species, certain sensory experiences evoke aversive responses and others comfort and pleasure. As the tool-using capabilities of our distant ancestors evolved, there was a concomitant refinement in perceptual judgement. The point at which we want to call this perceptual judgement an aesthetic sense is purely arbitrary. The hand axes produced from 500,000 years ago to 100,000 years ago show a definite trend toward greater and greater symmetry and beauty (Schick & Toth, 1993). Of course, it could be argued that the increasing beauty of these tools was just an incidental by-product of their ever-increasing efficiency. However, evidence for the emergence of a true aesthetic sense comes from a site in Southeastern England dated at about 200,000 years before the present (Oakley, 1981). A hand axe was found at this site that had been deliberately shaped around a fossil sea urchin embedded in a piece of flint. In addition to this naturally ornamented stone tool, there were pieces of chert containing fossil corals that had been transported to another site some 200 kilometers away. The pieces of coral had been deliberately stained with red ocher, the iron-bearing mineral that has a long history of cosmetic usage, particularly ritual body painting. There is even some evidence that the *Homo erectus* populations in Africa may have been collecting red minerals for such purposes as early as 1.6 million years ago.

One of the oldest nonutilitarian objects (nonutilitarian in the sense of not directly enhancing survival) is a bone flute found in Northern Europe dating between 43,000 and 82,000 years in age (Wong, 1997). Remarkably, this flute is associated with the Neanderthal populations that occupied this region during that time. It is remarkable because, generally, almost no art artifacts have been found in association with the Neanderthals. Although the musical scale theory would not be developed until about 600 BC in Babylon, this Neanderthal flute may have been capable of producing four notes on a do-re-mi scale. Only a few other example of Neanderthal artwork have been found. For example, a mammoth's tooth that had been shaped into a decorative amulet was dated to about 100,000 years of age (Schwarcz & Skoflek, 1982). Unlike the modern humans that would displace them, the Neanderthals seemed to produce artwork only on an individual basis. The modern humans that would follow incorporated art into long-standing social traditions and rituals.

Modern humans living in Eastern Europe about 27,000 years ago created the first ceramic objects from clay fired in a kiln (Klima, 1990). Many of these clay figurines were in the form of humans and animals, and there is evidence that they were often deliberately broken in some form of ritual (Vandiver et al., 1989). One particulary distinctive category of representations produced by these people living in Eastern Europe at this time are the female statuettes. These statuettes are carved from such material as ivory, limestone, and calcite in addition to the ceramic figures that were fired in the kiln. These statuettes generally depict very robust female forms with extremely large breasts, buttocks, and belly. The statues appear to depict young women carrying a large reserve of adipose tissue or showing an advanced state of pregnancy. The lower legs end in points with no feet and faces are seldom depicted. The classic example of this type of statuette is referred to as the Venus of Willendorf found in lower Austria and dating to about 26,000 years ago. The statues are small and portable and most theorists believe they are associated with aspects of pregnancy and fertility. Supporting the hypothesis that these objects were used to either facilitate pregnancy or to maintain a successful pregnancy and birth is evidence garnered from a site in Russia dating to 26,000 years ago (Gvozdover, 1987). This site has yielded the majority of these female statuettes found in the world. They are carved from mammoth ivory, and they depict women in the terminal stages of pregnancy and childbirth.

When cave paintings were discovered on the Altamira Farm in Northern Spain in 1879, the scholars of the time dismissed these renderings as modern forgeries. The paintings depicted bison, horses, and other animals colored in red, yellow, and black upon the cave ceiling (see Figure 9.2). The artist had made use of the natural bulges and depressions in the rock to get a highly realistic three-dimensional quality to the animals depicted. The elegance and sophistication displayed in this artwork did not correspond to the preconceptions the European scholars had concerning the artistic capabilities of prehistoric humans. It was not until the turn of the century, after numerous other sites of Ice Age cave art were found in France and in Spain, that Altamira was accepted (Leakey, 1981). The cave paintings began about 35,000 years ago and persisted until the end of the ice age about 10,000 years ago. During the course of this 25,000-year period, the general pattern of artwork maintained great stability. This overall similarity is also maintained in the artwork across a great geographic range that encompasses much of Europe, although most of the sites are in France and Northern Spain. Although artistic styles remain highly stable during this period, there were consistent and dramatic innovations in tool industries occurring. The constancy of the art forms over such a long period of time suggests that they were part of a ritualistic tradition that carried great significance.

The most common subjects depicted in the Paleolithic paintings are animals, but there are also numerous abstract motifs of dots, lines, squares, and other symbolic renderings. The most common animals depicted are the horse, the bison, and the ox. There is not a direct relationship between the hunting of the animals depicted and their frequency of being rendered. For example, reindeer bones make up to 98% of animal remains found at these sites and yet this animal is almost never

FIGURE 9.2   Cave painting from Altamira, Spain cave of bison.

(Printed with permission of the American Museum of Natural History.)

displayed in cave paintings. One of the oldest cave paintings, Cosquer cave, which dates to over 30,000 years, depicts animals that would have been highly dangerous to hunt, such as cave bears, lions, and the wooly rhinoceros (Chauvet, Deschamps, & Hillaire, 1996). We can speculate that these dangerous animals symbolize power but understanding exactly what these paintings represented to the minds of the artists who created them, and to the minds of the audiences for which they were created, will never be known to us. We can however gain some insight into the general origin of this very unusual pattern of behavior, the creation of artwork.

The Adaptive Significance of Art

As was pointed out in the beginning of this chapter, there is a seeming paradox associated with explaining art as a product of natural selection. The goal of art is to manifest something eternal and subjective as some sort of concrete representation that can be perceived and possibly appreciated by others. The artwork produced is nonutilitarian and does not directly enhance survival. The question posed for evolutionary psychology is how does art indirectly enhance survival and reproductive success? Ellen Dissanayake (1989, 1992) has argued that the adaptive significance of art comes form its ability to cement societies together into unified wholes as a means of providing enhanced survival potential for individuals living within those groups. Looking at art from a cross-cultural and evolutionary perspective, she concludes that art is based on a universal inherited propensity in humans to make some objects and activities special. For Dissanayake, "making special" refers to the observation that humans, unlike other species, intentionally shape, embellish, and otherwise fashion aspects of their world to make these more than ordinary. Dissanayake makes the following observations:

> Each of the arts can be viewed as ordinary behavior made special (or extraordinary). This is easy to see in dance, poetry, and song. In dance, ordinary bodily movements of everyday life are exaggerated, patterned, embellished, repeated— made special. In poetry, the usual syntactic and semantic aspects of everyday spoken language are patterned (by means of rhythmic meter, rhyme, alliteration, and assonance), inverted, exaggerated (using special vocabulary and unusual metaphorical analogies), and repeated (e.g., in refrains)—made special. In song, the prosodic (intonational and emotional aspects of everyday language—the ups and

The terms Paleolithic, Mesolithic and Neolithic, Old, Middle and New Stone Ages, respectively, have been used to label broad swaths of human cultural development. The use of these terms reflects not only a bias resulting from the archaeological record, but it also perpetuates and amplifies a conceptual bias even in the scientists, who should know better. Implements of stone and bone are what remain from the distant past, for the simple reason that they are durable. When we try to reconstruct a picture of the culture and daily existence of the people that left these tools we must keep in mind the fact that what we have is a sample of durable artifacts and not a sample of representative artifacts. Objects such as spear throwers, carved from mammoth tusks and a wealth of stone spear points have fostered the image of late Pleistocene societies that revolved around male big-game hunting. Pictorial reconstructions of men and women in these societies typically depict them clad in animal skins.

Evidence that suggested something very different was overlooked. For example, the "Venus" figurines, thought to be fertility icons dating to over 25,000 years, are some of the most extensively studied of all archaeological objects. Yet despite all this study, prominent researchers failed to note features on many of the statuettes that indicated sophisticated clothing. It was not until widespread evidence of weaving technology dating back to over 28,000 years had been discovered that the apparel "worn" by some of the Venus statues could be identified. The carvings depict elaborately woven skirts, bandeaux, belts, and hats (Soffer & Adovasio, 2000).

Until recently, archaeologists had little information on Ice Age objects that degrade quickly—soft objects such as cordage and basketry—known as "perishable technologies." In 1953, fragments of rope sticking to the wall of Lascaux cave in southwestern France were dated at 15,000 years of age. In 1994, samples of cordage dating to 19,000 years were found in Israel. In 1998, impressions in hardened bits of clay found in the Czech Republic were identified as evidence of prehistoric textiles (rope, nets, baskets, and woven cloth) dating back to 28,000 years (Adovasio, Soffer, & Klima, 1996). Recent findings indicate that these early textile industries were widespread over ice age Europe (Soffer & Adovasio, 2000). The origins of the textile industry may date back to over 40,000 years ago when people learned to twist plant fibers together. This time period marks the beginning of the so-called "Creative Explosion" when widespread artwork begins to appear.

While woven objects have numerous utilitarian functions, such as baskets for carrying foraged plant foods and nets for capturing small game, the act of constructing them lends itself to artistic expression. This is particularly true for clothing. Although clothing has an obvious utilitarian function in cold climates, it may have originated as a form of body ornament and display rather than a heat insulator. Many modern hunter-gatherer peoples who live in the tropics wear little or no clothing but put a lot of energy into body adornment in the form of body painting, tattooing, scarification and the use of jewelry. The first *Homo sapiens sapiens* populations arose in tropical Africa before invading the colder regions of Europe and Asia around 50,000 years ago. Archaeological evidence associated with the anatomically modern humans living in southern Africa 120,000 years ago suggests that ocher pigment was used for body adornment.

It is quite possible that, originally, clothing was purely an early form of artistic expression functioning to enhance displays of status and courtship. Exposure to colder and wetter environments would have quickly resulted in a shift to a more-functional role for clothing. Weaving technologies would have been readily co-opted for clothing production. No matter how utilitarian a particular garment, wearing it affects how others perceive an individual. Consequently, clothing has probably always been either a blending of art and utility or purely a form of art.

downs of pitch, pauses or rests, stresses or accents, crescendos and diminuendos of dynamics, accelerandos and rallentandos of tempo—are exaggerated (lengthened and otherwise emphasized), patterned, repeated, varied, and so forth—made special. In the visual arts, ordinary objects like the human body, the natural surroundings, and common artifacts are made special by cultural shaping and elaboration to make them more than ordinary. (Cooke & Turner, 1999, p. 30)

Dissanayake notes the intimate association of art with two other behaviors that do not directly promote survival and reproductive success, namely play and ritual. Both play and ritual do however have a very real adaptive significance. When humans and other species engage in play, they are honing survival skills in a protected, consequence-free, environment so that these skills can be brought to bear later in very real scenarios. The purpose of ritualized behavior is to formalize, stylize, and exaggerate ordinary behaviors and confirm a special communitive function upon them thereby facilitating and smoothing out social interactions. For example, one function of ritualized behavior is to minimize aggressive encounters that can result from social misperceptions. Keep in mind that in all of these behaviors, art, play, and ritual the proximate stimulus for performing the behaviors is the self-reinforcement, or pleasure associated in doing it whereas the ultimate cause has to do with the enhanced reproductive success of the individuals. A human child engages in play not because they believe that they are developing skills that will serve them in their adult life, but rather because it is fun. Dissanayake believes that the propensities for play and ritual behavior that our ancestors shared with other primate species provided the framework for the evolution of a new adaptive behavior, i.e., art. One of the basic survival strategies opted for by our hominid ancestors was to exert control upon the environment. This is in part evidenced by the eons long history of tool-making behavior. The same skills that had developed for shaping these tools could be co-opted to decorate the tools with special symbols as well as the bodies of the users.

Art in its most incipient form was simply manifested as individual creative expression. It directly increased fitness by enhancing attractiveness to prospective mating partners and indirectly through gains in social status. Novel innovations in body adornment movement and the use of language represented the earliest precursors to the visual arts, dance, and poetry. As was pointed out in Chapters 4 and 5 a process of runaway sexual selection for creative behavior and language probably occurred in our species.

The use of creative innovation to make one's self more impressive and to problem solve is a phylogenetically old trait that was probably present in the common ancestors of humans and chimpanzees. Jane Goodall (1971) once observed a male chimpanzee rise to alpha status by "inventing" the technique of banging empty kerosene cans together creating a frightening sound. The innovative problem-solving that Wolfgang Kohler (1976) witnessed in chimpanzees and that he referred to as insight learning also represents a form of creative expression. Although the innovations in these examples had a utilitarian payoff, the line separating this kind of creativity from true artistic expression is a very subtle one. In primitive people, the creation of visual images, special objects and special behaviors is often done for the practical purpose of controlling certain aspects of the environment through magic.

In our ancient ancestors, when special objects, such as talismans, were constructed for the magical control they were expected to exert over the environment, these objects invariably produced powerful psychological effects. The social power that belonged to the shamans who controlled the magic objects and rituals no doubt conferred enhanced reproductive success upon these individuals. Enhanced reproductive fitness, however, extended well beyond the individual welders of supernatural power (see Figure 9.3). Every group member stood to gain. Special rituals functioned to bond the group members to each other and effectively orchestrate their actions towards achieving desired goals, such a hunting success, or successful warfare against other groups. In addition to making groups more cohesive and effective in their actions, art and ceremonies made group knowledge more impressive and thus more compelling and memorable, helping to maintain vital information over the coarse of generations.

Nancy Aiken (1998) has examined the aesthetic response as part of our evolved psychology. The aesthetic response is partially influenced by learning, but it is also influenced by an innate releaser response package.

> Certain configurations of line, shape, color, and sound evoke emotional responses in observers of art. This occurs not because of the observer's learned associations with the configurations, but because of unconditioned reflexes. That is, each configuration is a stimulus which triggers a neural mechanism in the observer

FIGURE 9.3 "Sorcerer" from Les Trois Freres cave in French Pyrenees, dated at 16,000 BP.

(Printed with permission of the American Museum of Natural History.)

under adequate conditions and which, in turn, causes a particular behavior to be performed by the observer. In the case of observers of art, behavior consists of autonomic nervous system changes that are described by the observers as emotional or aesthetic responses. (p. 29)

Some releasing stimuli evoke pleasant reinforcing responses, such as open savanna-like landscapes. Other releasing stimuli produce an aversive response or defense reaction. Eyespots, sharp as opposed to curved lines, and the color of red, for example, are potentially aversive releasers. These noxious or threatening stimuli become reinforcing when displayed as art because they are presented in controlled, nondangerous contexts.

When the neural structures that process these releasing stimuli become spontaneously active, the basic visual components of these releasers are experienced as hallucinations (Aiken, 1998). These emergent visual patterns consist of grids, dots, spirals, zigzags, circles and curved lines and are referred to as geometric entoptic (meaning inner vision) phenomena or phosphenes. These particular images are universally reported by people who have entered an altered state of consciousness, regardless of whether this state has been induced by psychotropic drugs, fever, food or sleep deprivation, brain pathology or electrical brain stimulation. Contemporary shamanistic societies such as the San of the Kalahari desert recreate these images in their rock art (Lewis-Williams & Dowson, 1988) and Paleolithic cave art displays these patterns amid the representational images of animals (see Figure 9.4). Phosphene patterns also appear in the drawings of children and even to some degree in the drawings made by great apes. The universality of the entoptic images is due to the shared neural architecture of the higher primate brain. Note the wealth of entoptic images depicted in Figure 9.5, a black ink composition created by a 12-year-old American girl.

Determining exactly how certain basic phosphene patterns form the building blocks for certain biological meaningful stimuli is the challenge of future neurological research. For example, one hypothesis to be tested would be whether seeing the bared fangs of a predator triggers activity in the same part of the brain that becomes active when an entoptic, zig-zag pattern is generated.

The ideas outlined above, were anticipated early in the twentieth century by the psychologist Carl Jung (1969). Jung conceived of a collective unconscious that is biologically inherited and consists of pre-existent forms, the archetypes. The archetypes were considered to be indefinite structures, which were crystallized into a particular form as a result of an individual's personal experience. Furthermore, Jung believed that every individual inherited preformed patterns of apperception that guided and circumscribed the conscious processing of certain experiences. Thus, for Jung, concepts such as good and evil, death and immortality, soul and God, were part of the innate psychological architecture typical of the human species. Most Pleistocene art may have been produced to express such spiritual concepts. Groups that could produce and rally around such symbols may have been more unified and therefore more likely to survive than other groups that lacked this general pattern of behavior.

FIGURE 9.4 Entopic images found universally in artwork by modern children, contemporary hunter-gatherers, Paleolithic humans, great apes, and humans in altered states of consciousness.

FIGURE 9.5 Example of rich use of entopic imagery in ink composition by a gifted 12-year-old girl.

(Printed with permission of Nani Faye Palmer.)

Consciousness and the Symbolic Universe

Although a developed aesthetic sense and good manipulative skills are necessary for the production of art, they are not sufficient in and of themselves. What sets true artistic expression apart from the behavior of an animal, such as a bowerbird that decorates its nest in order to attract a mate, is that artistic expression requires higher-order consciousness. Higher-order consciousness means that artists are not only aware of aesthetic differences, but they are also aware of their own awareness and hence the possibility that others share this awareness or experiential world. One way to get a handle on the evolution of higher-order consciousness is through a phylogenetic comparison.

The German scientist, Jacob Von Uexkull (1909) used the term *Umwelt* to describe the perceptional world that is experienced by different species. The perceptual world of a bloodhound for example, would be much more dominated by information relating to olfaction than information from other sensory modalities including vision. Uexkull believed that as organisms evolved more sense organs and greater neurological complexity their overall awareness increased. Thus, the *Umwelt* of an earthworm would be of a very rudimentary nature consisting of simple somatosensory information. Just increasing the number of sense organs necessitated an increase in neurological complexity to some degree. However, once the senses that we are familiar with had evolved in vertebrates, there was a great deal of brain evolution still to take place. A system of cross-referencing across the different sense modalities was a critical aspect of this neurological evolution. For example, the sound of a snapping twig could be localized for visual scanning and then the olfactory senses could be brought to bear to determine if indeed an intruder was in the general vicinity. There is evidence that certain cross-modal associations have become hardwired possibly to improve perceptual efficiency and to lower response times. English children were compared to children from Kenya in a task that required them to match a nonsense word with a pictoral display (Davis, 1961). Children from both groups matched the word "malume" with a curved shape and the word "takete" with a pointed shape.

As was pointed out in the chapters on brain development and language, the exigencies of functioning in a social environment greatly accelerated brain evolution and consequently the general level of consciousness or awareness. It was speculated that the development of a theory of mind, i.e., possessing the idea that others have a mind similar to one's own and using this concept to try to manipulate the behavior of the others, was a key factor in the evolution of higher primates. Unfortunately, it has been difficult to demonstrate the existence of theory of mind in nonhuman primate species to date. If theory of mind exists in other primate species, it may be in an incipient form, which is to say it may be a completely nonconscious process. Since theory of mind is currently conceptualized as being a fully conscious process, we may need another term to describe what various species of monkeys and apes are actually doing when they try to manipulate the behavior of others.

The first requisite in having a bonafide theory of mind, i.e., a conscious theory of mind, is self-awareness. By self-awareness we mean that an individual has a mental construct of oneself as a distinct entity, separate from everyone and everything else. In 1970, Gordon Gallup reported an experiment which he claimed to demonstrate self-awareness in chimpanzees. His experiment was a variation of the rouge test, which had been used by developmental psychologists for many years to demonstrate the point in human development when very young children first demonstrate self-awareness. In the developmental test, a mark of rouge, or some other distinctive coloring, is clandestinely placed on the forehead of the young child. The child is then placed in front of a mirror. Very young children, around one year in age, will typically look at the mirror image and react to it as if they were looking at another child. They will attempt to play with this other child they see in the mirror. Most human children around 18 months of age show a different response. They look in the mirror, note there is a mark of coloring upon their foreheads, and then they try to wipe it away. This response is seen as being indicative of a concept of self. More conservative critics say it does not really demonstrate self-concept but only mirror recognition, which may be a different quality.

Gallop (1970) used this same procedure when a chimpanzee was anesthetized for its periodical medical checkup; an odorless red dye was applied to the chimps forehead while it lay unconscious. When the animal regained consciousness a mirror was placed next to its cage, and the chimpanzee showed all the behaviors indicative of mirror self-recognition. The animal tried to wipe the dye from its forehead and it also positioned its body at various angles in front of the mirror in order to see places it could not ordinarily see on its own body. Since Gallop's early experiment, numerous other chimpanzees have passed the mirror test, as well as other species of great apes including the orangutan and some gorillas that had been reared by humans (Gallup & Suarez, 1986; Patterson & Cohn, 1994; Patterson, 1984; Povinelli, 1993). Because of the inherent adaptive differences in intelligent marine species such as the bottlenose dolphin, procedures used to demonstrate self-awareness in primates are highly problematic with cetacean species (Marino, Reiss, & Gallup, 1994). Nevertheless, studies using mirrors and TV monitors in mirror mode make a compelling case for the existence of self-recognition in the bottlenose dolphin (Marten & Psarakos, 1994). Not all great apes immediately pass the mirror test, and often they require prolonged exposure to mirrors before they understand what they are looking at. However, regardless of the length of time that the individuals are exposed to mirrors, no member of any other species, outside of the humans, great apes, and possibly bottlenose dolphins have ever passed this mirror recognition test (Gallup, 1994). Monkeys can be in the presence of a mirror for thousand of hours without ever acquiring this level of awareness (Gallup, 1977). At first they react to it as an intruding member of their own species, but eventually they habituate and ignore the mirror all together. Based on these findings, it would seem that the best place to look for theory of mind in nonhuman species would be in our close relatives the chimpanzees.

In 1978, David Premack and Guy Woodruff reported the results of a study on an adult chimpanzee named Sarah. The investigators showed Sarah a series of videotapes with human actors portraying various problems. For example, the videotape might show a human actor jumping up and down trying to reach a bunch of bananas hanging from the ceiling that were just out of reach. Following this videotape, Sarah would be given a set of photographs, one of which showed a solution to the problem, in this case, several boxes stacked on top of each other just below the bunch of bananas. Sarah would consistently choose the photograph that represented a viable solution to the problem shown in the videotape. Interestingly, Sarah's was much more likely to choose a "good", i.e., correct, outcome if the actor in the videotape was a trainer that she liked. If the videotape depicted an individual whom Sarah was suspected of disliking, she would typically choose an outcome that displayed the actor in some mishap such as lying under cement blocks. Based on these findings, the investigators concluded that Sarah recognized the videotape as representing a problem, understood the actor's purpose, and chose solutions compatible with that purpose except in those instances that involved a particular individual that she disliked. This, Premack and Woodrup argued, demonstrated theory of mind in chimpanzees. Unfortunately, additional, corroborating evidence for theory of mind in chimpanzees has not been forthcoming.

Daniel Povinelli has worked extensively on the problem of demonstrating theory of mind in chimpanzees but generally his results have been nil (Povinelli and Preuss, 1995). Although he has time and time again confirmed Gallop's original findings of self-awareness, or at least mirror self-recognition in chimpanzees (Povinelli, Gallup, Eddy, & Bierschwale, 1997) the outcomes of the theory of mind studies have not corroborated Premack's earlier (1978) findings. Povinelli and Eddy (1996) investigated theory of mind in chimpanzees by having their chimp subjects observe two human trainers who were present when food was cashed in a certain secret location. The chimps could see the trainers but not the location of the food. In one human trainer, the cloth covered the eyes like a blindfold, while in the other, the cloth was placed lower on the face acting as a gag. All of the chimpanzees tested showed no discrimination between the two trainers and were just as likely to beg for food from the blindfolded individual, who had no knowledge of the food's location, as from the sighted individual. On the other hand, human children as young as two years of age easily discriminated between the two experimenters and preferentially choose the experimenter whose vision was unimpeded for the reinforcer, in this case, stickers.

By age four, the theory of mind concept is well developed in human children. For example, a child is given a crayon box only to find the box is full of candles instead of crayons. When the experimenter asks the child what another child would expect to find in the same box, a child who is over four years of age will answer "crayons," and a younger child, will answer "candles." Based on these findings, it is assumed children under four years of age do not have a fully developed theory of mind concept. Autistic individuals typically fail this sort of false belief test and an absence of theory of mind has been proposed to explain many of the symptoms of autism.

Autism is characterized by extreme deficits in social behavior and under-standing. Children with autism display an emotional indifference to others and treat close family members exactly the same way they treat complete strangers. Verbal and nonverbal communication is extremely impaired. These individuals also display no imagination or creativity. They prefer a sameness of routine and are very disturbed by any slight changes. Autistic individuals interpret speech very literally, for example, if one asks "Can you pass the salt?" a child with autism might reply "Yes" as though they were being queried about their ability to do this rather than being requested to actually pass the salt to the individual (Mitchell, 1997). Certain high-functioning autistic individuals show great abilities in making mathematical calculations or in memorizing a great amount of seemingly irrele-vant information, such as the contents of phone books. There is a very mechani-cal, machine-like quality in these abilities. For example, two young autistic artists, Steven Wiltshire and Nadia, produce extremely realistic and detailed line draw-ings. These drawing have an extreme photographic quality about them, as if they were produced by a camera rather than a thinking, feeling being. Many of these deficits seem to be directly linked to a lack of theory of mind in autistic individu-als. A failure to understand other peoples beliefs would restrict a child to exces-sive literal interpretations of the speech of others. Their problems of relating socially to others and understanding the emotions of others could also be directly linked to their failure to understand theory of mind.

Although some of the symptoms of autism can be directly causally linked to a poorly developed theory of mind, it is probably more accurate to view the deficits in theory of mind and the other deficits as part of a global impairment. These global deficits are due to neurological abnormalities, particularly in a region of the brain known as the cerebellum. As was pointed out in Chapter 2, the cere-bellum is involved in the precise sequencing of motor movements, particularly ballistic movements. This was the basis of Calvin's so-called, ballistic hypothesis, namely that the development of the cerebellum due to the selection for more ac-curate throwing movements provided the requisite neurological substrates for language evolution. The cerebellar abnormalities that result in autism suggest the cerebellum plays a critical role, not only in ballistic motor sequencing, but also in the sequencing of language, social intelligence, imagination and creativity, theory of mind and intentionally. It would seem that there has been a long history of co-evolutionary development between all of these traits.

The efforts of a few autistic artists not withstanding, the key features of the creativity that have characterized our species since the late Pleistocene are higher-order consciousness, theory of mind, and intentionally. A developed aesthetic sense and symbolic reasoning are, of course, also necessary elements in producing art but they are not sufficient in and of themselves. As we have seen, an aesthetic sense evolves directly from adaptive preferences, which are exhibited in other an-imal species. Our phylogenetic cousins, the great apes, are quite adept at manip-ulating and understanding symbols and although there are examples of chimpanzee paintings, such endeavors are not a part of the normal repertoire of the species. Only in our species is a effort made to creatively manipulate elements of the outer world such that they can express something of our inner subjective state as individuals, or collectively, as groups of individuals.

As we noted earlier, there is an intimate link between art and play and ritual. These elements of art and play and ritual come full circle when we ritualize play into athletic competitions and these competitions are appreciated as expressions of art in a very real sense. When a football fan delights in watching a receiver stretch out to catch a pass over the middle before being pummeled violently by a pair of linebackers, this is just as much a form of artistic appreciation as that experienced by thousands of painting enthusiasts who visit the Louvre each day in Paris. The essence of art is its ability to captivate. Modern sports do just that by displaying grace and elegance often juxtaposed with violence. The innate preferences that maintain the complex cultural traditions that manifest as sporting events probably arose through the adaptive advantage accrued from having a very active interest in intertribal skirmishes. The central function of sporting contests, in terms of evolved adaptations, is not to produce aesthetic responses but these responses are certainly a common phenomenon.

The same is true of entertainment. Despite the label of "entertainment arts," the primary function of entertainment is not to produce art, although this is often an outcome incidental and sometimes integral to the production of entertainment. Entertainment taps into our innate interest in the social behavior of our fellow humans. In particular, we are interested in sex, courtship, competition, and danger. Narrative, the telling of stories, is probably as old as language itself. A keen interest in attending to stories would have been essential for assimilating the cultural database. A powerful adaptive advantage would belong to individuals possessing such an interest in narrative, while, conversely, individuals who lacked such an interest would have been at severe disadvantage. The existence of thousands of myths, legends, folk tales, novels, plays, and movies is the result of our having descended from ancestors who had a definite preference for attending to stories. As to what percentage of "entertainment" represents art is open to debate. If we use Dissanayake's definition of art, as something made special, then the sheer banality of most works of entertainment excludes them from the category, art.

Art enriches virtually every aspect of human existence. It can exist as something in and of itself. More often it is embedded in other features of human life. Entertainment, religion, body adornment, architecture, transportation, and play are all enhanced by art. Even science is enhanced by elegant creativity. Art is made possible by a combination of inner aesthetic values (a feature we share with other species) and higher order consciousness (a feature known to exist only in humans) that gives us the capacity to act intentionally. The highly developed human brain is capable of generating complex mental representations including elaborate visual images. Higher order consciousness gives us the capacity to be aware of our own mental representations and also, to be aware that consciousness and mental attributes can exist in others. This provides the impetus to shape matter in such a way that it can convey something of our inner experience to others. The ways in which matter can be shaped for this purpose are myriad. Painting, sculpture, music, and narrative, are categories for artistic expression with a very ancient history. As our technological sophistication increases, more and more categories for artistic expression are added. But regardless of whether the medium is paint, photographic film, or electronic digital information the basic motivation for creative expression lies in our evolved psychology.

Summary

Our success as a species is largely due to our use of technology to master the physical environment. This sort of utilitarian technology is distinguished from non-utilitarian technology or art. Utilitarian technology, ie., tool-use is not restricted to humans and occurs widely though not commonly throughout the animal kingdom. The only nonhuman primate to regularly use tools is our closest phylogenetic relative, the chimpanzee. This suggests that tool-using behavior is over five million years old in our lineage, going back to the common ancestor of humans and chimpanzees.

The oldest tools, that can be definitively identified as such, date to over 2.5 million years in age. These are pebble tools of the Oldowon tradition. This was followed by the Acheuleun tool industry characterized by bifacial forms such as the hand axe. The Acheulean industry lasting from 1.7 million years ago to 200,000 years ago demonstrates the existence of a cultural tradition almost impervious to change. The most sophisticated stone-tool industries coincide with the entry of *Homo sapiens sapiens* into Europe about 40,000 years ago. The rate of innovation dramatically increased at this point and has continued to increase exponentially ever since.

Humans show special anatomical adaptations in the hands and brains demonstrating that tool-use has been a selective force in our evolutionary history. Our species also shows a unique pattern of right-handedness bias (about 90%) that may be the result of a long history of tool-using cultural transmission. It is possible that learning the toolmaking procedures from a mentor was greatly facilitated by both mentor and apprentice being right-handed. A shift to the construction of more symmetrical stone tools about 300,000 years ago may indicate a rise in general cognitive ability from a preoperational (prelogical) level to a concrete operational (logical) level.

Although there is evidence of an emerging aesthetic sense based on artifacts dated to about 200,000 years before the present, consistent evidence of artwork does not appear until 50,000 years ago. Between 35,000 and 10,000 years ago, cave paintings displaying great elegance and stylistic sophistication persisted with great stability. The constancy of the art forms over such a long period suggest that they were part of a ritualistic tradition.

The use of creative innovations to make one's self more impressive and to problem solve is a phylogenetically old trait that was probably present in the common ancestors of humans and chimpanzees. The first art probably took the form of novel innovations in body adornment, movement, or the use of language to enhance attractiveness to prospective mating partners or to increase social status.

Later, art was co-opted for the development of rituals and traditions that facilitated group solidarity and effectiveness.

True artistic expression requires higher-order consciousness, an awareness of one's own awareness and hence the possibility that others share this awareness. A preliminary step toward higher order consciousness is self-awareness, which has been demonstrated through mirror self-recognition in great apes and bottlenose dolphins. Human children demonstrate mirror self-recognition by 18 months of age. By four years of age, normal children have a well-developed theory of mind concept, i.e., understanding that others have a mind similar to one's own and adjusting one's own behavior in accordance with this view. The existence of theory of mind in nonhuman species has not been reliably demonstrated as yet. Art is made possible by a combination of inner aesthetic values (a feature we share with other species) and higher order consciousness (a feature known to exist only in humans) that gives us the capacity to act intentionally.

Discussion Questions

1. Discuss the development of technology from 2.5 million years ago until 10,000 years ago. What clues does the archaeological record give regarding culture and cognitive development?

2. What aspects of Pleistocene cave paintings are suggestive of ritual significance? How does art promote group survival?

3. How does Carl Jung's idea of the collective unconscious relate to the idea of shared neural architecture and entoptic images?

Key Terms

Acheulean	hand axe	*Scala Natura*
archetypes	handedness	self-awareness
autism	Mousterian	termite fishing
blade-tool	Oldowan	theory of mind
cognitive development	Piaget' system	tool-use
collective unconscious	preoperational	Umwelt
entoptic image	rouge test	Venus of Willendorf

Additional Reading

Art and the Brain by Joseph Goguen (Editor) (1999).

Biopoetics: Evolutionary Explorations in the Arts by Brett Cooke and Frederick Turner (Editors) (1999).

Sociobiology and the Arts by J. B. Bedaux and Brett Cook (1999).

The Biological Origins of Art by Nancy E. Aiken (1998).

From Complexity to Creativity: Explorations in Evolutionary, Autopoietic, and Cognitive Dynamics by Ben Goertzel (1997).

Biomusicology: Neurophysiological, Neuropsychological, and Evolutionary Perspectives on the Origins and Purposes of Music by Nils L. Wallin (1992).

The Symbolic Species: The Co-Evolution of Language and the Brain by Terrence W. Deacon (1998).

Laughter: A Scientific Investigation by Robert R. Provine (2000).

Origins of Genius: Darwinian Perspectives on Creativity by Dean Keith Simonton (1999).

A Universe of Consciousness: How Matter Becomes Imagination by Gerald M. Edelman and Giulio Tononi (2000).

Why We Feel: The Science of Human Emotions by Victor S. Johnston (1999).

The Feeling of What Happens: Body and Emotion in the Making of Consciousness by Antonio R. Damasio (1999).

The Biology of Mind: Origins and Structures of Mind, Brain, and Consciousness by M. Deric Bownds (1999).

Evolving the Mind: On the Nature of Matter and the Origin of Consciousness by A. G. Galexander Cairns-Smith (1998).

The Radiance of Being: Complexity, Chaos and the Evolution of Consciousness by Allan Combs (1997).

Consciousness and the Brain by Michael Gazzaniga (1996).

Consciousness Explained by Daniel Clement Dennett (1992).

10

Ancient Mammal
in a Brave New World

For we which now behold these present days
Have eyes to wonder, but lack tongues to praise.
—William Shakespeare, *Sonnet 106*

This strange disease of modern life,
With its sick hurry, its divided aims.
—Matthew Arnold, *The Scholar-Gipsy.*

O brave new world
That has such people in't!
—William Shakespeare, *The Tempest* (1611)

Chapter Questions

1. Why was there a general decline in human health after the rise of agriculture?
2. Why is the stress response an adaptive trait despite its potentially harmful health effects?
3. How do our stone-age minds and bodies sabotage our mental and physical health in the modern world?
4. How could something as maladaptive as a propensity for drug addiction evolve through the process of natural selection?
5. Will the next phase of human evolution be the result of genetic engineering?

Despite the inherent difficulties of tracing our evolutionary origins, we know far more about where we came from and what we are, than about where we are going and what we will become. Morphologically, physiologically, and behaviorally we have been shaped by evolution to live the life of hunter-gatherers for hundreds of thousands of years. For millions of years preceding that, our ancestors lived the life of social primates living in small hierarchically organized groups. With the rise of agriculture and civilization beginning some ten thousand years ago, most of humanity began to abandon the hunter-gatherer lifestyle. Since the advent of the industrial revolution a few centuries ago there has been an exponential explosion in the rate of technological innovations. Today we live in a world that is quite alien relative to the one that has been the home of our species for the vast majority of its existence. Although in truth, it is a world that we, ourselves, are largely responsible for having created, in many respects, it is a world for which we are ill-suited as a result of our evolutionary legacy. We must come to grips with this simple fact before we face an even greater challenge. In the past, our technological inventiveness has allowed us to shape the outer world to suit our own ends but now certain technological advances have put us on the threshold of something never before tried. Soon we will be able to shape ourselves by manipulating our own genomes. Before we step into that ultimate brave new world of re-creating ourselves, we need to have a firm understanding of exactly what we are and where we have come from.

Mismatch Theory

The skeletal remains of people living during the last Ice Age (30,000 to 15,000 years ago) indicate that these individuals were taller on average than modern humans (Eaton, Eaton, & Konner, 1999). They had powerful, robust physiques, excellent teeth with no indication of dental caries, and even their brain capacity was larger than the average brain capacity of modern humans. These are comparisons made between Pleistocene individuals and people today, but when we compare them to people living before modern Western industrial times, the differences are even greater. With the advent of agriculture around 10,000 years ago, there is a marked deterioration in physical health that can be inferred from the skeletal remains. There is a great decline in overall stature and robusticity, and the skeletons indicate signs of degenerative disease. These indications of dietary deficiencies persist right up until relatively recent modern times. Most modern men would find it impossible to fit into a suit of armor from the middle ages, and the Civil War general, Robert E. Lee, was said to tower commandingly over his troops at a height of 5'10".

This shift to agriculture was probably a result of the large-scale depletion of game animals that forced a change in lifestyle rather than some eureka-like discovery in basic horticulture. The idea that edible plants would grow from their seeds planted in soil was probably common knowledge long before extensive agriculture became a common practice. Whatever its origin, the shift to the agricultural lifestyle put humanity along a path for which there was no turning back. What agriculture did was to allow for the production of large quantities of a single or a few types of food commodities, typically cereal grains. With a large staple base of calories, human populations could increase dramatically in number. Unfortunately, although there was a general increase in calories, the one-dimensional aspects of the diet often produced profound nutritional deficiencies. Even when the dietary deficiencies did not produce diseases or abnormalities, it generally resulted in much smaller stature. It was not until the twentieth century advances in transportation, food production, and food storage (i.e., refrigeration) were developed, that the majority of individuals living in our society had access to a diet as rich, varied, and nutritionally complete as that available to our ancestors living twenty thousand years ago. Even with these modern advances, individuals in our society must make a conscious effort to pursue a lifestyle that does not result in health deficits. These health problems are a direct result of the mismatch between our ancient genome and our modern lifestyle.

People today are put at risk by the modern lifestyle and diet. Modern Westerners typically average cholesterol levels of 200 mg/dl, and in the recent past levels as high as 300 mg/dl were considered normal (Elliot, 1989). The cholesterol levels of modern hunter-gatherers average around 125 mg/dl, which is comparable to that found in free-living nonhuman primates (Eaten, Eaten, & Konner, 1999). Hunter-gatherers obtain about 20 to 25 percent of their total energy from fats, which is a very low average by modern standards. Their cholesterol intake is estimated at 480 milligrams per day, which is nearly 200 milligrams per day greater than modern day recommendations. Apparently the active lifestyle of the hunter-gatherer plus the proportionally different types of fats in the diet offset the adverse effects of their high cholesterol intake. The game eaten by hunter-gatherers has much less capacity to raise serum cholesterol levels than does meat from today's supermarkets. The flesh from domesticated animals, which have been selectively bred for centuries for greater and greater fat content, contains about 20 grams of fat per 100 grams of meat, whereas the flesh from wild game animals has about 4 grams of fat per 100 grams of meat. Moreover, in hunter-gatherers the high animal-protein intake occurs in association with low-fat and high fruit and vegetable consumption as contrasted to industrialized countries where high-protein diets are consumed in concordance with low levels of plant foods, particularly fruits, vegetables, and fiber (see Figure 10.1).

A number of cancers including breast and colon cancer have been linked to the high-fat consumption of modern Westerners. The carcinogenic effects of the fat are further exacerbated by the absence of the antioxidant and other anticarcinogenic influences directly associated with fruits and vegetables. Moreover, the absence of fiber in the diet as a result of consuming refined foods and oils further increases the susceptibility to colon cancer and diverticulitis. Although hunter-gatherers obtain a similar number of their calories from carbohydrates compared with modern Westerners, the sources are very different. For Westerners, most of their carbohydrate calories come from refined sugars and flours that have a

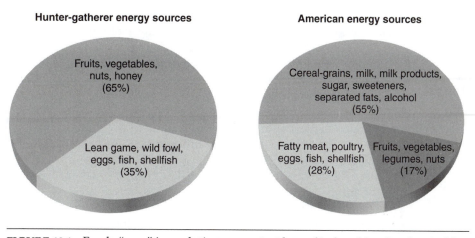

FIGURE 10.1 Foods "new" in evolutionary context have displaced/replaced a sizable fraction of the "original" foods that fueled 99% of human evolution.

(Adapted from "Evolutionary Aspects of Diet: Old Genes, New Fuels" by S. B. Eaton and L. Cordain, in *Evolutionary Aspects, Children's Health, Programs and Policies*, Fig. 1, p. 27, © 1997 by S. Karger AG; used by permission of S. Karger AG.)

glycemic index very similar to that of pure sugar. For the hunter-gatherer, the carbohydrate calories come from fresh fruits and vegetables. As a result, it is estimated that the vitamin and mineral intake of a typical hunter-gatherer far exceeds the recommendations for these vitamin and mineral levels that have been approved by modern nutritionists.

One nutrient that was a rarity in Paleolithic times but is now common to the point of excess is sodium salt. Sodium is absolutely essential to neurological and muscular functioning, and life cannot be sustained without it. The same can be said of potassium but, of these two nutrients, the body actively conserves only sodium. When sodium levels in the body drop, a peptide hormone called aldosterone is secreted by the adrenal cortex, which causes the kidneys to reabsorb the circulating sodium. Although potassium is equally essential to life, the body does not have elaborate physiological mechanisms for the retention of potassium. It is constantly secreted through the urine. These differences are a product of our evolutionary history. With the exception of the seacoast, most ancestral environments were fairly devoid of sodium salt. Consequently, we have an appetite for salt, and our body has mechanisms for retaining it. Potassium on the other hand is commonly found in plant foods, particularly fruits. It has always been such a common part of our environment that we do not have specific physiological adaptations to hold on to it. It has never been a necessity in our evolutionary past. In the modern world, salt is everywhere, and we typically use far more of it than is necessary. One consequence of this excessive sodium intake is hypertension or high blood pressure which effects nearly 20% of the adult population in the United States (Elliot, 1987). Hypertension can exacerbate cardiovascular problems accrued from high cholesterol/high fat diets greatly increasing the potential for heart attacks and strokes. Hypertension is also a primary cause of kidney failure.

Compounding the negative effects of improper diet is physical activity, or the lack there of, in our modern existence. For hunter-gatherers, a sedentary lifestyle is a possibility only occasionally available to a few highly privileged individuals. In the modern world, a sedentary lifestyle is not a privilege but rather a direct and unavoidable consequence of industrial civilization. A sedentary lifestyle is such a common part of the modern world that for most individuals it can only be avoided through conscious effort. For many office-bound Westerners, physical activity is something that is engaged in as a peripheral activity to improve health and appearance with no direct relation to the attainment of food, shelter, or other necessities of survival. Even among today's fitness buffs only a select few approach levels of aerobic fitness that were average for our Paleolithic ancestors. One reason hunter-gatherers have such low levels of cholesterol in their blood despite their relatively high dietary intake of this substance is the generally high level of physical activity they engage in. A sedentary lifestyle coupled with a diet high in cholesterol and fat greatly increases the risk for coronary artery disease as well as stroke. Furthermore, when the body is not subjected to the demands of weight-bearing exercise the bones become weaker and thinner. This condition is particularly problematic in postmenopausal women where the extreme thinning of the bones is referred to as osteoporosis. The susceptibility of elderly women to hip fractures is a direct result of osteoporosis. In osteoporosis, as with cardiovascular disease, a sedentary lifestyle interacts with improper diet to amplify the effect. Because of their consumption of green leafy vegetables Paleolithic peoples had, on average, a much higher dietary intake of calcium than modern Westerners (Eaton, Eaton, & Konner, 1999).

Since humanity first ventured on the path toward agriculture and civilization, there has been an ever-increasing mismatch between our evolved genome and the world in which we find ourselves. The five thousand year old "iceman" who was found freeze-dried in a glacier in the Swiss Alps tells us something about this mismatch (Dorfer, Spindler, & Bahr, 1998; Loy, 1998). Painstaking forensic analysis of the iceman's remains indicates that he became frozen in the glacier when he was in early middle age. Despite his relative youth, his arterial system shows signs of relatively advanced atherosclerosis. His tissues contain high levels of the heavy metal poison, arsenic; probably the result of the metallurgical procedures he used to produce the copper axe found near his body. His body also shows the signs of a parasitic infestation. Heavy levels of parasitism are also associated with a shift to an agricultural existence. Highly concentrated human populations living in the same area, generation after generation, greatly facilitated the spread of such parasites. What the iceman tells us is that even in the relatively pristine world of five thousand years ago, the "more advanced" human cultures were already engaged in a lifestyle that was at odds with their biological heritage. The health-compromising effects of this mismatch are further worsened by the disparity between modern stressors and our ancient evolved stress-coping mechanisms.

Stress: Then and Now

For the vast majority of our natural history, stress could be defined in terms of a direct physical threat. Typical stressors during the Pleistocene would be attacking predators, threatening conspecifics, or environmental hazards such as slipping off a steep cliff face. In each case the response would be the same, a generalized activation of the autonomic nervous system referred to as the fight/flight response. The fight/flight appellation is an accurate description of the functional aspects of this general response. The sympathetic nerve fibers of the autonomic nervous system, which mediates the fight/flight response, target a variety of organs effecting them in a manner to facilitate fighting or fleeing. For example, the heart rate is stepped up, the blood vessels constrict directing more blood flow to the large muscles of the body, the pupils of the eyes dilate taking in more information, and other systems not essential to dealing with a momentary physical emergency are inactivated or inhibited, such as the digestive system, the immune system and the reproductive system (Carlson, 1998). The fight/flight response is also associated with the release of stress hormones such as the glucocorticoid, cortisol, and epinephrine (adrenaline). Epinephrine enhances the sympathetic nervous system effects, increasing the heart rate and blood pressure. And as a blood-borne hormone, it is carried to tissues that are not directly connected to sympathetic fibers. In addition, stress hormones act as gluconeogenic agents. In other words, they promote the production of new glucose (gluconeogenesis) by breaking down stored animal starches in the liver and muscle tissues, which provides a quick source of fuel for the muscles and brain to utilize during an emergency. These same stress hormones also break down stored adipose tissue (body fat) into fatty acids, which provide an energy source for muscle tissues. Furthermore, the glucocorticoids and epinephrine also break down body proteins such as muscle tissue into their constituent amino acids. These amino acids can be further broken down to become glucose, or they can serve as a handy supply of tissue-building material to repair wounds and other injuries that may be suffered during a physical emergency.

Through countless generations of our ancestors, the fight/flight response provided the necessary physical boost that was needed to survive emergency situations. Even in today's world this activation of the sympathetic nervous system can be critical to survival. For example, a woman pulling out of her driveway accidentally backed over her two-year-old toddler. She jumped out of her car and the slight 120-pound woman lifted the vehicle completely off of her son facilitating his rescue. In yet another occurrence, a giant tractor toppled over, pinning a man's twelve-year-old son. The man was able to lift the tractor from his son but broke his back in the process. Even in the course of day-to-day existence, the autonomic nervous system plays a vital role. If not for this system we would be unable to adjust to slight environmental changes, for example, going outside and back inside, or adjust to changes in work load such as having a term paper due on a particular day.

However, despite the critical role this system plays in the context of modern human life, it often produces maladaptive consequences. When an individual becomes angry or agitated at being stuck in traffic or enraged by the actions of another driver, the sympathetic nervous system and endocrine system produces the ancient fight/flight response. The body is flooded with stress hormones, the heart races, the blood pressure goes up, and the blood stream is flooded with fatty acids mobilized from adipose tissue. Sitting behind the steering wheel of a car there is little outlet for these physiological responses. The blood pressure may remain high hours after the event that triggered it. The fatty acids that had been mobilized as fuel to the bloodstream are not utilized and, consequently, they precipitate out on the inner lining of the arteries to form a plaque buildup leading to atherosclerosis.

The work place is another modern arena where this age-old response now produces maladaptive consequence. When a person's boss or superior finds fault with their work, the same sort of fight/flight mechanism is triggered. Unfortunately, if the individual does pursue a physical pattern of responding congruent with his bodies physiological pattern he is probably in store for a great deal of trouble. Physically attacking one's boss is frowned upon in our culture and almost inevitably leads to incarceration for any individuals who opt for this particular strategy.

In the modern world we often get news of stressful events via electronic equipment that allows for remote communication. A powerful stress response can be induced by a telephone call from a relative living hundreds of miles away or even the images of a current war being beamed into our living-room television set. This constant triggering of the stress response without an appropriate physical outlet has an extremely deleterious effect upon the body.

Atherosclerosis is clearly one consequence of having a hair-trigger sympathetic response. It is estimated that some 20% of Americans are predisposed by their personality type to be at risk for heart disease resulting from their quick anger and generally cynical view of human nature (Donner, 1996). These individuals are a subset of the so-called Type A personality, which is characterized by frantic, hard-driving, goal-oriented behavior. Being hard driving in itself is not a risk factor, but in those individuals in which it is linked to hostility, there is a clear association with heart disease. Chronic anger and frustration lead to periodic triggering of the stress response, resulting in the arterial plaque build-up known as an atherosclerosis. The chronic surges in blood pressure and heart rate experienced by people who are already developing atherosclerosis may cause the plaque in a coronary artery to rupture producing a blood clot and thereby precipitating a heart attack (The Stress Connection, 1994).

In addition to potentiating heart disease, chronic stress responses compromise numerous other body systems. Chronic stress plays havoc with the digestive system because one function of sympathetic arousal is to inhibit digestive functioning. When the parasympathetic division of the autonomic nervous system becomes active, in order to return the digestive system to functioning level, it can result in an excessive secretion of stomach acids. With chronic overrelease of stomach acid there is a potential for peptic ulcers to form. Viral infection has been implicated as one factor in the formation of peptic ulcers but this is also linked to the stress response. The inhibition of the immune system that occurs during sympathetic arousal compromises the body's ability to defend against infectious agents.

The chronic shutdown of the immune system makes the individual vulnerable to numerous bacterial and viral pathogens. The result is a pattern of chronic illness that makes coping with the stressful events even more problematic, setting up a vicious cycle where stress impairs health making the existing stressors even more stressful and difficult to cope with.

Making matters even worse are the effects of chronic stress upon the brain. In the modern world most of our day-to-day problems are of a complex nature and require a relatively high degree of mental acuity to deal with. One of the proximate functions of the stress response is to elevate cognitive functioning. This is achieved by increasing the blood plasma levels of glucose available to central nervous system neurons. The stress hormones mobilize glucose from stored sources via their gluconeogenic properties and shunt this fuel to the brain by elevating blood pressure. Hormones such as epinephrine probably also increase the permeability of the neuron membranes to their essential fuel, glucose. All this has the effect of increasing the speed and efficiency in neural functioning. The down side is that, in the long term, chronic exposure to the glucocorticoids such as cortisol make the neurons much more vulnerable to physiological insults leading to neuron death and cognitive deficits (Sapolsky, 1999).

Individuals diagnosed with clinical depression typically secrete abnormally high levels of glucocorticoids such as cortisol (Sapolsky, 1999). High-resolution MRI brain scans of such depressed individuals indicate significant reductions in hippocampal size ranging from 12 to 15 percent when compared to matched nondepressed controls. The hippocampus is a brain structure critical in mediating the storage of long-term memories. It could be argued that individuals with smaller that normal hippocampi become depressed because of their impaired cognitive functioning. This however seems unlikely because subjects were matched for level of education in the study referred to. Examinations of hippocampal volume in individuals with post-traumatic stress disorder (PTSD) also show indications of atrophy with a seven to eight percent reduction in normal volume. There is also evidence of a direct positive correlation between duration of exposure to combat and hippocampal atrophy regardless of whether the individuals were diagnosed with PTSD or not.

Even in ancient ancestral environments, chronic activation of the fight/flight response undoubtedly produced detrimental health defects. One must keep in mind that the process of natural selection is not about producing ideal organisms or ideal systems. Natural selection is about maintaining physiological and behavioral traits that allow individual organisms to survive long enough to reproduce viable offspring. The cumulative effects of chronic stress are generally not lethal in an individual until after the prime reproductive years have passed. Consequently, in the calculus of natural selection, having a stress-response system that will get you through an occasional emergency, even though in the long term it produces a relatively early death, will always be selected for.

In practical terms, we as modern humans must keep in mind that the stress response is evoked by a perception of threat. Whether or not something sensed is actually perceived as threatening is a consequence of the calculations and filtering that take place in our cognitive system. A conscious realization that becoming angry and frustrated at another driver's irrational actions is only inflicting harm upon ourselves is the first step in circumventing the cascade of physiological events associated with the stress response. Psychologists have identified a personality type that appears to be relatively unaffected by adverse stress responses. This type is called the "hardy personality," and they typically view stressors not as threats or punishing events but rather as challenges (Dobasa, Maddi, & Kahn, 1982). Such individuals seem to have a naturally positive outlook on life, accepting each new stressor as a kind of obstacle to be overcome in the game of life. While most of us are probably not blessed with this natural inclination towards hardiness, we would be well advised to try to inculcate this outlook as much as it is possible to do so. Since the vast majority of the stressors experienced in the modern world are of an abstract mental nature, to respond to them with an ancient pattern of physical metamorphosis is not only maladaptive it is also potentially lethal.

Mental Health

One indication of the validity of mismatch theory is the progressive decline in mental health over the past century. Each successive generation appears to be growing more susceptible to bouts of major depression. For Americans born before 1905 only one percent had suffered an episode of major depression by age 75 (Meyer & Deitsch, 1996). Of Americans born after 1955 six percent had suffered major depression by age 30. This same historical trend is evident in other Western industrial nations such as New Zealand, Taiwan and Lebanon. Currently, it is estimated that 23.1% of the U.S. population will develop symptoms of depression during their lifetime.

Depression also powerfully interacts with other aspects of health and well being. For people 45 years of age and older, who are in otherwise perfect health, depression makes them 50% to 100% more likely to have a heart attack than their nondepressed cohorts (Marano, 1999). Moreover, people who have heart attacks and develop symptoms of depression over the following 18 months, are three and one-half times more likely to die than those individuals who do not become depressed following a heart attack.

The etiology of clinical depression is highly complex and convoluted. However some causal patterns are self-evident. As pointed out earlier, chronic stress creates a vicious cycle of physiological decline. The brain areas most directly damaged by chronic cortisol secretion are the same areas most likely to contribute to worsening symptoms of depression, namely the prefrontal cortex, the amygdala, and the hippocampus. These areas all show significant atrophy in chronically depressed individuals. Clearly, the modern environment is becoming increasingly stressful.

But why should this necessarily be the case? Compared to our Paleolithic forebears, the life we lead is one of ample food, creature comforts, and leisure. Unfortunately, excessive food and physical leisure compromise the body's ability to cope with stress. The health problems associated with our modern diet and sedentary lifestyle have already been discussed. The question that remains, however, is why should the physically undemanding modern lifestyle be such a stressful one, one that is growing increasingly stressful with each successive generation.

Part of the problem is that as work has become less and less physically demanding, we have had to do more and more of it. With the invention of each new "labor saving" device, the sum total of daily and weekly labor has increased. The work patterns of hunter-gatherer peoples are very different from the 40-plus hours per week of labor typical in our society. Most foraging peoples work for one or two days with one or two days off in between, usually working only a few hours per day (Elliot, 1998). This pattern has probably held true for the vast majority of human existence.

Traditional peoples also show seasonal variations in the workload. Activity levels are generally much higher in the spring and summer months when food is abundant and weather conditions are favorable. Conversely, winter season is generally a time of rest and conserving resources. One form of depression, called seasonal affective disorder (SAD), probably represents an adaptation to this pattern of conserving resources during the winter. People suffering the symptoms of seasonal affective disorder become very lethargic during the winter months when nights are long and days are short. In addition to feeling listless, they have a strong craving for carbohydrates and a tendency to store excess adipose tissue during the winter months.

SAD is often treated with prolonged exposure to artificial lighting. The physiological changes associated with this disorder are probably the result of an endocrine gland in the brain called the pineal gland, which produces a hormone called melatonin. Melatonin is continuously produced during periods of darkness and production shuts down during light periods. Melatonin has the effect of inducing sleep and suppressing sex hormones thus insuring energy conservation during the winter months.

One major source of modern stress is that we live in a world peopled by strangers. Traditional tribal groups are seldom comprised of more than a few hundred individuals and are generally much smaller than that. Practically everyone in such a group is known to everyone else, and the degree of familiarity is often closely associated with the degree of kinship. Even the people of neighboring tribes are generally somewhat familiar to foraging peoples. Overall, encounters with complete strangers are very rare occurrences. The life of modern people is a very different one. Often times, more strangers are encountered during a daily outing than friends or even acquaintances. Usually, most or all of the people in our work environment have no kinship relationships to us at all. It is a paradox of the modern world, with its population in the teeming billions, that many individuals experience minimal social support and often have feelings of extreme isolation.

Indoctrination, Nationalism, and War

So far in this chapter we have discussed evolved predispositions that may create maladaptive tendencies in the modern world and ultimately compromise the physical and mental health of individual humans. Unfortunately, our evolutionary legacy has shaped other predispositions that put not only individual lives at risk but also the lives of millions of individuals and possibly our entire species. The lives of countless nonhuman organisms are also in jeopardy. We live in a world bristling with weapons of mass destruction. An enormous amount of time, energy, and intelligence has gone into the construction of these weapons, which in objective analysis appears to be completely irrational. Given the state of things as they are, it could be argued that nonparticipation in the arms race opens the door to conquest or annihilation. This is true when the situation is viewed from the limited perspective taken by most world leaders. It would require an inordinate degree of dedication, discipline, and sacrifice to extricate ourselves from the current mess. However, when viewed from a perspective that transcends the current generation and encompasses all the generations of humanity, such tremendous investment into the art of destruction appears very foolish. Why would so much intelligence be devoted to such a stupid undertaking? What is the origin of the human capacity to wage war?

One of the first gender differences that emerges in humans as well as nonhuman primates is the tendency for young males to engage in bouts of rough-and-tumble play much more so than females (Maccoby, 1999). Rough-and-tumble play quickly develops into play fighting which appears to be an important socialization tool for males. Experimental studies of nonhuman primates in which subjects are either allowed to play fight or denied the opportunity indicate that play fighting is a critical developmental experience necessary for the development of the social intelligence and skills required for existing in a hierarchical group. Play fighting allows young males to learn the give and take of dominance relationships, the proper communication signals involved in those relationships, and when to fight and with whom to fight. Not only does it allow them to learn to control their aggressive tendencies but it is critical to their ability to learn cooperation and collaboration.

On January 7, 1994, in Gombe National Park, Tanzania, one of Jane Goodall's field assistants observed a group of eight chimpanzees consisting of seven males and one adult female walking towards the border of their territory (Goodall, 1986). When the group reached the boundary of their normal range, they did not stop but stealthily crossed over to the territory of a neighboring chimpanzee group. Just inside the neighboring territory, a young male chimpanzee from the neighboring group was encountered. By the time this young male detected the presence of the ape interlopers, it was too late. Although he fled, his pursuers chased after him, grabbed him and held him captive. While one male held him face down on the ground, the others rushed in pummeling his body and biting and tearing bits of flesh from him. Of the ape intruders, the only two who did not participate in the attack were the female and an adolescent male. After a few minutes of this vicious assault, the attack ended, and the intruders left their victim to die. This is undoubtedly what happened since the animal was never seen again following this encounter.

This observation was the first of many that would completely turn around the prevailing view of great apes as passive, peace-loving creatures consistent with Jean Jacques Rousseau's ideal of the noble savage. Subsequently, numerous field observations have shown that chimpanzees actively defend their territories, often going in gangs of six to ten individuals into neighboring territories and ambushing lone animals from neighboring groups. When such "raiding parties" encounter larger odds, usually more than one animal, they generally retreat immediately.

The basic chimpanzee pattern of territorial defense, gang raids, and ambush, bear striking resemblance to some of the core warfare tactics employed by the Yonomamo people of the Venezuelan Amazon basin. Studies of the Yonomamo are of particular interest because, unlike the majority of the hunter-gatherer people still in existence in today's world, the Yonomomo are culturally autonomous. In other words, they do not fall directly under the political sway or influence of outside cultures, particularly modern Western industrial cultures.

The Yonomamo war technique that most closely resembles the chimpanzee pattern is called *Wayu Huu* or raid (Chagnon, 1988, 1992). A Yonomamo raid begins after a party of 10 to 20 men agrees to kill selected enemies. After going through ceremonial rituals to prepare them for the raid, they set out for the enemy village, which is often a distance of four or five days on foot. Upon reaching the outskirts of the enemy village the raiding party scouts out the situation waiting quietly in ambush for a lone victim. If the raiders cannot find an isolated individual, they simply fire a volley of arrows into the village and run away. However, should an unfortunate individual cross their path, they immediately shoot him with lethal curare-tipped arrows and then immediately flee back to their own village.

The second Yonomamo war technique is even more appalling by Western ethical standards than the *Wayu Huu*. It is called *Nomohori*, the dastardly trick (Chagnon, 1988, 1992). In this scenario, the men pretend that the enemy villagers are actually their allies and invite them to a feast. Once their supposed guests have completely relaxed their guard and are lying in repose, the hosts turn and slaughter them, cleaving their skulls with axes, beating them with clubs, and shooting them with arrows. All the males are killed outright, and the females are taken captive. This tactic strongly resembles a similar deceptive strategy employed by some Scottish Highlanders over the centuries, and examples of dastardly tricks in a general sense can be found in the histories of virtually all existing cultures.

Women are also taken captive when they are encountered during *Wayu Huu* raids. Anthropologist, Napoleon Chagnon (1988, 1992), who studied the Yonomamo extensively through the 1960s and 1970s, has argued that the conflict exhibited by the Yonomamo relates to reproductive fitness. Chagnon discovered in his data analysis that Yonomamo males, who had been honored for killing enemy tribesmen, had more than two and one-half times the average number of wives and more than three times the average number of children as men who had not killed. Thus, successful raiding, which is generally related to superior fighting skills and aggressive tendencies, enhances reproductive fitness

If human tendencies toward violent behavior were limited to individual actions or even the actions of small groups (gangs), we would still have needless tragedies on a daily basis but there would be no such thing as war. The chimpanzee raids described above are sometimes referred to as "wars" but in reality they are really acts of gang violence. The ape raiding behavior, does however, give us an important insight into the origin of the human capacity to wage war (Wrangham & Peterson, 1996). The chimp raiding behavior is predicated on male coalition building and aggressive defense of group territories against outside groups of conspecifics. In humans these patterns of coalition building and in-group versus out-group territorial defense have been tremendously augmented by language and its corollary, enhanced cultural transmission. Consequently, the history of civilized humans is a record of wars, both great and small. Of the modern hunter-gatherer societies studied, only ten percent have been found that do not participate in war on a regular basis. Because we share a common ancestry with chimpanzees dating to seven million years ago, it is likely that bellicose, territorial male coalitions also existed in the ancestral species. If this is true, it means that inter-group conflict has been an ongoing selective force in our evolution for over five million years. Inter-group conflict has been proposed as one explanation for the rapid encephalization seen in human evolution (see Chapter 3).

This raises the question as to why the human lineage would experience a trebling of brain size, whereas relatively little encephalization has occurred in the chimp lineage since the two lines diverged. Inter-group conflict at the level that it occurs in forest-dwelling apes is not a particularly strong selective force, at least on time scales measured in millions of years. In the lineage leading to humans, rapid encephalization did not start until millions of years of savannah existence as a biped with a chimp-sized brain had already passed. Evidently, a certain critical level of population density and raiding effectiveness must be reached before inter-group conflict becomes a strong selective force. Once that critical threshold was reached an arms race ensued (figuratively at first and later literally). Brain-based skills such as ballistic throwing, language, creativity, and planning would have been traits critical to surviving such inter-group encounters. The exponential increase in brain size that has occurred in our lineage over the past 2.5 million years must be due, at least in part, to inter-group conflict and competition (see Chapter 3 for other factors). Unfortunately, this thesis suggests that some of the complex cognitive attributes that were selected for may predispose our species to some potentially highly maladaptive behaviors (e.g., world wars, genocide, nuclear arms races).

One such cognitive attribute is our species-specific capacity for indoctrination. The human ethologist, Irenaus Eibl-Eibesfeldt, has defined indoctrinability as a "special learning disposition allowing acceptance and identification with group characteristics which thus serves bonding and we-group demarcation" (Eibl-Eibesfeldt, 1998, p. 51). He argues that this facility for tribal bonding was evolutionarily derived from the primal capacity for forming mother-child dyads. The generally high level of resistance to abandoning cultural beliefs and loyalties inculcated at an early age makes human indoctrination very similar to the phenomenon of avian filial imprinting. In imprinting, avian species such as graylag geese learn to follow the first large moving object they perceive during the first 36 hours after they hatch. Whatever object the gosling imprints on during this critical period, whether it is an adult goose, a human researcher, or a windup toy, is likely to remain permanently etched into the animal's memory, powerfully influencing its behavior. Similarly, humans form group allegiances during sensitive periods in childhood and are very resistant to forming alternative allegiances in later life.

Frank Salter (1998), also a human ethologist agrees that indoctrination is dependent upon fixed species-typical principles. However, he defines indoctrination as the purposive inculcation of an identity or doctrine requiring repetition, deception and often coercion. This means that it is not like imprinting, which requires only minimal exposure to a releasing stimulus during the sensitive period. Salter argues that kin affiliation forms in an imprinting-like manner but larger nonkin group allegiances require a special concerted effort at indoctrination.

In studying the indoctrination techniques of the !Kung San of Botswana and the Enga of New Guinea, Polly Wiessner (1998) came to a similar conclusion. She believes that indoctrination is a very effort-intensive, formal process aimed at counteracting in-group tendencies by opening boundaries to the formation of broad social networks outside the small kinship groups. In traditional societies much of this indoctrination process is often focused into what is generally referred to as a rite of passage or puberty rite. It is during the rite of passage that individuals in traditional societies pass from childhood status to adult status.

Such rites of passage typically involve prolonged isolation, sleep deprivation, physical debilitation, physical coercion, threat, verbal inculcation of doctrine, and a show of compassion at the point of collapse (Salter, 1998). These same characteristics are common to full brainwashing techniques although brainwashing is generally much harsher, implementing a great deal of degradation and punishment. Both brainwashing and traditional initiation are highly effective in creating affiliative bonds. Salter gives the following summary:

> The most successful approaches to indoctrination challenge self-identity and induce a common set of psychological states that sway individuals toward identifying with a leader, group, or doctrine. The process induces intense emotions of fear, depression, guilt and loneliness combined with a state of dependency on the instructor. These combine to drive the subject into an affiliative bond with one or more representatives of the indoctrinating group. It is this bond, combined with the instructor's authority and the subject's altered physiological and psychological state that increases the likelihood of a new identity and set of loyalties being embraced. This pathway appears to be a common denominator of highly effective indoctrination. Furthermore, the behaviors, emotions and relationships that it evokes all belong to the species-typical repertoire, that is they are innate universals. The lack of variety of effective paths to indoctrination, especially at the functional level of cognition and emotion in the subject confirms the hypothesis that the means for indoctrinating humans, no matter how technically developed, are constrained by the necessity of keying into the human sensory and behavioral apparatus. This apparatus is a product of hominid and primate phylogeny stretching back over geological epochs. (p. 448)

These techniques have proved equally effective in unifying the populations of tribal groups, agrarian villages, and city-states. Remarkably, these same propensities for forming group alliances have created solidarity in nations comprised of hundreds of millions of people. Consequently, we now see the phenomena of young men going off to distant lands, to fight to the death against people they have never seen, for leaders they have never encountered personally and for reasons that are, at best, remote abstractions.

Better Living through Chemistry: Psychopharmacology

The Origins of Substance Abuse

One of the most obvious patterns of maladaptive behavior in modern life is substance abuse. Innumerable lives have been destroyed by tobacco addiction, alcoholism, heroin addiction, cocaine addiction, and addiction to and reliance upon numerous other substances that affect the functioning of the brain. It may seem paradoxical that evolution could produce organisms with a predilection for such maladaptive behavior but the explanation for it is quite simple and in perfect congruence with evolutionary theory.

In order to maintain survival-enhancing behaviors, the brain must have what are called reinforcement mechanisms to insure that when a necessary behavior is engaged in the organism is rewarded or reinforced for engaging in that behavior. These reinforcement centers are located in a part of the brain called the medial forebrain bundle and another center called the nucleus accumbens. The neurons in this area use a neurotransmitter called dopamine. When an organism engages in a behavior that promotes its survival, for example, eating food when hungry or drinking water when thirsty, these dopamine circuits in the reinforcement centers become active, and the organism experiences a sensation of pleasure or a satisfaction. Without these reinforcement centers and their activity there would be nothing to promote the regular continuance of behaviors that promote survival.

All drugs that have abuse potential either directly or indirectly stimulate these dopamine circuits and reinforcement centers of the brain (Carlson, 1998). For example, when someone uses crack cocaine, the cocaine is borne in the form of smoke up to the nasal mucosa where it is carried by the arterial system to these reinforcement centers. Cocaine exerts it effect by blocking the re-uptake of dopamine at the synapse. Normally when dopamine is released at a synaptic junction, it is removed immediately from the synapse by a process called re-uptake. When this process is disrupted the dopamine remains in the synapse, and the neural impulses continue to be transmitted along the circuit. Consequently, by using cocaine an individual can stimulate reinforcement centers of the brain without involving survival-oriented behavior.

Opiate drugs such as heroin exert their effects through their chemical similarity to naturally occurring endorphins in the brain (Carlson, 1998). These brain endorphins exist to moderate traumatic pain and thus have an analgesic effect on the body. It is the removal of this analgesic effect and the compensatory physio-logical adaptations that result in the withdrawal experienced by heroin addicts when they stop taking the drug. However, it is not fear of the adverse conse-quences of drug withdrawal that maintains the addictive process in heroin addic-tion. Often times heroin addicts will willingly quit using of their own volition, going "cold-turkey," if prices are too high on the street or if no drugs are available. Typically they resume the habit later, even though they essentially cleaned out their systems and are free of physiological dependence. What maintains the be-havior is the fact that stimulating the endorphin receptors with heroin or other opiate-like drugs has the indirect effect of stimulating the dopamine pathways in the medial forebrain bundle and the nucleus accumbens, thus inducing the plea-surable sensations associated with reinforcement. Similarly, all drugs with abuse potential, in some fashion stimulate these reinforcement centers.

With drugs such as ethanol (drinking alcohol) the positive reinforcement ef-fect is amplified by negative reinforcement (Carlson, 1998). The old adage of peo-ple drinking to forget is an example of negative reinforcement. Ethanol numbs the individual to both physical and psychological pain thereby cutting off the source of displeasure, this effect is referred to as negative reinforcement. Negative rein-forcement occurs when a behavior is engaged in to avoid something aversive as opposed to positive reinforcement where a behavior is engaged in order to acquire something desirable. The negative reinforcement associated with desensitization coupled with the positive reinforcement from the indirect stimulation of the nu-cleus accumbens creates the intense gripping effect of alcoholism.

For hunter-gatherers, the major causes of mortality are accidents and infec-tion (Elliot, 1989). For modern Westerners the primary causes of death are heart disease, cancer, and stroke. One primary risk factor linked to all three is tobacco smoking. As a plant indigenous to the New World, tobacco has been available to native Americans for thousands of years but for the rest of the world, only a few centuries (Smith, 1999). Tobacco, particularly in the form of smoke, is such a recent introduction into the human environment that there has not been adequate time to evolve physiological defenses to its toxic effects.

Smoking is linked to heart disease and stroke though its compromising ef-fects on the arterial system. Smoking accelerates atherosclerosis by depositing cho-lesterol on the walls of the arteries. The active ingredient of cigarette smoke is nicotine, a potent vasoconstrictor which further narrows the passageways for blood flow. This combination of clogging arteries as well as constricting them po-tentates heart attack and stroke. Moreover, tobacco is the most dangerous car-cinogen that our society is exposed to. It accounts for more cancer deaths than all other carcinogens combined. Although tobacco has been linked to cancer of the mouth, the larynx, the throat, the esophagus, pancreas, bladder, and kidney, the most common cancer resulting from tobacco use is lung cancer.

A variety of animals, including many primate and rodent species, that have had electrodes directly implanted into the reinforcement centers of their brain become addicted to the self-administration of electric shocks to these areas. They can also become addicted in the old-fashioned chemical fashion. Thus, not only humans but also all relatively complex animals have the potential for addiction and substance abuse. As to why some individuals succumb to this natural vulnerability and others do not, or why some will experiment briefly with such things and then put them aside, can best be explained in terms of genetic predispositions and ontogenetic histories.

Drug use by a mother during pregnancy can skew the neurological development of her developing offspring for optimal functioning in an environment in which that drug is present. Thus, children born to women who smoke throughout the pregnancy may be predisposed to take up cigarette smoking later in life. Ontogeny can also predispose individuals towards drug abuse through psychological trauma. A 1996 survey of over 3,600 female adolescents showed that those with a history of childhood sexual abuse were at much greater risk for substance abuse problems (Chandy, Blum, & Resnick). In general, negligence, abuse, and impoverished environments, predispose individuals towards substance abuse. When external reinforcement is often rare and unpredictable, direct stimulation of the brains reinforcement centers becomes a more-attractive option. Substance abuse is also more frequent in certain age groups, notably adolescence through young adulthood.

Jared Diamond (1992) has proposed an explanation for the prevalence of drug use among people during their peak reproductive years. Basically Diamond's theory is a variation of Zahavi's handicapping principle. The handicapping principle explains selection for gaudy nonfunctional traits such as the peacock's tail as a display that indicates quality genes. By displaying an obvious handicap the message is that the individual has such high-quality genes that it can maintain health despite the added burden of the nonfunctional handicap. Thus from Diamond's perspective, the teenager who can drive 120 miles per hour with high levels of ethanol, cocaine and other drugs in his system should be more attractive to perspective female mating partners than the nonintoxicated individual who drives his vehicle at legal speeds if all other characteristics are held equal. This would explain why "bad boys" occupy such a central role as the fascinating attractive forbidden fruit of literature and media.

Psychopharmacology

For many individuals, their first steps toward substance abuse began as an attempt at self-medication. Feelings of depression, anxiety, and low self esteem often prompt these individuals to seek relief through chemical means. In light of our current understanding of neurochemistry as the proximate mechanism underlying many mental disorders, the chemical solution sought by many anguished individuals may be ill-conceived only in the details of its implementation.

There are many ways in which nerve cells can be chemically defective, many of which are not yet well understood. However, it appears that two important conditions related to a number of psychiatric conditions are either a relative excess or a relative deficit in the functioning of a particular neurotransmitter. Consequently, many psychotropic medications appear to work because they increase or decrease the amount of neurotransmitter available at the synapse. Two ways drugs work to increase the amount of neurotransmitter are by blocking re-uptake (these medications inhibit the cell's ability to engage in re-uptake) or by blocking neurotransmitter metabolism (these medications block the action of the enzymes that cause neurotransmitters to change into other compounds).

For example, in the case of depression it is hypothesized that neural transmissions are not being passed on. Two neurotransmitters, norepinephrine and serotonin, are suspected to be deficient. Most antidepressant drugs inhibit re-uptake of either or both of these neurotransmitters. The tricyclics are a group of antidepressant drugs that work by inhibiting the re-uptake of both serotonin and norepinephrine, but predominately the latter. A more recent class of drugs, including Prozac and Zoloft, focus more on inhibiting the re-uptake of serotonin, and so are called serotonin selective re-uptake inhibitors (SSRIs) (Julian, 1998). Finally another group of drugs interfere with the action of a particular enzyme that metabolizes these neurotransmitters, called monoamineoxidase (MAO). The drugs are called MAO inhibitors. They also increase the amount of neurotransmitter available at the synapse by interfering with metabolism of the neurotransmitter.

For conditions in which it appears that there is a relative excess of neurotransmitter causing nerves to fire unnecessarily, psychoactive medications often work by blocking receptor sites. With this approach the drug has a chemical structure that locks into the receptor site but does not cause the nerve to fire. Because the receptor site is filled, the neurotransmitter can not fit into the receptor site. For example, it is hypothesized that a relative excess of the neurotransmitter dopamine causes schizophrenia. The drug chlorpromazine (Thorazine) blocks dopamine receptors and has proved effective in eliminating psychotic symptoms such as auditory hallucinations and delusional thinking.

During the past fifteen years there has been an increase in the prescribing of psychotropic medications. The reasons for the increase are numerous but undoubtedly related to the availability of more medications that are effective. These medications are also considered safe, with fewer side effects and a decreased risk of fatality from overdose. There is also a decreased stigma in taking psychotropic medication.

The first highly effective psychotropics were the antidepressants. The first group of antidepressants was the tricyclic antidepressants, which were popularized in the 1960s and 1970s (Julian, 1998). This group is still used, though they do have some shortcomings. Foremost is the risk of fatality when these medications are taken in overdose. The tricyclic antidepressants are known to cause ventricular arrhythmia and other cardiac anomalies. Other common side effects associated with these type antidepressants are dizziness, constipation, and weight gain.

The next class of antidepressant medication to be discovered and utilized was the monoamineoxidase inhibitors, or MAOI inhibitors for short (Julian, 1998). These antidepressants were found to be especially helpful for what we call "atypical depression," where people tend to eat and sleep more (not less) and where there is less anhedonia, or inability to enjoy life. They seemed especially helpful, as well, for people who experienced rejection sensitivity and for those suffering from panic attacks or agoraphobia, which is a fear of going outside.

The new generation of antidepressants began with fluoxetine (Prozac) (Julian, 1998). They are also called selective serotonin re-uptake inhibitors (SSRIs) because of the way in which they work. Their mechanism of action is to block the serotonin re-uptake pump that scavenges the released serotonin through the cell wall back into the presynaptic neuron. The other SSRI antidepressants that were developed after Prozac are paroxetine (Paxil), sertraline (Zoloft), and fluvoxamine (Luvox). These drugs are presently the best-selling prescriptions in the world. Side effects of the SSRIs include decreased sexual functioning and gastric distress.

Because of the desire to maintain the safety of the SSRIs but also to enhance their effectiveness and to combat the problem with sexual functioning, additional antidepressants have been developed. These new antidepressants are also considered "new generation," but they are actually a step closer to the tricyclics in their mechanism of action. These new or second-phase new-generation antidepressants target more than the SSRIs. They include buproprion (Wellbutrin), venlafaxin (Effexor), nefazadon (Serzone), and mirtazapine (Remeron). Though these newer model antidepressants offer some additional features, they still do not work in all patients.

Antipsychotic medications are those that blunt the symptoms of schizophrenia. All appear to work by blocking the re-uptake of dopamine (Julian, 1998). The first "classic" antipsychotic is chlorpromazine (Thorazine), which was the first popular antipsychotic, introduced in the 1950s. Many other neuroleptic medications have been developed. None were more effective, but they differed in terms of dosing and side effects. In the 1960s, haloperidol (Haldol), was developed. Since that time, Haldol has come to represent the drug of first choice for controlling psychotic disorders.

These "classic" antipsychotics have notable side effects (Julian, 1998). These include tremors, stiffness, muscle dystonias, and tardive dyskinesia, which is an irreversible movement disorder. Tardive dyskinesia is especially undesirable and devastating. This side effect is often irreversible and leads to involuntary persistent rhythmic movements of various muscles. One important point about the typical neuroleptics is that they are not effective at treating what we call the "negative" symptoms of schizophrenia. The negative symptoms include affective blunting, alogia (failure to think logically), anhedonia (not enjoying anything) and avolition (not doing anything.)

During the 1950s and 1960s, the "atypical" neuroleptics were developed (Julian, 1998). The atypical neuroleptics derive their name because they do not specifically block the D2 (dopamine 2) receptors as do the typical neuroleptics. The first of these atypical neuroleptics to be developed was Clozaril. However, it has not found great favor due to its propensity to cause agranulocytosis, which is a potentially fatal disease causing the patient to fail to develop blood cells and platelets. Advantages of atypical neuroleptics include reduced tremors and less muscle stiffness. There is also a reduced risk of tardive dyskinesia. One additional advantage to the atypical neuroleptics is that, unlike the typicals, they do help to reverse the negative symptoms of schizophrenia.

Anxiolytics are medications that reduce anxiety. The first types were barbiturates and nonbarbiturate medications such as glutethamide and meprobamate (Julian, 1998). Prior to the benzodiazepines, these were the prime medications used to reduce anxiety. The advantages of the benzodiazepine class of medications was safety. Whereas it was quite common for people to die from the pre-benzodiazepine-era anxiolytics, it was quite uncommon for someone to die from the benzodiazepine anxiolytics. Further, there later developed an antidote that would reverse the sedative effects of benzodiazepine medications in an individual who had taken an overdose. An additional welcome feature of the benzodiazepines was that tolerance did not develop. This meant that if a certain dose was effective to calm a certain level of anxiety in a particular person, it would continue to have the same degree of effectiveness despite the person taking the medication even for years. One such anxiolytic that has been developed is called buspirone (Buspar) (Julian, 1998). Additionally, other medications not specifically developed for tranquilization but which have sedative-type side effects are appropriate for selected cases. These medications included antihistamines, beta blockers, which block a subtype of norepinephrine, and serotonin (5HT) re-uptake inhibitors.

Mood stabilizers include lithium carbonate and several of the antiseizure drugs include valproate (Depakene) and carbamazepine (Tegretol). Researchers really do not understand how these drugs operate, but they suspect that they alter synaptic activity in neurons, though not in the same way as antidepressants (Julian, 1998). Recent research indicates that the changes appear to occur at the second messenger system, so-called because they intervene between the reaction of the original message and the firing of the neuron.

Before the appearance of psychiatric medications, there were virtually no effective techniques available to treat the symptoms of mental illness. Throughout the 1940s, 1950s, and even 1960s, patients with severe mental illness and some cases not-so-severe illness were treated by a surgical technique called a prefrontal lobotomy (Carlson, 1998). This surgical procedure in no way alleviated the subjective symptoms of mental illness. All it did was to leave these people docile and relatively easy to manage. The prefrontal cortex is a site in the brain involved in making plans and executing them. By destroying this region of the brain, the patient's ability to act upon their own volition was severely compromised. Clearly, the psychopharmalogical treatment of mental disorders is light years in advance of what passed for treatment previously.

Most would agree that many individuals suffering from severe mental psychological disorders have benefited greatly from the development of psychotropic medications. However, the current use of these drugs, particularly the antidepressants and anxiolitics, greatly exceeds the percentage of people diagnosed with severe or even moderate psychopathogy. In his 1932 anti-utopian novel, *Brave New World*, Aldous Huxley describes a future society where everyone maintains a state of happiness and contentment as a consequence of their use of a drug called soma (literally food of the gods) that is doled out to them daily by the government. The future government described in *Brave New World* actively promotes the use of soma with advertising slogans such as "a gram is better than a damn." The

BOX 10.1 • *Through a Glass Darwinian*   *Nootropics, The Smart Drugs: Can Genius Be Purchased in Pill Form?*

Using drugs to enhance cognitive performance is nothing new. The nineteenth century writer, Balzac, regularly dosed himself with massive amounts of coffee (caffeine) in order to maintain his prolificacy. Today, many thousands use caffeine to help them meet the cognitive demands of daily life. Thousands also use the drug nicotine, which stimulates excitatory acetylcholine receptors, as a cognitive aid despite the severe health hazards associated with it. These drugs and their cognitive effects were discovered serendipitously, but, currently, the search for new nootropics is a major goal of many major pharmaceutical laboratories.

The term nootropic comes from a Greek word meaning "acting on the mind" (Dean, 1993). The "grandfather" of nootropic drugs is piracetam which, in fact, carries the brand name Nootropyl. Piracetam was invented by UCB Laboratories in Belgium. Piracetam is reported to boost mental clarity and alertness, improve problem-solving ability and verbal ability and enhance memory and concentration. Remarkably, it may have a regenerative effect upon the nervous system. When piracetam was given to older mice for a two-week period, researchers found a 30 to 40 percent increase in the number of cholinergic receptors in their frontal cortexes. Piracetam may also improve creativity by increasing the flow of information between the right and left hemispheres of the brain. Moreover, these effects are achieved without promoting addiction. Few, if any negative side effects have been reported with short-term usage. The discovery of piracetam set off a competitive race in the pharmaceutical industry to find more nootropics. Some of the related compounds that have been produced include aniracetam, pramiracetam, and oxiracetam.

Most of the nootropics, to date, have been developed by European pharmaceutical companies. However, researchers Jerry Yin and Tim Tully of Cold Spring Harbor Labora-

tory of Long Island, New York, are on the verge of clinical trials for their own memory-enhancing drug (Weed, 2000). They have isolated a protein that helps nerve cells in the brain store memories. They created two genetically altered strains of fruit flies: one with extremely high levels of this protein and the other with almost none. They then looked at how rapidly individuals from the respective strains would learn to avoid a certain odor that presaged an electric shock. The high-protein strain learned in one trial. The low-protein strain never made the association. Fruit flies with normal levels of the memory protein needed an average of 10 trials to learn the association. Yin and Tully are close to developing a pill that will temporarily produce an overproduction of this memory protein in the human brain, thus permitting extreme memory enhancement upon demand. This memory protein does not enhance intelligence, so if its widespread use becomes a reality, we will have the prospect of numerous students who have indelibly stamped volumes of information into their memories but who remain clueless as to what it all means.

Nootropics can not really give you something you do not already have. What they do is make performance at the upper range of one's potential, in terms of problem solving, verbal fluency, clarity, and memory more available on a day-to-day basis. As any competitive athlete will attest, anything that allows one to consistently perform closer to their best is a major helping factor. Many individuals are capable of turning in an outstanding performance occasionally but it is consistent high-level performance, day in and day out that separates the champions from the also-rans. This is not to suggest that everyone with academic aspirations should rush out and purchase nootropic compounds.

Nootropic research is still in its infancy. Although, findings from animal research confirm the efficacy of existing nootropics,

BOX 10.1 • (Continued)

their mechanism of action is largely unknown. Moreover, the nature and magnitude of their effects on human cognition remains a mystery because of the lack of experimental studies with humans. One very serious consideration is the fact that almost nothing is known about the long-term effects of these drugs. The FDA has not approved most of these drugs. Paradoxically, one of the most commonly used nootropics, nicotine, is fully legal, highly addictive, and proven to cause cancer and heart disease. Given the labile nature of human rationalization, this last fact could be used to argue for either tighter controls or looser controls on nootropics.

protagonist of the novel, the Savage (a human bred and reared in an ordinary manner), struggles for his right to experience the full spectrum of human experience, including distress and unhappiness. This proves to be an almost impossible goal in a society that has virtually eliminated discomfort, danger, pain, and psychological distress.

The capacity to experience psychological distress evolved as a mechanism to guide our behavior in directions that generally enhanced survival and reproductive fitness. The general elimination of all psychological distress would be as disastrous as eliminating all sensations of physical distress. However, it must be remembered that the tweaking of a patient's neurochemistry is basically a relatively crude and second-hand adjustment of the most complex system known to exist in the physical universe. Each individual's brain/body is the product of a personal ontogeny interacting with genes that are the legacy of thousands of millions of years of evolution. We are on the verge of the deepest, most-invasive intervention into adjusting our minds and bodies ever attempted. These adjustments are so pervasive and overwhelming that they make the most extensive present-day chemical and surgical treatments look like mere cosmetic alterations. Taking into account the contingencies of personal ontogeny, our bodies and behavior can ultimately be reduced to the three billion nucleotide base-pairs that comprise our genome. The ability to directly tinker with this genome constitutes the single most significant technological innovation ever made by our species.

The New Eugenics: Genetic Engineering

The key difference between natural selection and selective breeding is that selective breeding is always based on value judgments. Natural selection is an automatic process that is wholly indifferent to concepts such as good and bad, beautiful and ugly, strong and weak, noble or loathsome. Natural selection revolves wholly around reproductive viability. Although reproductive viability is necessary in selective breeding, the selection is oriented toward increasing some characteristic or set of characteristics that have been judged to be of value. Eugenics, in its original sense, like other forms of selective breeding was conceptualized as a means of "improving" the stock, in this case, of the human race. Eugenics is a very old idea, dating back to Plato and even earlier. It has been embraced by many individuals throughout history. These individuals ranged from sensitive artists like George Bernard Shaw to the man whose name has become synonymous with evil, Adolf Hitler. Similarly, a number of different eugenics movements have risen throughout the course of history, also spanning the gamut in terms of general merit. However, none of these eugenics programs persisted for the time it would take to significantly alter the gene pool of the target population. Whether such a selective breeding program could ever be sustained for the requisite time is rapidly becoming a moot point. Soon we will have the technological know-how to transform the human genome in a single generation.

The science of genetic engineering originated in the late 1960s and early 1970s with the discovery of restriction enzymes (Avise, 1998). While investigating how viruses and rings of deoxyribonucleic acid (DNA) called plasmids infect bacterial cells, recombine, and reproduce themselves, scientists discovered that bacteria make enzymes, called restriction enzymes, that cut DNA chains at specific sites. Restriction enzymes recognize particular stretches of nucleotides arranged in a specific order and cut the DNA in those regions only. Each restriction enzyme recognizes a different nucleotide sequence. Thus, restriction enzymes form a molecular tool kit that allows the chromosome to be cut into various desired lengths, depending on how many different restriction enzymes are used. Each time a particular restriction enzyme or set of restriction enzymes is used, the DNA is cut into identical pieces of the same number allowing for precise replication. The 1978 Nobel prize for physiology went to the discoverer of restriction enzymes, Hamilton O. Smith, and the first people to use these tools to analyze the genetics of a virus, Daniel Nathans and Werner Arber.

Restriction enzymes make it possible to remove a bit of DNA from one organism's chromosome and to insert it into another organism's chromosome (Avise, 1998). This allows for the production of new combinations of genes that may not exist in nature. For example, a human gene can be inserted into a bacterium or a bacterial gene into a plant. So far, however, there are limits to this ability. Science fiction fantasies notwithstanding, scientists are currently unable to create a whole new organism starting solely with a test tube full of nucleotides. They must start with the complete genetic material of an already-existing organism. Thus, genetic engineering allows the addition of only one or a small number of new characteristics to an organism that remains essentially the same. In addition, only characteristics that are determined by one or a few genes can be transferred. The current knowledge of behavioral genetics is not sufficiently advanced to enable scientists to transfer behavioral traits, such as intelligence, that are a complex mixture of many genes and ontogenetic factors.

Several biologically useful peptides (chains of amino acids that act as neurotransmitters and hormones) were made and tested in clinical trials during the late 1970s and early 1980s (Bodmer & McKie, 1995). The first genetically engineered product to be approved for human use was human insulin made in bacteria. Insertion of the human insulin gene into bacteria was accomplished by the pioneer genetic engineering company, Genentech. Testing, approval for medical use, and large-scale production of genetically engineered human insulin were carried out, and the first diabetic patient in the world was injected with human insulin made in bacteria in December 1980, making this the first genetically engineered product to enter medical practice. Genetically engineered products are often identified by the prefix *r*, for "recombinant." Thus, genetically engineered insulin is sometimes written, *r*-insulin.

The interferons are another medically important group of peptides that became available in abundance only after the development of genetic engineering techniques (Bodmer & McKie, 1995). Interferon was useful for treating viral infections, and there were strong indications that it might be effective against some cancers. Before the advent of genetic engineering techniques, it took laborious processing of thousands of units of human blood to obtain enough interferon to treat a few patients. Other medically useful human peptides that have been made widely available because of genetic engineering are human growth hormone, which is used to treat persons with congenital dwarfism and tissue-type plasminogen activator (t-PA), which is a promising new treatment for persons who suffer a heart attack. With the development of retroviral vectors in the early 1980s, the possibility of efficient gene transfer into mammalian cells for the purpose of gene therapy became widely accepted.

On Sept. 14, 1990, the United States became the first country to allow new genes be introduced into human beings (Bodmer & McKie, 1995). A gene drug was used to treat a four-year-old girl with severe combined immune deficiency (SCID). Victims of SCID lack the gene that controls the production commands vital to immune functioning. SCID patients prior to gene treatment had to live inside sanitized plastic bubbles. In early 1991, a nine-year-old girl with SCID was also treated with the same gene therapy. In 2000 it was announced that three French infants born with SCID had been cured using a more refined version of this technique (D'Agnese, 2001).

Retroviruses are currently used as vehicles to carry gene drugs to cells within the patient's body. Such somatic forms of gene therapy do not affect germ cells and, consequently, the introduced genes are not passed on to the patient's offspring. Currently, more than a dozen different types of somatic gene drugs are being used in approved clinical trials throughout the world (Wekesser, 1996). Most of the treatments are for cancer and the remaining ones for single gene diseases such as hemophilia. The next major step in human genetic engineering will be germ-line gene therapy correcting genetic deficits present in the reproductive cells of prospective parents or in the embryos themselves (Taylor, 1998).

The line between germ-line correction of potential health problems and germ-line enhancement is a very blurred one. For example, it has been shown that people with two copies (alleles) of the long version of a gene for angiotensin-converting enzyme (ACE) have greater muscle efficiency and more stamina than people with a long ACE gene and a short ACE gene, who in turn have more physical endurance than people with two short ACE genes (Montgomery, 2000). If there are no negative pleiotropic effects associated with having two of the long genes and the germ-line procedure is largely risk free, many prospective parents, given the opportunity, will opt for their child to have greater stamina. Similarly, as more generally beneficial single gene effects are discovered the age of the "designer baby" will inevitable descend upon us.

These "designer humans" will also have access to vastly improved somatic techniques and pharmacological technologies allowing for very precise adjustments in hormones and neurotransmitters. Self-made man and woman will become a reality in a very concrete sense. Whether these beings will be more like demi-gods, monsters, or something as yet unimagined, no one can predict. That such experiments are part of human destiny seems very probable, assuming that our current civilization persists sufficiently long into the future.

Of course none of us can know the future with any certainty but if human history is any indicator of what to expect we should be quite concerned. The current state of the world is a direct result of countless actions driven by ancient animal motives. This is not to say that animal motives are necessarily bad or destructive. Our capacity for compassion and empathy is a product of our biology. Various science fiction writers and futurists have suggested that if an artificial intelligence (AI) reached a sufficient level of complexity to achieve self-awareness such a being would also automatically be incapable of harming other conscious beings. Their reasoning in this is an implicit assumption that a self-aware intelligence would have empathy for other conscious entities. This seems highly improbable. In all likelihood, a self-aware AI could know only cold detachment. If the AI valued its own existence, it would probably protect itself with absolute ruthlessness regardless of the effect on any sentient innocents that happened to get in the way.

It is only our eons old history as creatures developing under parental nurturance, living in social groups with close kin, and nurturing our young that gives us the capacity for anything other than cold indifference, or ruthless selfishness. That we are already fully capable of the latter behaviors is all too evident in our history. Our primate tendencies toward xenophobia, territorial defense and unrelenting hostility amplified by giant brains and cultural legacy have wrecked great havoc. As for the future, the real threat is that we completely abandon our animal selves (i.e., our evolved psychological natures). Our capacity for courage, passion, self-sacrifice, kindness and love is also firmly rooted in our biology. It is our biology, coupled with our higher-order consciousness that gives us our humanity and our hope for something better.

Summary

Since humanity first ventured on the path toward agriculture and civilization, there has been an ever-increasing mismatch between our evolved genome and the world in which we find ourselves. Modern lifestyle is generally associated with a diet high in cholesterol, refined flour, sugar, and salt, and low in fruits and vegetable. The poor nutrition is coupled with a marked absence of regular physical exercise. Moreover, modern psychological stressors evoke primitive stress responses that interact with and exacerbate the effects of poor diet and sedentary habits to create cardiovascular disease and other health problems. The loss of traditional tribal affiliations as a source of social support is associated with a general increase in the incidence of severe depression.

In modern humans ancient primate patterns of coalition building and in-group versus out-group territorial defense have been tremendously augmented by language and cultural transmissions. Consequently, the twentieth century was marked by two world wars, numerous smaller wars, and a nuclear arms race between global superpowers. The same propensities for cultural indoctrination that evolved to cement tribal groups together now create solidarity in nations of hundreds of millions of people. Unfortunately, aggressive territorial defense against other groups/nationalities is also part of this legacy.

One of the most pervasive problems to plague modern society is drug abuse. The capacity for drug abuse exists because reinforcement centers in the brain evolved to insure that behaviors essential to survival would be engaged in. Drugs with abuse potential, directly or indirectly stimulate these reinforcement centers, bypassing the typical patterns of survival promoting behavior such as eating and drinking. People in their peak reproductive years may be at particular risk for substance abuse, which may constitute an unconscious "mating display," congruent with Zahavis handicapping principle.

Recent advances in psychopharmacology have brought in a new era of managing psychological distress. Individuals suffering from severe psychological disorders have benefited greatly from these advances, but the development of these drugs has created another problem. The percentage of people using these medications in modern Western society greatly exceeds the percentage of people diagnosed with severe or moderate psychopathology. Problematic as they are, the neurochemical adjustments made possible by psychopharmacology must be viewed as crude and relatively minor when compared to the newest innovation in biotechnology—genetic engineering.

The science of genetic engineering originated in the late 1960s and early 1970s with the discovery of restriction enzymes that cut DNA chains at specific sites. Some genetic diseases have been treated in humans with somatic gene therapy, which uses retroviruses to carry normal functioning genes into the patients body. The next step in human genetic engineering will be germ-line gene therapy which will permanently alter the subjects genome and allow for the transmission of the altered genes to the subjects offspring. Although germ-line therapy will initially be used to correct potential health problems, the use of germ-line therapy for enhancement will probably quickly follow. As more beneficial single gene effects are discovered and as pleiotropic effects come to be better understood, the age of the "designer baby" will descend upon us.

Discussion Questions

1. Discuss how our evolved psychology and physiology can produce deleterious effects in the modern environment.

2. Develop a lifestyle plan designed to create optimal physical and mental health in the context of modern, day-to-day living.

3. Discuss the concept of an evolved capacity for indoctrination in relation to traditional ideas of patriotism, civic duty, and national defense.

4. Discuss the relationship between neurochemistry and psychological functioning. When are psychoparmacological interventions appropriate? Should psychological distress be considered a normal part of the "human experience"? Why or why not?

5. Discuss the inherent dangers of human germ-line genetic engineering. Can the potential benefits outweigh the risks?

Key Terms

antidepressant
antioxidant
antipsychotic
anxiolytics
atherosclerosis
carcinogenic
cholesterol
cortisol
designer humans
dopamine
epinephrine
eugenics
fight/flight response
germ-line therapy

gluconeogenesis
glycemic index
hardy personality
hippocampus
hypertension
indoctrination
MAO inhibitors
medial forebrain bundle
melatonin
mismatch theory
nicotine
nucleus accumbens
osteoporosis
pineal gland

Pleiotropic
posttraumatic stress disorder
reinforcement centers
restriction enzymes
retroviruses
rite of passage
seasonal affective disorder
    (SAD)
serotonin selective re-uptake
    inhibitors (SSRIs)
somatic gene therapy
tricyclics
type A personality
Yonomamo

Additional Reading

Evolution in Health and Disease by Stephen C. Stearns (Editor) (1999).

Evolutionary Aspects of Nutrition and Health: Diet, Exercise, Genetics, and Chronic Disease by A. P. Simopoulos (Editor) (1999).

Evolutionary Medicine by Wenda Trevathan, James J. McKenna, and Euclid O. Smith (Editors) (1999).

The Future of Disease: Predictions by Matt Ridley (1999).

Why We Get Sick: The New Science of Darwinian Medicine by George C. Williams and Randolph M. Nesse (1996).

Darwinism Applied by John Beckstrom (1993).

The Imitation Factor: Evolution Beyond the Gene by Lee Alan Dugatkin (2001).

Technological Innovation As an Evolutionary Process by John Ziman (Editor) (2000).

The Evolution of Culture: An Interdisciplinary View by R. I. M. Dunbar, Chris Knight, and Camilla Power (Editors) (1999).

That Complex Whole: Culture and the Evolution of Behavior by Lee Cronk (1999).

Cultural Selection by Agner Fog (1999).

A Sociobiology Compendium: Aphorisms Sayings Asides by Del Thiessen (1998).

The Third Culture: Beyond the Scientific Revolution by John Brockman (1996).

Engineering the Human Germline: An Exploration of the Science and Ethics of Altering the Genes We Pass to Our Children by Gregory Stock and John Campbell (Editors) (2000).

Genetics, Society & Clinical Practice by Peter Harper and Angus Clarke (1997).

In the Blood by Steve Jones (1996).

The Human Body Shop: The Engineering and Marketing of Life by Andrew Kimbrell (1993).

Wason Selection Tasks for Cheater Detection *(Cosmides & Tooby, 1992)*

Cheater Version

You are an anthropologist studying the Kaluame, a Polynesian people who live in small, warring bands on Maku Island in the Pacific. You are interested in how Kaluame chieftains wield power.

"Big Kiku" is a Kaluame chieftain who is known for his ruthlessness. As a sign of loyalty, he makes his subjects put a tattoo on their face. Members of other Kaluame bands never have facial tattoos. Big Kiku has made so many enemies in other Kaluame bands that being caught in another village with a facial tattoo is, quite literally, the kiss of death.

Four men from different bands stumble into Big Kiku's village, starving and desperate. They have been kicked out of their respective villages for various misdeeds and have come to Big Kiku because they need food badly. Big Kiku offers each of them the following deal:

"If you get a tattoo on your face, then I'll give you cassava root."

Cassava root is a very sustaining food cultivated by Big Kiku's people. The four men are very hungry, so they agree to Big Kiku's deal. Big Kiku says that the tattoos must be in place tonight but that the cassava root will not be available until the following morning.

You learn that Big Kiku hates some of these men for betraying him to his enemies. You suspect he will cheat and betray some of them. Thus, this is a perfect opportunity for you to see first hand how Big Kiku wields his power.

The cards below have information about the fates of the four men. Each card represents one man. One side of a card tells whether or not the man went through with the facial tattoo that evening and the other side of the card tells whether or not Big Kiku gave that man cassava root the next day.

These examples are reproduced from L. Cosmides and J. Tooby, "Cognitive adaptations for social exchange", from *The Adapted Mind*, edited by J. Barkow, L. Cosmides, and J. Tooby, copyright © 1992 by Oxford University Press; used by permission of Oxford University Press.

Did Big Kiku get away with cheating any of these four men? Indicate only those card(s) you definitely need to turn over to see if Big Kiku has broken his word to any of these four men.

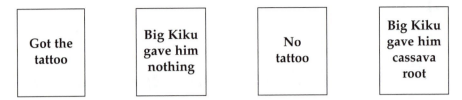

Altruistic Version

Imagine everything is the same except as follows:

The cards above have information about the fates of the four men. Each card represents one man. One side of a card tells whether or not the man went through with the facial tattoo that evening, and the other side of the card tells whether or not Big Kiku gave that man cassava root the next day.

Did Big Kiku behave altruistically towards any of these four men? Indicate only those card(s) you definitely need to turn over to see if Big Kiku has behaved altruistically towards any of these four men.

Appendix B

Neurotransmitters: A Primer

Neurotransmitters are small molecules that transmit information in the tiny spaces between neurons. They are released by a presynaptic neuron into a tiny area called the synaptic cleft. There they cause changes in the postsynaptic membrane potential or the ability of this membrane to conduct electricity. These change can be either a direct depolarization or hyperpolarization of the postsynaptic membrane. These changes can also be more indirect. Neurotransmitters can also often activate a "second messenger system" that eventually leads to more indirect changes in firing rates of the neuron. Other molecules, called neueromodulators, act on neurons to change more complex firing characteristics. These neuromodulators act from a distance and are not usually directly involved in synaptic transmission.

It is generally agreed that there are four criteria for a substance to be considered as a neurotransmitter. First, it has to be synthesized by the neuron that releases it. Neurotransmitters are synthesized in the cell body and are transported to the terminal synaptic buttons of the axon. Second, it has to be present in the presynaptic terminal and subsequently released. When an action potential occurs, an influx of calcium ions induces the vesicles to fuse with the presynaptic membrane. Its contents are then poured into the synaptic cleft. Third, and very important, when applied postsynaptically, it must mimic the effects of the neurons that release it. Finally, a specific mechanism or mechanisms must exist for removing it from the synapse. This is important because synaptic signal does not subside until the transmitter is removed from the synaptic cleft. The transmitter can be degraded in the cleft or absorbed by the postsynaptic neuron or a glial cell and then decomposed.

Each neurotransmitter has a particular biosynthetic pathway (or manner) in which it is synthesized in the brain. However, we can conveniently divide the synthesis of neurotransmitters into three principal classes. The first class is made up of acetylcholine. The second class are the biogenic amines, which are molecules formed by an amino acid losing a hydroxyl or carboxyl group. The third class is made up of amino acids. There is also a specific chain of enzymatic reactions that decompose the transmitter, either for destruction of the neurotransmitter or for its recycling.

Neurotransmitters can act as inhibitory or excitatory signals to the postsynaptic cell, by hyperpolarizing or depolarizing its membrane. The same molecule can function as an inhibitor or an excitatory. This happens because there are a small number of neurotransmitters but a great variety of their receptors on different types of cells. Acetylcholine, for instance can act as excitatory when it binds to one type of receptor, and as an inhibitor when bound on another kind, even if both types of receptors are present in the same cell.

Some of the well-studied neurotransmitters are described here. Others have been proposed, along with bioactive peptides, such as substance P and neuropeptide Y.

Acetylcholine (ACh) is mostly an excitatory neuron. It is synthesized by choline acetyltransferace. All vertebrate motor neurons use ACh. It is also found in cells of the basal ganglia. (These are the cells that tend to die in Alzheimer's disease.) ACh is extremely important in memory formation. Arthropod sensory neurons also use ACh.

The bioactive amines include the subgroup called the catecholamines. All of the catecholamines are synthesized by a similar path, which begins with tyrosine. These include dopamine, a neurotransmitter that is in evidence at many diverse sites in the brain. Too much dopamine is associated with the severe biobehavioral disorder schizophrenia. Drugs that block the bioavailablity of dopamine—or in other words, functional amount of dopamine at the receptor level—reduce the symptoms of schizophrenia. In fact, it has been known for the past 40 years that the potency of a drug to block dopamine receptors in a test-tube correlates very highly with the ability of the drug to reduce symptoms of schizophrenia.

Death of dopaminergic neurons in the substantia nigra results in Parkinson's disease, a serious movement disorder. Dopamine is also the neurotransmitter that mediates much of the activity of pleasure, largely through activity at the nucleus accumbens.

Norepinephrine is a major neurotransmitter that is found in the locus ceruleus and in the postganglionic neurons of the sympathetic nervous system. The former structure appears to operate like an alarm for general danger. Environmental events that are judged as potentially dangerous cause activity of the norepinephrine neurons (also known as noradrenergic neurons) at the nucleus accumbent. The role of the sympathetic nervous system in preparing higher animals for "fight or flight" is well known. Epinephrine is not commonly found as a neurotransmitter in mammals and usually has a more peripheral role. However, it is used by the adrenal medulla and may play other roles that are not well understood.

Serotonin (5-hydroxytryptamine or 5HT) is a catecholamine in the indolamine subclass. It is synthesized from tryptophan, an amino acid that is common in the typical diet. Serotonin is found in abundance in a number of sites in the brain including the raphe nuclei of vertebrates It is the site of action of antidepressants and hallucinogens. Additionally, it seems to play a role in sleep, sexual behavior, and satiety or the sense of fullness related to eating. Also important is the role it plays in social hierarchies.

Histamine, in addition to its role in systemic response to stress, is an invertebrate neurotransmitter found in arthropods.

In general, less is known about the amino acid transmitters. These include glutamate, which is a major vertebrate excitatory transmitter and an arthropod neuromuscular transmitter. Glycine is an inhibitory transmitter in spinal cord.

GABA (gamma-amino butyric acid) is a major inhibitory neurotransmitter in the brain that take up about 50% of brain neurons. It is synthesized from glutamate. Action at the GABA complex is important for the effects of anti-anxiety drugs and also for the effects of alcohol.

Neuropeptides are larger molecules that are synthesized in the cell body and transported to release sites. They also act as neurotransmitters, despite the fact that they are often many hundreds of times larger than neurotransmitters. They are synthesized from precursor polyproteins. More than 50 neuroactive peptides have been identified. Many were identified as hormones or gastrointestinal peptides prior to their identification as neurotransmitters. Important examples, which is involved in pain transmission. Perhaps the most interesting is the proopioidmelanocortin (POMC) chain that includes the enkephalin and the endorphins, which are involved in internal reward systems and in pain reduction. They also include adrenocortotrophic hormone, a major neurohumoral response to general stress.

When peptides and small molecule transmitters are synthesized and released by the same neuron, they are called cotransmitters. In addition, small molecules can be cotransmitters. The result of cotransmission is to produce a more-complicated postsynaptic response.

At least three mechanisms exist for removal of neurotransmitters from the synaptic cleft. Simple diffusion may account for some removal. However, high-affinity uptake of small molecule transmitters into the presynaptic terminal and glial cells is the fastest means of terminating the synaptic signal for most small transmitters (except acetylcholine). Uptake is mediated by transporter proteins.

Enzymatic degradation is the third mechanism of removal. Acetylcholine is broken down by acetylcholine esterase. Monoamine oxidase (MAO) breaks down dopamine and serotonin. MAO inhibitors are therapeutically important peptides that are broken down by proteolysis by peptidases. There is no reuptake mechanism for peptides, so their effects tend to be longer lasting than small molecule transmitters.

Glossary

Acheulean   of or relating to a Lower Paleolithic culture typified by bifacial tools with round cutting edges.

acromatopsia   loss of color vision, including the memory and conceptualization of color.

adrenocorticotropic hormone (ACTH)   a hormone released from the pituitary gland that stimulates production of hormones by the adrenal cortex.

agrammatism   a condition resulting from brain damage (such as trauma or stroke) in which the individual has impaired understanding of meaning that is normally derived from word order in a sentence.

agreeableness   ready or willing to agree or consent.

Allen's rule   states that animals of a given species show reductions in body extremities when living in colder climates.

alpha   the highest ranking animal in a dominance hierarchy.

altruism   unselfish behavior that favorably affects the survival, comfort, and state of mind of others. Can range from simple avoidance behavior to sacrificing ones' own life for another.

American Sign Language (ASL)   the main manual-visual language system of deaf persons in the United States.

android fat   fat deposits in the abdominal region stimulated by testosterone; readily mobilized for energy and depleted through physical activity. (Compare with gynoid fat.)

androsterone   a steroid metabolite having a weak masculinizing effect, somewhat similar to testosterone.

anomia   **1.** Knowing a particular word but unable to speak it; nominal aphasia. **2.** A defective moral sense.

anthropoid   **1.** Human-like. **2.** Pertaining to or resembling a human.

antidepressants   medicines used for a wide range of disorders, from hyperactivity and enuresis in children to panic disorder, obsessive-compulsive disorder, and bulimia in teenagers and adults.

antioxidant   a substance that inhibits oxidation or reactions promoted by oxygen or peroxides.

antipsychotics   drugs or medicines designed to treat the symptoms of psychosis, primarily schizophrenia.

antisocial personality disorder   a diagnosis of a personality disorder characterized by chronic and continuous antisocial or delinquent behavior not due to severe mental retardation, schizophrenia, or manic episodes. More common in males than females.

anxiety   a pervasive and unpleasant feeling of tension, dread, apprehension, and impending disaster. Whereas fear is a response to a clear and present danger, anxiety often is a response to an undefined or unknown threat that may stem from internal conflicts, feelings of insecurity, or forbidden impulses.

anxiolytics   drugs or medicines that reduce anxiety.

archetypes   a primitive or original plan from which other plans have evolved.

aromatization   to convert into one or more aromatic compounds.

atherosclerosis   a condition characterized by atheromatous deposits in and fibrosis of the inner layer of the arteries.

autism   retreat from reality into a private world of fantasies, thoughts, and, in extreme cases, delusions and hallucinations. The autistic person is turned inward, apparently completely preoccupied with his or her own needs and wishes, which are gratified largely or wholly in imagination.

avoidant personality disorder   a diagnosis assigned to a person showing a pattern of behavior characterized by hypersensitivity to rejection and criticism, social withdrawal, and low self-esteem. May impair the person's ability to work and maintain relationships.

avuncular relationships   having to do with or relating to an uncle.

babbling stage   a period of life of infants during which simple vocalization sounds are made. Typically occurs at about two months of age.

ballistic movements   sudden jerky movements over which the person has no control.

behaviorism   a school of psychology that takes the objective evidence of behavior (as measured responses to stimuli) as the only concern of its research and the only basis of its theory without reference to conscious experience.

Bergmann's rule   states that warm-blooded animals living in cold climates tend to be larger than their counterparts of the same species living in warm climates.

Big Bang theory   a theory positing that a cosmic explosion marked the beginning of the universe.

biological evolution   a theory that the various types of animals and plants have their origin in other preexisting types and that the distinguishable differences are due to modifications in successive generations.

borderline personality disorder   a serious psychological disorder indicating pattern of behavior characterized by a disturbed and fluctuating self-image, unstable and impaired interpersonal relationships, marked impulsivity that is usually damaging, and extremely reactive emotions. Other characteristics are irrational fear of abandonment, impulsive sex and other reckless behaviors, suicidal or self-mutilating behavior, inappropriate and intense hostility, and abnormal amounts of interpersonal conflict. Moods are often extreme, inappropriate, and change quickly. Unrealistic paranoia, severe dissociation, and impaired sense of reality may also be present. This disorder is one of the most difficult to treat.

Broca's aphasia   a condition due to a brain lesion in which a person finds it difficult or impossible to communicate by speaking or writing but is able to communicate by gestures. Also known as nonfluent aphasia.

Broca's area   an area of the left cerebral cortex that controls muscular movements of those organs used during articulation of speech and that is essential to the production of spoken language.

Comprehension of spoken or written language may not be affected if the area is damaged.

carcinogenic   cancer-causing.

cerebellum   located in the hindbrain. Controls muscle coordination and body balance, modulates muscular contractions to reduce jerking or tremors, and helps maintain equilibrium by predicting body positions ahead of actual body movements.

cholesterol   a substance, technically an alcohol, present in fats of some animal tissues. It is associated with circulatory disorders because of the high levels of cholesterol often found in obese individuals and in those afflicted by stress, tension, high blood pressure, and atherosclerosis.

chromosomes (diploid)   thread-like strands of deoxyribonucleic acid (DNA), ribonucleic acid (RNA), and other molecules that carry the genetic traits of an individual.

clever Hans phenomenon   animals appearing to perform high-level mental feats may actually be responding to subtle cues given unconsciously by the human trainer.

cognitive development   the growth and extension of thinking processes of all kinds, such as perceiving, remembering, concept formation, problem solving, imagining, and reasoning.

collective unconscious   the genetically determined part of the unconscious that, according to Carl Jung, is common to all humankind; comprised of the thousands or possibly millions of years of ancestral experiences.

communication   the process by which one person transmits an idea to another person by means of spoken or written words, pictures, sign language, gestures, and nonverbal communications such as body language.

conduction aphasia   a form of aphasia associated with lesions in the postcentral cortical area, characterized by difficulty in differentiating speech sounds and repeating them accurately, even though spontaneous articulation may be intact.

conscientiousness   governed by or conforming to the dictates of conscience.

conspecific   a member of the same species.

contralateral neglect   a syndrome usually caused by brain damage from trauma or stroke in which the person is unaware of portions of the body that are on the side of the body opposite from the side of the brain that is damaged. For example, a person with damage to the somatosensory portion of the right side of the brain may be unaware of his or her left leg.

copulins   a mixture of vaginal acids secreted by women at the time of ovulation that cause a rise in testosterone in men who are exposed to it.

corpus callosum   a thick band of nerve fibers connecting the cerebral hemispheres; the principal connection between the two sides of the brain.

correlational research   research on acts or processes in which two or more variables covary, usually with the objective of establishing an orderly relationship between the variables or of considering them together to find relationships.

cortical blindness   complete or partial blindness caused by ischemia (inadequate blood flow to occipital lobes, in the posterior areas of the cerebrum). Most cases of cortical blindness are accompanied by other neurological deficits usually associated with strokes.

cortisol   one of the glucocorticoid hormones secreted by the adrenal cortex. Blood levels of cortisol in humans vary according to wake-sleep cycles, being highest around 9 a.m. and lowest at midnight.

Creole   a new language ordinarily made up of words from two or more well-established languages, often with various terms pronounced differently from the original language, that becomes the language of choice of people in some social and economic groups.

critical period hypothesis   a postulate that certain abilities, such as learning language, are confined or maximized at certain time periods either for individuals or all members of a species.

Cro-Magnon   a tall erect race of hominids of the Upper Paleolithic known from skeletal remains found chiefly in southern France and classified as the same species (*Homo sapiens*) as present-day humans.

cultural relativist perspective   a perspective positing that attitudes, beliefs, values, concepts, and achievements must be understood in light of specific cultural milieu and social contexts and not judged according to another culture's standards. Proponents hold that no culture should be typified as primitive or inferior.

deoxyribonucleic acid (DNA)   any of various nucleic acids that are usually the molecular basis of heredity, are localized especially in cell nuclei, and are constructed of a double helix held together by hydrogen bonds between purine and pyrimidine bases, which project inward from two chains containing alternate links of deoxyribose and phosphate.

dependent personality disorder   a diagnosis for a pattern of allowing other people to take responsibility for major decisions in the person's life and agreeing with or following others with more dominant personalities.

depression   an emotional state of persistent dejection, ranging from relatively mild discouragement and gloominess to feelings of extreme despondency and despair. These feelings are usually accompanied by loss of initiative, listlessness, insomnia, loss of appetite, and difficulty in concentrating and making decisions.

designer humans   hypothesized individuals with special physical and behavioral traits that have been induced through genetic engineering and other advanced biomedical technologies.

dominance hierarchy   **1.** In behavior, the ordering of responses in terms of their priority or importance. **2.** In social psychology, the classification of group members as a function of their power or prestige.

dopamine   an important catecholamine neurotransmitter in the brain and also the precursor of epinephrine and norepinephrine. It is derived from dopa and is a primary form in which catecholamines are stored in tissues outside the nervous system.

Doppler effect   a change in the frequency with which waves (as sound or light) from a given source reach an observer when the source and the observer are in motion with respect to each other, so that the frequency increases or decreases according to the speed at which the distance is decreasing or increasing.

dysthymia   **1.** Any mood disorder. **2.** Morbid depression with obsessions. **3.** A depressive mood less severe than observed in cases of manic-depressive (bipolar) psychosis or major depression.

egalitarian   a social philosophy advocating the removal of inequalities among people.

empiricist   one who abides by a doctrine positing that all knowledge comes through experience.

encephalization   inflammation of the brain.

entoptic image   a visual experience due to stimuli or conditions within the eye itself.

epinephrine   a catecholamine hormone secreted in large amounts when an individual is stimulated by fear, anger, or a similar stressful situation. It increases the heart rate and force of heart contractions, relaxes bronchiolar and intestinal smooth muscle, and has varying effects on blood pressure. Also known as adrenaline.

ethology   **1.** A branch of knowledge dealing with human ethos and with its formation and evolution. **2.** The scientific and objective study of animal behavior especially under natural conditions

eugenics   Processes and methods aimed at improving the qualities of humans through better mate selection, sterilization, etc.

eukaryote   an organism composed of one or more cells containing visibly evident nuclei and organelles.

evolutionary psychology   a theory based on the recognition that the human brain consists of a large collection of functionally specialized computational devices that evolved to solve the adaptive problems regularly encountered by our hunter-gatherer ancestors.

extra-pair copulation (EPC)   copulating with someone other than one's long-term or committed mate.

extraversion   a tendency to direct interests and energies toward the outer world of people and things rather than the inner world of subjective experience.

extreme environmentalism   a doctrine that assumes that behavior is solely modifiable by changes in outward circumstances, in contrast to hereditarianism, that emphasizes the role of genetic inheritance in determining ability, intelligence, and personality.

factor analysis   a collection of techniques designed to uncover possible underlying variables that might have in part accounted for the relationships observed among a set of variables.

families   a group of things related by common characteristics such as a closely related series of elements or chemical compounds; a group of soils that have similar profiles and include one or more series; or a group of related languages descended from a single ancestral language.

female mate choice   a category of sexual selection. Darwin theorized that characteristics that females prefer in a mate would become more pronounced over evolutionary time. (Compare with male-male competition.)

field independence   the general capacity to orient the self correctly despite deceptive environmental cues. Field independence is highly correlated with analytic ability, high achievement motivation, and an active coping style.

fight-flight response   species-typical physiological response preparatory to fight or flight, synonymous with stress response.

fluctuating asymmetry (FA)   a method of assessing the relative symmetry of an organism. FA is computed by measuring a number of traits such as ankle breadth, wrist breadth, elbow breadth, and ear length. The difference between the right and left sides is computed, and the results are summed to form a composite score for all the measurements. The higher the score, the greater the lack of symmetry.

functionalism   **1.** A philosophy of design holding that form should be adapted to use, material, and structure. **2.** A doctrine or practice that emphasizes practical utility or functional relations.

gene imprinting   a theory that genes have different expressions depending on whether they are inherited via an egg or a sperm.

genetic determinism   a doctrine positing that behavior is inborn and can be predicted by the study of genetics.

genus   **1.** A class, kind, or group marked by common characteristics or by one common characteristic; *specifically:* a category of biological classification ranking between the family and the species, comprising structurally or phylogenetically related species or an isolated species exhibiting unusual differentiation. **2.** A class of objects divided into several subordinate species.

germ-line therapy   genetically engineered traits that can be transmitted to the patient's offspring.

gluconeogenesis   formation of glucose within the animal body especially by the liver from substances (as fats and proteins) other than carbohydrates.

Gondwanaland   hypothetical land area believed to have once connected the Indian subcontinent and the land masses of the Southern Hemisphere.

Gracile Australopithecines hominids that were slender and small and who had molars and incisors of similar size adapted to an omnivorous diet.

gynoid fat fat deposits in the region of the thighs and buttocks stimulated by estrogen and highly resistant to mobilization. Gynoid fat evolved as an energy reserve for pregnancy and lactation following birth. (Compare with android fat.)

Haeckel's biogenetic law posits the theory that as an individual organism passes through its early embryonic and fetal stages of development, it recapitulates the evolutionary history of its species; largely discredited by modern science.

handedness a tendency to prefer either the right or the left hand for performing certain tasks. Usually is related to a dominance effect of the motor cortex on the opposite side of the body.

handicapping principle Zahavi (1975) hypothesis that female animals select males with extravagant and costly physical displays because they are reliable indicators of genetic quality.

haploid pertaining to cells or similar structures that have a single set of unpaired chromosomes.

hardy personality one that has the capacity to survive physically and mentally in conditions of extreme environmental stress.

heterochrony a time and speed difference between two processes such as nerve impulses or the development of organs.

hippocampus a part of the limbic system of the brain associated with memory and emotional functions.

histrionic personality disorder a diagnosis of a pervasive personality disturbance characterized by excessive, extensive attention-seeking in highly emotional fashion usually beginning in early adulthood. Characterized by constantly seeking or demanding reassurance, approval, or praise from others and being uncomfortable in situations when not the center of attention. Often displays dramatic or striking physical appearance and grossly exaggerated emotions to gain attention. Considers relationships to be much more intimate than they actually are.

holophrase a single word being a sentence; a word sentence.

HOM genes an interrelated group of genes that control aspects of body differentiation in invertebrate animal embryos.

homeotherm a warm-blooded organism.

hominids any of a family (*Hominidae*) of erect bipedal primate mammals comprising recent humans together with extinct ancestral and related forms.

Homo antecessor distinguished by the characters of the midface. Provided lineage to both *Homo sapiens* and *Homo Heidelbergensis*. Midface contained a modern morphology a rather large nose, a strong brow ridge, and a receding forehead. Lived 400,000 years ago.

Homo erectus descendent of *Homo habilis*. Larger cranial size and thicker bone structure than its predecessor. Buttresses and crests are more prominent; brows over the orbits are especially thick and projecting; the rear of the cranium is strongly angled, the face and jaws are large relative to the overall size of the braincase, but the cheek and teeth are especially reduced from the Australopithecus. From Africa, *Homo erectus* migrated out to the Eurasian continent less than 1 million years ago.

Homo habilis branch of Australopithecus at the manufacturing of stone tools 2.5 to 2 million years ago. First appears at this time in both eastern and southern Africa. Delineated from other species by smaller facial bones, teeth, and skeleton showing a resemblance of the primitive Australopithecus.

Homo neanderthalensis lived 120,000 to 30,000 years ago. Larger brained, flatter forehead, broader, smaller at the front, and larger at the rear than that of the modern *Homo sapien*. Large bodied, short, stocky, and very muscular. Large heads dominated by a projecting nose, while the cheekbones were swept back. Large front teeth used as a clamp for food, tool making or skin processing.

Homo sapiens sapiens the subspecies of the genus 'Homo' in which modern humans are classified.

hormone a secretion from certain ductless glands introduced directly into the bloodstream and carried to other organs of the body where they stimulate functional activity.

HOX genes   an interrelated group of genes that control aspects of body differentiation in vertebrate animal embryos.

human chorionic gonadotropin (hCG)   a placental hormone.

human placental lactogen (hPL)   hormone that causes maternal insulin resistance in late pregnancy.

hypertension   technical term for high blood pressure.

hypoglossal nerve   originates in gray-matter nucleus on the floor of the fourth ventricle and controls the tongue, lower jaw, and areas of the neck and chest.

Ice Age   The Pleistocene glacial epoch.

ice age   a time of widespread glaciation.

imprinting   a rapid learning process that takes place early in the life of a social animal and establishes a behavior pattern (as recognition of and attraction to its own kind or a substitute).

inclusive fitness   ability or tendency of an individual to ensure the survival of its genes in future generations.

indoctrination   to imbue with a usually partisan or sectarian opinion, point of view, or principle.

in-group phenomenon   a tendency to favor the group to which a person belongs; in-group bias.

insulin   a hormone in the pancreas that controls glucose utilization.

intersexual selection   selectiveness in choosing a mate of the opposite sex; predicted to operate most strongly in the sex investing more highly in offspring, compelling it to be highly selective when choosing a partner of the sex that invests less in the offspring.

intrasexual competition   competition among the same sex for mates of opposite sex; predicted to be strongest among the sex that invests less in offspring. For example, human males compete with each other for female attention and choice.

kamikaze sperm   sperm that function to prevent the sperm of other males from reaching the egg, either by blocking or attacking; 99% of sperm perform this activity.

Kibbutzim   a cooperative or collective settlement in Israel based on the principles of idealistic socialism. Child rearing is shared by the parents and professional caretakers.

language   any means, vocal or other, of expressing or communicating thought or feeling.

larynx   a muscular and cartilaginous structure at the top of the trachea and below the tongue roots; the organ of voice consisting of nine cartilages connected by ligaments, and containing the vocal chords.

laterality   the preferential use of one side of the body for certain functions such as eating, writing, sighting, and kicking. The trait is associated with cerebral dominance.

limerance   commonly known as "being in love"; describes an obsessive state of desiring someone emotionally and sexually; often includes the desire to produce and raise offspring with them; usually involves delusional thinking that maximizes the desired one's positive traits and minimizes their negative ones.

Machiavellian intelligence   social behavior focused on gaining and maintaining power through manipulation and ruthlessness.

major histocompatibility complex (MHC)   a group of genes that create transport molecules vital to destroying and removing pathogens from the body as an important part of the immune system.

male-male competition   a category of sexual selection. Darwin theorized that characteristics that help a male out-compete other males would become more pronounced over evolutionary time. (Compare with female mate choice.)

MAO inhibitors   a class of psychotropic drugs that counter or inhibit the monoamine oxidases. In so doing, they effectively allow more monoamine presence, which contributes to an antidepressant effect.

mate guarding   actions such as physical intimidation and violence elicited when a person perceives or believes that someone else is interested in taking his or her mate. These actions may be directed toward the perceived rival or toward the mate. Subtle forms of mate guarding include making oneself more attractive to the mate or acting in a subordinate fashion to the mate.

matriarchy   a society ruled by women who are the symbols of power or of love and motherhood.

medial forebrain bundle   a group of sensory fibers located between the dorsal ganglion and the spinal cord. The medial bundle fibers communicate with the dorsal column of white matter.

melatonin a neurohormone secreted into the blood by the pineal gland that affects circadian rhythms. In humans, production is affected by light, with more production during the night than during the day. Thought to affect sexual development, sleep and appetite.

menarche a female's first menstruation, usually occurring between the eleventh and the seventeenth year, marking the onset of puberty.

menopause a period during which menstruation ceases; the end of the reproductive cycle in women.

menstrual synchronicity the gradual harmonizing of menstrual cycles in women living close together.

modular brain the idea that the brain consists of individual components with specific functions.

modular mind the idea that the mind consists of a number of specialized mechanisms designed by evolution to cope with certain recurring adaptive problems.

monogamy having only one mate. In humans, implies exclusive commitment to each other, and/or marriage to only one person.

morphology **1a.** A branch of biology that deals with the form and structure of animals and plants **b.** The form and structure of an organism or any of its parts. **2a.** A study and description of word formation (as inflection, derivation, and compounding) in language. **b.** The system of word-forming elements and processes in a language. **3.** A study of structure or form.

Mousterian of or relating to a Middle Paleolithic culture that is characterized by well-made flake tools often considered the work of Neanderthal humans.

mutations **1.** A significant and basic alteration. **2a.** A relatively permanent change in hereditary material involving either a physical change in chromosome relations or a biochemical change in the codons that make up genes; *also:* the process of producing a mutation **b.** An individual strain or trait resulting from mutation.

narcissistic personality disorder a clinical diagnosis of a disorder characterized by grandiose ideas of self-importance, need for attention and admiration, feeling entitled to special favors, and exploitation of others.

nativist one adhering to a doctrine positing that mental and behavioral factors, as well as physical traits, are inherited.

naturalistic fallacy confusion of "is" with "ought."

neocortex a part of the cerebral cortex assumed to be the most recent evolutionary stage of the brain development in mammals.

neural Darwinism a theory that groups of neurons are selected by experience to form the basis of cognitive operations such as memory and learning. This selectionism is seen as an explanation for the functioning of the brain.

neuroticism proneness to neurosis; also a mild condition of neurosis characterized by a high level of anxiety and other distressing emotional symptoms.

neurotransmitter chemicals that carry the "messages" of the nerves from one nerve cell to another.

nicotine a prevalent addictive substance, a chemical obtained from the tobacco plant.

nucleus accumbens a region of the basal forebrain generating dopamine during pleasurable behavior.

obsessive-compulsive personality disorder a diagnosis of patterns of behavior that interfere with the ability to function characterized by obsessions, compulsions, or both. Obsessions are persistent, recurrent ideas and impulses that appear senseless to the person but cannot be ignored or suppressed. Compulsions are repetitive acts, such as hand washing, counting, and touching that must be performed to relieve tension.

ontogeny the development or course of development especially of an individual organism.

openness to experience a personality characteristic that describes receptiveness and responsiveness to ideas, situations, people, and places, even when particularly novel or unusual.

operant conditioning conditioning in which the desired behavior or increasingly closer approximations to it are followed by a rewarding or reinforcing stimulus.

orders **3a:** A rank, class, or special group in a community or society. **b:** A class of persons or things grouped according to quality, value, or natural characteristics: as (1): A category of taxonomic classification ranking above the family and below the class.

osteoporosis   a condition that affects especially older women and is characterized by decrease in bone mass with decreased density and enlargement of bone spaces producing porosity and fragility.

out-group phenomenon   when a group emphasizes their solidarity by calling attention to how they are different from other groups.

oxytocin   a pituitary hormone that stimulates especially the contraction of uterine muscle and the secretion of milk.

Pangaea   hypothetical land area believed to have once connected the land masses of the Southern Hemisphere with those of the Northern Hemisphere.

paranoid personality disorder   a diagnosis of patterns of behavior that is characterized by an attitude of general suspiciousness or overwariness of other people; the attitude that other people are most likely to be dangerous, or looking to take advantage of the paranoid person.

parent-infant conflict theory   the idea that parents and infants have somewhat divergent fitness concerns, which creates an escalating arms race of evolved strategies and counterstrategies.

particulate inheritance   inheritance of characters specifically transmitted by genes in accord with Mendel's laws.

personality   a complex psychological construct that serves as a heuristic for understanding how an individual or collective entity of persons typically behaves in situations that present to them differing affordances and demands.

pheromones   glandular odoriferous secretions by male or female used for identification of territory or for communication purposes. Especially important for survival of the species since a female's pheromones lead males to her during mating time.

phonemes   fundamental structural units of sound, audible speech, or group of speech sounds combined into syllables and words, each language having a limited number and each phoneme having relevance only for that language.

phonology   1. The study of sounds in a language. 2. The sound system of a language. 3. The history of sound changes in a language.

phylogeny   the evolutionary development of a species.

pineal gland   a gland found near the center of the brain assumed to connect the soul to the body. Its function in humans is not certain—possibly the source of melatonin.

pleiotropic   producing more than one genic effect; having multiple phenotypic expressions.

poikilotherm   an organism (as a frog) with a variable body temperature that is usually slightly higher than the temperature of its environment; a cold-blooded organism.

polyandry   marriage of a woman to more than one husband at any time.

polygamy   marriage to more than one spouse at a time.

polygyny   marriage of a man to more than one wife at any time.

posttraumatic stress disorder   a mental and emotional condition resulting from exposure to severe stresses whereby a person has experienced or witnessed an event or events involving actual death or threat of death to self or others. Can be acute or chronic.

preparedness theory   a theory positing that there exists in organisms a conditioning predisposition in which the individual has a biological sensitivity to certain stimuli that are associated, in turn, with an unconditioned stimulus. For instance, primates may have an inherent preparedness to associate objects such as snakes, spiders, and enclosed spaces, with aversive events.

prisoner's dilemma   a game used in social-psychological studies in which participants must choose between competition and cooperation. It derives from a standard detective ploy (used when incriminating evidence is lacking) in which two suspects are first separated and then told that the one who confesses will go free or receive a light sentence. The prisoner may choose silence, hoping that the other suspect does the same (a cooperative motive) or that the other prisoner may confess, hoping to improve his or her own situation (competitive motive).

prosidy   the emotional aspects of speech; how something is said rather than what is said.

prosimians   any of a suborder (prosimii) of lower primates (as lemurs).

proximate causation a doctrine positing that in a sequence of events it is the final one that has the direct effect.

psychoticism a factor developed as a means of assessing the dimensions of personality that includes a disposition toward psychosis and psychopathy, distinguishing persons considered normal, schizophrenic, or manic-depressive from each other. The system uses tests of judgment of spatial distance, reading speed, level of proficiency in mirror drawing, and adding rows of numbers.

reciprocal altruism aid given by one organism to another nonrelated organism in which the reason for such aid is not readily apparent nor is there an indication that the aid will be reciprocated.

red queen hypothesis the idea that competing organisms continually evolve to counter the evolutionary advances of the other, resulting in no change in status for either.

regulator genes master-control genes that express or inhibit the actions of other sets of genes according to a development timetable.

restriction enzymes chemicals that identify a particular sequence of the chain of nucleotide bases on a DNA molecule and cut the DNA at that location.

retroviruses any of a family (Retroviridae) of RNA viruses (as HIV) that produce reverse transcriptase by means of which DNA is produced using their RNA as a template and incorporated into the genome of infected cells.

rite of passage the formal acknowledgments of transitions of a person's life course from one level of status to another by formal ceremonies.

robust australopithecines hominids that were large and heavyset, with heavy molars and small incisors, adapted to a vegetarian diet.

runaway sexual selection a process in which a positive feedback loop becomes established between female preference for certain male traits and the male traits themselves, causing the trait to develop in an unchecked fashion.

Scala Natura an Aristotelian idea in which all living things are ranked in a series, with humans at the top, apes and monkeys somewhat below, and so on down the scale to the simpler organisms.

schizoid personality disorder a personality disorder characterized by long-term emotional coldness, absence of tender feelings for others, indifference to praise or criticism and to the feelings of others, friendships with no more than two persons; but there are no eccentricities of speech, behavior, or thought.

schizophrenia a functional psychotic disorder characterized by disturbances of thinking often with delusions. Bizarre behavior and inappropriate moods such as apparent lack of emotional feelings are also included in this diagnosis.

schizotypal personality disorder a personality disorder characterized by various oddities of thought, perception, speech, and behavior not severe enough to warrant a diagnosis of schizophrenia.

seasonal affective disorder (SAD) depression-like states resulting from lack of sunlight, experienced by some people during the dark seasons of the year; alleviated by natural or artificial light.

selective breeding an attempt to achieve certain physical structure and temperament of living organisms by picking certain desired characteristics from samples of the organisms and permitting their reproduction, as in the breeding of cows for milk.

self-awareness consciousness of one's own existence.

semantics a doctrine and educational discipline intended to improve habits of response of human beings to their environment and one another, especially by training in the more critical use of words and other symbols.

serotonin a neurotransmitter that functions as a smooth-muscle stimulator, a constrictor of blood vessels, and inducer of nightly sleep. Brain levels of serotonin have been associated with psychiatric symptoms such as depression, bulimia, aggressiveness, obsessions and compulsions.

serotonin selective reuptake inhibitors (SSRIs) a class of medicines that is widely prescribed as antidepressants. Prozac was the first, introduced in the mid-1980s. Used for treating depression and in the treatment of obsessive-compulsive disorder, bulimia, and other conditions.

sexual selection choosing a mate, or competing with others for a mate. (See female mate choice and male-male competition.)

Simpua marriages a system of arranged marriages in Chinese culture where the prospective bride is brought into the household of the prospective groom when both are still children.

social Darwinism an extension of Darwinism to social phenomena, specifically a theory in sociology where sociocultural advance is the product of intergroup conflict and competition and the socially elite classes (as those possessing wealth and power) possess biological superiority in the struggle for existence.

sociobiology the comparative study of social organization in animals including humans especially concerning its genetic basis and evolutionary history.

somatic gene therapy the medical treatment of mental disorders by organic methods, such as electroshock therapy, psychotropic drugs, or megavitamins.

species a class of individuals having common attributes and designated by a common name, specifically a logical division of a genus or more comprehensive class. A category of biological classification ranking immediately below the genus or subgenus, comprising related organisms or populations potentially capable of interbreeding.

split-brain surgery a surgical split of the brain at the corpus callosum performed to end serious epileptic episodes. Postoperatively, the left and right hemispheres do not communicate with each other.

subordinate placed in or occupying a lower class, rank, or position.

symbolic reasoning to think logically about things not immediately present.

syntax the way in which linguistic elements (as words) are put together to form constituents (as phrases or clauses).

Systema Natura a book published in 1758 by Carolus Linnaeus, in which he attempted to classify all living organisms.

tabula rasa **1.** The mind in its hypothetical primary blank or empty state before receiving outside impressions. **2.** Something existing in its original pristine state.

taxonomy **1.** The study of the general principles of scientific classification: systematics. **2.** Classification: *especially* orderly classification of plants and animals according to their presumed natural relationships.

teleological error the belief that traits evolve in order to achieve a future goal.

temperament an individual organism's constitutional pattern of reactions. Characteristics include the general energy level, emotional make-up and intensity, and tempo of response.

testosterone a male sex hormone and one of the most active of the androgens produced by the testes. Stimulates the development of male reproductive organs, including the prostate, and secondary features such as the beard and bone and muscle growth.

the five-factor model of personality a model of personality including neuroticism, extraversion, openness, agreeableness, and conscientiousness.

the three-factor model of personality a model of personality that includes the primary factors of psychoticism, neuroticism, and extraversion; developed by Eysenck.

theory of evolution a theory that the various types of animals and plants have their origin in other preexisting types and that the distinguishable differences are due to modifications in successive generations.

theory of mind a theory that other entities have mental states that allows prediction of their behavior.

theory of natural selection a natural process that results in the survival and reproductive success of individuals or groups best adjusted to their environment and that leads to the perpetuation of genetic qualities best suited to that particular environment.

TIT FOR TAT a computer program designed by Anatole Rapoport that creates a successful strategy for the iterated prisoner's dilemma based on reciprocal altruism.

tool-use the ability of animals including humans to use objects as tools.

trait theory a point of view that personality is a collection of traits.

tricyclics antidepressants named for three-ring chemical structure, include amitriptyline (Elavil), imipramine (Tofanil), desipramine (Norpramin), doxepin (Sinequan), and nortriptyline (Pamelor).

type A personality behavior that is highly competitive in all aspects of life, such as work, recreation, friendship, and love, and a tendency to be hostile when frustrated.

umwelt **1.** Relating to the world in terms of its physical and biological aspects. **2.** The perceptual world in which an organism lives.

Venus of Willendorf a sculptured stone female figurine carved with emphasis on the reproductive organs, the breasts, and the buttocks; thought to symbolize fertility (25,000–30,000 BP).

visual agnosia an inability to recognize visual stimuli, such as objects.

Von Baer's law a theory that different kinds of organisms are at first similar and develop along similar lines, those of organisms least closely related, diverging first; the others diverging at later periods in proportion to the closeness of relationship.

waist-hip ratio (WHR) a measure of health and fertility in the human female, computed by dividing the hip measurement by the waist measurement. Ratios around 0.7 in women were found to be preferred by men in many cultures. Ratios above 0.9 in women are associated with increased risk of various illnesses.

Wason Selection Task Peter Wason developed this procedure in order to test if people used scientific-hypothetico-deductive reasoning in their day-to-day problem solving.

Wernicke's aphasia loss of the ability to comprehend sounds or speech, and in particular, to understand or repeat spoken language.

Wernicke's area an area of the left cerebral cortex that lies immediately behind and below the primary receptive area for hearing and that is essential to the comprehension of meaning language. Damage to this area results in an inability to comprehend spoken language and, at times, written language.

Westermark's hypothesis the idea that long-term familiarity during the early developmental process between children brought up together inhibits their having sexual interest in each other later in life.

William's syndrome a condition of mental retardation in which the cerebral cortex is about 80% the size of normal. However, the cerebellum is normal in size, and the neocerebellum is larger than normal. Individuals suffering from this disorder have IQs around 50, but their language abilities are remarkably normal.

Yonomamo the largest unacculturated Brazilian tribe today, numbering more than 16,000 people.

Bibliography

Ahlstrom, R., Berglund, B., Berglund, U., Engen, T., & Lindvall, T. (1987). A comparison of odor perception in smokers, nonsmokers, and passive smokers. *American Journal of Otolaryngology, 8,* 1–6.

Aiello, L. C., & Collard, M. (2001). Our newest oldest ancestor? *Nature, 410,* 526–527.

Aiken, N. (1998). *The biological origin of art.* Westport, CT: Praeger.

Alcock, J. (1984). *Animal behavior: An evolutionary approach.* Sunderland, MA: Sinauer Assoc.

Alexander, R. (1987). *The biology of moral systems.* New York: Aldine de Gruyter.

Alexander, R. (1974). The evolution of social behavior. *Annual Review of Ecology and Systematics, 5,* 325–383.

Alexander, R., Hoodland, J., Howard, R., Noonan, K., & Sherman, P. (1979). Sexual dimorphism and breeding systems in pinnepeds, ungulates, primates and humans. In N. A. Chagnon & W. Irons (Eds.), *Evolutionary biology and human social behavior.* North Scituate, MA: Duxbury Press.

Allee, W., Collias, N., & Lutherman C. (1939). Modification of the social order in flocks of hens by the injection of testosterone proprionate. *Physiological Zoology, 12,* 412–430, 436–440.

Allen, L. S., & Gorski, R. A. (1992). Sexual orientation and the size of the anterior commissure in the human brain. *Proceedings of the National Academy of Science, 89,* 7199–7202.

Allman, W. F. (1995). *The stone age present: How evolution has shaped modern life—from sex, violence, and language to emotions, morals, and communities.* New York: Touchstone.

Allport, G. (1937). *Personality: A psychological interpretation.* New York: Holt, Rinehart & Winston.

American Psychiatric Association. (1994). *Diagnostic and statistical manual of mental disorders* (4th ed.). Washington, DC: American Psychiatric Association.

Andersson, H. W., Sommerfelt, K., Sonnander, K., & Ahlsten, G. (1996). Maternal child-rearing attitudes, IQ, and socioeconomic status as related to cognitive abilities of five-year-old children. *Psychological Reports, 79,* 3–14.

Aristophanes (1962). *The frogs.* Ann Arbor, MI: University of Michigan Press. (Original work published 405 B.C.)

Aristotle (1937). *Parts of animals.* Cambridge, MA: Harvard University Press. (Original work published 350 B.C.)

Atkinson, J. W. (1958). *Motives in fantasy action and society.* Princeton: Van Nostrand.

Atran, S. (1998). Folk biology and the anthropology of science: Cognitive universals and cultural particulars. *Behavioral-and-Brain-Sciences, 21,* 547–609.

Atran, S. (1999). The universal primacy of generic species in folkbiological taxonomy: Implications for human biological, cultural, and scientific evolution. In R. A. Wilson (Ed.), *Species: New interdisciplinary essays* Cambridge, MA: MIT Press.

Austin, W., & Bates, F. (1974). Ethological indicators of dominance and territory in a human captive population. *Social Forces, 52,* 447–455.

Avise, C. J. (1998). *The genetic gods: Evolution and belief in human affairs.* Cambridge, MA: Harvard University Press.

Bailey, J. M., Willerman, L., & Parks, C. (1991). A test of the maternal stress theory of human male homosexuality. *Archives of Sexual Behavior, 20,* 277–293.

Baker, R. (1996). *Sperm wars: The science of sex.* New York: Basic Books.

Baker, R. R., & Bellis, M. A. (1995). *Human sperm competition: Copulation, masturbation, and infidelity.* London: Chapman and Hall.

Baker, R. R., & Bellis, M. A. (1993). Human sperm competition: Ejaculate manipulation by females and a function for the female orgasm. *Animal Behaviour, 46,* 887–909.

Barber, J. T. (1989). The use of tools for food transportation by the imported fire ant (Solnopsis invicta). *Animal Behavior, 38,* 550–552.

Barkow, J., Cosmides, L., & Tooby, J. (Eds.). (1992). *The adapted mind: Evolutionary psychology and the generation of culture.* New York: Oxford University Press.

Barrow, J. D. (1994). *The origin of the universe.* New York: Basic Books.

Battaglia, M., Przybeck, T., Bellodi, L., & Cloninger, R. (1996). Temperament dimensions explain the comorbidity of psychiatric disorders. *Comprehensive Psychiatry, 37,* 292–298.

Bayer, A. E. (1965). Birth order and attainment of the doctorate: A test of an economic hypothesis. *American Journal of Sociology, 72,* 540–550.

Beck, B. B. (1986). Tools and intelligence. In R. J. Hoage & L. Goldman (Eds.), *Animal Intelligence.* Washington, D.C. & London: Smithsonian Press.

Beck, B. B. (1980). *Animal tool behavior: The use and manufacture of tools by animals.* New York: Garland.

Begley, S. (1995, March 27). Gray matters. *Newsweek,* 48–54.

Bellis, M. A., & Baker, R. R. (1990). Do females promote sperm competition? Data for humans. *Animal Behaviour, 40,* 997–998.

Belmont, L., & Marolla, A. F. (1973). Birth order, family size, and intelligence. *Science, 182,* 1096–1101.

Belsky, J., Steinberg, L., & Draper, P. (1991). Childhood experience, interpersonal development, and reproductive strategy: An evolutionary theory of socialization. *Child Development, 62,* 647–670.

Bereczkei, T., Voros, S., Gal, A., & Bernath, L. (1997). Resources, attractiveness, family commitment: Reproductive decisions in human mate choice. *Ethology, 103,* 681–699.

Bermudez de Castro, J., Arsuaga, J., & Carbonell, E. (1997). A hominid from the Lower Pleistocene of Atapuerca, Spain: Possible ancestor to Neanderthals and modern humans. *Science, 276,* 1392–1395.

Bertenthal, B., Proffitt, D., Kramer, S., & Spetner, N. (1987). Infants' encoding of kinetic displays varying in relative coherence. *Developmental Psychology, 23,* 171–178.

Betzig, L. (1993). Sex, succession, and statification in the first six civilizations. In Ellis, L. (Ed.) *Social Stratification and Socioeconomic Inequality: Vol. I.* Westport, CT: Praeger Publishers.

Bodmer, W., & McKie, R. (1994*). The book of man: The Human Genome Project and the quest to discover our genetic heritage.* New York: Scribner.

Boesch, C. & Boesch, H. (1981). Sex difference in the use of natural hammers by wild chimpanzees: A preliminary report. *Journal of Human Evolution, 10,* 585–593.

Boring, E. G. (1950). *A history of psychology.* Cambridge, MA: Harvard University Press.

Botchin, M., Kaplan, J., Manuck, S., & Mann, J. (1994). Neuroendocrine responses to fenfluramine challenge are influenced by exposure to chronic social stress in adult male cynomolgus macaques. *Psychoneuroendocrinology, 19,* 1–11.

Bower, B. (1997). Lowly status proves infections in monkeys. *Science News, 151,* 381.

Bowlby, J. (1967). *Attachment and loss: Vol.1. Attachment.* New York: Basic Books

Box, H. O. (1984). *Primate behaviour and social ecology.* New York: Chapman and Hall Ltd.

Bradie, M. (1994). *The Secret Chain: Evolution and Ethics.* Albany, NY: State University of New York Press.

Brannon, E. M., & Terrace, H. S. (1998). Ordering of the numerosities 1 to 9 by monkeys. *Science, 282,* 746–749.

Brothers, L. (1989). A biological perspective on empathy. *American Journal of Psychiatry, 146,* 10–19.

Brothers, L. (1990). The neural basis of primate social communication. *Motivation and Emotion, 14,* 81–91.

Brunner, E. (1997). Stress and the biology of inequality. *British Medical Journal, 314,* 1472–1476.

Buss, A., & Plomin, R. (1986). The EAS approach to temperament. In R. Plomin & J. Dunn (Eds.), *The study of temperament: Changes, continuities and challenges* Mahwah, NJ: Erlbaum.

Buss, D. M. (1989a). Sex differences in human mate preferences: Evolutionary hypotheses tested in 37 cultures. *Behavioral and Brain Sciences, 12,* 1–49.

Buss, D. M. (1989b, June). *A theory of strategic trait usage: Personality and the adaptive landscape.* Paper presented at the Invited Workshop on Personality Language, University of Groningen, Groningen, The Netherlands.

Buss, D. M. (1991). Evolutionary personality psychology. *Annual Review of Psychology, 42,* 459–491.

Buss, D. M. (1994). *The evolution of desire.* New York: Basic Books.

Buss, D. M. (1995). Evolutionary psychology: A new paradigm for psychological science. *Psychological Inquiry, 6,* 1–30.

Buss, D. M. (1998). The psychology of human mate selection: Exploring the complexity of the strategic repertoire. In C. Crawford & D. L. Krebs (Eds.), *Handbook of evolutionary psychology: Ideas, issues, and applications.* Mahwah, NJ: Erlbaum.

Buss, D. M., & Schmitt, D. P. (1993). Sexual strategies theory: An evolutionary perspective on human mating. *Psychological Review, 100,* 204–232.

Buss, D. M., & Shackelford, T. K. (1997). From vigilance to violence: Mate retention tactics in married couples. *Journal of Personality and Social Psychology, 72,* 346–361.

Buss, D. M., Larsen, R., Westen, D., & Semmelroth, J. (1992). Sex differences in jealousy: Evolution, physiology, and psychology. *Psychological Science, 3,* 251–255.

Buunk, B. P., Angleitner, A., Oubaid, V., & Buss, D. M. (1996). Sex differences in jealousy in evolutionary and cultural perspective: Tests from the Netherlands, Germany, and the United States. *Psychological Science, 7,* 359–363.

Calder, N. (1983). *Timescale: An atlas of the fourth dimension.* New York: The Viking Press.

Calvin, W. H., & Bickerton, D. (1998). *Lingua ex machina: Reconciling Darwin and Chomsky with the human brain.* Cambridge, MA: MIT Press.

Calvin, W. H. (1982). *The throwing Madonna: Essays on the brain.* New York: McGraw-Hill.

Candland, D. K. (1993). *Feral children and clever animals: Reflections on human nature.* New York: Oxford University Press.

Caramazza, A. (2000). The organization of conceptual knowledge in the brain. In M. S. Gazzaniga (Ed.), *The new cognitive neurosciences, 2nd ed.* Cambridge, MA: The MIT Press.

Carlson, N. R. (1998). *Physiology of behavior* (6th ed.). Boston: Allyn and Bacon.

Carter, C. S. (1992). Hormonal influences on human sexual behavior. In J. B. Becker, S. M. Breedlove, & D. Crews (Eds.), *Behavioral endocrinology* Cambridge, MA: MIT Press.

Cartmill, M. (1974). Rethinking primate origins. *Science, 184,* 436–442.

Cartmill, M. (1998a). Oppressed by evolution. *Discover, 19,* 78–83.

Cartmill, M. (1998b). The gift of gab. *Discover, 19,* 56–64.

Cattell, R. B. (1965). *The scientific analysis of personality.* London: Penguin Books, Limited.

Cattell, R. B. (1972a). *A new morality from science: Beyondism.* Elmsford, NY: Pergamon Press Inc.

Cattell, R. B. (1972b). *Measurement of mood and personality by questionnaire.* New York: Random House.

Chagnon, N. A. (1988). Life histories, blood revenge, and warfare in a tribal population. *Science, 239,* 985–992.

Chagnon, N. A. (1992). *Yanomamo: The last days of Eden.* New York: Harcourt Brace.

Chandy, J. Blum, R., & Resnick, M. (1996). Female adolescents with a history of sexual abuse: Risk outcome and protective factors. *Journal of Interpersonal Violence, 11,* 503–518.

Chavet, J. M. C., Deschamps, E. B., & Hillaire, C. (1996). *Dawn of art: The Chauvet Cave.* New York: Abrams.

Chen, C., Burton, M., Greeberger, E., & Dmitieva, J. (1999). Population migration and the variation of dopamine D4 receptor (D4D4) allele frequencies around the globe. *Evolution and Human Behavior, 20,* 309–324.

Cheney, D. L., & Seyfarth, S. M. (1990). *How monkeys see the world.* Chicago: Chicago University Press.

Cheney, D. L., & Seyfarth, R. M. (1991). Truth and deception in animal communication. In C. A. Ristau (Ed.), *Cognitive ethology: The minds of other animals.* Hillsdale, NJ: Erlbaum.

Cheney, D. L., Seyfarth, R. M., & Smuts, B. (1986). Social relationships and social cognition in non-human primates. *Science, 234,* 1361–1366.

Chess, S., & Thomas, A. (1982). Infant bonding: Mystique and reality. *American Journal of Orthopsychiatry, 52,* 213–222.

Chess, S., & Thomas, A. (1984). *Origins and evolution of behavior disorders.* New York: Brunner/Mazel.

Chevalier-Skolnikoff, S., & Liska, J. (1993). Tool use by wild and captive elephants. *Animal Behavior, 46,* 209–219.

Chevalier-Skolnikoff, S., Galdikas, M. F., & Skonikoff, A. Z. (1982). The adaptive significance of higher intelligence in wild orangutans: A preliminary report. *Journal of Human Evolution, 11,* 639–652.

Choi, J., & Silverman, I. (1996). *Sex differences in spatial mapping strategies.* Paper presented at the meeting of the Human Behavior and Evolution Society Conference presented in Evanston, IL.

Chown, M. (1997). The alien spotters. *The New Scientist, 154,* 28–31.

Cloninger, C. R. (1987). A systematic method for clinical description and classification of personality variants. *Archives of General Psychiatry, 44,* 57–588.

Clutton-Brock, T. (Ed.). (1988). *Reproductive success: Studies of individual variation in contrasting breeding systems.* Chicago: University of Chicago Press.

Cohen, D. B. (1999). *Stranger in the nest: Do parents really shape their child's personality, intelligence, or character?* New York: John Wiley & Sons.

Collins, D. A., & McGrew, W. C. (1987). Termite fauna related differences in tool-use between groups of chimpanzees (Pan troglodytes). *Primates, 28,* 457–471.

Corballis, M. C. (1991). *The lopsided ape: Evolution of the generative mind.* New York: Oxford University Press.

Cosmides, L. (1989). The logic of social exchange: Has natural selection shaped how humans reason? *Cognition, 31,* 187–276.

Cosmides, L., & Tooby, J. (1992). Cognitive adaptations for social exchange. In J. Barkow, L. Cosmides, & J. Tooby (Eds.), *The adapted mind: Evolutionary psychology and the generation of culture.* New York: Oxford University Press.

Cosmides, L., & Tooby, J. (1997). *Evolutionary psychology: A primer* [On-Line]. Available: http://www.psych.ucsb.edu/research/cep/primer.htm

Cosmides, L., & Tooby, J. (2000). The cognitive neuroscience of social reasoning. In M. S. Gazzaniga (Ed.), *The New Cognitive Neurosciences, 2nd ed.* Cambridge, MA: MIT Press.

Costa, P., & McCrae, R. (1992). The five-factor model of personality and its relevance to personality disorders. *Journal of Personality Disorders, 6,* 343–359.

Costa, P. T., Jr., & McCrae, R. R. (1998). Trait theories of personality. In D. F. Barone & M. Hersen (Eds.), *Advanced personality. The Plenum series in social/clinical psychology.* New York: Plenum Press.

Crick, F. (1981). *Life itself: Its origin and nature.* New York, NY: Simon and Schuster.

Crick, F. (1994). *The astonishing hypothesis: The scientific search for the soul.* New York: Charles Scribner's Sons.

Cronin, C. (1980). Dominance relations and females. In D. Omark, F. Strayer, & D. Freeman (Eds.), *Dominance Relations: An Ethological View of Human Conflict and Social Interaction.* New York: Garland Publishing, Inc.

Culotta, E. (1995). New hominid crowds the field. *Science, 269,* 918.

Cummins, D. (1996). Evidence for the innateness of deontic reasoning. *Mind and Language, 11,* 160–190.

Curtiss, S. (1989). The independence and task-specificity of language. In A. Bornstain & J.

Bruner (Eds.). *Interaction in human development.* Hillsdale, NJ: Erlbaum.

Cutler, W. B., Friedmann, E., & McCoy, N. L. (1998). Pheromonal influences on sociosexual behavior in men. *Archives of Sexual Behavior, 27,* 1–13.

Cutler, W. B., Preti, G., Krieger, A., Huggins, G. R., Garcia, C. R., & Lawley, H. J. (1986). Human axillary secretions influence women's menstrual cycles: The role of donor extract from men. *Hormones and Behavior, 20,* 465–473.

D'Agnese, J. (2001). The year in science: 2000. *Discover, 22,* 49–65.

Daly, M., & Wilson, M. (1995). Discriminative parental solicitude and the relevance of evolutionary models to the analysis of motivational systems. In M. S. Gazzaniga (Ed.). *The cognitive neurosciences.* Cambridge, MA: MIT Press.

Daly, M., & Wilson, M. (1998) The evolutionary social psychology of family violence. In C. B. Crawford, D. L. Krebs, et al. (Eds.), *Handbook of evolutionary psychology: Ideas, issues, and applications.* Mahwah, NJ: Erlbaum.

Daly, M., Wilson, M., & Weghorst, S. J. (1982). Male sexual jealousy. *Ethology and Sociobiology, 3,* 11–27.

Darwin, C. (1859). *On the origin of species by means of natural selection.* London: Murray.

Darwin, C. (1868). *The voyage of the beagle.* London: Heron books.

Darwin, C. (1871). *The descent of man, and selection in relation to sex* (2nd ed.). London: Murray.

Darwin, C. (1872). *The expression of the emotions in man and animals.* London: Murray.

Darwin, F. (1887). *The life and letters of Charles Darwin.* New York: Appleton.

Dasser, V. (1985). Cognitive complexity in primate social relationships. In R. A. Hinde, A. N. Perret-Clemont, & J. Stevenson-Hinde (Eds.), *Social relationships and cognitive development.* Oxford: Clarendon Press.

Dasser, V. (1988). A social concept in Java monkeys. *Animal Behaviour, 36,* 225–230.

Davies, P. (1994). *The last three minutes.* New York: Basic Books.

Davis, K. (1948). *Human society.* New York: MacMillan.

Davis, R. (1961). The fitness of names to drawings: A cross-cultural study in Tanganyika. *British Journal of Psychology, 52,* 259–268.

Dawkins, R. (1989). *The selfish gene* (2nd ed.). Oxford: Oxford University Press

De Vries G., & Boyle P. (1998). Double duty for sex differences in the brain. *Behavioural Brain Research, 92,* 205–213.

De Waal, F. (1982). *Chimpanzee politics.* London: Jonathan Cape.

Dehaene, S., Spelke, E, & Pinel, P. (1999). Sources of mathematical thinking: Behavioral and brain-imaging evidence. *Science, 284,* 970–974.

Dennett, D. (1995). *Darwin's dangerous idea: Evolution and the meaning of life.* New York: Simon & Schuster.

Dewsbury, D. (1982). Dominance rank, copulatory behavior and differential reproduction. *Quarterly Review of Biology, 57*(2), 135–159.

Diamond, J. M. (1992). *The third chimpanzee: The evolution and future of the human animal.* New York: Harper Collins.

Diamond, J. M. (1996). Why women change. *Discover, 17,* 130–138.

Diamond, M. C. (1988). *Enriching heredity: The impact of the environment on the anatomy of the brain.* New York: Free Press.

Digman, J., & Shmelyov, A. (1996). The structure of temperament and personality in Russian children. *Journal of Personality and Social Psychology, 71,* 341–351.

Diesendruck, G., & Gelman, S. A. (1999). Domain differences in absolute judgments of category membership: Evidence for an essentialist account of categorization. *Psychonomic Bulletin and Review, 6,* 338–346.

Diesendruck, G., Gelman, S. A., & Lebowitz, K. (1998). Conceptual and linguistic biases in children's word Learning. *Developmental Psychology, 34,* 823–839.

Dissanayake. E. (1988). *What is art for?* Seattle, WA: University of Washington Press.

Dissanayake, E. (1992). *Homo Aestheticus: Where art comes from and why.* New York: Free Press.

Dissanayake, E. (1999). "Making Special": An undescribed human universal and the core of a behavior of art. In B. Cooke & F. Turner

(Eds.), *Biopoetics: Evolutionary exploration in the arts.* Icus Books Pub.

Dittmann, R. W., Kappes, M. E., & Kappes, M. H. (1992). Sexual behavior in adolescent and adult females with congenital adrenal hyperplasia. *Psychoneuroendocrinology, 17,* 153–170.

Dobasa, S. C., Maddi, S., & Kahn, S. (1982). Hardiness and health: A prospective study. *Journal of Personality and Social Psychology, 42,* 168–177.

Dollard, J., & Miller, N. (1950). *Personality and psychotherapy: An analysis in terms of learning, thinking, and culture.* New York: McGraw-Hill.

Doner, K. (1996). Heal your angry heart. *American Health, 15,* 74–77.

Dorfer, L., Spindler, K., & Bahr, F. (1998). 5,200-year-old acupuncture in central Europe? *Science, 282,* 242–243.

Doupe, A., & Kuhl, P. (1999). Birdsong and human speech: Common themes and mechanisms. *Annual Review of Neuroscience, 22,* 567–631.

Dunbar, R. (1992). Neocortex size as a constraint on the behavioral ecology of primates. *Journal of Human Evolution, 20,* 469–493.

Dunbar, R. (1996). *Grooming, gossip, and the evolution of language.* Cambridge, MA: Harvard University Press.

Eaton, B. S., Eaton, S. B., III, & Konner, M. J. (1999). Paleolithic nutrition revisited. In W. R. Trevathan, E. O. Smith, & J. J. Mckenna (Eds.), *Evolutionary medicine.* New York: Oxford University Press.

Edelman, G. M. (1987). *Neural Darwinism.* New York: Basic Books.

Ehrenkranz, J., Bliss, E., & Sheard, M. (1974). Plasma testosterone: Correlation with aggressive behavior and social dominance in man. *Psychosomatic Medicine, 36,* 469–475.

Ehrnhardt, A. A., Meyer-Bahlburg, H. F. L., Rosen, L. R. Feldman, J. F., & Veridiano, N. P. (1990). The development of gender-related behavior in females following prenatal exposure to diethylstilbestrol (DES). *Hormones and Behavior, 23,* 526–541.

Eibl-Eibesfeldt, I. (1989). *Human ethology.* Chicago: Aldine.

Eibl-Eibesfeldt, I. (1998). Us and the others: The familial roots of ethnonationalism. In I. Eible-Eibesfeldt, & F. K. Salter, (Eds.), *Indoctrinability, ideology, and warfare: Evolutionary perspectives.* New York: Berghahn Books.

Elliott, W. T. (1989, Winter). Fitness and our forebears: Insights into the health of the modern human. *CUPA Journal, 40,* 1–6.

Elliott-Smith, G. (1927). *The evolution of man. Essays.* (2nd ed.) London: Oxford University Press.

Ellis, B. J., & Garber, J. (in press). Psychosocial antecedents of pubertal maturation in girls: Parental psychopathology, stepfather presence, and family and marital stress. *Child Development.*

Ellis, B. J., McFayden-Ketchem, S., Dodge, K. A., Pettit, G., & Bates, J. (1999). Quality of early family relationships and individual differences in the timing of pubertal maturation in girls: A longitudinal test of an evolutionary model. *Journal of Personality and Social Psychology, 77,* 387–401.

Ellis, L. (1993). *Social stratification and socioeconomic inequality.* (Vol I.) Westport, CT: Praeger Publishers.

Ellis, L., Ames, M. A., Peckham, W., & Burke, D. (1988). Sexual orientation of human offspring may be altered by severe maternal stress during pregnancy. *Journal of Sex Research, 25,* 152–157.

Erdal, D., & Whiten, A. (1994). On human egalitarianism: An evolutionary product of Machiavellian status escalation? *Current Anthropology, 35,* 175–183.

Eysenck, H. J. (1983). A biometrical-genetical analysis of impulsive and sensation seeking behavior. In M. Zuckerman (Ed.), *Biological bases of sensation seeking, impulsivity, and anxiety.* Hillside, NJ: Erlbaum.

Eysenck, H. J. (1997). Addiction, personality and motivation. *Human Psychopharmacology, Clinical and Experimental, 12*(Suppl. 2), 79–87.

Eysenck, H. J. (1999). *The psychology of politics.* New Brunswick, NJ: Transaction Publishers.

Eysenck, H. J., & Eysenck, M. W. (1985). *Personality and individual differences: A natural science approach.* New York: Plenum.

Falk, D. (1987). Brain lateralization in primates and its evolution in hominids. *American Journal of Physical Anthropology, 30*(Suppl. 8), 107–125.

Feingold, A. (1998). Cognitive gender differences are disappearing. *American Psychologist, 43,* 95–103.

Feldman, R. S. (1999). *Child development: A topical approach.* Upper Saddle River, NJ: Prentice-Hall.

Fiddick, L. (1999). The deal and the danger: An evolutionary analysis of deontic reasoning. *Dissertation Abstracts International: Section B: the Sciences & Engineering, 60*(3-B), 1322.

Fisher, H. (1998). *Anatomy of love: The natural history of monogamy, adultery and divorce.* New York: Norton.

Fisher, R. A. (1930). *The genetical theory of natural selection.* Oxford: Clarendon.

Flamsteed, S. (1997). Impossible planets. *Discover, 18,* 78–83.

Flaxman, S., & Sherman, P. (2000). Morning sickness: a mechanism for protecting mother and embryo. *The Quarterly Review of Biology, 75,* 113–148.

Francis, J. L. (1977). Towards the management of heterosexual jealousy. *Journal of Marriage and Family Counseling, 3,* 61–69.

Gallup, G. G. (1970). Chimpanzees: Self-recognition. *Science, 167,* 86–87.

Gallup, G. G. (1978). Self-recognition in primates: A comparative approach to the bidirectional properties of consciousness. *American Psychologist, 32,* 329–338.

Gallup, G. G. (1994). Self-recognition: Research strategies and experimental design. In S. T. Paker and R. W. Mitchell, M. L. Boccia (Eds.), *Self-awareness in animals and humans: Developmental perspectives.* New York: Cambridge University Press.

Gallup, G. G., & Suarez, S. D. (1986). Self-awareness and the emergence of mind in humans and other primates. In J. Suls & A. G. Greenwald (Eds.). ETC.

Gangestad, S. W., & Simpson, J. S. (1990). Toward an evolutionary history of female sociosexual variation. *Journal of Personality, 58,* 69–96.

Gangestad, S. W., & Thornhill, R. (1998). Menstrual cycle variation in women's prefer-

ences for the scent of symmetrical men. *Proceedings of the Royal Society of London, 265,* 927–933.

Gangestad, S. W., Thornhill, R., & Yeo, R. A. (1994). Facial attractiveness, developmental stability, and fluctuating asymmetry. *Ethology and Sociobiology, 15,* 73–85.

Garcia-Velasco, J., & Mondragon, M. (1991). The incidence of the vomeronasal organ in 1,000 human subjects and its possible clinical significance. *Journal of Steroid Biochemistry and Molecular Biology, 39,* 561–563.

Gardner, R. (1998). *The Biology of leadership.* Presented at the NLU Psi Chi Distinguished Speaker Series, Northeast Louisiana University, Monroe, LA.

Gaulin, S., FitzGerald, R., & Wartell, M. (1990). Sex differences in spatial ability and activity in two vole species (Microtus ochrogaster and M. pennsylvanicus). *Journal of Comparative Psychology, 104,* 88–93.

Gelman, S. A., Coley, J. D., & Gottfried, G. M. (1994). Essentialist beliefs in children: The acquisition of concepts and theories. In L. A. Hirschfeld, S. A. Gelman, et al. (Eds.), *Mapping the mind: Domain specificity in cognition and culture.* New York: Cambridge University Press.

Gelman, S. A., & Markman, E. M. (1987). Young children's inductions from natural kinds: The role of categories and appearances. *Child Development, 58,* 1532–1541.

Ghesquiere, J., Martin, R. D., & Newcombe, F. (Eds.). (1985). *Human sexual dimorphism.* Washington, DC: Taylor & Francis.

Giedd J., Castellanos F., Rajapakse J., Vaituzis A., & Rapoport J. (1997). Sexual dimorphism of the developing human brain. *Progress in Neuro-Psychopharmacology & Biological Psychiatry, 21,* 1185–1201.

Gillan, D. (1981). Reasoning in the chimpanzee: II. Transitive inference. *Journal of Experimental Psychology: Animal Behavioral Processes, 7,* 150–164.

Gillis, J. (1982). *Too tall, too small.* Champaign, Il. Institute for Personality and Ability Testing.

Gisiner, R., & Schusterman, R. (1992). Sequence, syntax, and semantics: Responses of a language trained sea lion (*Zalophus californi-*

anus) to novel sign combinations. *Journal of Comparative Psychology, 106,* 78–91.

Gold, D. C., & Maple, T. L. (1994). Personality assessment in the gorilla and its utility as a management tool. *Zoo-Biology 13,* 502–522.

Goldsmith, H., Buss, A., Plomin, R., Rothbart, M., Thomas, A., Chess, Hinde, R., & McCall, R. (1987). Roundtable: What is temperament? Four approaches. *Child Development, 58,* 505–529.

Goodall, J. (1971). *In the shadow of man.* Boston: Houghton Mifflin.

Goodall, J. (1986a). *The chimpanzees of Gombe.* Cambridge: Belknap Press.

Goodall, J. (1986b). *The chimpanzees of Gombe: Patterns of behavior.* Cambridge, MA: Harvard University Press.

Goodall, J. (1986c). The behavior of free-living chimpanzees in the Gombe stream area. *Animal Behavior Monographs, 1,* 161–311.

Gordon T., Rose, R., Grady, C., & Berstein, I. (1979). Effects of an increased testosterone secretion on the behavior of adult male rhesus living in a social group. *Folia primatologica, 32,* 149–160.

Gosling, S. D. (1998). Personality dimensions in spotted hyenas (Crocuta crocuta). *Journal of Comparative Psychology 112,* 107–118.

Graham, C. A., & McGrew, W. C. (1980). Menstrual synchrony in female undergraduates living on a co-educational campus. *Psychoneuroendocrinology, 5,* 245–252.

Graham-Rowe, D. (1998). How was it for you? *New Science, 159,* 20.

Grammer, K. (1996, June). *The human mating game: The battle of the sexes and the war of signals.* Paper presented at the 8th annual Human Behavior and Evolution Society meetings, Evanston, Illinois.

Grammer, K., & Jutte, A. (1997). Battle of odors: Significance of pheromones for human reproduction. *Gynakol Geburtshilfliche Rundsch, 37,* 150–153.

Grammer, K., & Thornhill, R. (1994). Human (Homo Sapiens) facial attractiveness and sexual selection: The role of symmetry and averageness. *Journal of Comparative Psychology, 108,* 233–242.

Gray, J. (1987). *The neuropsychology of stress and anxiety.* London: Oxford University Press.

Gray, J., & Buffery, A. (1971). Sex differences in emotional and cognitive behaviour in mammals including man: Adaptive and neural bases. *Acta-Psychologica, 35,* 89–111.

Gregory R. L. (Ed.). (1987). *The oxford companion to the mind.* Oxford: Oxford University Press.

Gruter, M. (1991). *Law and the mind: Biological origins of human behavior.* Newbury, CA: Sage Pub.

Gur R., Turetsky B., Matsui M., Yan M., Bilker W., Hughett P., & Gur R. (1999). Sex differences in brain gray and white matter in healthy young adults: correlations with cognitive performance. *Journal of Neuroscience, 19,* 4065–4072.

Gust, D., Gordon, T., Hambright, M., & Wilson, M. (1993). Relationship between social factors and pituitary-adrenocortical activity in female rhesus monkeys (Macaca mulatta). *Hormonal Behavior, 27,* 318–331.

Gvozdover, M. (1987). The typology of female figurines of the Kostenki Paleolithic culture. *Soviet Anthropology and Archaeology, 27,* 32–94.

Haig, D. (1993). Genetic conflicts in human pregnancy. *The Quarterly Review of Biology, 68,* 495–532.

Hamilton, W. D. (1963). The evolution of altruistic behavior. *The American Naturalist, 97,* 354–356.

Harpending, H., & Sobus, J. (1987). Sociopathy as an adaptation. *Ethology and Sociobiology, 8*(Suppl. 3), 63–72.

Hartung, J. (1985). Matrilineal inheritance: New theory and analysis. *Behavioral Brain Science, 8,* 661–688.

Hausfater, G. (1975). Dominance and reproduction in baboons (Papio cynocephalus): A quantitative analysis. *Contributions in Primatology, 7,* 1–150.

Hecht, J., & Concar, D. (1996). Earth oddities tell their tale. *New Scientist, 151,* 7.

Helmreich, R. (1968). Birth order effects. *Naval Research Reviews, 21,*

Henschell, J. R. (1995). Tool use by spiders: Stone selection and placement by corolla spiders

Ariadna (Segestriidae) of the Namib Desert. *Ethology, 101,* 187–199.

Hergenhahn, B. R. (1997). *An introduction to the history of psychology.* (3rd Ed.). Boston: Brooks/Cole Publishing Company.

Herman, L. M. (1987). Receptive competencies of language-trained animals. In J. S. Rosenblatt, C. Beer, M. C. Busnel, & P. J. B. Slater (Eds.), *Advances in the study of behavior* (Vol.17, pp. 1–55). San Diego, CA: Academic Press.

Heyes, C. (1994). Social cognition in primates. In Mackintosh, N. (Ed.). *Animal learning and cognition. Handbook of perception and cognition series.* San Diego, CA: Academic Press.

Higley, D., Suomi, S., & Linnoila, M. (1996). A nonhuman primate model of Type II alcoholism? Part 2. Diminished social competence and excessive aggression correlates with low cerebrospinal fluid 5-hydroxyindoleacetic acid concentration. *Alcoholism, Clinical and Experimental Research, 20,* 643–649.

Hirschfeld, L. A. (1996). *Race in the making: Cognition, culture, and the child's construction of human kinds.* Cambridge, MA: MIT Press.

Hockett, C. F. (1960). Logical considerations in the study of animal communication. In W. E. Lanyon & W. N. Tavolga (Eds.), *Animal sounds and communication.* Washington, DC: American Institute of Biological Sciences.

Holloway, M. (1997). The paradoxical legacy of Franz Boas. *Natural History, 106,* 86–89.

Holloway, R. (1981). Culture, symbols, and brain evolution: A synthesis. *Dialectical Anthropology, 5,* 287–303.

Hook, E. B. (1976). Changes in tobacco smoking and ingestion of alcohol and caffeinated beverages during early pregnancy: Are those consequences, in part, of feto-protective mechanisms diminishing maternal exposure to embryotoxins? In S. Kelly, E. B. Hook, D. T. Janerich, & I. H. Porter (Eds.), *Birth defects: Risks and consequences.* New York: Academic Press.

Horn, J. (1983). The Texas Adoption Project: Adopted children and their intellectual resemblance to biological and adoptive parents. *Child Development, 54,* 268–275.

Hrdy, S. B. (1988). The primate origins of human sexuality. In R. Bellig & G. Stevens (Eds.), *The evolution of sex.* San Francisco: Harper & Row.

Hrdy, S. B. (1997). Raising Darwin's consciousness: Female sexuality and the prehominid origins of patriarchy. *Human Nature, 8,* 1–49.

Hunt, G. R. (1996). Manufacture and use of hook-tools by New Caledonian crows. *Nature, 379,* 249–251.

Huntingtonford, F. (1976). The relationship between anti-predatory behavior and aggression among conspecifics in the three-spined stickleback, *Gasterosteus aculeatus. Animal Behavior, 24,* 245–260.

Hurd, J. (ed.). (1996). *Investigating the biological foundations of human morality.* Lewiston, NY: Edwin Mellen Press.

Hutchison, J. B., Beyer, C., Hutchison, R. E., & Wozniak, A. (1995). Sexual dimorphism in the developmental regulation of brain aromatase. *Journal of Steroid, Biochemistry, and Molecular Biology, 53,* 307–313.

Huxley, A. (1994). *Brave New World.* London: Flamingo.

Ingman, M., Kaessmann, H., Paabo, S., & Gyllensten, U., (2000). Mitochondrial genome variation and the origin of modern humans. *Nature, 408,* 708–713.

Ingold, T. (Ed.) (1994). *Companion encyclopedia of anthropology.* London: Routledge.

Jaeger J., Lockwood A., Van Valin R., Kemmerer D., Murphy B., & Wack D. (1998). Sex differences in brain regions activated by grammatical and reading tasks. *Neuroreport, 9,* 2803–2807.

James, W. (1890). *The principles of psychology.* New York: Henry Holt and Company.

Johanson, D., & Edey, M. (1981). *Lucy: The beginnings of humankind.* New York: Warner Books.

Johanson, D., & Shreeve, J. (1989). *Lucy's child: The discovery of a human ancestor.* New York: William Morrow and Company, Inc.

John, O. (1990). The search for basic dimensions of personality: A review and critique. In P. McReynolds, & J. Rosen (Eds.), *Advances in psychological assessment,* (Vol. 7., pp. 1–37). New York: Plenum Press.

Johnson, J. S., & Newport, E. L. (1989). Critical period effects in second language learning: The influence of maturational state and the acquisition of English as a second language. *Cognitive Psychology, 21,* 60–99.

Jones, D. (1999). Evolutionary psychology. *Annual Review of Anthropology, 28,* 553–575.

Jones, P. E. (1995). Contradictions and unanswered questions in the Benie case: A fresh look at the linguistic evidence. *Language and Communication, 15,* 261–280.

Judge, D., & Hrdy S. (1992). Allocation of accumulated resources among close kin: Inheritance in Sacramento, CA, 1890–1984. *Ethological Sociobiology, 13,* 409–442.

Julien, R. M. (1998). *A primer of drug action: A concise, nontechnical guide to the actions, uses, and side effects of psychoactive drugs.* New York: W. H. Freeman and Company.

Jung, C. G. (1969). *The archetypes and the collective unconscious.* (Vol. 9) Princeton: Princeton University Press.

Kalat, J. (1997). *Biological Psychology* (6th ed.). Pacific Grove, CA: Brooks/Cole Publishing Co.

Kandel, E. R., Schwrtz, J. H., & Jessell, T. M. (1991). *Principles of Neural Science.* New York: Elsevier Science Publishing Company.

Kant, I. (1927). *Kant's inaugural dissertation and early writings on space.* Westport, CT: Hyperion Press, Inc.

Kaplin, S. (1992). Environmental preference in a knowledge-seeking, knowledge-using organism. In J. Barkow, L. Cosmides, & J. Tooby (Eds.), *The adapted mind.* New York: Oxford University Press.

Kay, R., Cartmill, M., & Balow, M. (1998). The hypoglossal canal and the origin of human vocal behavior. *Proceedings of the National Academy of Sciences of the United States of America, 95,* 5417–5419.

Keil, F. C. (1989). *Concepts, kinds, and cognitive development.* Cambridge, MA: MIT Press.

Kellman, P. J., & Spelke, E. S. (1983). Perception of partly occluded objects in infancy. *Cognitive Psychology, 15,* 483–524.

Kenrick, D. T., Sadalla, E. K., Groth, G., & Trost, M. R. (1990). Evolution, traits, and the stages of human courtship: Qualifying the parental investment model. *Journal of Personality, 58,* 97–116.

Kerr, R. A. (1997). Once, maybe still, an ocean on Europa. *Science, 277,* 764–765.

Kimble, J. W. (1994). *Biology* (6th ed.). Oxford: Wm. C. Brown Publishers.

Klaus, M. H., & Kennell, J. H. (1976). *Maternal-infant bonding* (2nd ed.). St. Louis, MO: Mosby.

Klima, B. (1990). Chronologie de l'art mobilier paleolithique en Europe centrale. In J. Clottes (Ed.), *L'art des objets au paleolithique* (Vol. 1, pp. 133–141). Foix: French Ministry of Culture.

Kohler, W. (1976). *The mentality of apes* (E. Winter, Trans., Rev. ed.). New York: Liveright. (Original work published 1927)

Kortlandt, A. (1986). The use of stone tools by wild-living chimpanzees and earliest hominids. *Journal of Human Evolution, 15,* 77–132.

Kramer, P. (1993). *Listening to Prozac.* New York: Viking Press.

Kuhl, P. (1991). Human adults and human infants show a "perceptual magnet effect" for the prototypes of speech categories, monkeys do not. *Perception & Psychophysics, 50,* 93–107.

Kuhl, P. (2001). Speech, language, and developmental change. In F. Lacerda, C. von Hofsten, et al. (Eds.), *Emerging cognitive abilities in early infancy.* Mahwah, NJ: Erlbaum.

Kuhl, P., & Metzoff, A. (1982). The bimodal perception of speech in infancy. *Science, 218,* 1138–1141.

Langlois, J. H., & Roggman, L. A. (1990). Attractive faces are only average. *Psychological Science, 1,* 115–121.

Leakey, M. G., & Harris, J. M. (1987). *Laetoli: A Pliocene site in northern Tanzania.* New York: Oxford University Press.

Leakey, M. G., Feibel, C. S., & McDougall, I. (1995). New four-million-year-old hominid species from Kanapoi and Allia Bay, Kenya. *Nature, 376,* 565–571.

Leakey, M. G., Spoor, F., Brown, Frank, H., Gathogo, P. N., Kiarie, C., Leakey, L. N., & McDougall, I. (2001). New hominin genus from eastern Africa shows diverse middle Pliocene lineages. *Nature, 410,* 433–440.

Leakey, R. (1981). *The making of mankind.* New York: Dutton.

Leakey, R. (1994). *The origin of humankind.* New York: BasicBooks.

Leakey, R., & Lewin, R. (1992). *Origins reconsidered: In search of what makes us human.* New York: Doubleday.

Lenneberg, E. H. (1967). *Biological foundations of language.* New York: Wiley.

LeVay, S. (1991). A difference in hypothalamic structure between heterosexual and homosexual men. *Science, 253,* 1034–1037.

LeVay, S. (1993). *The sexual brain.* Cambridge, MA: MIT Press.

Levy, J., & Heller, W. (1992). Gender differences in human neuropsychological function. In A. A. Gerall, H. Moltz, & I. L. Ward (Eds.), *Handbook of behavioral neurobiology.* New York & London: Plenum Press.

Lewin, R. (1997). Distant cousins. *New Scientist, 155,* 5.

Lewis-Williams, J. D., & Dowson, T. A. (1988). The signs of all times: Entoptic phenomena in upper Palaeolithic art. *Current Anthropology, 29,* 201–245.

Little, R. E., & Hook, E. B. (1979). Maternal alcohol and tobacco consumption and their association with nausea and vomiting during pregnancy. *Acta Obstetrica et Gynecologica Scandinavica, 58,* 15–17.

Loehlin, J. (1992). *Genes and environment in personality development: Sage series on individual differences and development* (Vol. 2). Newbury Park, CA: Sage Publications, Inc.

Lorenz, K. Z. (1965). *Behind the mirror.* New York and London: Harcourt Brace Jovanovich.

Loy, T. (1998). Blood on the axe. *New Scientist, 159,* 40–43.

Lucas, A., Morley, R., & Cole, T. J. (1999). Randomized controlled trial of early diet in preterm babies and later intelligence quotient. *Journal of Neonatal Nursing, 5,* 22.

Ludolph, P. S., Westen, D., Misle, B., Jackson, A., Wixom, J., & Wiss, F. C. (1990). The borderline diagnosis in adolescents: Symptoms and developmental histories. *American Journal of Psychiatry, 147,* 470–476.

Maccoby, E. E. (1998). *The two sexes: Growing up apart, coming together.* Cambridge, MA: The Belknap Press of Harvard University Press.

Machiavelli, N. (1532). *The Prince.* New York: Norton.

Maier, R. A. (1998). *Comparative animal behavior: An evolutionary and ecological approach.* Chicago: Allyn and Bacon.

Mandler, J. M., & Bauer, P. J. (1988). The cradle of categorization: Is the basic level basic? *Cognitive Development, 3,* 247–264.

Marano, H. E. (1999). Depression: Beyond serotonin. In B. M. Jubilan (Ed.), *Biopsychology* (5th ed.). Guilford, CT: Dushkin/McGraw-Hill.

Marchant, L. F., McGrew, W. C., & Eibl-Eibesfeldt, I. (1995). Is human handedness universal? Ethological analyses from three traditional cultures. *Ethology, 101,* 239–258.

Markovitz, P. (1995). Pharmacotherapy of impulsivity, aggression, and related disorders. In E. Hollander & D. Stein (Eds.), *Impulsivity and aggression.* West Sussex, England: John Wiley & Sons.

Marks, I. M. (1987). *Fears, phobias, and rituals.* New York: Oxford University Press.

Marino, L., Reiss, D., & Gallup, G. G., Jr. (1994). Mirror self-recognition in bottlenose dolphins: Implications for comparative investigations of highly dissimilar species. In S. T. Parker, R. W. Mitchell, & M. L. Boccia (Eds.), *Self-awareness in animals and humans: Developmental perspectives.* New York: Cambridge University Press.

Marten, D., & Psarakos, S. (1994). Evidence of self-awareness in the bottlenose dolphin (Tursiops truncatus). In S. T. Parker, R. W. Mitchell, & M. L. Boccia (Eds.), *Self-awareness in animals and humans: Developmental perspectives.* New York: Cambridge University Press.

Marzke, M., & Shackley, M. (1986). Hominid hand use in the Pliocene and Pleistocene: Evidence from experimental archaeology and comparitive morphology. *Journal of Human Evolution, 15,* 439–460.

Mather, J., & Anderson, R. (1993). Personalities of octopuses (*Octopus rubescens*). *Journal of Comparative Psychology, 107,* 336–340.

Matthys, W., Cohen-Kettenis, P., & Berkhout, J. (1994). Boys' and girls' perceptions of peers in middle childhood: Differences and similarities. *Journal of Genetic Psychology, 155,* 15–24.

Mazur, A., & Lamb, V. (1980). Testosterone, status, and mood in human males. *Hormones and Behavior, 14,* 236–246.

McBeath, N. M., & McGrew, W. C. (1982). Tools used by wild chimpanzees to obtain termites at Mt Assirik, Senegal: The influence of habitat. *Journal of Human Evolution, 11,* 65–72.

McClintock, M. K. (1971). Menstrual synchrony and suppression. *Nature 229,* 244–245.

McGinnis, W., & Kuziora, M. (1994). The molecular architects of body design. *Scientific American, 270,* 58–61.

McGuire, M. T., & Troisi, A. (1998). *Darwinian psychiatry.* New York: Oxford University Press.

Mealy, L. (1993). *Selective memory for faces of cheaters?* Presented at the Evolution and Human Science conference, London.

Mehlman, P., Higley, J., Faucher, I, Lilly, A., Taub, D., Vickers. J., Suomi, S., & Linnoila, M. (1994). Low CSF 5-HIAA concentrations and severe aggression and impaired impulse control in nonhuman primates. *American Journal of Psychiatry, 151,* 1485–1491.

Meltzoff, A. N., & Borton, R. W. (1979). Intermodal matching by human neonates. *Nature, 282,* 403–404.

Meyer, R. G., & Deitsch, S. E., (1996). *The clinician's handbook: Integrated diagnostics, assessment, and intervention in adult and adolescent psychopathology* (4th ed.). Boston: Allyn and Bacon.

Miller, G. F. (1995). *Darwinian demographics of cultural production.* Paper presented at the Human Behavior and Evolution Society 7th annual meeting, University of California, Santa Barbara.

Miller, G. F. (1998). How mate choice shaped human nature: A review of sexual selection and human evolution. In C. Crawford & D. L. Krebs (Eds.), *Handbook of evolutionary psychology: Ideas, issues, and applications.* Mahwah, NJ: Erlbaum.

Milner, R. (1990). *The encyclopedia of evolution: Humanity's search for its origins.* New York: Facts on File.

Minturn, L., & Weiher, A. W. (1984). The influence of diet on morning sickness: A cross-cultural study. *Medical Anthropology, 8,* 71–75.

Mitchell, P. (1997). *Introduction to theory of mind: Children, autism, and apes.* New York: Arnold.

Money, J., Schwartz, M., & Lewis, V. G. (1984). Adult herotosexual status and fetal hormonal masculinization and demasculinization: 46, XX congenital virilizing adrenal hyperplasia (CVAH) and 46, XY androgen-insensitivity syndrome (AIS) compared. *Psychoneuroendocrinology, 9,* 405–414.

Montgomery, H. (2000). Gene boosts athletic performance. *Nature 403,* 614.

Morgan, B. A. (1997). Hox genes and embryonic development. *Poultry Science, 76,* 96–104.

Morris, D. (1967). *The naked ape.* New York: Dell.

Newmeyer, F. (1991). Functional explanation in linguistics and the origin of language. *Language and Communication, 11,* 3–96.

Newport, E. (1986, November). *Maturational constraints on language learning.* Paper presented at the meeting of the Psychonomic Society, New Orleans.

Newport, E. (1990). Maturational constraints on language learning. *Cognitive Science, 14,* 11–28.

Newport, E., & Supalla, T. (In press). A critical period effect in the acquisition of primary language. *Science.*

Nopoulos P., Flaum M., O'Leary D., & Andreasen N. (2000). Sexual dimorphism in the human brain: evaluation of tissue volume, tissue composition and surface anatomy using magnetic resonance imaging. *Psychiatry Research, 98,* 1–13.

Notman, M. T., & Nadelson, C. C., (1990). *Women and men: New perspectives on gender differences.* Washington, DC: American Psychiatric Press, Inc.

Oakley, K. P. (1981). Emergence of higher thought. *Philosophical Transactions of the Royal Society, 292B,* 205.

Ogata, S. N., Silk, K. R., Goodrich, S., Lohr, N. E., Westen, D., & Hill, E. M. (1990). Childhood sexual and physical abuse in adult patients with borderline personality disorder. *American Journal of Psychiatry, 147,* 1008–1013.

Orians, G. H., & Heerwagen, J. H. (1992). Evolved responses to landscapes. In J. Barkow, L. Cosmides, & J. Tooby (Eds.), *The adapted mind.* New York: Oxford University Press.

Palmer, J., McCown, W., & Kerby, D. (1997). *The adaptive significance of "dysfunctional impulsivity."* Presented at the Human Behavior and Evolution Society conference, Tucson, AZ.

Palmer, J., McCown, W., & Thornburgh, T. (1998). *The ontogenetic priming of social hierarchical functioning.* Presented at the International Society for Human Ethology conference, Victoria, BC.

Patterson, F. (1984). Self-recognition by *Gorilla gorilla gorilla. Gorilla [Newsletter published by the Gorilla Foundation], 7,* 2–3.

Patterson, F., & Cohn, R. H. (1994). Self-recognition and self-awareness in lowland gorillas. In S. T. Parker, R. W. Mitchell, & M. L. Boccia (Eds.), *Self-awareness in animals and humans: Developmental perspectives.* New York: Cambridge University Press.

Pepperberg, I. M. (1992). Proficient performance of a conjunctive, recursive task by an African gray parrot (*Psittacus erithacus*). *Journal of Comparative Psychology, 106,* 295–305.

Pepperberg, I. M. (1993). Cognition and communication in an African Grey parrot (*Psittacus erithacus*): Studies on a nonhuman, nonprimate, nonmammalian subject. In H. L. Roitblat, L. M. Herman, & P. Nachtigall (Eds.). *Language and communication: Comparative perspectives. Comparative cognition and neuroscience* (pp. 221–248). Hillsdale, NJ: Erlbaum.

Pepperberg, I. M. (1994). Numerical competence in an African gray parrot. *Journal of Comparative Psychology, 108,* 36–44.

Pepperberg, I. M. (1996). Categorical class formation by an African Grey parrot (Psittacus erithacus). In T. R. Zentell & P. M. Smeets (Eds.), *Stimulus class formation in humans and animals. Advances in psychology* (No. 17, pp. 71–91). Amsterdam, Netherlands: Elsevier Science Publishing Co., Inc.

Pillard, R. C., & Bailey, J. M. (1998). Human sexual orientation has a heritable component. *Human Biology, 70,* 347–365.

Pinker, S. (1994). *The language instinct.* New York: Harper Collins.

Pinker, S. (1997). *How the mind works.* New York: Norton.

Pinker, S., & Bloom, P. (1990). Natural language and natural selection. *Behavioral and Brain Sciences, 13,* 707–784.

Plomin, R. (1976). Extroversion: Sociability and impulsivity? *Journal of Personality Assessment, 40,* 24–30.

Poizner, H., Klima, E. S., & Bellugi, U. (1987). *What the hands reveal about the brain.* Cambridge, MA: MIT Press.

Porter, R., & Moore, J. (1981). Human kin recognition by olfactory cues. *Physiology of Behavior, 27,* 493–495.

Porter, R., Cernoch, J., & Balogh, R. (1985). Odor signature and kin recognition. *Physiology of Behavior, 34,* 445–448.

Povinelli, D. J. (1993). Reconstructing the evolution of mind. *American Psychologist, 48,* 493–509.

Povinelli, D. J., & Eddy, D. J. (1996). What young chimpanzees know about seeing. *Monographs of the Society for Research in Child Development, 61,* 1–52.

Povinelli, D. J., & Preuss, T. M. (1995). Theory of mind: Evolutionary history of a cognitive specialization. *Trends in Neuroscience, 18,* 418–424.

Povinelli, D. J., Gallup, G. G., Eddy, T. J., & Bierschwale, D. T. (1997). Chimpanzees recognize themselves in mirrors. *Animal Behavior, 53,* 1083–1088.

Premack, D. (1971). On the assessment of language competence in the chimpanzee. In A. M. Schrier & F. Stollnitz (Eds.), *Behavior of nonhuman primates* (Vol. 4). New York: Academic Press.

Premack, D., & Woodruff, G. (1978). Does the chimpanzee have a theory of mind? *Behavioral and Brain Sciences, 1,* 515–526.

Prentice, A. M., & Whitehead, R. G. (1987). The energetics of human reproduction. In A. S. I. Loudon & P. A. Racey (Eds.), *Reproductive energetics in mammals.* Oxford: Clarendon Press.

Pretie, G., Cutler, W. B., Garcia, C. R., Huggins, G. R., & Lawley, H. J. (1986). Human axillary secretions influence women's menstrual cycles: The role of donor extract of females. *Hormones and Behavior, 20,* 474–482.

Preuss, T. M. (2000). Evolution. In M. S. Gazzaniga (Ed.), *The New Cognitive Neurosciences.* Cambridge, MA: MIT Press.

Prochaska, J., & Norcross, J, (1994). *Systems of psychotherapy: A transtheoretical analysis.* (3rd ed.). Pacific Grove, CA: Brooks/Cole Publishing.

Profet, M. (1992). Pregnancy sickness as adaptation: A deterrent to maternal ingestion of teratogens. In J. Barkow, L. Cosmides, & J. Tooby (Eds.), *The adapted mind.* New York: Oxford University Press.

Pusey, A., Williams, J., & Goodall, J. (1997). The influence of dominance rank on the reproductive success of female chimpanzees. *Science, 277,* 828–831.

Quadagno, D. M., Shubeita, H. E., Deck, J., & Francoeur, D. (1981). Influence of male social contacts, exercise and all female living conditions on the menstrual cycle. *Psychoneuroendocrinology, 6,* 239–244.

Quinn, P., & Eimas, P. (1996). Perceptual cues that permit categorical differentiation of animal species by infants. *Journal of Experimental Child Psychology, 63,* 189–211.

Radetsky, P. (1997). Y?. *Discover, 18,* 88–93.

Ragland J., Coleman A., Gur R., Glahn D., & Gur R. (2000). Sex differences in brain-behavior relationships between verbal episodic memory and resting regional cerebral blood flow. *Neuropsychologia, 38,* 451–461.

Raleigh, M. (1991). Serotonergic mechanisms promote dominance acquisition in adult male vervet monkeys. *Brain Research, 559,* 181–190.

Reddy, V., Hay, D., Murray, L., & Trevarthen, C. (1997). Communication in infancy: Mutual regulation of affect and attention. In G. Bremner, A. Slater, et al. (Eds.), *Infant development: Recent advances.* Hove, England: Psychology Press/Erlbaum.

Regan, P. C. (1998). Minimum mate selection standards as a function of perceived mate value, relationship context, and gender. *Journal of Psychology & Human Sexuality, 10,* 53–73.

Rejeski, W., Gagne, M., Parker, P., & Koritnik, D. (1989). Acute stress reactivity from contested dominance in dominant and submissive males. *Behavioral Medicine, 15,* 118–124.

Richards, M. P., Pettitt, P. B., Trinkaus, E., Smith, F. H., Paunovic, M., & Karavanic, I. Neanderthal diet at Vindija and Neanderthal predation: The evidence from stable isotopes. *Proceedings of the National Academy of Science USA, 97,* 7663–7666.

Ridley, M. (1996). *The Origins of Virtue.* New York: Viking.

Rolls, E. T. (1984). Neurons in the cortex of the temporal lobe and in the amygdala of the monkey with responses selective for faces. *Human Neurobiology, 3,* 209–222.

Ross, C., & Garnett, S. (Eds.). (1989). *Crocodiles and alligators.* New York: Facts on File.

Rottschaefer, W. (1998). *The biology and psychology of moral agency.* New York: Cambridge University Press.

Roy, A., & Linnoila, M. (1988). Suicidal behavior, impulsiveness and serotonin. *Acta Psychiatrica Scandinaviea 78,* 529–535.

Rozin, P. (1976). Psychological and cultural determinants of food choice. In T. Silverstone (Ed.), *Appetite and food intake.* Berlin: Dahlem Konferenzen.

Rumbaugh, D. M., & Gill, T. V. (1976). The mastery of language-type skills by the chimpanzee Pan. *Annals of the New York Academy of Sciences, 280,* 572–578.

Rushton, J. P. (1989). Genetic similarity, human altruism, and group selection. *Behavioral Brain Science, 12,* 503–559.

Russell, M. J., Switz, G. R., & Thompson, K. (1980). Olfactory influences on the human menstrual cycle. *Pharmacological and Biochemical Behavior, 13,* 737–738.

Rymer, R. (1993). *Genie: An abused child's flight from silence.* New York: HarperCollins.

Salter, F. K. (1998). Indoctrination as institutionalized persuasion: Its limited variability and cross-cultural evolution. In I. Eible-Eibesfeldt, & F. K. Salter, (Eds.), *Indoctrinability, ideology, and warfare: Evolutionary perspectives.* New York: Berghahn Books.

Samuels, C. A., Butterworth, G., Roberts, T., Graupner, L., & Hole (1994). Facial aesthetics: Babies prefer attractiveness to symmetry. *Perception, 23,* 823–831.

Sandstrom, N., Kaufman, J., & Huettel, S. A. (1998). Males and females use different distal cues in a virtual environment navigation task. *Brain Research. Cognitive Brain Research, 6,* 351–360.

Sapolsky, R. M., (1997). Stress in the wild. In R. W. Sussman (Ed.), *The biological basis of human behavior.* Needham Heights, MA: Simon & Schuster Custom Publishing.

Sapolsky, R. M. (1999). Why stress is bad for your brain. In B. M. Jubilan (Ed.), *Biopsychology* (5th ed.). Guilford, CT: Dushkin/McGraw-Hill.

Sarich, V. M. (1983). A personal perspective on hominoid macromolecular systematics. In R. L. Ciochon and R. S. Corruccini (Eds.), *New interpretations of ape and human ancestry.* New York: Plenum Press.

Savage-Rumbaugh, S., Shanker, S. G., & Taylor, T. J. (1998). *Apes, language, and the human mind.* New York: Oxford University Press.

Scarr, S., & Weinberg, R. (1983). The Minnesota adoption study: Genetic differences and malleability. *Child Development, 54,* 260–267.

Schick, K. D., & Toth, N. (1993). *Making silent stones speak.* New York: Simon & Schuster.

Schiller, P. H. (1952). Innate constituents of complex responses in primates. *The Psychological Review, 59,* 177–191.

Schiller, P. H. (1957). Innate motor action as a basis of learning. In C. Schiller (Ed.), *Instinctive Behavior.* New York: International Universities Press.

Schuster, A. M. H. (1997). World's oldest stone tools. *Archaeology, 50,* 13.

Schwarcz, H. P., & Skoflek, I. (1982). New dates for the Tata, Hungary, archaeological site. *Nature, 295,* 590.

Selye, H. (1956). *The stress of life.* New York: McGraw Hill.

Sharkey, M., Graba, Y., & Scott, M. P. (1997). Hox genes in evolution: Protein surfaces and paralog groups. *Trends in Genetics, 13,* 145–151.

Sheehy, N., Chapman, A., & Conroy, W. (1997). *Biographical dictionary of psychology.* London: Routledge.

Sherman, P. (1977). Nepotism and the evolution of alarm calls. *Science, 197,* 1246–1253.

Sherman, P. (1980). The limits of ground squirrels' nepotism. In Barlow, G., & Silverberg, J. (Eds.), *Sociobiology: Beyond nature/nurture?* Boulder, CO: Westview Press.

Silverman, I., & Eals, M. (1992). Sex differences in spatial abilities: Evolutionary theory and data. In J. Barkow, L. Cosmides, & J. Tooby (Eds.), *The adapted mind.* New York: Oxford University Press.

Simpson, J. A., & Gangestad, S. W. (1992). Sociosexuality and romantic partner choice. *Journal of Personality, 60,* 31–52.

Singh, D. (1993). Adaptive significance of waist-to-hip ratio and female attractiveness. *Journal of Personality and Social Psychology, 51,* 181–190.

Singh, D. (1993). Adaptive significance of female physical attractiveness: Role of waist-to-hip ratio. *Journal of Personality and Social Psychology, 65,* 293–307.

Singh, D. (1994). Is thin really beautiful and good? Relationship between waist-to-hip ratio (WHR) and female attractiveness. *Personality and Individual Differences, 16,* 123–132.

Singh, D. (1995). Female judgment of male attractiveness and desirability for relationships: Role of waist-to-hip ratio and financial status. *Journal of Personality and Social Psychology, 69,* 1089–1101.

Singh, D., & Luis, S. (1995). Ethnic and gender consensus for the effect of waist-to-hip ratio on judgment of women's attractiveness. *Human Nature, 6,* 51–65.

Slater, A., & Johnson, S. (1998). Visual sensory and perceptual abilities of the newborn: Beyond the blooming, buzzing confusion. In F. Simion, G. Butterworth, et al. (Eds), *The development of sensory, motor and cognitive capacities in early infancy: From perception to cognition.* Hove, England: Psychology Press/Erlbaum.

Small, M. (1995). Rethinking human nature (again). *Natural History, 104,* 8.

Smith, E. (1988). Risk and uncertainty in the 'original affluent society.' In T. Ingold, D. Riches, & J. Woodburn, (Eds.), *Hunters and gatherers: Vol. 1. History, evolution, and social change.* Oxford: Berg.

Smith, E. O. (1999). Evolution, substance abuse, and addiction. In W. R. Trevathan, E. O. Smith, & J. J. Mckenna (Eds.), *Evolutionary medicine.* New York: Oxford University Press.

Smith, J. M. (1982). *Evolution and the theory of games.* Cambridge, England: Cambridge University Press.

Smith, J. R., & Brooks-Gunn, J. (1997). Correlates and consequences of harsh discipline for young children. *Archives of Pediatric and Adolescent Medicine, 151,* 758–760.

Smuts, B. B., Cheney, D. L., Seyfarth, R. M., Wrangham, R. W., & Struhsaker, T. T. (Eds.), (1987). *Primate societies.* Chicago: University of Chicago Press.

Sober, E. (1994). *From a biological point of view: Essays on evolutionary philosophy.* New York: Cambridge University Press.

Spelke, E. S. (1998). Where perceiving ends and thinking begins: The apprehension of objects in infancy. In A. Yonas, et al. (Eds.), *Perceptual development in infancy. The Minnesota symposia on child psychology, Vol. 20.* Hillsdale, NJ: Erlbaum.

Spiro, M. E. (1958). *Children of the kibbutz.* Cambridge, MA: Harvard University Press.

Sroufe, L. A., & Waters, E. (1976). The ontogenesis of smiling and laughter: A perspective on the organization of development in infancy. *Psychological Review, 83,* 173–189.

Sroufe, L. A., & Wunsch, J. P. (1972). The development of laughter in the first year of life. *Child Development, 43,* 1324–1344.

Stevens, A., & Price, J. (1996). *Evolutionary psychiatry: A new beginning.* London: Routledge.

Stevenson-Hinde, J., & Zunz, M. (1978). Subjective assessment of individual rhesus monkeys. *Primates, 19,* 473–482.

Strickberger, M. W. (1990). *Evolution.* Boston: Jones and Bartlett Publishers.

Stronks, K., van-de-Mheen, H., Looman, C., & Mackenbach, J. (1998). The importance of psychosocial stressors for socio-economic inequalities in perceived health. *Social Science and Medicine, 46,* 611–623.

Sugiyama, Y., Fushimi, T., Sakura, O., & Matsuzawa, T. (1993). Hand preference and tool use in wild chimpanzees. *Primates, 34,* 151–159.

Sulloway, F. J. (1996). *Born to rebel: Birth order, family dynamics, and creative lives.* New York: Pantheon Books.

Suomi, S., Scanlan, J., Rasmussen, K., Davidson, M., Boinski, S., Higley, J., & Marriott, B. (1989). Pituitary-adrenal response to capture in Cayo Santiago-derived group M rhesus monkeys. *Public Relations Health Science Journal, 8,* 171–176.

Sutton-Smith, B. (1982). Birth order and sibling status effects. In M. E. Lamb & B. Sutton-Smith (Eds.), *Sibling relationships: Their nature and significance across the life span.* Hillsdale, NJ: Erlbaum.

Svitil, K. (1997). When earth tumbled. *Discover, 18,* 48.

Svrakic, N., Svrakic, D., & Cloninger, R. (1996). A general quantitative theory of personality development: Fundamentals of a self-organizing psychobiological complex. *Development and Psychopathology, 8,* 247–272.

Swaab, D. F., & Hofman, M. A. (1990). An enlarged suprachiasmatic nucleus in homosexual men. *Brain Research, 537,* 141–148.

Symons, D. (1979). *The evolution of human sexuality.* New York: Oxford University Press.

Tanaka, T. (1980). *The San, hunter-gatherers of the Kalahari.* (D. W. Hughes, Trans.). Tokyo: University of Tokyo Press.

Tattersall, I., Delson, E., & Couvering, J. V. (Eds.). (1988). *Encyclopedia of human evolution and prehistory.* New York and London: Garland.

Taubes, G. (1997). Echo of the big bang. *Discover, 18,* 110–117.

Teicher, M. H. (2000). Wounds that time won't heal: The neurobiology of child abuse. *Cerebrum, 2.*

Tellegen, A. (1993) Folk concepts and psychological concepts of personality and personality disorder. *Psychological Inquiry, 4,* 122–130.

Tennov, D. (1979). *Love and limerence.* New York: Stein and Day.

The stress connection. (1994). *Prevention, 46,* 62.

Thomas, A., & Chess, S. (1977). *Temperament and development.* New York: Brunner/Mazel.

Thomas, A., Chess, S., & Birch, H. (1970). The origins of personality. *Scientific American, 223,* 102–109.

Thompson, P. R. (1980). And who is my neighbor? An answer from evolutionary genetics. *Social Science Information, 19,* 341–384.

Thornhill, R., & Gangestad, S. W. (1993). Human facial beauty. *Human Nature, 4,* 237–269.

Thornhill, R., & Gangestad, S. W. (1994). Human fluctuating asymmetry and sexual behavior. *Psychological Science, 5,* 290–302.

Thornhill, R., Gangestad, S. W., & Comer, R. (1995). Human female orgasm and mate fluctuating asymmetry. *Animal Behavior, 50,* 1601–1615.

Thornhill, R., & Gangestad, S. W. (1996). Human female copulatory orgasm: A human adaptation or phylogenetic holdover. *Animal Behavior, 52,* 853–855.

Tiger, L. (1979). *Optimism: The biology of hope.* New York: Kodansha Globe.

Tiger, L. (1991). *Manufacture of evil: Ethics, evolution in the industrial system.* New York: Marion Boyers.

Tiger, L., & Fox, R. (1971). *The imperial animal.* New York: Transactive Publishing.

Tinbergen, N. (1951). *The study of instinct.* Oxford: Oxford University Press.

Tooby and Cosmides (2000). Toward Mapping the Evolved Functional Organization of Mind and Brain. In M. S. Gazzaniga (Ed.), *The New Cognitive Neurosciences.* Cambridge, MA: MIT Press.

Trevarthen, C., Kokkinaki, T., & Fiamenghi, G. (1999). What infants' imitations communicate: With mothers, with fathers and with peers. In J. Nadel, G. Butterworth, et al. (Eds.), *Imitation in infancy: Cambridge studies in cognitive perceptual development.* New York: Cambridge University Press.

Trinkaus, E., & Shipman, P. (1993). *The Neanderthals.* New York: Alfred A. Knopf, Inc.

Trivers, R. (1971). The evolution of reciprocal altruism. *Quarterly Review of Biology, 46,* 35–56.

Trivers, R. (1972). Parental investment and sexual selection. In B. Campbell (Ed.), *Sexual selection and the descent of man: 1871–1971.* Chicago: Aldine.

Trivers, R. (1985). *Social evolution.* Reading, MA: Benjamin/Cummings.

Trivers, R. (1991). Deceit and self-deception: The relationship between communication and consciousness. In M. Robinson, & L. Tiger, (Eds.), *Man and beast revisited.* Washington, DC: Smithsonian Press.

Turlejski, K. (1996). Evolutionary ancient roles of serotonin: Long-lasting regulation of activity and development. *Acta-neurobiol-Exp-Warsz. 56,* 619–636.

Turnbull, C. (1965). *Wayward servants.* London: Eyre and Spottiswoode.

Uexküld, J. Von. (1909). Umwelt und innenwelt der tiere. Berlin: Springer.

United States Surgeon General's Office (1999). *Mental health: A report of the Surgeon General.* Washington, DC: United States Government Printing Office.

Vandiver, P., Soffer, O., & Klima, B. (1989). The origins of ceramic technology at Dolni Vestonice, circ 26,000 B.P. Studio Potter.

Van-Noordwijk, M., & Van-Schaik, C. (1987). Competition among female long-tailed macaques. *Animal Behaviour, 35,* 577–589.

von Frisch, K. (1971). *Bees: Their vision, chemical senses and language.* Ithaca, NY: Cornell University Press.

Vrba, E. S., (1996). Climate, heterochrony, and human evolution. *Journal of Anthropological Research, 52,* 1–28.

Walker, A., Shipman, P. (1996). *The wisdom of the bones: In search of human origins.* New York: Alfred A. Knopf, Inc.

Ward, I. L. (1977). Exogenous androgen activates female behavior in noncopulating, prenatally stressed male rats. *Journal of Comparative and Physiological Psychology, 91,* 465–471.

Ward, I. L., & Reed, J. (1985). Prenatal stress and prepubertal social rearing conditions interact to determine sexual behavior in male rats. *Behavioral Neuroscience, 99,* 301–309.

Ward, I. L., & Ward, O. B. (1985). Sexual behavior differentiation: Effects of prenatal manipulations in rats. In N. Adler, D. Pfaff, & R. W. Goy (Eds.), *Handbook of behavioral neurobiology* (Vol. 7, pp. 77–98). New York: Plenum Press.

Ward, I. L., Ward, B., Winn, R. J., & Bielawski, D. (1994). Male and female sexual behavior potential of male rats prenatally exposed to the influence of alcohol, stress, or both factors. *Behavioral Neuroscience, 108,* 1133–1195.

Ward, O. B., Monaghan, E. P., & Ward, I. L. (1986). Naltrexon blocks the effects of prenatal stress on sexual behavior differentiation in male rats. *Pharmacology Biochemistry & Behavior, 25,* 573–576.

Wedekind, C., & Furi, S. (1997). Body odor preferences in men and women: do they aim for specific MHC combinations or simply heterozygosity? *Proc-R-Soc-Lond-B-Biol-Science, 264,* 1471–1479.

Wekesser, C. (Ed.), (1996). *Genetic engineering: Opposing viewpoints.* San Diego, CA: Greenhaven Press, Inc.

Westermark, E. A. (1891). *The history of human marriage.* London: MacMillan.

White, T., Suwa, G., & Asfaw, B. (1994). Australopithecus ramidus, a new species of early hominid from Aramis, Ethiopia. *Nature, 371,* 306–312.

Whitten, W. K. (1959). Occurrence of anestrus in mice caged in groups. *Journal of Endocrinology, 18,* 102–107.

Wierzbicka, A. (1992). The semantics of interjection. *Journal of Pragmatics, 18,* 159–192.

Wierzbicka, A. (1998). The semantics of English causative constructions in a universal-typological perspective. In M. Tomasello (Ed.), *The new psychology of language: Cognitive and functional approaches to language structure.* Mahwah, NJ: Erlbaum.

Wiessner, P. (1998). Indoctrinability and the evolution of socially defined kinship. In I. Eible-Eibesfeldt, & F. K. Salter, (Eds.), *Indoctrinability, ideology, and warfare: Evolutionary perspectives.* New York: Berghahn Books.

Williams, G. (1966). *Adaptation and natural selection: A critique of some current evolutionary thought.* Princeton, NJ: Princeton University Press.

Willis, C., (1993). *The runaway brain: The evolution of human uniqueness.* New York: Basic Books.

Wilson, A. C., & Cann, R. L. (1992). The recent African genesis of humans. *Scientific American, 266,* 68–73.

Wilson, D., Clark, A., Coleman, K., & Dearstyne, T. (1994). Shyness and boldness in humans and other animals. *Trends in Ecology and Evolution, 9,* 442–446.

Wilson, E. (1975). *Sociobiology: The new synthesis.* Cambridge, MA: Harvard University Press.

Wilson, E. (1978). *On human nature.* Cambridge, MA: Harvard University Press.

Wilson, E. (1998). *Consilience: The unity of knowledge.* New York: Alfred A. Knopf, Inc.

Wilson, R. S. (1983). The Louisville Twin Study: Developmental synchronies in behavior. *Child Development, 54,* 298–316.

Woldegabriel, G., Haile-Selassie, Y., Renne, P., Hart, W., Ambrose, S., Asfaw, B., Heiken, G., & White, T. (2001). Geology and palaeontology of the Late Miocene Middle Awash valley, Afar rift, Ethiopia. *Nature* 412, 175–178.

Wolf, A. P., & Huang, C. S. (1980). *Marriage and adoption in China, 1845–1945.* Stanford, CA: Stanford University Press.

Wong, K. (1997). Neanderthal notes. *Scientific American, 277,* 28–30.

Wrangham, R., & Peterson, D. (1996). *Demonic males: Apes and the origins of human violence.* Boston: Houghton Mifflin.

Wright, R. (1972). Imitative learning of a flaked tool technology: The case of an orangutan. *Mankind, 8,* 296–306.

Wright, R. (1994). *The moral animal: The new science of evolutionary psychology.* New York: Random House Inc.

Wynn, T. (1979). The intelligence of later Acheulean hominids. *Man, 14,* 371–379.

Wynn, T. (1981). The intelligence of Oldowan hominids. *Journal of Human Evolution, 10,* 529–541.

Wynn, T. (1994). Tools and tool behavior. In T. Ingold (Ed.), *Companion Encyclopedia of Anthropology.* New York: Routledge.

Xu, F., & Spelke, E. (2000). Large number discrimination in 6-month-old infants. *Cognition, 74,* B1–B11.

Yoshikubo, S. (1985). Species discrimination and concept formation by rhesus monkeys (Macaca mulatta). *Primates, 26,* 285–299.

Zahavi, A. (1975). Mate selection—a selection of handicap. *Journal of Theoretical Biology, 53,* 205–214.

Zimmerman, I., & McEwen, B. S. (1985). Sexual orientation after prenatal exposure to exogenous estrogen. *Archives of Sexual Behavior, 14,* 57–77.

Zuckerman, M. (1999). *Vulnerability to psychopathology: A biosocial model.* Washington, DC: American Psychological Association.

Index

Abnormal behavior, personality and, 204–214
Abstract reasoning, 46
Abuse, 175
  changes in brain function with, 159
Acheulean period, tool use, 227
ACTH. *See* Adrenocorticotropic hormone
Adaptability, mating selection and, 113
Adenine, 9, 10
Adler, Alfred, 192
Adrenocorticotropic hormone, 178
Adult personality, childhood experience and,
    155–156
Adult reproductive strategy, childhood
    experience and, 154–155
Aesthetic manipulation, 227–241
  adaptive significance of art, 230–235
  Pleistocene art, 228–230
Aesthetic response, 233
Affiliation, 165–172
Africa, 34–38
Age of universe, 27
Aggression, 73, 165–172
Agnosia, visual, 63
Agreeableness, 197, 199
Agriculture, advent of, 245
Aiken, Nancy, 233
Alcohol
  in American diet, 247
  during pregnancy, 144
Alcoholism, 258–260
Aldosterone secretion, 247
Allen's rule, 54
Alpha animal, 165
Alpha fetoprotein, 75
Altruism, 15–16, 97, 169, 183–185, 200, 277, 285

American energy sources, percentage of diet,
    247
American sign language, 83, 90, 92, 95
Amino acids, 9
Amygdala, 63, 73
  effect of chronic cortisol secretion on, 252
Androstenone, 123
Anger, atherosclerosis and, 250
Anterior commissure, 131
Antidepressants, 261
Antigens, 123
Antipsychotic medications, 262
Antisocial personality disorder, 210–211
Anxiety, 208–209, 263
Anxiolytics, 263
Aphasia, 94
Appeasement signals, 168
Arboreal theory, encephalization, 51
Archetypes, 147, 234
Archeulean stone tool industry, 223
Arcuate fasciculus, 94
Aristophanes, 1
Aristotle, 26, 220
Art
  adaptive significance of, 230–235
  aesthetic manipulation, 227–241
    adaptive significance of art, 230–235
    Pleistocene art, 228–230
  definition of, 240
  play, ritual, link between, 240
  Pleistocene, 228–230
ASL. *See* American sign language
Assortment, independent, Mendel's law of, 7
Atherosclerosis, stress response and, 250
Attachment theory, 203

Attraction, sexual, aesthetics of, 115–119
Australopithecus, 54
Authoritarian personality, 201
Autism, 239
Autonomy, 203
Aversion, 144
Avoidant personality disorder, 212
Axe, hand, 224, 225
Axis I psychiatric diagnoses (DSM), 205–209
Axis II personality disorders (DSM), 209–214

Babbling stage, 88
Background, radiation, cosmic, 28
Von Baer, Ken, 141
Ballistic hunting, 56–57
Bee, "language" of, 14
Behaviorism, 12, 13, 67
Bequeathal, 179
Bergmann's rule, 54
Big Bang theory, 28
Biogenetic law, of Haeckel, 141
Biosphere, of Earth, 26
Bipedalism, 38–41
Birth order, adult personality and, 156–158
Blending inheritance, 6
Blood pressure, salt intake and, 247
Blood sugar levels, maternal, 146
Blushing, 168
Boas, Franz, 13
Body symmetry, mating and, 115–116
Bone flute, of Neanderthal, 228
Borderline personality disorder, 156, 175, 211–212
Bowlby, John, 203
Brain evolution, 44–47
Brain stem pons, 63
Breast, in sexual selection, 129
Breast cancer, incidence of, 246
Broca, Paul, 93
Broca's aphasia, 93
Broca's area, 62, 93
    language production center in, 93
Buproprion, 262
Buss, David, 16

Caffeinated drinks, during pregnancy, 144

Cancer, incidence of, 246
Capitalism, 12
Carbohydrate consumption, 246–247
Carroll, Lewis, 79
Cat, brain development, 52
Cather, Willa, 217
Cattell, Raymond, 195
Cave paintings, 46, 229
    Cosquer cave, 230
Cephalocaudal pattern, developmental process, 151
Cereals, in American diet, 247
Cerebellum, 63
Chauvinism, cultural, 13
Cheater detection, 19
    Wason selection tasks, 271–272
Chemical environment, early earth, 29
Chimpanzee, brain development, 52
Chlorpromazine, 205
Cholesterol, levels of, 246
Chomsky, Noam, 91
Choticism, 196
Chromosomes, 6, 7
Clever Hans phenomenon, 84
Clothing, origin of, 231
Cocaine addiction, 258–260
Coffee, during pregnancy, 144
Collective unconscious, 234
Colon cancer, incidence of, 246
Communication, animal, 81–82
Compassion, 180–187
Comprehension, reading, in women, 73
Conceptual knowledge, 103
Confirmatory factor analysis, 197
Conflicts of interest, parent–infant, 150–152
Conscientiousness, 197, 199
Consciousness, 236–241
Conservative doctrines, firstborn valuation of, 157
Contralateral neglect, 63
Copernicus, 158
Copulins, 124
Corpus callosum, 63, 65
    sexual abuse and, 159
Correlational research, factor analysis, 194–196

Cortical blindness, 62
Cortisol, 179
 chronic secretion, effects of, 252
Cosmic background radiation, 28
Cosmides, Leda, 16
Cosquer cave, cave paintings, 230
Creative impulse, 217–243
 aesthetic manipulation, 227–241
  adaptive significance of art, 230–235
  Pleistocene art, 228–230
 tool use, 218–227
  assessment of hominid cognitive ability, 227
  hominid archaeological record, 223–225
  in nonhuman animals, 218–223
  selective force in evolution, 225–227
Creativity, mating selection and, 113
Crick, Francis, 9
Critical-period hypothesis, in language
  acquisition, 90
Cro-Magnon man, 46
Cultural relativism, 13
Cultural supremacy anthropology, 13
Cytosine, 10

Darwin
 Charles, 2–12, 33, 59, 72, 82, 91, 95, 107, 141,
  156–158, 183
 Erasmus, 4
Deoxyribonucleic acid. *See* DNA
Dependency, 203
Dependent personality disorder, 213
Depression, 176, 207–208, 252
 drug use and, 261
 heart attack and, 252
Descartes, Rene, 66
Desire for children, mating selection and, 113
Destiny, genes as, 12
Determinism, environmental, 12–23
Diabetes, gestational, 146
Diethylstilbestrol, 131
Dissanayake, Ellen, 230
Diverticulitis, incidence of, 246
Division of cell, 8
Divorce, timing of, 134
DNA, 9–11, 29, 142

ability to replicate, 9
 genetic engineering and, 266
Dobzhansky, Theodosius, 7
Domestic animals, selective breeding in, 5
Dominance hierarchies, 166
Dopamine, 199, 205
Doppler effect, 28
Dunbar, Robin, 100
Dysthymia, 207

Earning capacity, mating selection and, 113
Earth, biosphere of, 26
Eating disorders, 156, 175
Economic resources, female mate preference for,
  psychological mechanism, 19
Egg cells, creation of, 8
Eggs
 in hunter-gatherer, American, diets, 247
Embedded figures test, 74
Emotion, expression of, 157
Empathy, 200
Encephalization, 49–78
Endorphins, 130
Energy sources, hunter-gatherer, percentage of
  diet, 247
Entertainment, 240
Environmental determinism, 12–23
Epilepsy, 65
Epinephrine, sympathetic nervous system and,
  249
Equality, concepts of in latter-born siblings, 157
Estradiol, 75
Estrogen, 73
Ethology, 14–15
Eugenicists, 12
Euphoria, 175
Europa, 27
Evolution of interest, 69
Existentialist theory, 192
Expression, facial, 82
 interpretation of, 74
Extra-marital affairs, 116
Extraterrestrial intelligences, 27
Extraversion, 196, 198
Eysenck, H. J., 196

Fabre, Jean Henri, 120
Facial blushing, 168
Facial expression, 82
    interpretation of, 74
Factor analysis, personality theory, 194–196
Factor rotation, 195
Fairness, concepts of in latter-born siblings,
        157
Fats
    in American diet, 247
    in mother's milk, 158
    preference for, psychological mechanism, 19
Fear learning, 67–69
Feminine mating ideal, 120
Feral children, language ability, 85–88
Field dependency, 74
Field independence, 74
Fight/flight response, 179, 249
    immune system and, 178
Filial imprinting, 14
Fingers, masculinized brain and, 143
Fish
    in hunter-gatherer, American diets, 247
Fisher, R. A., 109
Fluoxetine, 173, 262
Food-sharing customs, 172
Forgiveness, 200
Fowl, wild, in hunter-gatherer diet, 247
Freud, Sigmund, 192
Von Frisch, Karl, 14, 81
Frontal cortex, 64
Frontal lobe, 63
Fruits
    in hunter-gatherer, American diets, 247

Galapagos Islands, 2
Gallup, Gordon, 237
Galton, Sir Francis, 192
Game, in hunter-gatherer diet, 247
Gamete production, 8
Gender differences, 72–77
    in mating, 109–111
Gene, defined, 11
Gene mutation, 6–7, 10

Gene pool, 7
Gene recombination, 7
Gene theory, 6
Generalized anxiety, 208
Genetic determinism, 12
Genetic engineering, 265
Genetic information, translation of, 10
Gestaltist theory, 192
Gestational diabetes, 146
Glucose levels, 146
Gonads, 128–130, 130
Gondwanaland, 33
Grains, in American diet, 247
Grass snake, brain development, 52
Grooming, 171
    language acquisition and, 101
Guanine, 10
Guilt, 168

Haeckel, Ernst, 12
Haldane, J. B. S., 7
Hamilton, W. D., 15
Hand axe, 224, 225
Handicapping principle
    drug use and, 260
    in mating, 109
Haplodiploidy, 181
Health
    deterioration of, with agriculture, 245
    mating selection and, 113
Heart attack, depression and, 252
Height, 169
Heredity, molecule of, 9
Heroin addiction, 258–260
Heterochrony, 55
Heterozygotes, 6
Hindbrain, 63
Hippocampus, 63, 73
    effect of chronic cortisol secretion on, 252
Histrionic personality disorder, 210–211, 211
Hitler, Adolph, 12
Hockett, Charles, 80
HOM genes, 142
Homeothermy, 32

Homer, 21
Hominid evolution, 34–47
Homo Antecessor, 43, 46
Homo Erectus, 42, 43, 54, 100, 223
Homo Ergaster, 43
Homo Habilis, 42, 223
Homo Rudolfensis, 42
Homo Sapiens, 27, 43, 46, 54, 60, 80, 100, 224
Homosexual behavior, 131
Honey, in hunter-gatherer diet, 247
Hooker, Sir Joseph, 5
Horney, Karen, 192
HOX genes, 142
Human chorionic gonadotropin, 145–146
Hunter-gatherer, energy sources, percentage of
    diet, 247
Huxley, Aldous, 263
Hybridization experiments, of Mendel, 6
Hypertension, salt intake and, 247
Hypoglossal nerve, language acquisition and,
    100
Hyposerotonergic activity, 156, 175
Hypothalamus, 63

Ice Age, 53–56, 60
Illiad, 21
Immune system, fight/flight response, 178
Imprinting, 14
Impulse control, 175
Impulsive behavior, 174
Impulsivity, 155
Incest avoidance, 152–153
Inclusive fitness, 15, 182
Independent assortment, Mendel's law, 7
Indoctrination, 256–258
Insensitivity, 196
Insight learning, 219
Instinct blindness, 11, 21
Intelligence, mating selection and, 113
Interferons, 267
Intraspecific competition, 59–60
Introversion extraversion, 196
Irish sheep boy, language ability, 87
Isolation, in modern society, 253

James, William, 11, 21
Jealousy, 124–126
Jung, Carl, 147, 192, 234

Kamikaze sperm, 127
Kant, Immanuel, 146
Kenyanthropus Platyops, 39, 40, 42
Kibbutzim, 153
Kidney failure, hypertension and, 248
Kin selection, 15
Kindness, mating selection and, 113
Koestler, Arthur, 217

Lactogen, placental, 146
Laissez-faire capitalism, 12
Language, 57–59, 79–105, 282
    acquisition of, 88–91
    animal communication, 81–82
    animal language studies, 82–85
    centers, left hemisphere, 93
    critical periods, 90–91
    developmental stages, 88–89
    evolution, 91–104
        ancient origins, 97–102
        conceptual domains, 102–104
        universals, 92–97
    feral children, 85–88
    language acquisition, 88–91
    natural, 19
    nature of, 80–88
    reception, 93
    studies, animal, 82–85
Larynx, 83, 95
Laterality of brain, 65–66
Laughing, development of, 151
Left hemisphere, language centers of, 93
Legumes, in American diet, 247
Leopard frog, brain development, 52
Light red shift, 28
Limbic system, 63, 196
Limerence, 132–135
Linnaeus, Carolus, 34, 87
Lithuanian bear boy, language ability, 87
Lobotomy, 64

Localization of function, brain, 62–65
Logical reasoning, perception, distinction, 63
London school, 192
Lorenz, Konrad, 14, 147
Luvox, 262
Lyell, Charles, 5, 33

Macaque monkey, brain development, 52
Machiavellian intelligence, 51–53, 59, 100
Major histocompatibility complex preferences, 122–123
Male-male competition, 107, 110
Malthus, Thomas, 4
Mars, microbial forms, 27
Marx, Karl, 193
Marxism, 12
Masculine mating ideal, 119–120
Mate-guarding, 124–126
Mate selection criteria, 111–114
Maternal nurturance, 180
Mating, 106–139
    attraction, 115–119
    body symmetry, 115–116
    feminine ideal, 120
    jealousy, 124–126
    limerence, 132–135
    long-term pair bonding, 135–136
    major histocompatibility complex, 122–123
    masculine ideal, 119–120
    mate-guarding, 124–126
    mate selection criteria, 111–114
    menstrual synchronicity, 121
    pair-bonding strategies, 132–136
    pheromones, 120–124
    sex differences, 109–111
    sexual selection, 107–114
    sperm wars, 126–129
    waist-hip ratio, 116–119
Mead, Margaret, 13
Medulla, 63
Medulla oblongata, 63
Megatherium, 3
Meiosis, zygote formation, and cell division, cellular, 8
Meiotic division, 8

Melatonin, seasonal affective disorder and, 253
Men, mating preferences of, 111–112
Menarche stress hormones, onset of, 155
Menarcheal timing, 154
Mendel, Father Gregor, 6
Mendel's laws, 6–7
Menopause, adaptive function of, 160
Menstrual synchronicity, 121
Mental health, stress and, 252–253
Milk, in American diet, 247
Millennium man, 38
Mirtazapine, 262
Mismatch theory, 245–248
Modular brain model, 60–66
Modular mind, 67–77
Modularity, brain, 63–64
Molecular compounds, early earth atomosphere, 29
Molecule of heredity, 9
Monoamineoxidase inhibitors, 261
Monogamy, 125
Monotreme, reproductive physiology, 3
Mood stabilizing pharmaceuticals, 263
Mood state, 173–180, 175
Moon, 29
Morality, 185–187
Morning sickness, adaptive function of, 142–145
Mother-fetus competition, 145–146
Mousterian tool industry, 224
Multicellular organisms, formation of, 30
Music, modern brain and, 61–62
Mutationism, 7

Narcissistic personality disorder, 212
Nationalism, 253–258
Natural language, 19
Natural selection, theory of, 5, 286
Nazis, 12
Neanderthal man, 44–46, 224
    bone flute, 228
Nefazadon, 262
Neglect, changes in brain function, 159
Neocortex, 58, 63, 100
Neocortical expansion, 59
Nervous system, physiology of, 60

Neural Darwinism, 89
Neuroimaging techniques, 23
Neuroleptics, 262
Neurons, 173
Neuroticism, 196, 198, 204
Neurotransmitters, 173, 273–275
Nomothetic method, personality research, 194
Noninvasive neuroimaging techniques, 23
Nucleotides, 9
Nuts
  in hunter-gatherer, American diets, 247

Obsessionality, 156, 175
Obsessive-compulsive personality disorder, 209,
    213–214
Occipital lobe, brain, 63
Oldowan tool users, 227
Ontogeny
  birth order, adult personality, 156–158
  childhood experience
    adult personality, 155–156
    adult reproductive strategy, 154–155
  cognitive potential, optimizing, 158–160
  evolved contingency mechanisms, 153–158
  incest avoidance, 152–153
  menopause, adaptive function of, 160
  morning sickness, adaptive function of,
    142–145
  mother–fetus competition, 145–146
  parent–infant conflicts of interest, 150–152
  phylogeny, of personality, 200–204
  postnatal development, 146–160
  prenatal development, 141–146
  recapitulating phylogeny, 141–142
  regulator genes, 142
Openness to experience, 197
Opossum, brain development, 52
Order of birth, adult personality and, 156–158
Orgasm, 127
  as adaptive mechanism, 116
Origin of Species, 7, 33, 95, 157
Orrorin Tugenensis, 38
Orthogonality, 195
Osteoporosis, incidence of, 248
Oxytocin, 116

Paintings, cave, 229
Pair bonding
  long-term, 135–136
  short-term, 132–135
  strategies, 132–136
Paleolithic paintings, 229
Pangaea, 33
Panic disorder, 208
Paranoid personality disorder, 212
Parasitism, with shift to agriculture, 248
Parietal lobe, brain, 63
Particulate inheritance, 4–7
Pavlov, Ivan, 12
Paxil, 176, 262
Pearson, Karl, 193
Pecking order, 166
Penis, 128–130
Perception, logical reasoning, distinction, 63
Personality, 191–216
  childhood experience and, 155–156
  mating selection and, 113
Personality research, nomothetic method, 194
Personality theory, 192–193
Personality traits, adaptive significance of,
    198–200
Pharmaceuticals, 176
Pheromones, 81, 120–124
Phobias, 67, 209
  extinguishing, 13
Phonemes, 88, 98, 148
Phrenology, 60
Phylogeny, ontogeny, of personality, 200–204
Physical attractiveness, mating selection and,
    113
Physical health, deterioration of, with
    agriculture, 245
Piaget, Jean, 149
Pigeon, brain development, 52
Pinker, Steven, 92
Pituitary, 63
Placental gestation, 145
Placental lactogen, 146
Planets, Earth, compared, 26
Play, art, ritual, link between, 240
Pleistocene art, 228–230

Plotinus, 191
Poikilotherm, 32
Polyandry, 125
Polygamy, 124
Polygyny, 124
Postmenopausal women, 160
Postnatal development, 146–160
Posttraumatic stress disorder, 208
Potassium intake, 247
Poultry, in American diet, 247
Prefrontal lobotomy, 64
Pregnancy, 144
  drug use during, 260
Prelinguistic vocalizations, 88
Premack, David, 84, 238
Prenatal development, 141–146
Pride, evolutionary origin of, 168
Primates, appearance on earth, 34
Prisoner's dilemma, 183
Product moment correlation, 193
Programmed tool use, 220
Prosidy, 95
Proteins, transcription of, 10
Prozac, 173, 176, 262
Psychopathology, 191–216
Psychopharmacology, 260–265
Psychoticism, 196, 199
Pubertal timing, 154
Purgatorius, 32

Racism, 13
Raiding, practices of, 254–255
Reading speed, in women, 73
Reciprocal altruism, 16, 169, 183–185
Recombination, gene, 7
Red queen hypothesis, 145
Regulator genes, 142
Reinforcement centers, brain, 258
Relativism, cultural, 13
Religious orientation, mating selection and,
  113
Replicator molecule, 9
Reproduction, 106–139
  attraction, 115–119
  body symmetry, 115–116

feminine ideal, 120
jealousy, 124–126
limerence, 132–135
long-term pair bonding, 135–136
major histocompatibility complex, 122–123
masculine ideal, 119–120
mate-guarding, 124–126
mate selection criteria, 111–114
menstrual synchronicity, 121
pair-bonding strategies, 132–136
pheromones, 120–124
sex differences, 109–111
sexual selection, 107–114
sperm wars, 126–129
strategy of, childhood experience and,
  154–155
waist-hip ratio, 116–119
Restriction enzymes, genetic engineering and,
  266
Retroviruses, 267
Right-handedness, tool use and, 226
Right-wing authoritarianism scale, 201
Ritual, play, art, link between, 240
RNA, 29
Rod and frame test, 74
Rumbaugh, Dwayne, 84
Runaway sexual selection, 59

Sacks, Oliver, 63
SAD. *See* Seasonal affective disorder
Salt intake, 247
Savanna-like environments, landscape
  preferences for, psychological
  mechanism, 19
Schizoid personality disorder, 212
Schizophrenia, 196, 205–207, 206, 262
Schizotypal personality disorder, 213
Search for extraterrestrial intelligence project.
  See SETI project
Season of birth, schizophrenia and, 206
Seasonal affective disorder, 253, 285
Sedentary lifestyle, effects of, 248
Segregation, law of, Mendel's, 6
Selection
  natural, theory of, 5, 286

sexual behavior and, 59
Selective breeding, 2–4
Self-awareness, 237
Self-esteem, 168
Selfless service, 15
Sense of smell, pregnancy, 144
Serotonin, 155, 173–177, 209
Serotonin reuptake inhibitors, 156, 175, 176, 207, 262
SETI project, 27
Sexual abuse, 175
    corpus callosum and, 159
Sexual attraction, aesthetics of, 115–119
Sexual behavior, 106–139
    attraction, 115–119
    body symmetry, 115–116
    feminine ideal, 120
    jealousy, 124–126
    limerence, 132–135
    long-term pair bonding, 135–136
    major histocompatibility complex, 122–123
    masculine ideal, 119–120
    mate-guarding, 124–126
    mate selection criteria, 111–114
    menstrual synchronicity, 121
    pair-bonding strategies, 132–136
    pheromones, 120–124
    sex differences, 109–111
    sexual selection, 107–114
    sperm wars, 126–129
    waist-hip ratio, 116–119
Sexual jealousy, male, psychological mechanism, 19
Sexual orientation, 129–132
Sexual selection, 107–114, 286
Sexual variety, male desire for, 19
Shakespeare, William, 244
Shamanistic societies, 234
Shame, evolutionary origin of, 168
Shellfish
    in hunter-gatherer, American diet, 247
Simpua marriage, 153
Skinner, B. F., 12
Slow-to-warm-up child, 202
Smiling, development of, 151

Smoking
    effects of, 259
    during pregnancy, 144
Snakes, fear of, psychological mechanism, 19
Social Darwinism, 12
Social intelligence, 51, 53
Social order, 164–190
    altruism, 180–187
    compassion, evolution of, 180–187
    dominance hierarchies, 165–172
    ethics, 185–187
    kin selection, 180–187
    morality, universal, 185–187
    reciprocal altruism, 183–185
    serotonin, 173–177
    status, mood states and, 173–180
    stress hormones, 178–180
    testosterone, 177–178
Social reasoning, 69–72
Sociobiology, 15–16, 16
Sociopathy, 210
Sodium intake, 247
Solar system, 26–27
Soma, 263
Spatial ability, 74
Spatial-location memory, of female, psychological mechanism, 19
Spatial relations, male manipulation of, 73
Spearman, Charles, 193
Spelling ability, women, 73
Spencer, Herbert, 11
Sperm
    creation of, 8
    wars, 126–129
Split brain, 65–66
SRIs. *See* Serotonin reuptake inhibitors
Star system, 27
Status, mood states, 173–180
Stone tools, 223
    examples of, 225
Stress, negative effects of, 179, 249–252
Stress hormones, 175, 178–180
    menarche, onset of, 155
Structural equation modeling, 197
Substance abuse, 258–260

Sugar
   in American diet, 247
   preference for, psychological mechanism, 19
Suicidal ideation, 207
Sun, birth of, 29
Survival of fittest, 12
Sweeteners, in American diet, 247
Symbolic expression, 46
Symbolic universe, 236–241
Symmetry, body, mating and, 115–116
Synchronicity, menstrual, 121
Systema Natura, 34

Tabula rasa, 13, 16
Talismans, 233
Technology, development of
   aesthetic manipulation, 227–241
      adaptive significance of art, 230–235
      Pleistocene art, 228–230
   tool use, 218–227
      assessment of hominid cognitive ability, 227
      hominid archaeological record, 223–225
      in nonhuman animals, 218–223
      selective force in evolution, 225–227
Temper tantrum, 152
Temperament, 203
Testicles, 127
Testosterone, 177–178
Textiles, origin of, 231
Thalamus, 63
Theory of mind, 59, 100, 237
   in chimpanzees, 238
Theory of natural selection, 1–25, 286
Thorazine, 205
Thymine, 10
Tinbergen, Nikolaas, 14
Tissue-type plasminogen activator, development
   of, 267
TIT FOR TAT, 183, 184
Tobacco addiction, 258–260
Tongue, movements of, language acquisition
   and, 100
Tooby, John, 16
Tool industry, Mousterian, 224

Tool use, 218–227
   assessment of hominid cognitive ability, 227
   hominid archaeological record, 223–225
   learned, 220
   in nonhuman animals, 218–223
   programmed, 220
   selective force in evolution, 225–227
Tough mindedness, 196
Trachea, 95
Trait theory, 194
Transcription of proteins, 10
Tricyclic antidepressants, 261
Trivers, R., 16, 109
Type A personality, 250

Von Uexkull, Jacob, 236
Umwelt, 236
Unconscious, collective, 234
Understanding, mating selection and, 113
Universals, language evolution, 92–97
Universe, age of, 27

Vegetables
   in hunter-gatherer, American diet, 247
Venlafaxin, 262
Venus of Willendorf, 229
Verbal fluency, in women, 73
Vertebrate life, 31–34
Violent behavior, 253–258
Viral infection, schizophrenia and, 206
Visual agnosia, 63
Visual process, 62
Visuospatial relations, 74
De Vries, Hugo, 7

Waist-hip ratio, 116–119
Wallace, Alfred Russell, 5, 6
War, 253–258
Wason selection tasks, cheater detection,
   271–272
Watson, J., 9, 12
Wells, H. G., 49
Wernicke, Carl, 94
Wernicke's aphasia, 94

Wernicke's area, 93
Westermark, Edward, 152
Whitten effect, 121
William's syndrome, 58
Wilson, E. O., 16
Wolf boy, language ability, 87
Women, mating preferences of, 112–114
Woodruff, Guy, 238
Work, increase in hours expended on, 253
Woven objects, 231
Wright, Sewall, 7

Youth, male mate preference for, psychological
    mechanism, 19

Zenophobia, 201
Zoloft, 176, 262
Zygote, formation of, 8